Pigeon pea farmer Esther Saizi in Malawi, with bread rolls made from pigeon pea flour. She's joined a local farming cooperative, Nandolo Farmers Association, a Christian Aid partner.

Put global social justice at the heart of your church.

Find prayer, campaign and fundraising resources at **caid.org.uk/Scotland** or scan the QR code

Please get in touch:
edinburgh@christian-aid.org or 0131 220 1254

Christian Aid is a key member of ACT Alliance. Eng and Wales charity no. 1105851 Scot charity no. SC039150 Company no. 5171525. The Christian Aid name and logo are trademarks of Christian Aid. © Christian Aid July 2023.

Registered with FUNDRAISING REGULATOR

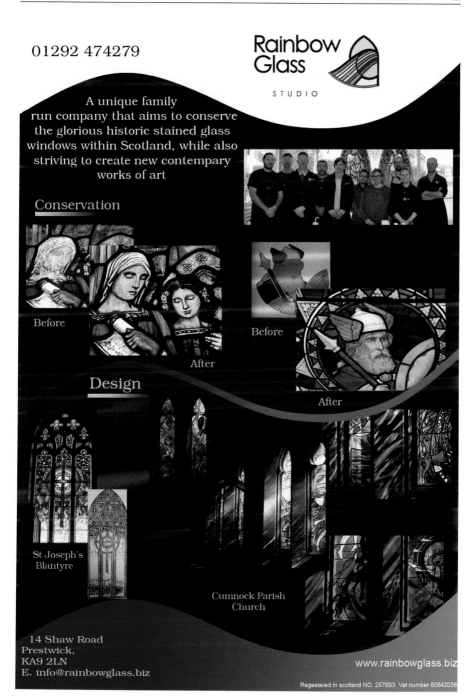

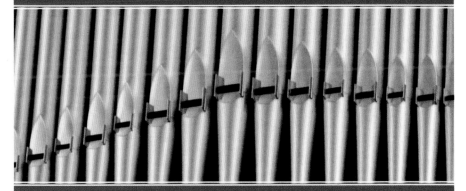

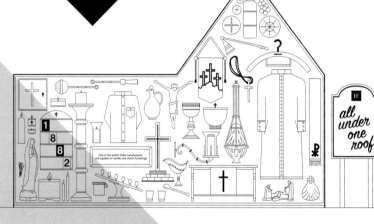
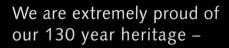

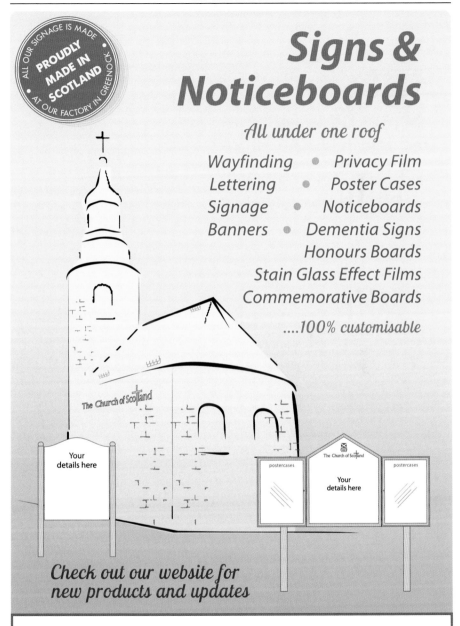

© Andrew O'Brien Photography   The Right Reverend Sally Foster-Fulton BA BD   © Church of Scotland
MODERATOR

The Church of Scotland
YEAR BOOK
2023–2024

138th year of issue

Editor

David A. Stewart

Published on behalf of
THE CHURCH OF SCOTLAND
by SAINT ANDREW PRESS
121 George Street, Edinburgh EH2 4YN

THE OFFICES OF THE CHURCH

121 George Street, Edinburgh, EH2 4YN
0131 225 5722
Fax: 0131 220 3113
www.churchofscotland.org.uk

Office Hours: Monday–Friday 9:00am–5:00pm

CrossReach operates from Charis House, 47 Milton Road East, Edinburgh, EH15 2SR
0131 657 2000
Fax: 0131 657 5000
info@crossreach.org.uk
www.crossreach.org.uk

Scottish Charity Numbers

The Church of Scotland: unincorporated Councils and Committees	SC011353
The Church of Scotland General Trustees	SC014574
The Church of Scotland Investors Trust	SC022884
The Church of Scotland Trust	SC020269

For the Scottish Charity Numbers of presbyteries and congregations, see Section 7

Corrections and alterations to the Year Book
Contact the Editor, David A. Stewart:
yearbookeditor@churchofscotland.org.uk
0131 441 3362

The General Assembly of 2024 will convene on
Saturday 18 May

First published in 2023 by SAINT ANDREW PRESS, 121 George Street, Edinburgh EH2 4YN on behalf of THE CHURCH of SCOTLAND

Copyright © THE CHURCH of SCOTLAND, 2023

ISBN 978 1 80083 039 4

It is the Publisher's policy only to use papers that are natural and recyclable and that have been manufactured from timber grown in renewable, properly managed forests. All of the manufacturing processes of the papers are expected to conform to the environmental regulations of the country of origin.

Acceptance of advertisements for inclusion in *The Church of Scotland Year Book* does not imply endorsement of the goods or services or of any views expressed within the advertisements.

British Library Cataloguing in Publication Data
A catalogue record for this book is available from the British Library.

Printed and bound by Bell and Bain Ltd, Glasgow

CONTENTS

4

FROM THE MODERATOR

The Year Book is more than a list of names and places, contact numbers and addresses. It is more than a record of congregations and Presbyteries, of trustees, agencies, committees, forums and departments. It is more than a memo of past Moderators or a guide to church procedure. The Year Book is a reminder that we are all a small part of something so much bigger, that there are friends and colleagues willing to roll up their sleeves and help out, that there is wisdom at work throughout the Church of Scotland and we all are called to live out our faith as part of the body of Christ.

My theme for this year is based on a South African phrase – 'Ubuntu', most closely translated as 'I am because you are.' We cannot be fully human without each other, cannot become who we are meant to be without other human beings to become with. We are completely and intricately intertwined, set together on one beautiful and fragile planet home and called to cherish it and each other.

So, when you pick up this book, when you use it to get on with the work of the church, remember it represents sisters and brothers who love you and are serving their communities. And be inspired!

Sally Foster-Fulton

BHON MHODARÀTAIR

Tha barrachd san Leabhar Bhliadhnail na liosta ainmean is àiteachan, àireamhan fòn is sheòlaidhean. Tha barrachd ann na clàr de choitheanalan is chlèirean, de dh'urrasairean, bhuidhnean, chomataidhean, fhòraman is roinnean. Tha barrachd ann na cunntas de Mhoderàtoran a bh' ann no iùl gu modhan-obrach eaglaise. Tha an Leabhar Bliadhnail a' cur nar cuimhne gu bheil sinn nar pàirt bheag de rudeigin mòran nas motha, gu bheil caraidean agus companaich ann a tha deònach am muilichinnean a thrusadh is taic a thoirt, gu bheil gliocas ri lorg are feadh Eaglais na h-Alba agus gu bheil sinn uile air ar gairm gus ar creideamh a chur an gnìomh mar phàirt de bhodhaig Chrìosd.

Tha mo chuspair airson na bliadhna seo bonntaichte air abairt bho Africa a Deas – 'Ubuntu', a tha eadar-theangaichte nas fhaisge mar "Tha mise ann seach gu bheil thusa." Chan urrainn dhuinn a bhith gu lèir daonna gun chàch-a-chèile, chan urrainn dhuinn a bhith mar a tha sùilichte dhuinn gun a bhith an lùib mhuinntir eile. Tha sinn fighte-fuaighte ri chèile, air ar suidheachadh còmhla air an aon dachaigh planaid bhrèagha is chugallach agus fo uallach sùim a ghabhail dheth is do chàch-a-chèile.

Mar sin, nuair a thogas sibh an leabhar seo, nuair a chleachdas sibh e airson obair na h-eaglaise a chur air adhart, cuimhnichibh gu bheil e a' riochdachadh peathraichean is bràithrean aig a bheil gràdh dhuibh agus a tha frithealadh an coimhearsnachdan. Agus bithibh air ur brosnachadh!

Sally Foster-Fulton
Translation by Professor Boyd Robertson

EDITORIAL

Given the further progress now made in the restructuring of presbyteries, this edition now reflects the new structure, beside the usual extensive updating across most pages.

In the Presbytery listings in Section 5:

- presbyteries have been renumbered 1 to 14;

- the Presbyteries of Lothian (3), Melrose and Peebles (4), Duns (5), and Jedburgh (6) have been united as the Presbytery of Lothian and Borders (2);

- the Presbyteries of Stirling (23), Dunkeld and Meigle (27), Perth (28), Dundee (29) and Angus (30) have been united as the Presbytery of Perth (8);

- the Presbyteries of Aberdeen and Shetland (31), Kincardine and Deeside (32), Gordon (33), Buchan (34), Moray (35) and Orkney (45) have been united as the Presbytery of the North East and the Northern Isles (9);

- the number (10) has been reserved for the forthcoming Presbytery Clèir Eilean Ì: Highlands and Hebrides, to be formed by the union in January 2024 of the Presbyteries of Argyll, Abernethy, Inverness, Lochaber, Ross, Sutherland, Caithness, Lochcarron-Skye and Uist. Meanwhile those presbyteries are listed separately but temporarily numbered (10.1) to (10.9); and

- opportunity has been taken by the restructuring to bring together under the relevant presbytery those previously listed in Section 6 Lists D and E (Ministers registered by presbytery but not members of presbytery), H (Readers) and I (Ministries Development Staff).

The lists of Additional Personnel in Section 6 are consequentially now fewer, and re-lettered. The Forces List now includes reference to Veterans Chaplaincy Scotland, while the former List M has been deleted, following the winding up of Work Place Chaplaincy Scotland.

Sections 7, 8, 9, 10 and the Indexes have been revised to reflect the presbytery restructuring.

In Section 3 the guidance on the conduct of funeral services: fees (3E), and pulpit supply fees and expenses (3F) has been restored to the printed book.

As always, I am grateful to those readers who sent corrections and updates. Many people contribute to the Year Book. My thanks to the Presbytery Clerks and their administrators, the staff in the Church offices (in particular Karen Keil and Angus Mathieson of Faith Action), and those who compile some sections or subsections: Boyd Robertson and Duncan Sneddon (Gaelic), Sheena Orr (Prison Chaplains), Madelaine Sproule (legal names and Scottish charity numbers), Roy Pinkerton (church grid references, parishes and congregations: names no longer in use, index of parishes and places, and editorial advice), and Fiona Tweedie, Karen Bass and Sandy Gemmill (statistics). Thanks also to Claire Ruben of FairCopy for diligently tackling the substantial amount of additional copy editing required for this edition and to our contacts at Hymns Ancient and Modern who publish the book via the St Andrew Press.

Corrections, amendments and suggestions are always welcome.

David Stewart
yearbookeditor@churchofscotland.org.uk

SECTION 1

Assembly Trustees, Agencies, Committees and Departments

The symbol > used in website information indicates the headings to be selected as they appear

1. OFFICE OF THE GENERAL ASSEMBLY

The Office supports the General Assembly, Presbyteries and Kirk Sessions, the Moderator and the process of Presbytery reform. In addition, the staff service the following: Assembly Business Committee, Legal Questions Committee, Nomination Committee, Judicial Commission, Judicial Panel, Appeals Committee of the Commission of Assembly, Ministries Appeal Panel, Mission Plan Review Group, the Committee to Nominate the Moderator, the Chalmers Lectureship Trust, the Committee on Overtures and Cases, the Delegation of Assembly, the Committee on Classifying Returns to Overtures, the Ecumenical Relations Committee and the Theological Forum. The Clerks of Assembly are responsible for consultation on matters of Church Law, Practice and Procedure.

Secretaries:

Principal Clerk of the General Assembly:	Rev. Fiona E. Smith LLB BD
Depute Clerk:	Ms Christine Paterson LLB DipLP
Presbytery Resource Adviser:	Rev. Victoria J. Linford LLB BD
Senior Public Sector Policy Adviser:	Mr Robert Marshall BMus LLB WS
Executive Assistant to the Principal Clerk:	Mrs Nicola Nicholls, 0131 376 1137
Senior Administration Officer	Miss Catherine McIntosh MA, 0131 376 1594
(Assembly Arrangements	
and Moderatorial Support):	
Secretary, Ecumenical Relations Committee:	Rev. Dr John L. McPake
Secretary, Theological Forum:	Rev. Dr Alasdair J. Macleod (till Dec 2023)
	(from Jan 2024) Ms Nathalie A. Mareš
	MacCallum MA MTh

Personnel in this department are also listed with the bodies and Committees that they serve.
Contact: pcoffice@churchofscotland.org.uk   0131 225 5722

2. OFFICE OF THE ASSEMBLY TRUSTEES

The Trustees have responsibility for governance, finance and stewardship, budgeting and general oversight of the agencies of the Church. They assist the General Assembly to determine the strategy and priorities of the Church, and seek to ensure the implementation of the policies, priorities and strategic objectives of the General Assembly through working with the agencies of the Church to achieve a collaborative approach to the nurturing of the people of the Church in their witness, worship and service. They are the Charity Trustees of the Church of Scotland (the Unincorporated Entities) Scottish Charity No. SC011353.

Assembly Trustees:

Convener:	Rev. David S. Cameron
Vice-Convener:	David Harrison

Administrative Trustee: Ann Nelson
Other Trustees: Jean Couper CBE
                         Ian Forrester
                         Miranda Heggie
                         Rev. Barry J. Hughes
                         Jennifer MacDonald
                         Rev. Michael J. Mair
                         Rev. Dr Peter McEnhill
                         Geoff Miller
                         Rev. Norman A. Smith
                         Rev. Prof. Philip G. Ziegler

Chief Officer: Dave Kendall
Head of Analysis and Programme Development: Catherine Skinner
Head of Faith Action Programme: Rev. Dr Scott J.S. Shackleton
  (see 3. below)
Head of Estates and Procurement: Liam Fennell   0131 376 1131
  (see 11. below)
Executive PA to the Chief Officer: Carron Lunt
Programme Support Officer: Lynn Hall
Statistician: Rev. Dr Fiona J. Tweedie
Research Officer: Karen Bass
Grants Manager: David Williams   0131 376 5846
                                                       grants@churchofscotland.org.uk
Health and Safety Manager: Jacqueline Collins

Contact: OATadmin@churchofscotland.org.uk   0131 225 5722

Further information:
www.churchofscotland.org.uk > About us > Our structure > The Assembly Trustees
www.churchofscotland.org.uk > Resources > Statistics for Mission

---

3. FAITH ACTION PROGRAMME

The Faith Action Programme is an integrated programme which incorporates the work of the former Faith Nurture and Faith Impact Forums. The Programme exists to equip people to live out the mission of God. Over the next five years, we are looking to:

- Build and launch an integrated training programme for members of local churches, carrying in the first instance resources for faith, life and mission;
- Create pathways that attract and allow us to recruit the required number of resilient and emotionally intelligent leaders for the recognised ministries for which they are suited and called;
- Establish a programme to develop and support churches to grow in Christian faith and deliver missional activity throughout the year and establish 100 new worshipping communities;
- Establish and deliver with all presbyteries a comprehensive programme of support to equip all those responsible for evolving fresh forms of worship including digitized ministry alongside continued support for developing best practice in existing worship;

- Contribute to public life and social justice on behalf of the church;
- Deliver the Presbytery Mission Plan Act – with a configuration of ministries and congregational estates which is sustainable and affordable; and
- Decrease annually, by amounts agreed through the Assembly Trustees' budgeting process, the operating costs of national programmes as work is devolved or ended, and generate income to fulfil the Programme and further the wider work of the Church.

FAITH ACTION PROGRAMME LEADERSHIP TEAM

Convener:	Rev. Tommy MacNeil
Deputy Convener and Resource and Presence Programme Group Leader:	Rev. Alistair Cumming
Vice-Convener and Mission Support Programme Group Leader:	Richard Lloyd
Vice-Convener and People and Training Programme Group Leader:	Rev. Bill M. Wishart
Vice-Convener and Public Life and Social Justice Programme Group Leader:	Emma Jackson
Presbytery Mission Plan Implementation Group Convener:	Rev. Dr Karen K. Campbell

FAITH ACTION PROGRAMME STAFF

Head of Faith Action Programme:	Rev. Dr Scott J.S. Shackleton
Mission Support Senior Manager:	Shirley Grieve
Presbytery and Partnership Support Senior Manager:	Rev Angus R. Mathieson
People and Training Senior Manager:	Kay Cathcart
Public Life and Social Justice Senior Manager:	David Bradwell
Resource and Presence Senior Manager (including centres in Israel & Palestine):	Kenny Roger

Contact: FaithAction@churchofscotland.org.uk 0131 225 5722

Further information:
www.churchofscotland.org.uk > About us > Forums, committees and departments > Forums
www.churchofscotland.org.uk > Connect > Interfaith; Global Partnerships; Priority Areas; Campaigns; Scottish Faiths Action for Refugees
www.churchofscotland.org.uk > Resources > Presbytery Planning; Exploring Discipleship; Children and Young People; Learn Online
www.churchofscotland.org.uk > Serve > Recognised Ministries; Training for Ministry
www.ascend.churchofscotland.org.uk

---

4. CROSSREACH

Charis House, 47 Milton Road East, Edinburgh EH15 2SR
0131 657 2000   Fax: 0131 657 5000
info@crossreach.org.uk   www.crossreach.org.uk

CrossReach, overseen by the CrossReach Board (formally recognised as the Social Care Council), provides social care services as part of the Christian mission and ministry of the Church to the people of Scotland, and engages with other bodies in responding to emerging areas of need. CrossReach provides social care services throughout Scotland: www.crossreach.org.uk/our-locations

Convener:	Rev. Thomas S. Riddell
Vice-Convener:	Mike Cantlay
Chief Executive Officer:	Viv Dickenson (viv.dickenson@crossreach.org.uk)
Director of Services to Older People:	Allan Logan (allan.logan@crossreach.org.uk)
Director of Adult Care Services:	Vic Walker (vic.walker@crossreach.org.uk)
Director of Children and Families:	Sheila Gordon (sheila.gordon@crossreach.org.uk)
Director of Finance and Resources:	Eoin McDunphy (eoin.mcdunphy@crossreach.org.uk)
Director of Human Resources and Organisational Development:	Claire Hay (claire.hay@crossreach.org.uk)

Further information: www.crossreach.org.uk

5. ASSEMBLY BUSINESS COMMITTEE

The Committee makes the arrangements and ordering of business for the General Assembly and Commissions of Assembly. It keeps under review the functions, membership, processes and procedures of the Assembly, and monitors the implementation of Assembly decisions. It has responsibility for the Assembly Hall and the Moderator's residence and oversight of presbytery restructuring.

Convener:	Rev. Michael J. Mair MStJ BD MTh
Vice-Convener:	Rev. Sheila M. Kirk BA LLB BD
Secretary:	Principal Clerk
	cmcintosh@churchofscotland.org.uk 0131 376 1594

Further information:
www.churchofscotland.org.uk > About us > General Assembly
www.churchofscotland.org.uk > About us > Forums, committees and departments > Committees > Assembly Business

6. AUDIT COMMITTEE

Remit: to oversee the financial and other relevant reporting processes implemented by management; to work with the Assembly Trustees in setting appropriate standards of financial management and in overseeing compliance; and to keep under review the effectiveness of the systems for internal financial control, financial reporting and risk management, including compliance with the legal and regulatory environment.

Convener: Kenneth Baldwin

Contact: OATadmin@churchofscotland.org.uk   0131 225 5722

Further information:
www.churchofscotland.org.uk > About us > Forums, committees and departments > Committees
> Audit

7. CHURCH OF SCOTLAND TRUST

The Trust's function is to hold properties outwith Scotland and to act as trustee in a number of
third-party trusts.

Chairman: Mr Leon M. Marshall CA
Vice-Chairman: Mrs Morag Angus MA DipLS FRICS
Treasurer: Mrs Anne F. Macintosh BA CA
Secretary and Clerk: Mrs Madelaine Sproule LLB MSc DipLP NP
                     msproule@churchofscotland.org.uk   0131 376 1307; 0131 225 5722

Further information:
www.churchofscotland.org.uk > About us > Stewardship, finance and trusts > Church of
Scotland Trust

8. COMMITTEE TO NOMINATE THE MODERATOR

Convener: The immediate past Moderator
Secretary: Principal Clerk
Contact: pcoffice@churchofscotland.org.uk
             0131 225 5722

9. COMMUNICATIONS DEPARTMENT

Head of Communications: Ruth MacLeod Ruth.Macleod@churchofscotland.org.uk
Communications Manager: Helen Silvis HSilvis@churchofscotland.org.uk
Senior Communications Officer: Cameron Brooks CBrooks@churchofscotland.org.uk
Communications Officer: Jane Bristow JBristow@churchofscotland.org.uk
Communications Officer: Calum Macleod CMacleod@churchofscotland.org.uk
Web Editor: Vacant
Web Developer: Alan Murray

Design Team Leader: Chris Flexen
Senior Designer: Steve Walker

Contact the Media Team after hours: 07854 783539
Contact department: 0131 225 5722
Further information:
www.churchofscotland.org.uk > About us > Forums, committees and departments >
Departments > Communications

---

10. ECUMENICAL RELATIONS COMMITTEE

The Committee is composed of Convener, Vice Convener and eight members appointed by
the General Assembly, plus representatives of other denominations in Scotland and Church of
Scotland members elected to British and international ecumenical bodies.

Convener: Rev. I. Ross Blackman BSc MBA BD CertTh
Vice-Convener: Pauline E.D. Weibye MA FCIPD
Secretary and Ecumenical Officer: Rev. Dr John L. McPake

Contact: ecumenical@churchofscotland.org.uk   0131 225 5722

Further information:
www.churchofscotland.org.uk > About us > Forums, committees and departments > Committees
> Ecumenical Relations Committee
www.churchofscotland.org.uk > Connect > Ecumenical relations
World Council of Churches: www.oikumene.org
Churches Together in Britain and Ireland: www.ctbi.org.uk
Action of Churches Together in Scotland: www.acts-scotland.org
For other international ecumenical bodies see Committee's web pages as above
See also 'Other Churches in the United Kingdom' at Section 2.2.

---

11. ESTATES AND PROCUREMENT DEPARTMENT

Remit: to provide property, facilities, and procurement services to the Agencies and Departments
of the central administration of the Church, and to manage the church offices.

Head of Estates and Procurement: Liam Fennell
Facilities Manager, Church Offices: Eunice Smith   0131 380 3054
                                     eunice.smith@churchofscotland.org.uk
Contact: cpd@churchofscotland.org.uk   0131 225 5722

Further information:
www.churchofscotland.org.uk > About us > Forums, committees and departments > Departments > Estates and Procurement

12. FORCES CHAPLAINS COMMITTEE

The Committee has responsibility for the recruitment of chaplains and takes an interest in their welfare and that of their families. It makes a contribution to the formulation of Ministry of Defence policy as it concerns the spiritual well-being of the women and men of the Armed Forces.

Convener:	Rev. Scott J. Brown CBE
Vice-Convener:	Group Captain Andrew G. Tait CEng FRAeS RAF(Ret'd)
Secretary:	Daran Golby, Faith Action Staff
	DGolby@churchofscotland.org.uk 0131 225 5722

Further information:
www.churchofscotland.org.uk > About us > Forums, committees and departments > Forces Chaplains Committee
A list of Chaplains is found at Section 6 D

13. GENERAL TRUSTEES

The General Trustees hold properties and investments for the Church as a whole. They are charged with ensuring church buildings and funds are managed in the best interest of the Church as a whole and in support of parish ministry. The Trustees offer practical advice and guidance on maintaining and improving Church properties, manses and glebes. They also offer a limited amount of financial aid to congregations facing expenditure on their buildings.

Chair:	Mr Alan F.K. Kennedy BSc FFA
Vice-Chair:	Rev. Scott M. Rennie MA BD STM FRSA
Chief Executive:	Mr Brian D. Waller LLB DipLP
PA to Chief Executive &	
Head of Business Support:	Mrs Eva Elder
Head of Land & Estates:	Mrs Morag J. Menneer BSc MRICS
	Ms Claire L. Cowell LLB
Head of Buildings & Projects:	Vacant
Finance Manager:	Ms Jennifer Law BSc CA
Buildings insurance,	Church of Scotland Insurance Services Ltd.
all enquiries to	121 George Street, Edinburgh EH2 4YN
	enquiries@cosic.co.uk 0131 220 4119

Chief Executive (COSIS):   Mr Barry Clarkson

Contact: gentrustees@churchofscotland.org.uk   0131 225 5722
Further information:
www.churchofscotland.org.uk > About us > Forums, committees and departments > Departments > General Trustees
www.churchofscotland.org.uk > Resources > Building and property resources

14. THE GUILD

The Church of Scotland Guild is a movement within the Church of Scotland whose aim is 'to invite and encourage both women and men to commit their lives to Jesus Christ and to enable them to express their faith in worship, prayer, action and fellowship'.

Convener:	Rae Lind, Irvine and Kilmarnock Guilds Together
Vice-Conveners:	Flora Buthlay, Gordon Guilds Together
	Kay Coull, Edinburgh Guilds Together
	Morag Duncan, Lewis Guilds Together
	Christina Patterson, Stirling and Clackmannshire Guilds Together
General Secretary:	Karen Gillon
Administrator:	Mandy Moir

Contact: guild@churchofscotland.org.uk   0131 380 6306

Further information:
www.cos-guild.org.uk
www.churchofscotland.org.uk > Serve > The Guild

15. HOUSING AND LOAN FUND

Chair:	Rev. Dorothy U. Anderson LLB DipLP BD
Deputy Chair:	Rev. Bruce H. Sinclair BA BD
Secretary:	Hazel Bett
	HBett@churchofscotland.org.uk
	0131 225 5722; 07929 418762
Project Manager:	Mark Learmonth
Property Manager:	Hilary J. Hardy
Property Assistant:	Selena MacArthur

Further information:
www.churchofscotland.org.uk > About us > Forums, committees and departments > Departments > Housing and Loan Fund

16. HUMAN RESOURCES DEPARTMENT

Head of Human Resources: Elaine McCloghry
Human Resources Managers: Karen Smith
                             Angela Ocak
Human Resources Advisers: Sarah-Jayne McVeigh
                             Stephanie Thomson

Contact: hr@churchofscotland.org.uk   0131 225 5722

Further information:
www.churchofscotland.org.uk > About us > Forums, committees and departments >
Departments > Human Resources

17. INFORMATION TECHNOLOGY DEPARTMENT

Head of IT: Richard MacLennan
               0131 376 1597

Contact: itdept@churchofscotland.org.uk   0131 376 1597

Further information:
www.churchofscotland.org.uk > About us > Forums, committees and departments >
Departments > IT

18. INVESTORS TRUST

The Trust provides the Church's agencies, committees and congregations with a simple and
economical facility for the investment of their funds.

Chairman: Robert D. Burgon
Vice-Chairman: Elaine Crichton
Treasurer: Anne F. Macintosh BA CA
Executive Officer: June Lee
                       investorstrust@churchofscotland.org.uk   0131 376 3678

Further information:
www.churchofscotland.org.uk > About us > Stewardship, finance and trusts > Departments >
Investors Trust

19. LAW DEPARTMENT

The Law Department gives advice and acts in legal matters for the Church and its courts, agencies, committees, congregations, the General Trustees, the Church of Scotland Trust and the Investors Trust. It is responsible for buying and selling churches, manses and other buildings/land on behalf of the Church's agencies, committees and congregations. The Department also provides advice and assistance to congregations and other Church bodies on a diverse range of issues including employment law, contract matters, trusts, charity law, data protection and litigation of various sorts and prepares circulars on legal topics affecting congregations such as health and safety, employment and discrimination law and data protection.

Solicitor of the Church and of the General Trustees:	Mary Macleod LLB DipLP NP
Depute Solicitor:	Elspeth Annan LLB DipLP NP
Solicitors:	Anne Steele LLB DipLP NP
	Jennifer Campbell LLB LLM DipLP NP
	Gregor Buick LLB DipLP WS NP
	Madelaine Sproule LLB MSc DipLP NP
	Gordon Barclay LLB DipLP BSc MSc MPhil PhD FRSA
	David di Paola LLB DipLP NP
	Shirley Davidson LLB DipLP
	John Wilson LLB DipLP NP
	Kirsty Wilson LLB DipLP
Data Protection Officer:	Alice Wilson BA PCDP

Contact: lawdept@churchofscotland.org.uk   0131 225 5722 ext. 2230

Further information:
www.churchofscotland.org.uk > About us > Forums, committees and departments > Departments > Law

20. LEGAL QUESTIONS COMMITTEE

Remit: to advise on legal questions of Church and civil law, assist in formulating responses to consultations by the Scottish and UK governments, provide the legislative drafting service for Agencies of the General Assembly, advise on reform to Church law in terms of practice and procedure, report on proposed amendments to Standing Orders, and inspect annually the records of Agencies and Presbyteries.

Convener:	Rev. Dr Marjory A. MacLean
Vice-Convener:	Rev. Alan D. Reid MA BD
Secretary:	Principal Clerk
Depute Clerk:	Ms Christine Paterson LLB DipLP

Contact: NNicholls@churchofscotland.org.uk   0131 376 1137

Further information:
www.churchofscotland.org.uk > About us > Forums, committees and departments > Committees > Legal Questions

---

21. LIFE AND WORK
the Church of Scotland's monthly magazine

The magazine's purpose is to keep the Church informed about events in church life at home and abroad and to provide a forum for Christian opinion and debate on a variety of topics. It has an independent editorial policy. Contributions which are relevant to any aspect of the Christian faith are welcome. The website, www.lifeandwork.org, includes up-to-date news, extracts from the magazine and additional features. To subscribe to the magazine through your church, speak to your Life and Work co-ordinator. To receive by post, call the number below or visit the website. A digital download, for reading on PC, tablet and smartphone, is also available.

Editor: Lynne McNeil   magazine@lifeandwork.org   0131 225 5722

Further information:
www.lifeandwork.org
www.churchofscotland.org.uk > News and Events > Life and Work

---

22. NOMINATION COMMITTEE

Remit: to bring before the General Assembly names of persons to serve on the Standing Committees of the General Assembly; to work with the Standing Committees to ensure an open, fair and robust process for identifying suitable persons to serve as Conveners; and to comment on recommendations for the appointment of Assembly Trustees.

Convener:	Rev. Dr Andrew Gardner BSc BD
Vice-Convener:	Rev. Bryan Kerr BA BD
Secretary:	Rev. Victoria J. Linford LLB BD

Contact: Nominations@churchofscotland.org.uk   0131 225 5722

Further information:
www.churchofscotland.org.uk > About us > Forums, committees and departments > Committees > Nomination Committee

23. PENSION TRUSTEES

The Trustees are responsible for the Church's three defined benefit pension schemes, now closed to future accrual and new members. The schemes are for: Ministers and Overseas Missionaries (including sections for Ministers Main Pension Fund, Widows and Orphans and the Contributors Fund); Staff (including sections for staff of the Social Care Council and of the Central Services Committee); and Ministries Development Staff (previously Presbytery and Parish Workers).

Chair:	Mr Stuart Stephen BSc
Vice-Chair:	Miss Lin J. Macmillan MA
Scheme Secretary and Pensions Manager:	Miss Jane McLeod BSc FPMI
Senior Pensions Administrator:	Mrs Fiona McCulloch-Stevenson
Pensions Administrators:	Ms Birgit Mosemann
	Mrs Lesley Elder
	Mrs Ruth Farquharson

Contact: pensions@churchofscotland.org.uk   0131 225 5722

Further information:
www.churchofscotland.org.uk > About us > Stewardship, finance and trusts > Pension Trustees

---

24. REGISTRATION OF MINISTRIES COMMITTEE

The Committee considers applications from ministers who wish to have the status of Category O, which entitles them to be inducted to a charge.

Convener:	Rev. Robert A. Hamilton BA BD
Vice-Convener:	Rev. Hilary N. McDougall MA PGCE BD
Registrar:	Rev. Angus R. Mathieson MA BD

Contact: RegistrationofMinistries@churchofscotland.org.uk 0131 376 6388

Further information:
www.churchofscotland.org.uk > Forums, committees and departments > Committees > Registration of Ministries Committee

---

25. SAFEGUARDING SERVICE

The service ensures that the Church has robust structures and policies in place for the prevention of harm and abuse of children and adults at risk; and to ensure a timely and appropriate response when harm or abuse is witnessed, suspected or reported.

Convener: Rev. Adam J. Dillon BD ThM
Vice-Convener: Judy Wilson
Service Manager: Ms Julie Main BA DipSW

Contact: safeguarding@churchofscotland.org.uk   0131 225 5722

Further information:
www.churchofscotland.org.uk > About us > Forums, committees and departments >
Departments > Safeguarding Service

26. SAINT ANDREW PRESS

Saint Andrew Press is managed on behalf of the Church of Scotland by Hymns Ancient and
Modern Ltd and publishes a broad range of titles, focussing principally on resources for the
mission and ministry of the contemporary church but also including backlist favourites such as
William Barclay's much-loved *Daily Study Bible* commentaries. The full list of publications
can be viewed on the Saint Andrew Press website (see below).

Contact: Christine Smith, Publishing Director christine@hymnsam.co.uk   0207 776 7546

Further information: www.standrewpress.com

27. SCOTTISH CHURCHES PARLIAMENTARY OFFICE
121 George Street, Edinburgh EH2 4YN

The purpose of the Scottish Churches Parliamentary Office is to build good relations between
Scottish Churches, the Scottish and UK Parliaments and the Scottish and UK Governments. It
aims to do this by: creating space for ecumenical fellowship and encounter on parliamentary
and political affairs in Scotland; facilitating and enabling Scottish Churches to speak on
legislation and political developments; and sharing news of parliamentary and political developments timeously and to the right people in the Churches.

Scottish Churches Parliamentary Officer: David Bradwell

Contact: DBradwell@churchofscotland.org.uk   0131 376 9104

Further information: www.scpo.scot

28. SCOTTISH STORYTELLING CENTRE (THE NETHERBOW)
43–45 High Street, Edinburgh EH1 1SR

The integrated facilities of the **Netherbow Theatre** and the **John Knox House**, together with the outstanding conference and reception areas, form an important cultural venue on the Royal Mile in Edinburgh. The Centre captures both the historical roots of storytelling and the forward-looking mission to preserve it: providing an extensive year-round cultural and literary programme. Faith Nurture Forum is pleased to partner with TRACS (Traditional Arts and Culture Scotland), a grant-funded body which provides advice and assistance nationally in the use of traditional arts in a diversity of settings.

Contact: reception@scottishstorytellingcentre.com   0131 556 9579

Further information: www.scottishstorytellingcentre.com

29. STEWARDSHIP AND FINANCE DEPARTMENT

The Department provides financial, governance and accounting advice to congregations and accounting, banking, payroll and budgeting services to the Church's agencies, committees and its statutory corporations - General Trustees, Investors Trust, Church of Scotland Trust – and to the Pension Trustees. It promotes Christian stewardship throughout the Church.

General Treasurer:	Anne F. Macintosh BA CA
Deputy Treasurer (Unincorporated Entities):	Gillian E. Coghlan MA CA
Deputy Treasurer (Wider Church and Statutory Corporations):	Leanne Thompson BSc CA
Finance Managers:	Lisa Erskine BA FCCA
	Jennifer Law BSc CA
	Elaine Macadie BA CA
	Suzanne Nolte
Stewardship Team Leader:	Pauline Wilson MA

Contact: sfadmin@churchofscotland.org.uk
Further information and details of consultants:
www.churchofscotland.org.uk > About us > Forums, committees and departments > Stewardship and Finance
www.churchofscotland.org.uk > Resources > Finance resources
www.churchofscotland.org.uk > Resources > Stewardship
www.churchofscotland.org.uk > About us > Stewardship Finance and Trusts

30. THEOLOGICAL FORUM

The purpose of the Forum is to continue to develop and bring to expression doctrinal understanding of the Church with reference to Scripture and to the confessional standards of the Church of Scotland, and the implications of this for worship and witness in and beyond contemporary Scotland. It responds to requests to undertake enquiries as they arise, draws the Church's attention to particular matters requiring theological work, and promotes theological reflection throughout the Church.

Convener:	Rev. Liam J. Fraser LLB BD MTh PhD
Vice-Convener:	Professor Paul T. Nimmo MA DipIA BD MTh PhD FHEA
Secretary:	Rev. Alasdair J. Macleod MA MLitt PhD (till Dec 2023)
	(from Jan 2024) Nathalie A. Mareš MacCallum MA MTh

Contact: AMacleod@churchofscotland.org.uk; NMaresMacCallum@churchofscotland.org.uk
Further information:
www.churchofscotland.org.uk > About us > Forums, committees and departments > Committees > Theological Forum

SECTION 2

General Information

1. GAELIC DEVELOPMENT IN THE CHURCH OF SCOTLAND

Leasachadh na Gàidhlig ann an Eaglais na h-Alba

Tha Comataidh na Gàidhlig air a bhith ag obair tron bhliadhna gus taic a thoirt do leasachadh na Gàidhlig anns an Eaglais.

B' e am pròiseact as motha taic a thoirt do Chomann Bhìoball na h-Alba (CBA) agus Faith Comes By Hearing ann an clàradh leabhar-fuaim eadar-theangachadh ùr dhen Tiomnaidh Nuaidh. Chaidh seo a chlàradh an uiridh ann an Dùn Èideann agus Steòrnabhagh agus tha e a-nis ri fhaotainn. Chaidh na clàraidhean an cleachdadh cuideachd airson fiolmaichean nan Soisgeul le Lumo, agus tha an dà chuid na clàraidhean agus na bhideothan rim faotainn air làrach-lìn CBA. Chaidh fàilte a chuir air na goireasan ùra le gluasad ann am Pàrlamaid na h-Alba, le taic o BPA ann an diofar pàirtaidhean.

Tha sinn cuideachd ag obair còmhla ri CBA gus goireasan a bharrachd a leasachadh. Nam measg, bidh ath-fhoillseachadh a' Bhìobaill Ghàidhlig (1992) agus goireasan chloinne suidhichte air a' Bhìoball ri chleachdadh ann an eaglaisean, dachaighean agus sgoiltean FMG.

Thug sinn taic cuideachd do bhideothan Lego ag innse sgeulachdan na Nollaige agus na Càisge airson cloinne, leis a' bhuidhinn Go Chatter.

'S e ar n-ùrnaigh gum beannachadh Dia na goireasan seo, gus an tèid Fhacal am meud am measg luchd-labhairt agus luchd-ionnsachaidh na Gàidhlig.

Tha Na Duilleagan Gàidhlig fhathast air fhoillseachadh gach ràith. Am bliadhna-sa, fhuair Na Duilleagan maoineachadh o Bhòrd na Gàidhlig gus leth-bhreacan a lìbhreagadh ann an clò, agus tha sinn ag obair gus an toirt do dh'eaglaisean agus buidhnean eile far am biodh iad gu feum.

Tha an dà bhuidheann-leughaidh air loidhne fhathast a' coinneachadh a h-uile seachdain (buidheann do luchd-tòiseachaidh, buidheann eile dhan fheadhainn a tha nas fhileanta), a cleachdadh an t-eadar-theangachadh ùr dhen Tiomnaidh Nuaidh.

Ann an 2020 bha sinn ag amas air sgoil shamhraidh a chuir air dòigh do mhinistearan agus do sheamonaichean eile a bha ag iarraidh Gàidhlig a chleachdadh ann an seirbheisean agus obar na h-eaglaise aca san fharsaingeachd, ach cha d'thàchair sin air sgàth COVID-19. Aig an àm sgrìobhaidh, tha sinn a-rithist ag amas air bùth-obrach fad latha a chuir air dòigh as t-samhradh am bliadhna-sa, agus an dòchas gun tèid sin a leasachadh san àm ri teachd.

An t-Oll. Donnchadh Sneddon

Gaelic Development in the Church of Scotland

The Gaelic Committee has continued to work in the past year to support and develop provision for Gaelic worship.

The biggest project has been supporting the Scottish Bible Society and Faith Comes By Hearing in developing the audio version of the new translation of the New Testament. This was recorded last summer in Edinburgh and Stornoway, and has now been released. The recordings have also been used to provide Gaelic audio for the Lumo films of the four Gospels. Both the audio and video forms can be accessed for free on the Scottish Bible Society's website. The launch of the audio version was marked by a motion in the Scottish Parliament, supported by MSPs from a range of parties.

We are also working with the Scottish Bible Society for the production of further materials. These include a forthcoming reprint of the 1992 Gaelic Bible and sets of Bible-based Gaelic resources for children that can be used in churches, family worship and Gaelic-medium education.

We have also helped to produce and share the Gaelic version of the Christmas and Easter stories with Lego videos for children, with the group Go Chatter.

We pray that God will bless these new resources which give access to his word to Gaelic speakers and learners.

Na Duilleagan Gàidhlig, the Gaelic supplement to Life and Work, continues to be produced on a quarterly basis. This year funding was secured from Bòrd na Gàidhlig to produce print copies Na Duilleagan, and we are working to distribute these to churches and other organisations where they will be welcomed.

The online weekly reading groups for Gaelic learners (one for beginners, one for advanced learners) continue to run, using the new translation of the New Testament.

It had been intended to run a short summer school for ministers and other preachers looking to use Gaelic in services and the work of their churches more broadly for the summer of 2020. Due to the COVID-19 pandemic that did not take place, but at the time of writing we were intending to run a pilot day-long workshop in summer 2023, which we hope can be developed and expanded in future.

Dr Duncan Sneddon

2. OTHER CHURCHES IN THE UNITED KINGDOM

ASSOCIATED PRESBYTERIAN CHURCHES: Assistant Clerk of Scottish Presbytery: Rev. J.R. Ross Macaskill (077110 648665; jrrm@gmail.com; www.apchurches.org).

BAPTIST UNION OF SCOTLAND: General Director: Rev. Martin Hodson, 48 Speirs Wharf, Glasgow G4 9TH (0141 433 4555; martin@scottishbaptist.org.uk; www.scottishbaptist.com).

CHURCH OF ENGLAND: Secretary General of General Synod: Mr William Nye, Church House, Great Smith Street, London SW1P 3AZ (020 7898 1000; enquiry@churchofengland. org).

CONGREGATIONAL FEDERATION IN SCOTLAND: Secretary: Miss Margaret McGuiness, Coatdyke Congregational Church, Kippen Street, Airdrie ML6 9AX (www. congregational.org.uk).

FREE CHURCH OF SCOTLAND: Principal Clerk: Rev. Callum Macleod, 15 North Bank Street, Edinburgh EH1 2LS (0131 226 5286; offices@freechurch.org; www.freechurch.org).

FREE CHURCH OF SCOTLAND (CONTINUING): Principal Clerk: Rev. Graeme Craig, Free Church Manse, 46A Craigie Road, Ayr KA8 0HA (01292 737447; principalclerk@ fccontinuing.org; www.freechurchcontinuing.org).

FREE PRESBYTERIAN CHURCH OF SCOTLAND: Clerk of Synod: Rev. Keith M. Watkins, Free Presbyterian Manse, Ferry Road, Leverburgh, Isle of Harris HS5 3UA (kmwatkins@fpchurch.org.uk; www.fpchurch.org.uk).

METHODIST CHURCH IN SCOTLAND: District Administrator: Sue Marshall-Jennings, Methodist Church District Office, Old Churches House, 1 Kirk Street, Dunblane FK15 0AL (07884 236761; DistrictAdmin@methodistchurchinscotland.net; methodistchurchinscotland.net).

PRESBYTERIAN CHURCH IN IRELAND: Clerk of the General Assembly and General Secretary: Rev. Trevor D. Gribben, Assembly Buildings, 2–10 Fisherwick Place, Belfast BT1 6DW (028 9041 7208; clerk@presbyterianireland.org; www.presbyterianireland.org).

PRESBYTERIAN CHURCH OF WALES: General Secretary: Rev. Meirion Morris, Tabernacle Chapel, 81 Merthyr Road, Whitchurch, Cardiff CF14 1DD (02920 627465; swyddfa. office@ebcpcw.org.uk; www.ebcpcw.cymru).

REFORMED PRESBYTERIAN CHURCH OF SCOTLAND: Clerk of Presbytery: Rev. Peter Loughridge, 7 West Pilton Road, Edinburgh EH4 4GX (07791 369626; peterloughridge@ hotmail.com; www.rpcscotland.org).

RELIGIOUS SOCIETY OF FRIENDS (QUAKERS): Clerk to the General Meeting for Scotland: Michael Hutchinson (scotfriends@gmail.com; www.quakerscotland.org).

ROMAN CATHOLIC CHURCH: Fr. Gerard Maguiness, General Secretary, Bishops' Conference of Scotland, 64 Aitken Street, Airdrie ML6 6LT (01236 764061; gensec@bcos. org.uk; www.bcos.org.uk).

SALVATION ARMY: Lt-Col. Carol Bailey, Secretary for Scotland, Scotland Office, 12A Dryden Road, Loanhead EH20 9LZ (0131 440 9109; carol.bailey@salvationarmy.org.uk; www.salvationarmy.org.uk).

SCOTTISH EPISCOPAL CHURCH: Secretary General: Mr John F. Stuart, 21 Grosvenor Crescent, Edinburgh EH12 5EE (0131 225 6357; secgen@scotland.anglican.org; www. scotland.anglican.org).

UNITED FREE CHURCH OF SCOTLAND: Principal Clerks: Rev. Martin C. Keane and Rev. Colin C. Brown, United Free Church Offices, 11 Newton Place, Glasgow G3 7PR (0141 332 3435; office@ufcos.org.uk; www.ufcos.org.uk).

UNITED REFORMED CHURCH: General Secretary: Rev. Dr John Bradbury, Church House, 86 Tavistock Place, London WC1H 9RT (020 7916 2020; john.bradbury@urc.org.uk; www.urc.org.uk).

UNITED REFORMED CHURCH SYNOD OF SCOTLAND: Synod Clerk: Rev. Jan Adamson, United Reformed Church, 3/2 Atlantic Chambers, 45 Hope Street, Glasgow G2 6AE (0141 248 5382; clerk@urcscotland.org.uk; www.urcscotland.org.uk).

---

3. OVERSEAS CHURCHES

See www.churchofscotland.org.uk > Connect > Global Partnerships > Partner Churches

---

4. HIS MAJESTY'S HOUSEHOLD IN SCOTLAND
ECCLESIASTICAL

Dean of the Order of the Thistle and Dean of the Chapel Royal:	Very Rev. Prof. David A.S. Fergusson OBE MA BD DPhil DD FRSE FBA
Domestic Chaplains:	Rev. Kenneth I. Mackenzie DL BD CPS Rev. Neil N. Gardner DL CStJ MA BD
Chaplains in Ordinary:	Very Rev. Angus Morrison MA BD PhD DD Very Rev. E. Lorna Hood OBE MA BD DD Very Rev. Susan M. Brown BD DipMin DUniv Rev. Elizabeth M. Henderson OBE MA BD MTh Rev. George J. Whyte OBE BSc BD DMin KSG Rev. Marjory A. MacLean LLB BD PhD Rev. S. Grant Barclay LLB DipLP BD MSc PhD Rev. Prof. John Swinton BD PhD RMN RNMD FRSE FBA Rev. Moira McDonald MA BD

Extra Chaplains:

Rev. John MacLeod MA
Very Rev. James A. Simpson BSc BD STM DD
Very Rev. James Harkness KCVO CB OBE MA DD
Rev. John L. Paterson MA BD STM
Rev. Charles Robertson LVO MA
Very Rev. John B. Cairns KCVO LTh LLB LLD DD
Very Rev. Gilleasbuig I. Macmillan
            KCVO MA BD Drhc DD FRSE HRSA FRCSEd
Very Rev. Finlay A.J. Macdonald MA BD PhD DD
Rev. Alastair H. Symington MA BD
Rev. James M. Gibson TD LTh LRAM
Very Rev. Prof. Iain R. Torrance KCVO Kt DD FRSE
Rev. Norman W. Drummond CBE MA BD DUniv FRSE
Rev. Alistair G. Bennett BSc BD
Very Rev. John P. Chalmers BD CPS DD

5. LORD HIGH COMMISSIONERS
TO THE GENERAL ASSEMBLY

* deceased

1980/81	The Earl of Elgin and Kincardine KT DL JP
1982/83	*Colonel Sir John Edward Gilmour Bt DSO TD
1984/85	*Charles Hector Fitzroy Maclean, Baron Maclean of Duart and Morvern KT GCVO KBE
1986/87	*John Campbell Arbuthnott, Viscount of Arbuthnott KT CBE DSC FRSE FRSA
1988/89	*Sir Iain Mark Tennant KT FRSA
1990/91	The Rt Hon. Donald MacArthur Ross FRSE
1992/93	The Rt Hon. Lord Macfarlane of Bearsden KT FRSE
1994/95	*Lady Marion Fraser KT
1996	Her Royal Highness the Princess Royal KG KT GCVO GCStJ
1997	The Rt Hon. Lord Macfarlane of Bearsden KT FRSE
1998/99	*The Rt Hon. Lord Hogg of Cumbernauld CBE DL JP
2000	His Royal Highness the Prince Charles, Duke of Rothesay KG KT GCB OM
2001/02	*The Rt Hon. Viscount Younger of Leckie KT KCVO TD PC
	*Her Majesty Queen Elizabeth II attended the opening session in 2002
2003/04	The Rt Hon. Lord Steel of Aikwood KT KBE
2005/06	The Rt Hon. Lord Mackay of Clashfern KT
2007	His Royal Highness the Prince Andrew, Duke of York KG KCVO
2008/09	The Rt Hon. George Reid PC MA
2010/11	Lord Wilson of Tillyorn KT GCMG PRSE
2012/13	The Rt Hon. Lord Selkirk of Douglas KC MA LLB
2014	His Royal Highness the Prince Edward, Earl of Wessex KG GCVO
2015/16	The Rt Hon. Lord Hope of Craighead KT PC FRSE
2017	Her Royal Highness the Princess Royal KG KT GCVO GCStJ QSO
2018/19	The Duke of Buccleuch and Queensberry KT KBE DL FSA FRSE

2020   *The General Assembly in May was cancelled due to the pandemic*
2021   His Royal Highness the Prince William, Earl of Strathearn KG KT MA
2022/23   The Rt Hon. Lord Hodge PC KC MA LLB

6. MODERATORS
OF THE GENERAL ASSEMBLY

* deceased

1992   Hugh R. Wyllie MA DD FCIBS, Hamilton: Old
1993   *James L. Weatherhead CBE MA LLB DD, Principal Clerk of Assembly
1994   James A. Simpson BSc BD STM DD, Dornoch Cathedral
1995   James Harkness KCVO CB OBE MA DD, Chaplain General (Emeritus)
1996   *John H. McIndoe MA BD STM DD, London: St Columba's linked with
              Newcastle: St Andrew's
1997   *Alexander McDonald BA DUniv CMIWSc, General Secretary, Department of
              Ministry
1998   Alan Main TD MA BD STM PhD DD, University of Aberdeen
1999   John B. Cairns KCVO LTh LLB LLD DD, Dumbarton: Riverside
2000   Andrew R.C. McLellan CBE MA BD STM DD, Edinburgh: St Andrew's and
              St George's
2001   John D. Miller BA BD STM DD, Glasgow: Castlemilk East
2002   Finlay A.J. Macdonald MA BD PhD DD, Principal Clerk of Assembly
2003   Iain R. Torrance KCVO Kt DD FRSE, University of Aberdeen
2004   Alison Elliot CBE MA MSc PhD LLD DD FRSE, Associate Director, Centre
              for Theology and Public Issues, University of Edinburgh
2005   David W. Lacy DL BA BD DLitt, Kilmarnock: Henderson
2006   Alan D. McDonald LLB BD MTh DLitt DD, Cameron linked with St Andrews:
              St Leonard's
2007   Sheilagh M. Kesting BA BD DD DSG, Secretary of Ecumenical Relations
              Committee
2008   David W. Lunan MA BD DLitt DD, Clerk to the Presbytery of Glasgow
2009   William C. Hewitt BD DipPS, Greenock: Westburn
2010   John C. Christie BSc BD CBiol MRSB, Interim Minister
2011   A. David K. Arnott MA BD, St Andrews: Hope Park linked with Strathkinness
2012   Albert O. Bogle BD MTh, Bo'ness: St Andrew's
2013   E. Lorna Hood OBE MA BD DD, Renfrew: North
2014   John P. Chalmers BD CPS DD, Principal Clerk of Assembly
2015   Angus Morrison MA BD PhD DD, Orwell and Portmoak
2016   G. Russell Barr BA BD MTh DMin, Edinburgh: Cramond
2017   Derek Browning MA BD DMin, Edinburgh: Morningside
2018   Susan M. Brown BD DipMin DUniv, Dornoch Cathedral
2019   Colin A.M. Sinclair BA BD, Edinburgh: Palmerston Place
2020   W. Martin Fair BA BD DMin, Arbroath: St Andrew's
2021   James R. Wallace, The Rt Hon. Lord Wallace of Tankerness PC KC FRSE MA
              LLB DUniv

2022   Iain M. Greenshields BD CertMin DipRS ACMA MSc MTh DD, Dunfermline:
                 St Margaret's
2023   Sally Foster-Fulton BA BD, Head of Christian Aid Scotland

MATTER OF PRECEDENCE
The Lord High Commissioner (while the Assembly is sitting) ranks next to the Sovereign and
before the rest of the Royal Family. The Moderator ranks next to the Lord Chancellor of Great
Britain and before the Keeper of the Great Seal of Scotland (the First Minister) and the Dukes.

7. SCOTTISH DIVINITY FACULTIES
* denotes a Minister of the Church of Scotland

ABERDEEN
School of Divinity, History and Philosophy
50–52 College Bounds, Old Aberdeen AB24 3DS
01224 272366; divinity@abdn.ac.uk

Master of Christ's College: Rev. Professor John Swinton* BD PhD RMN RNMD FRSE FBA
                                     christs-college@abdn.ac.uk
Head of School: Professor Beth Lord MA PhD
Head of Divinity: Professor Paul T. Nimmo MA DipIA BD MTh PhD FHEA
Co-ordinator,
 Centre for Ministry Studies   Rev. Emma Percy BA MA PhD
Senior Lecturer: Rev. Kenneth S. Jeffrey* BA BD PhD DMin
                                     ksjeffrey@abdn.ac.uk

For other teaching staff and further information see www.abdn.ac.uk/sdhp/

ST ANDREWS
University College of St Mary
The School of Divinity, South Street, St Andrews, Fife KY16 9JU
01334 462850; divinity@st-andrews.ac.uk

Principal and Head of School: Professor Oliver Crisp BD MTh LLM PhD DLitt
Professor of World Christianity: Professor Sabine Hyland BA MPhil PhD

For other teaching staff and further information see www.st-andrews.ac.uk/divinity/people

EDINBURGH
School of Divinity and New College
New College, Mound Place, Edinburgh EH1 2LX
0131 650 8959; divinity@ed.ac.uk

Head of School:	Professor Jeremy R. Carette
Principal of New College:	Rev. Professor Alison M. Jack* MA BD PhD SFHEA
Vice Principal of New College:	Rev. Professor Susan Hardman Moore* MA MAR PhD FRHistS
Senior Teaching Fellow, Practical Theology and Missiology:	Rev. Alexander C. Forsyth* LLB DipLP BD MTh PhD

For other teaching staff and further information see www.ed.ac.uk/divinity/our-people

---

GLASGOW
School of Critical Studies
Theology and Religious Studies
4 Professors' Square, University of Glasgow, Glasgow G12 8QQ
0141 330 6526; trinitycollegeglasgow@gmail.com

Head of Subject:	Dr Mia Spiro
Professor of Theology and Creative Practice:	Professor Heather Walton
Principal of Trinity College:	Rev. Doug C. Gay* MA BD PhD
Clerk of Trinity College and Tutor in Pastoral Studies:	Rev. Mark G. Johnston* BSc BD DMin

For other teaching staff and further information see www.gla.ac.uk/subjects/theology and www.trinitycollegeglasgow.co.uk

---

HIGHLAND THEOLOGICAL COLLEGE UHI
High Street, Dingwall IV15 9HA
01349 780000; htc@uhi.ac.uk

Principal of HTC:	Rev. Hector Morrison* BSc BD MTh Cert ITL
Vice-Principal (Academic):	Jamie Grant LLB MA PhD
Vice Principal (Finance and Operations):	Blair Gardner BSc PGDip
Access Course Leader, Lecturer in Youth, Church and Culture:	Rev. Jonathan Fraser* MA(Div) MTh ThM PhD

Lecturer in Evangelism: Rev. Thomas MacNeil* MA BD

For other teaching staff and further information see www.htc.uhi.ac.uk

8. SOCIETIES AND ASSOCIATIONS
* Church of Scotland Societies

ACTION OF CHURCHES TOGETHER IN SCOTLAND (ACTS): ACTS was formed in 1990 as Scotland's national ecumenical instrument. It brings together nine denominations in Scotland who share a desire for greater oneness between churches, a growth of understanding and common life between churches, and unified action in proclaiming and responding to the gospel in the whole of life. The Member Churches of ACTS are in the process of transitioning the organisation into the Scottish Christian Forum, which would take forward the charitable purposes of ACTS.

* ASSEMBLY AND PRESBYTERY CLERKS FORUM: Secretary: Rev. Bryan Kerr, Greyfriars Parish Church, Bloomgate, Lanark ML11 9ET (01555 437050; 01555 663363; clerksforum@churchofscotland.org.uk).

BOYS' BRIGADE: A volunteer-led Christian youth organisation which was founded in Scotland in 1883 and now operates in many different countries around the world. Our vision is that children and young people experience life to the full (John 10:10). We provide opportunities for young people to learn, grow and discover in a safe, caring and fun environment. Contact: John Sharp, Carronvale House, Carronvale Road, Larbert FK5 3LH (01324 562008; support@boys-brigade.org.uk; www.boys-brigade.org.uk). Scottish Chaplain: Rev Derek Gunn (scottishchaplain@boys-brigade.org.uk).

BROKEN RITES: Support group for divorced and separated clergy spouses. Scottish representative: Janet Forbes (07398 222118; janetruth018@gmail.com; www.brokenrites.org).

CHRISTIAN AID SCOTLAND: Val Brown, Interim Head of Christian Aid Scotland, 41 George IV Bridge, Edinburgh EH1 1EL (0131 220 1254; edinburgh@christian-aid.org; www.christianaid.org.uk/get-involved-locally/scotland).

* CHURCH OF SCOTLAND ABSTAINERS' ASSOCIATION: Recognising that alcohol is a major – indeed a growing – problem within Scotland, the aim of the Church of Scotland Abstainers' Association, with its motto 'Abstinence makes sense', is to encourage more people to choose a healthy alcohol-free lifestyle. Further details are available from 'Blochairn', 17A Culduthel Road, Inverness IV24 4AG (jamwall@talktalk.net; www.kirkabstainers.org.uk).

* CHURCH OF SCOTLAND MILITARY CHAPLAINS' ASSOCIATION: The Association consists of serving and retired chaplains to HM Forces. It holds an annual meeting and lunch on Shrove Tuesday, and organises the annual Service of Remembrance in St Giles' Cathedral. Hon. Secretary: Rev. Stephen A. Blakey BSc BD CStJ, Balduff House, Kilry, Blairgowrie PH11 8HS (01575 560226; SBlakey@churchofscotland.org.uk).

* CHURCH OF SCOTLAND RETIRED MINISTERS' ASSOCIATION: The Association meets in St. Andrew's and St. George's West Church, George St., Edinburgh, normally on the first Monday of the month, from October to April. The group is becoming increasingly ecumenical. Meetings include a talk, which can be on a wide variety of topics, which is followed by afternoon tea. Details of the programme from Hon. Secretary: Rev. Douglas A.O. Nicol, 1/2 North Werber Park, Edinburgh EH4 1SY (07811 437075; Douglas.Nicol@churchofscotland.org.uk).

* CHURCH SERVICE SOCIETY: Founded in 1865 to study the development of Christian worship through the ages and in the Reformed tradition, and to work towards renewal in contemporary worship. It has published since 1928, and continues to publish, a liturgical journal, archived on its website. Secretary: Rev. Dr Scott McKenna (01292 226075; SMcKenna@churchofscotland.org.uk; www.churchservicesociety.org).

* COVENANT FELLOWSHIP SCOTLAND (formerly FORWARD TOGETHER): An organisation for evangelicals within the Church of Scotland. Contact the Chairman, Rev. Mark Malcolm (07731 737377; MMalcolm@churchofscotland.org.uk; https://www.facebook.com/covenantfellowshipscotland).

DAY ONE CHRISTIAN MINISTRIES: Day One has produced Christian literature for over 40 years. A variety of books are published for both adults and young people, as well as cards, bookmarks and stationery items. Ryelands Road, Leominster, Herefordshire HR6 8NZ. Contact Mark Roberts for further information (01568 613740; mark@dayone.co.uk; www.dayone.co.uk).

ECO-CONGREGATION SCOTLAND: An ecumenical environmental charity supporting the largest movement of community-based environment groups across Scotland to care and act for God's creation. Eco-Congregation Scotland offers a programme to help local congregations reduce their impact on climate change and live sustainably. 121 George Street, Edinburgh EH2 4YN (0131 240 2274; manager@ecocongregationscotland.org; www.ecocongregationscotland.org).

FELLOWSHIP OF ST ANDREW: The fellowship promotes dialogue between Churches of the east and the west in Scotland. Further information available from the Secretary, Rev. Dr Robert Pickles, The Manse, Thomas Telford Road, Langholm DG13 0BL (01387 380252; RPickles@churchofscotland.org.uk).

* FRIENDS OF ST ANDREW'S JERUSALEM & TIBERIAS: In co-operation with the Faith Action Programme, the Friends seek to provide support for the work of the Congregation of St Andrew's Scots Memorial Church, Jerusalem, St Andrew's House Hotel, Jerusalem and St Andrew's Church, Tiberias. Hon. Secretary: Carol Miller, c/o Faith Action Programme, 121 George Street, Edinburgh, EH2 4YN.

* FRIENDS OF TABEETHA SCHOOL, JAFFA: The Friends seek to support the only school run by the Church of Scotland in the world. Based in Jaffa, Israel, it seeks to promote tolerance and understanding amongst pupils and staff alike. President: Irene Anderson. Hon. Secretary: Rev. David J. Smith, 1 Cawdor Drive, Glenrothes KY6 2HN (01592 611963; David.Smith@churchofscotland.org.uk).

FRONTIER YOUTH TRUST: A movement journeying with young people on the margins of church and society. We host a community of practice for those working with young people in the community. We are resourcing the church to take pioneering risks in their work with young people. And we are calling others to join the pioneer movement to reach young people on the margins. Contact us for training and coaching, or find practical resources on our website at www. fyt.org.uk. Contact us at info@fyt.org.uk, 0121 771 2328 or find us on social media.

GIRLGUIDING SCOTLAND: 16 Coates Crescent, Edinburgh EH3 7AH (Tel: 0131 226 4511; administrator@girlguiding-scot.org.uk; www.girlguidingscotland.org.uk).

GIRLS' BRIGADE SCOTLAND: 11A Woodside Crescent, Glasgow G3 7UL (0141 332 1765; caroline.goodfellow@girls-brigade-scotland.org.uk; www.girls-brigade-scotland.org.uk).

INTERSERVE GREAT BRITIAN AND IRELAND: An international, evangelical and interdenominational organisation with 160 years of Christian service. The purpose of Interserve is 'to make Jesus Christ known through *wholistic* ministry in partnership with the global church, among the neediest peoples of Asia and the Arab world', and our vision is 'Lives and communities transformed through encounter with Jesus Christ'. Interserve supports over 800 people in cross-cultural ministry in a wide range of work including children and youth, the environment, evangelism, Bible training, engineering, agriculture, business development and health. We look to support churches and individuals as they seek to serve the Lord cross-culturally both locally and throughout Asia and the Arab world. (03333 601600; enquiries@interserve.org. uk; www.interserve.org.uk).

IONA COMMUNITY: We are an ecumenical Christian community with a dispersed worldwide membership, and an international network of supporters and volunteers. Inspired by our faith, we pursue justice and peace in and through community. Our Glasgow centre is the base for Wild Goose Publications and the Wild Goose Resource Group. The Iona Community welcomes thousands of visitors each year to its daily worship in Iona Abbey, and to its Welcome Centre and Community shop. It also welcomes guests to share in the common life on Iona and at Camas outdoor centre on Mull, which mainly hosts youth groups. Leader: Rev. Ruth Harvey, Suite 9, Fairfield, 1048 Govan Road, Glasgow, G51 4XS (0141 429 7281, admin@iona.org.uk; www. iona.org.uk; Facebook: Iona Community; Twitter: @ionacommunity). Iona Warden: Caro Penney, Iona Abbey, Isle of Iona, Argyll, PA76 6SN (01681 700404; enquiries@iona.org.uk).

* IRISH GATHERING: An informal annual meeting with a guest speaker; all those having a connection with or an interest in the Presbyterian Church in Ireland are very welcome. Treasurer: Rev. Richard Baxter, 31 Hughenden Gardens, Glasgow G12 9YH (07958 541418; RBaxter@ churchofscotland.org.uk).

LEPROSY MISSION SCOTLAND: Working in over 30 countries, The Leprosy Mission is a global fellowship united by our Christian faith and commitment to finishing what Jesus started and making leprosy a thing of the past. The Leprosy Mission Scotland, Suite 2, Earlsgate Lodge, Livilands Lane, Stirling FK8 2BG (01786 449266; contactus@leprosymission.scot; www. leprosymission.scot).

PLACE FOR HOPE: exists to accompany and equip people and faith communities so that all may reach their potential as peacemakers, able to navigate change and conflict well. For over 10 years, Place for Hope has provided high quality mediation and training services in faith-based peace and reconciliation, supporting faith communities to notice brokenness and division, nurture relationships and community, navigate conflict with graciousness and nourish wholeness

in themselves and their communities. In times of change and challenge, we know that practical support can help. Place for Hope supports the Church of Scotland through the Living Peace Programme which offers:
- support for groups and individuals experiencing conflict
- facilitation of sensitive or difficult group conversations, such as preparing for change or transition
- individual or team coaching
- community dialogues on difficult, potentially divisive issues
- training, workshops and resources for understanding and working with conflict and change.

Please get in touch for information, or a confidential conversation: 07884 580359; info@placeforhope.org.uk; www.placeforhope.org.uk.

PRISON FELLOWSHIP SCOTLAND is a Christian charity working with those in Scotland's 15 prisons from Dumfries in the south to Inverness in the north. We run weekly Bible study groups for men and women in prison to explore faith and the Bible. We deliver a 6-week Restorative Justice/Victim awareness course that helps offenders look at the consequences of their offending. We run a letter-writing programme helping alleviate loneliness and isolation felt especially by older prisoners. Through our Angel Tree programme, we provide Christmas presents for the children of those in prison and we partner with SU and Circle to help Children affected by imprisonment to attend an adventure holiday. We would be happy to come to speak or provide information about work in prisons close to you. Contact Executive Director: John Nonhebel, Connect House, 42 Hollowglen Road, Glasgow G32 0DP (0141 266 0136; office@pfscotland.org; www.pfscotland.org).

RELATIONSHIPS SCOTLAND: Scotland's largest provider of relationship counselling, family mediation and child contact centre services. Chief Executive: Mr Stuart Valentine, 18 York Place, Edinburgh EH1 3EP (Tel: 0345 119 2020; Fax: 0845 119 6089; enquiries@relationships-scotland.org.uk; www.relationships-scotland.org).

ST COLM'S FELLOWSHIP: An association for all from any denomination who have trained, studied or been resident at St Colm's, either when it was a college or later as International House. There is an annual retreat and a meeting for Commemoration; and some local groups meet on a regular basis. Hon. Secretary: Rev. Margaret Nutter, 'Kilmorich', 14 Balloch Road, Balloch G83 8SR (01389 754505; maenutter@gmail.com).

SCOTTISH BIBLE SOCIETY: Chief Executive: Elaine Duncan, 7 Hampton Terrace, Edinburgh EH12 5XU (0131 337 9701; info@scottishbiblesociety.org; https://scottishbiblesociety.org).

SCOTTISH CHURCH HISTORY SOCIETY: Promoting interest in the history of Christianity in Scotland. Journal: *Scottish Church History*. Secretary: Dr Ben Rogers (schssec@outlook.com; www.scottishchurchhistory.org.uk).

* SCOTTISH CHURCH SOCIETY: Founded in 1892 to 'defend and advance Catholic doctrine as set forth in the Ancient Creeds and embodied in the Standards of the Church of Scotland', the Society meets for worship and discussion at All Saints' Tide, holds a Lenten Quiet Day, an AGM, and other meetings by arrangement; all are open to non-members. The Society is also now working closely with the Church Service Society and is arranging meetings which are of joint interest. Secretary: Rev. W. Gerald Jones MA BD MTh, The Manse, Patna Road, Kirkmichael, Maybole KA19 7PJ (01655 750286; WJones@churchofscotland.org.uk).

* **SCOTTISH CHURCH THEOLOGY SOCIETY:** The Society encourages theological exploration and discussion of the main issues confronting the Church in the twenty-first century. Rev. Alec Shuttleworth, 62 Toll Road, Kincardine, Alloa FK10 4QZ (01259 731002; AShuttleworth@churchofscotland.org.uk).

SCOTTISH CHURCHES ORGANIST TRAINING SCHEME (SCOTS): Established in 1995, SCOTS is run by the Royal College of Organists in partnership with the Scottish Federation of Organists, the Royal School of Church Music and the Scottish Churches. It is a self-propelled ecumenical scheme by which organists and those called upon to play the organ in churches follow a three-stage syllabus, receiving a certificate at each stage. Participants each have an Adviser whom they meet occasionally for help and assessment, and also take part in one of the Local Organ Workshops which are held in different parts of Scotland each year. Syllabus information at www.rco.org.uk/scots; information from Andrew Macintosh (01382 521210); andrew.macintosh@rco.org.uk.

SCOTTISH EVANGELICAL THEOLOGY SOCIETY: Seeks to promote theology which serves the church, is faithful to Scripture, grounded in scholarship, informed by worship, sharpened in debate, catholic in scope, with a care for Scotland and its people. Secretary: Rev. M.G. Smith, 0/2, 2008 Maryhill Road, Glasgow G20 0AB (0141 570 8680; sets.secretary@gmail.com; www.s-e-t-s.org.uk).

SCOTTISH REFORMATION SOCIETY: Exists to defend and promote the work of the Protestant Reformation in Scotland by organising meetings, publishing literature and running an essay competition. Chairman: Rev. John Keddie. Vice-Chairman: Mr Allan McCulloch. Secretary: Rev. Dr Douglas Somerset. Treasurer: Mr Hugh Morrison. The Magdalen Chapel, 41 Cowgate, Edinburgh EH1 1JR (0131 220 1450; info@scottishreformationsociety.org; www. scottishreformationsociety.org).

SCOUTS SCOTLAND: Scottish Headquarters, Fordell Firs, Hillend, Dunfermline KY11 7HQ (01383 419073; hello@scouts.scot; www.scouts.scot).

SCRIPTURE UNION SCOTLAND: Scripture Union Scotland's vision is to see every child and young person in Scotland exploring the Bible and responding to the significance of Jesus. SU Scotland works in schools running SU groups and supporting Curriculum for Excellence. Its three activity centres, Lendrick Muir, Alltnacriche and Gowanbank, accommodate school groups and weekends away during term-time. During the school holidays it runs an extensive programme of events for school-age children – including residential holidays (some focused on disadvantaged children and young people), missions and church-based holiday clubs. In addition, it runs discipleship and training programmes for young people and is committed to promoting prayer for, and by, the young people of Scotland through a range of national prayer events and the *Pray for Schools Scotland* initiative. Scripture Union Scotland, 70 Milton Street, Glasgow G4 0HR (0141 332 1162; info@suscotland.org.uk; www.suscotland.org.uk).

STUDENT CHRISTIAN MOVEMENT: SCM is a student-led movement inspired by Jesus to act for justice and show God's love in the world. As a community we come together to pray, worship and explore faith in an open and non-judgemental environment. The movement is made up of a network of groups and individual members across Britain, as well as link churches and chaplaincies. As a national movement we come together at regional and national events to learn more about our faith and spend time as a community, and we take action on issues of social justice chosen by our members. SCM provides resources and training to student groups, churches and chaplaincies on student outreach and engagement, leadership and social action. Chief Executive: Rev. Naomi Nixon, SCM, Grays Court, 3 Nursery Road, Edgbaston, Birmingham B15 3JX (0121 426 4918; scm@movement.org.uk; www.movement.org.uk).

TEARFUND: A Christian charity which partners with local churches and organisations in more than 50 of the world's poorest countries. It tackles poverty and injustice by responding to disasters, through sustainable community development, and by challenging unjust policies and practices at a local, national and global level. Head of Tearfund Scotland: Lorna McDonald, Baltic Chambers, Suite 529, 50 Wellington Street, Glasgow G2 6HJ (0141 332 3621; scotland@tearfund.org; www.tearfund.org).

WALDENSIAN MISSIONS AID SOCIETY FOR WORK IN ITALY: Supporting the outreach of the Waldensian Churches, including important work with immigrant communities in the *Mediterranean Hope* project. Scottish Charity No. SC001346. David A. Lamb SSC, 36 Liberton Drive, Edinburgh EH16 6NN (0131 664 3059; david@dlamb.co.uk; www.scottishwaldensian.org.uk).

WORLD DAY OF PRAYER: SCOTTISH COMMITTEE: Convener: Mary Welsh, 4 Tweedsmuir, Bishopbriggs, Glasgow G64 1EE (07516 310394; marypwelsh@icloud.com). Secretary: Marjorie Paton, Muldoanich, Stirling Street, Blackford, Auchterarder PH4 1QG (01764 682234; marjoriepaton.wdp@btinternet.com; www.wdpscotland.org.uk).

YMCA SCOTLAND: Offers support, training and guidance to churches seeking to reach out to love and serve young people's needs. Chief Executive – National General Secretary: Mrs Kerry Reilly, YMCA Scotland, 1 Chesser Avenue, Edinburgh EH14 1TB (0131 228 1464; kerry@ymca.scot; www.ymca.scot).

YOUTH FOR CHRIST: Youth for Christ is a national Christian charity who are about seeing young people's lives change by Jesus. In Scotland there are 4 locally governed, staffed and financed centres, communicating and demonstrating the Christian faith. We also produce a wide variety of resources for churches and seek to serve the local church across Scotland as they seek to support and share the gospel with the young people in their communities. Local Ministries Development Manager for Scotland: Sandra Blair (0121 502 9620; sandra.blair@yfc.co.uk; www.yfc.co.uk/local-centres/scotland).

YOUTH SCOTLAND: Balfour House, 19 Bonnington Grove, Edinburgh EH6 4BL (0131 554 2561; office@youthscotland.org.uk; www.youthscotland.org.uk).

9. TRUSTS AND FUNDS

ABERNETHY ADVENTURE CENTRES: Full board residential accommodation and adventure activities available for all Church groups, plus a range of Christian summer camps, gap year programmes and adventure leadership training courses at our three centres in Scotland. 01479 821279; info@abernethy.org.uk; www.abernethy.org.uk).

BAIRD TRUST: Assists in the building and repair of churches and halls, and generally assists the work of the Church of Scotland. Apply to Iain A.T. Mowat CA, 182 Bath Street, Glasgow G2 4HG (0141 332 0476; info@bairdtrust.org.uk; www.bairdtrust.org.uk).

Rev. Alexander BARCLAY BEQUEST: Assists a family member of a deceased minister of the Church of Scotland who at the time of his/her death was acting as his/her housekeeper and who is in needy circumstances, and in certain circumstances assists Ministers, Deacons, Ministries Development Staff and their spouses facing financial hardship. Applications can only be submitted to the trustees by the Faith Action Ministries Support Team, 121 George Street, Edinburgh EH2 4YN (pastoralsupport@churchofscotland.org.uk).

BELLAHOUSTON BEQUEST FUND: Gives grants to Protestant denominations in the City of Glasgow and certain areas within five miles of the city boundary for building and repairing churches and halls and the promotion of religion. Apply to Mitchells Roberton, 36 North Hanover Street, Glasgow G1 2AD (0141 552 3422; info@mitchells-roberton.co.uk).

BEQUEST FUND FOR MINISTERS OF CHURCH OF SCOTLAND: Provides financial assistance to ministers towards the cost of manse furnishings, pastoral efficiency aids, and personal and family medical or educational costs. Apply to A. Linda Parkhill CA, 60 Wellington Street, Glasgow G2 6HJ (0141 226 4994; mail@parkhillmackie.co.uk).

CARNEGIE TRUST FOR THE UNIVERSITIES OF SCOTLAND: The Carnegie Trust invites applications by students who have had at least two years education at a secondary school in Scotland (or can demonstrate evidence of a substantial link to Scotland), for Tuition Fee Grants towards tuition fee costs for a first undergraduate degree at a Scottish university. For more information and a link to the online application form visit the Trust's website (https://www.carnegie-trust.org/award-schemes/undergraduate-tuition-fee-grants/) or contact the Carnegie Trust for the Universities of Scotland, Andrew Carnegie House, Pittencrieff Street, Dunfermline KY12 8AW (01383 724990; admin@carnegie-trust.org; www.carnegie-trust.org).

CHURCH HYMNARY TRUST: The trust is 'formed for the advancement of the Christian Faith through the promotion and development of hymnody in Scotland with particular reference to the Church of Scotland by assisting in the development, promotion, provision and understanding of hymns, psalms and paraphrases suitable for use in public worship, and in the distribution and making available of the same in books, discs, electronically and in other media for use by the Church of Scotland ….' The trust wishes to encourage applications for projects or schemes which are consistent with its purposes. These can include training courses, provision of music and guides to music, but the trust is not limited to those activities. The trust usually meets annually in February, though applications may be considered out of committee. Applications should be made to the Secretary and Treasurer Anne Steele, 121 George Street, Edinburgh EH2 4YN (0131 380 1970; asteele@churchofscotland.org.uk).

CHURCH OF SCOTLAND INSURANCE SERVICES LTD: Insurance intermediary, authorised and regulated by the Financial Conduct Authority, which arranges and manages the facility providing insurance protection for Church of Scotland congregations, including their activities and assets. Cover can also be arranged for other religious groups, charities, and non-profitmaking organisations. All profits are distributed to the General Trustees of the Church of Scotland through Gift Aid. Contact 121 George Street, Edinburgh EH2 4YN (0131 220 4119; b.clarkson@cosic.co.uk; www.cosic.co.uk).

CHURCH OF SCOTLAND MINISTRIES BENEVOLENT FUND: Makes grants to the following beneficiaries who are in need:
(a) any retired person who has been ordained or commissioned for the Ministry of the Church of Scotland;
(b) Ministers inducted or introduced to a charge or appointment, Probationer Ministers, Admissions Candidates during Familiarisation Placement or Ordained National Ministers appointed to posts under approval of Presbytery;
(c) Ministries Development Staff appointed to a Presbytery planned post (including Deacons);
(d) Ordained Local Minsters, Auxiliary Ministers or Deacons serving under the appointment of Presbytery;
(e) Readers set apart by Presbytery to carry out the work of the Church;
(f) any widow, widower and/or orphan of any person categorised in (a) to (e) above;
(g) any spouse or former spouse and/or child (natural or otherwise) of any person categorised by (a) to (e) above.
Contact pastoralsupport@churchofscotland.org.uk for an application form. Enquiries to Alison Stewart, Senior Administrator, Faith Action Ministries Support Team, 121 George Street, Edinburgh EH2 4YN (0131 376 3685).

CHURCH OF SCOTLAND SEEDS FOR GROWTH FUND: Provides grants from a fund of £25m over 7 years from 2023 onwards for projects which seek the numerical and spiritual growth of the Church through: (i) planting new worshipping communities; (ii) work focussed on the development of new forms and fresh expressions of church life; (iii) creative engagement with all sectors of society, especially those 40 and under; and (iv) enabling community transformation motivated by Christian service. Applications must come from presbyteries or groups of presbyteries. Guidance at: www.churchofscotland.org.uk/connect/seeds-for-growth Contact: David Williams, Grants Manager, grants@churchofscotland.org.uk

CHURCH OF SCOTLAND SMALL GRANTS FUND: Provides grants of up to £1000 for short-term project funding of between 3 and 12 months for developing mission through new worshipping communities, engaging and attracting those aged under 40, addressing pressing issues in the church, and innovation in church practices. Also provides grants of up to £5000 for 'winter support' to help communities through the winter at a time of increased need. Individual Church of Scotland churches and presbyteries and groups of churches or presbyteries may apply. Churches and presbyteries are also able to work with ecumenical partners, though the application will need to come from the Church of Scotland church or presbytery. Guidance on applications at: www.churchofscotland.org.uk/connect/small-grants-fund Contact: David Williams, Grants Manager, SGF@churchofscotland.org.uk

CINTRA BEQUEST: See 'Tod Endowment Trust ...' entry below.

CLAREMONT TRUST: aims to assist small, innovative projects of Christian witness, renewal and social action in their very early stages of development. Typically grants are of £500–£600 and not more than £1000. Completed application forms must be received by the last working day of April for consideration in May. Application forms available on www.claremonttrust.org.uk or the Secretary, Sylvia Marchant (01592 890986; smarchant1944@gmail.com)

CLARK BURSARY: Awarded to accepted candidate(s) for the ministry of the Church of Scotland whose studies for the ministry are pursued at the University of Aberdeen. Applications or recommendations for the Bursary to the Clerk to the Presbytery of the North East and the Northern Isles, Suite 2, Ocean Spirit House West, 33 Waterloo Quay, Aberdeen AB11 5BS.

CRAIGCROOK MORTIFICATION: The Trust has power to award a pension to men and women of 60 years of age or over born in Scotland or who have resided in Scotland for not less than 10 years who appear to be in poor circumstances. The Trust awards pensions of £1,230 payable per annum in half-yearly instalments. Ministers are invited to notify the Clerk and Factor, Anna Bennett, The WS Society, The Signet Library, Parliament Square, Edinburgh EH1 1RF (0131 220 3249; abennett@wssociety.co.uk) of deserving persons and should be prepared to act as a referee on the application form.

DRUMMOND TRUST: Makes grants towards the cost of publication of books of 'sound Christian doctrine and outreach'. The Trustees are also willing to receive grant requests towards the cost of audio-visual programme material, but not equipment, software but not hardware. Requests for application forms should be made to the Secretaries, Hill and Robb Limited, 3 Pitt Terrace, Stirling FK8 2EY (01786 450985; catherineberrill@hillandrobb.co.uk). Manuscripts should *not* be sent.

DUNCAN McCLEMENTS TRUST FOR ECUMENICAL TRAINING: Makes grants towards the cost of attendance at ecumenical assemblies and conferences; gatherings of young people; short courses or conferences promoting ecumenical understanding. Also to enable schools to organise one-off events to promote better understanding among differing communities and cultures with different religious backgrounds. The Trust also helps towards the cost of resources and study materials. Enquiries to: Committee on Ecumenical Relations, Church of Scotland, 121 George Street, Edinburgh EH2 4YN (ecumenicalofficer@churchofscotland.org.uk).

David DUNCAN TRUST: Makes grants annually (December) to students for the ministry and students in training to become deacons in the Church of Scotland in the Faculties of Arts and Divinity. All applications are considered with slight preference given to those born or educated within the bounds of the former Presbytery of Arbroath. Applications to be received no later than 24 October to Thorntons Law LLP, Brothockbank House, Arbroath DD11 1NE (reference: Glyn Roberts (Trust Manager); 01382 346299; groberts@thorntons-law.co.uk).

ERSKINE CUNNINGHAM HILL TRUST: Donates its annual income to charities and to CrossReach. Individual donations are in the region of £1,000. Priority is given to charities administered by voluntary or honorary officials, in particular charities registered and operating in Scotland and relating to the elderly, young people, ex-service personnel or seafarers. Application forms from the Secretary, Alan Ritchie, 121 George Street, Edinburgh EH2 4YN (0131 225 5722; aritchie@churchofscotland.org.uk).

ESDAILE TRUST: Assists the education and advancement of daughters of ministers, missionaries and widowed deaconesses of the Church of Scotland between 12 and 25 years of age. Applications are to be lodged by 31 May in each year with the Clerk and Treasurer, Kirsty Ashworth, Exchange Place 3, Semple Street, Edinburgh EH3 8BL (0131 473 3500; SM-Charity@azets.co.uk).

FERGUSON BEQUEST FUND: Assists with the building and repair of churches and halls and, more generally, with the work of the Church of Scotland. Priority is given to the Counties of Ayr, Kirkcudbright, Wigtown, Lanark, Dunbarton and Renfrew, and to Greenock, Glasgow, Falkirk and Ardrossan; applications are, however, accepted from across Scotland. Apply to Iain A.T. Mowat CA, 182 Bath Street, Glasgow G2 4HG (0141 332 0476; info@fergusonbequestfund.org.uk; www.fergusonbequestfund.org.uk).

James GILLAN'S BURSARY FUND: Bursaries are available for male or female Candidates for the Ministry in the Church of Scotland who are currently resident in, or were born and had their home for not less than three years continually in the Parishes of Dyke, Edinkillie, Forres St Leonard's and Rafford. In certain circumstances the Trustees may be able to make a grant to Church Candidates resident in the old counties of Moray or Nairn, but only while resident. Apply to Roy Anderson, royand@btinternet.com.

GLASGOW SOCIETY OF THE SONS AND DAUGHTERS OF MINISTERS OF THE CHURCH OF SCOTLAND: The Society's primary purpose is to grant financial assistance to children (no matter what age) of deceased ministers of the Church of Scotland. Applications for first grants can be lodged at any time. Thereafter annual applications must be lodged by 31 December for consideration by Council in February. To the extent that funds are available, grants are also given for the children of ministers or retired ministers, although such grants are normally restricted to university and college students. These latter grants are considered in conjunction with the Edinburgh-based Societies. Limited funds are also available for individual application for special needs or projects. Applications are to be submitted by 31 May in each year. Emergency applications can be dealt with at any time when need arises. More information can be found at www.mansebairnsnetwork.org. Application forms may be obtained from the Secretary and Treasurer, Kirsty Ashworth, Exchange Place 3, Semple Street, Edinburgh EH3 8BL (0131 473 3500; SM-Charity@azets.co.uk).

GUNTRIP TRUST: for the advancement of education and training in the field of human relations and bursary help for ministers, priests and rabbis; also, including those in roles of religious leadership, in Scotland and the North of England; and wishing to use the resources of psychotherapists accredited by appropriate bodies, as approved by the Trustees. Trustees normally meet at least three times each year to consider policy and projects and assess bursary applications. Individual applications are assessed confidentially by the Bursar and one other trustee. If deemed to satisfy the Trust's qualifying criteria, a recommendation to award a bursary for financial assistance towards payment of psychotherapist fees will be made to a meeting of the trustees. Grants may also be made to fund projects aimed at furthering the Trust's objects. SC051488. Enquiries to the Secretary, Mrs Joyce Watkinson, 20 Stirling Street, Tillycoultry FK13 6EA; joyce.watkinson@gmail.com; www.guntriptrust.com

HAMILTON BURSARY: Awarded, subject to the intention on graduation to serve overseas under the Church of Scotland Faith Action Programme or to serve with some other Overseas Mission Agency approved by the Church, to a student at the University of Aberdeen (failing whom to Accepted Candidate(s) for the Ministry of the Church of Scotland whose studies for the Ministry are pursued at Aberdeen University). Applications or recommendations for the Bursary to the Clerk to the Presbytery of the North East and the Northern Isles, Suite 2, Ocean Spirit House West, 33 Waterloo Quay, Aberdeen AB11 5BS.

Martin HARCUS BEQUEST: Makes annual grants to candidates for the ministry resident within the Presbytery of Edinburgh and West Lothian and currently under the jurisdiction of the Presbytery. Applications by 20 October each year to the Principal's Secretary, New College, Mound Place, Edinburgh EH1 2LX (NewCollege@ed.ac.uk) by 15 October.

HOPE TRUST: Gives support to organisations that (1) advance the cause of temperance through the promotion of temperance work and the combatting of all forms of substance abuse and (2) promote Reformed theology and Reformed church life especially in Scotland and the social mission of charities with historical or contemporary links to the Reformed tradition, and includes a scholarship programme, the appointment of a part-time post-doctoral fellowship and support for students in full time training. Apply to the Secretary, Lyn Sutherland, Glenorchy House, 20 Union Street, Edinburgh, EH1 3LR (Tel: 0131 226 5151; Fax: 0131 556 5354 or Email: hopetrust@drummondmiller.co.uk).

KEAY THOM TRUST: The purposes of the Trust are:
1. To benefit impoverished widows, widowers, surviving civil partners or relatives of deceased ministers, or of spouses or civil partners who have been deserted by ministers or have grounds for divorce or separation, who have been wholly dependent upon and assisted the minister in the fulfilment of his or her duties and who, by reason of death, divorce or separation, have been required to leave the manse. The Trust can assist in the purchase of a house or by providing financial or material assistance.
2. To assist financially in the education or training of the above relatives or children of deceased ministers.
Further information and application forms are available from Miller Hendry, Solicitors, 10 Blackfriars Street, Perth PH1 5NS (01738 637311; johnthom@millerhendry.co.uk).

LADIES' GAELIC SCHOOLS AND HIGHLAND BURSARY ASSOCIATION: Distributes small grants to students, preferably with a Highland/Gaelic background, who are training to be ministers in the Church of Scotland. Apply by 15 October in each year to the Secretary, Mrs Marion McGill, 61 Ladysmith Road, Edinburgh EH9 3EY (0131 667 4243; marionmcgill61@gmail.com).

LYALL BEQUEST: Offers grants to ministers:
1. Grants to individual ministers, couples and families, for a holiday where the purpose is recuperation or relaxation for a minimum of seven nights. No reapplication within a three-year period; and thereafter a 50 per cent grant to those reapplying.
2. Grants towards sickness and convalescence costs so far as not covered by the National Health Service.
Applications should be made to the Secretary and Clerk, The Church of Scotland Trust, 121 George Street, Edinburgh EH2 4YN (0131 376 1307; msproule@churchofscotland.org.uk).

Gillian MACLAINE BURSARY FUND: Open to candidates for the ministry of the Church of Scotland of Scottish or Canadian nationality. Preference is given to Gaelic-speakers. Application forms available from Mr W Stewart Shaw DL BSc, Clerk to the Presbytery of Argyll, 59 Barone Road, Rothesay, Isle of Bute PA20 0DZ (07775 926541; argyll@churchofscotland.org.uk). Closing date for receipt of applications is 31 October.

Alexander J. MacLEOD GAELIC FUND: This historic bequeathed fund is able to support Ministers who wish to study Gaelic for preaching purposes or to enable Gaelic learning projects within a parish. Church of Scotland Ministers of full-time word and sacrament can apply for funding. The fund is administered by Faith Action Programme. Applications must be received by the end of the second week in January to be considered for the annual allocation of grants. Decisions will be made in late January and grants will be paid upon the submission of receipts. A 300 word report on the impact of the work should be submitted along with receipts. Contact via ascend@churchofscotland.org.uk

E. McLAREN FUND: The persons intended to be benefited are widows and unmarried ladies, preference being given to ladies above 40 years of age in the following order:

(a) Widows and daughters of Officers in the Highland Regiment, and
(b) Widows and daughters of Scotsmen.
Further details from the Secretary, The E. McLaren Fund, Messrs Wright, Johnston & Mackenzie LLP, Solicitors, St Vincent Plaza, 319 St Vincent Street, Glasgow G2 5RZ (Tel: 0141 248 3434; Fax: 0141 221 1226; rmd@wjm.co.uk).

MEIKLE AND PATON TRUST: Grants are available to Ministers and Missionaries for rest and recuperation at the following hotels: Crieff Hydro; Murraypark Hotel, Crieff; Peebles Hydro; Park Hotel, Peebles; Ballachulish Hotel and Isle of Glencoe Hotel. Grants are in addition to any regular discount offered by the hotels, but not seasonal offers; and give a subsidy for overnight residence, such subsidy being decreed by the Trustees at any given time, subject to a limit of seven nights in any one calendar year. Booking should be made online, via the respective hotel's website, quoting the promotion code MEIKLE22 and should be made no more than six months in advance in order to obtain Meikle Paton benefit. Chairman: Rev. Iain F. Paton (iain.f.paton@ btinternet.com).

MORGAN BURSARY FUND: Makes grants to candidates for the Church of Scotland ministry studying at the University of Glasgow. Apply to the Clerk to the Presbytery of Glasgow, 260 Bath Street, Glasgow G2 4JP (0141 332 6606; glasgow@churchofscotland.org.uk). Closing date October 31.

NEW MINISTERS' FURNISHING LOAN FUND: Makes loans (of £1,000) to ministers in their first charge to assist with furnishing the manse. Apply to ministriesfinance@churchofscotland. org.uk. Enquiries to Faith Action Finance Team, 121 George Street, Edinburgh EH2 4YN (0131 225 5722).

NOVUM TRUST: Provides small short-term grants – typically between £300 and £2,500 – to initiate projects in Christian action and research which cannot readily be financed from other sources. Trustees welcome applications from projects that are essentially Scottish, are distinctively new, and are focused on the welfare of young people, on the training of lay people or on new ways of communicating the Christian faith. The Trust cannot support large building projects, staff salaries or individuals applying for maintenance during courses or training. Application forms and guidance notes from novumt@cofscotland.org.uk or Mrs Susan Masterton, Blair Cadell LLP, The Bond House, 5 Breadalbane Street, Edinburgh EH6 5JH (0131 555 5800; www.novum.org.uk).

PARK MEMORIAL BURSARY FUND: Provides grants for the benefit of candidates for the ministry of the Church of Scotland from the Presbytery of Glasgow under full-time training. Apply to the Clerk to the Presbytery of Glasgow, 260 Bath Street, Glasgow G2 4JP (0141 332 6606; glasgow@churchofscotland.org.uk). Closing date November 15.

PRESBYTERY OF ARGYLL BURSARY FUND: Open to students who have been accepted as candidates for the ministry and the readership of the Church of Scotland. Preference is given to applicants who are natives of the bounds of the Presbytery, or are resident within the bounds of the Presbytery, or who have a strong connection with the bounds of the Presbytery. Application forms available from Mr W Stewart Shaw DL BSc, Clerk to the Presbytery of Argyll, 59 Barone Road, Rothesay, Isle of Bute PA20 0DZ (07775 926541; argyll@churchofscotland.org.uk). Closing date for receipt of applications is 31 October.

Margaret and John ROSS TRAVELLING FUND: Offers grants to ministers and their spouses for travelling and other expenses for trips to the Holy Land where the purpose is recuperation or relaxation. Applications should be made to the Secretary and Clerk, The Church of Scotland Trust, 121 George Street, Edinburgh EH2 4YN (0131 376 1307; msproule@churchofscotland. org.uk).

SCOTLAND'S CHURCHES TRUST: Strives to preserve, promote and protect Scotland's rich ecclesiastical built heritage. In addition to providing an advocacy and advice service for the owners and users of Scotland's religious built heritage, the Trust focusses much of its efforts on improving the long-term sustainability of Scotland's places of worship. It is currently involved in a collaboration with Historic Environment Scotland in the recording of church buildings facing closure, and continues to develop new and existing initiatives that strengthen the ties between the country's ecclesiastical built heritage, the communities that surround these buildings and the wider tourist economy. Scotland's Churches Trust, 15 North Bank Street, Edinburgh EH1 2LP (office@scotlandschurchestrust.org.uk; www.scotlandschurchestrust.org.uk).

SMIETON FUND: To assist ministers who would benefit from a holiday because of a recent pastoral need. Contact pastoralsupport@churchofscotland.org.uk for an application form. Enquiries to Alison Stewart, Senior Administrator, Faith Action Ministries Support Team, 121 George Street, Edinburgh EH2 4YN (0131 376 3685).

Mary Davidson SMITH CLERICAL AND EDUCATIONAL FUND FOR ABERDEENSHIRE: Assists ministers who have been ordained for five years or over and are in full charge of a congregation in Aberdeen, Aberdeenshire and the north, to purchase books, or to travel for educational purposes, and assists their children with scholarships for further education or vocational training. Apply to Messrs Peterkins, 100 Union Street, Aberdeen AB10 1QR (01224 428000; maildesk@peterkins.com).

SOCIETY FOR THE BENEFIT OF THE SONS AND DAUGHTERS OF THE CLERGY OF THE CHURCH OF SCOTLAND: Annual grants are made to assist in the education of the children (normally between the ages of 12 and 25 years) of ministers of the Church of Scotland. The Society also gives grants to aged and infirm daughters of ministers and ministers' unmarried daughters and sisters who are in need. Applications are to be lodged by 31 May in each year with the Secretary and Treasurer, Kirsty Ashworth, Exchange Place 3, Semple Street, Edinburgh EH3 8BL (0131 473 3500; SM-Charity@azets.co.uk).

SOCIETY IN SCOTLAND FOR PROPAGATING CHRISTIAN KNOWLEDGE: The SSPCK gives grants to: 1. Resourcing mission within Scotland; 2. The training and education of Christians in Commonwealth countries overseas, aimed to equip them for service in the mission and outreach of the Church; 3.The training of British young people volunteering for periods of service in Christian mission and education overseas; 4. The resourcing of new initiatives in worldwide Christian mission. Chairman: Rev. Michael W. Frew; Secretary: Rev. Ian W. Alexander, SSPCK, c/o 121 George Street, Edinburgh EH2 4YN (SSPCK@churchofscotland. org.uk; www.sspck.co.uk).

Nan STEVENSON CHARITABLE TRUST FOR RETIRED MINISTERS: Provides loans and grants at or after retirement to ministers and others in a recognised ministry for the purchase, maintenance, repair or alteration of a property, primarily for those with a North Ayrshire connection. Secretary and Treasurer: Mrs Christine Thomas, 18 Brisbane Street, Largs KA30 8QN (01475 338564; 07891 838778; cathomas54@gmail.com).

SYNOD OF GRAMPIAN CHILDREN OF THE CLERGY FUND: Makes annual grants to children of deceased ministers. Apply to Rev. G. Euan D. Glen, Secretary and Treasurer, The Manse, 26 St Ninians, Monymusk, Inverurie AB51 7HF (01467 651470; GGlen@churchofscotland.org.uk).

SYNOD OF GRAMPIAN WIDOWS' FUND: Makes annual grants (currently £450 p.a.) to widows or widowers of deceased ministers who have served in a charge in the former Synod. Apply to Rev. G. Euan D. Glen, Secretary and Treasurer, The Manse, 26 St Ninians, Monymusk, Inverurie AB51 7HF (01467 651470; GGlen@churchofscotland.org.uk).

TOD ENDOWMENT TRUST; CINTRA BEQUEST; TOD ENDOWMENT SCOTLAND HOLIDAY FUND: The Trustees of the Cintra Bequest and of the Tod Endowment Scotland Holiday Fund can consider an application for a grant from the Tod Endowment funds from any ordained or commissioned minister or deacon in Scotland of at least two years' standing before the date of application, to assist with the cost of the beneficiary and his or her spouse or partner and dependants obtaining rest and recuperation in Scotland. The Trustees of the Tod Endowment Scotland Holiday Fund can also consider an application from an ordained or commissioned minister or deacon who has retired. Application forms are available from Madelaine Sproule, Law Department at msproule@churchofscotland.org.uk (for the Cintra Bequest), and from Alison Stewart, Senior Administrator, Faith Action Ministries Support Team at pastoralsupport@churchofscotland.org.uk (for the Tod Endowment Scotland Holiday Fund). The address in both cases is 121 George Street, Edinburgh EH2 4YN (0131 225 5722).

WEST OF SCOTLAND BIBLE SOCIETY: A charity whose purpose is the distribution of bibles all across Scotland. Bibles of choice are provided and delivered to your door at a 50% discount. Secretary: Rev. Robert Craig (01501 519085; secretary@westofscotlandbiblesociety@gmail.com; www.Facebook: West of Scotland Bible Society).

Stephen WILLIAMSON & ALEX BALFOUR FUND: Offers grants to Ministers in Scotland, with first priority being given to Ministers in the boundaries of the former Presbyteries of Angus and Dundee, followed by the Presbytery of Fife, to assist with the cost of educational school/ college/university trips for sons and daughters of the Manse who are under 25 years and in full time education. Application for trips in any year will be considered by the Trustees in the January of that year, when the income of the previous financial year will be awarded in grants. The applications for trips in that calendar year must be submitted by 31 December of the preceding year. For applications from outwith the 3 priority Presbyteries the total cost of the trip must be in excess of £500, with the maximum grant which can be awarded being £200. The trustees will always give priority to new applicants. If funds still remain for distribution after the allocation of grants in January further applications for that year will be considered. Applications from the Presbyteries of Angus, Dundee and Fife will be considered at any time of year as the Trustees have retained income for these grants. Applications should be made to the Secretary and Clerk, The Church of Scotland Trust, 121 George Street, Edinburgh EH2 4YN (0131 376 1307; msproule@churchofscotland.org.uk).

10. LONG SERVICE CERTIFICATES

Long Service Certificates, signed by the Moderator, are available for presentation to elders and voluntary office bearers in respect of not less than thirty years of service. At the General

Assembly of 2015, it was agreed that further certificates could be issued at intervals of ten years thereafter. It should be noted that the period is years of *service*, not (for example) years of ordination in the case of an elder. In the case of those volunteers engaged in children's and youth work, the qualifying period is twenty-one years of service. Certificates are not issued posthumously, nor is it possible to make exceptions to the rules, for example by recognising quality of service in order to reduce the qualifying period, or by reducing the qualifying period on compassionate grounds, such as serious illness. Applications for Long Service Certificates should be made in writing to the Principal Clerk at 121 George Street, Edinburgh EH2 4YN by the parish minister, or by the session clerk on behalf of the Kirk Session. Certificates are not issued from this office to the individual recipients, nor should individuals make application themselves. If a note of the award of the Certificate is to be inserted in *Life and Work* contact should be made with that publication direct.

11. RECORDS OF THE CHURCH OF SCOTLAND

Church records more than fifty years old, unless still in use, should be sent or delivered to the Principal Clerk for onward transmission to the National Records of Scotland. Where ministers or session clerks are approached by a local repository seeking a transfer of their records, they should inform the Principal Clerk, who will take the matter up with the National Records of Scotland.

12. FASTI ECCLESIAE SCOTICANAE

The *Fasti Ecclesiae Scoticanae* ('The Register of Officials of the Church of Scotland') is an ongoing series of volumes which documents the succession of the ordained ministry in the Church of Scotland. The initial volumes, published in the second half of the nineteenth century, offered a comprehensive account of the ministers of the church throughout the previous three hundred years. Since then there have been several updates, and the whole series now presents a complete record from the Reformation in the mid-sixteenth century to the present day of those who have served in parishes, as chaplains, as missionaries, and in academic, administrative and other appointments, including auxiliary and ordained local ministers. Since the bulk of the work is arranged by parishes, the *Fasti* also forms the only permanent record of unions, linkages and other forms of parish readjustment within the church.

The latest volume, volume XII, edited by Roy M. Pinkerton, covering the period from 1 October 1999 to 30 September 2020, was published in June 2021, and gives information about those who served as ordained ministers during the previous twenty years. The cost of this volume is £30 plus p&p: to obtain a copy, please e-mail fasti@churchofscotland.org.uk confirming that you wish to purchase a copy and giving your full postal address. The book will then be despatched to you together with instructions about payment.

SECTION 3

Church Procedure

A. THE MINISTER AND BAPTISM

See www.churchofscotland.org.uk > Resources > Yearbook > Section 3A

B. THE MINISTER AND MARRIAGE

See www.churchofscotland.org.uk > Resources > Yearbook > Section 3B

C. CONDUCT OF MARRIAGE SERVICES (CODE OF GOOD PRACTICE)

See www.churchofscotland.org.uk > Resources > Yearbook > Section 3C

D. MARRIAGE AND CIVIL PARTNERSHIP (SCOTLAND) ACT 2014

See www.churchofscotland.org.uk > About us > Our views > Same-sex-marriage
Following the decision of the 2022 Assembly on same-sex marriage, the Legal Questions Committee prepared a guidance document, which is available from Presbytery Clerks.

E. CONDUCT OF FUNERAL SERVICES: FEES

The Report of the Legal Questions Committee to the 2007 General Assembly included a statement regarding fees for funerals, prepared in the light of approaches from two Presbyteries seeking guidance on the question of the charging of fees (on behalf of ministers) for the conduct of funerals. It had seemed to the Presbyteries that expectations and practice were unacceptably varied across the country, and that the question was complicated by the fact that, quite naturally and legitimately, ministers other than parish ministers occasionally conduct funeral services. That statement was engrossed in the Minutes of the General Assembly, and it was felt helpful to include it also in the Year Book.

The statement
The Committee believes that the question is two-fold, relating firstly to parish ministers (including associate and assistant ministers, deacons and the like) within their regular ministry, and secondly to ministers and others taking an occasional funeral, for instance by private invitation or in the course of pastoral cover of another parish.

Ministers in receipt of a living
The Committee believes that the position of the minister of a parish, and of other paid staff on the ministry team of a parish, is clear. The Third Declaratory Article affirms the responsibility

of the Church of Scotland to provide the ordinances of religion through its territorial ministry, while the stipend system (and, for other staff members, the salary) provides a living that enables that ministry to be exercised without charging fees for services conducted. The implication of this principle is that no family in Scotland should ever be charged for the services of a Church of Scotland minister at the time of bereavement. Clearly, therefore, no minister in receipt of a living should be charging separately (effectively being paid doubly) for any such service. The Committee is conscious that the position of congregations outside Scotland may be different, and is aware that the relevant Presbyteries will offer appropriate superintendence of these matters.

A related question is raised about the highly varied culture of gift-giving in different parts of the country. The Committee believes it would be unwise to seek to regulate this. In some places, an attempt to quash a universal and long-established practice would seem ungracious, while in other places there is no such practice, and encouragement in that direction would seem indelicate.

A second related question was raised about Funeral Directors charging for the services of the minister. The Committee believes that Presbyteries should make it clear to Funeral Directors that, in the case of Church of Scotland funerals, such a charge should not be made.

Ministers conducting occasional services
Turning to the position of ministers who do not receive a living that enables them to conduct funerals without charge, the Committee's starting point is the principle articulated above that no bereaved person should have to pay for the services of a minister. The territorial ministry and the parish system of this Church mean that a bereaved family should not find itself being contingently charged because the parish minister happens to be unavailable, or because the parish is vacant.

Where a funeral is being conducted as part of the ministry of the local parish, but where for any reason another minister is taking it and not otherwise being paid, it is the responsibility of the congregation (through its financial body) to ensure that appropriate fees and expenses are met. Where that imposes a financial burden upon a congregation because of the weight of pastoral need, the need should be taken into account in calculating the resource-needs of that parish in the course of updating the Presbytery Plan.

It is beyond the remit of the Committee to make judgements about the appropriate level of payment. The Committee suggests that the [now] Faith Action Programme should give the relevant advice on this aspect of the issue.

The Committee believes that these principles could be applied to the conduct of weddings and are perfectly compatible with the Guidelines on that subject [in Section 3C of the Year Book].

In its Report to the General Assembly of 2023 the Faith Nurture Forum reiterated that:

Where a congregation calls upon the services of a Minister not already in receipt of a stipend, or other suitably qualified person, to conduct a funeral, a fee of £100 [set at GA 2023] may be paid by the congregation. On no account should such a fee be charged to the family of the deceased. For the avoidance of doubt, no fee may be offered to or received by a serving Parish Minister for the conduct of a funeral service, whether in their own or another parish.

F. PULPIT SUPPLY FEES AND EXPENSES

The Pulpit Supply Regulations (Regulations 6, 2008, as amended) are set out below, with the fee levels as approved by the 2023 General Assembly inserted.

1. In Charges where there is only one diet of worship, the Pulpit Supply Fee shall be a Standard Fee of £100 (or as from time to time agreed by the Faith Action Programme).

2. In Charges where there are additional diets of worship on a Sunday, the person fulfilling the Supply shall be paid £50 for each additional Service (or as from time to time agreed by the Faith Action Programme). (Where two ministers are involved, they each receive half the total fee).

3. Where the person is unwilling to conduct more than one diet of worship on a given Sunday, he or she shall receive a pro-rata payment based on the total available Fee shared on the basis of the number of Services conducted.

4. The Fee thus calculated shall be payable in the case of all persons permitted to conduct Services under section 7(1) to (9) of Act 2, 2018.

5. In all cases, Travelling Expenses shall be paid. Where there is no convenient public conveyance, the use of a private car shall be paid for at the rate of 45p per mile for Travelling Expenses. In exceptional circumstances, to be approved in advance, the cost of hiring a car may be met.

6. Where weekend board and lodging are agreed as necessary, these may be claimed for the weekend at a maximum rate of that allowed when attending the General Assembly, currently £75 per night. The Fee and Expenses should be paid to the person providing the Supply before he or she leaves on the Sunday.

G. PROCEDURE IN A VACANCY

See www.churchofscotland.org.uk > Serve > Faith Nurture Forum > Ministries handbooks, forms and guidance notes:
Vacancy Guidelines for Kirk Sessions and Interim Moderators (also covers appointing locums)
Guidelines for Nominating Committees
Guidelines for Advisory Committees
Guidance Notes on compiling Parish Profiles

SECTION 4

General Assembly 2023

The General Assembly of 2023 was held from 20-25 May with the majority of commissioners in the Assembly Hall, but some participating online via Zoom.

OFFICE-BEARERS OF THE GENERAL ASSEMBLY

The Lord High Commissioner:	The Rt Hon. Lord Hodge PC KC
Moderator:	Rt. Rev. Sally Foster-Fulton
Chaplains to the Moderator:	Rev. Dr H. Martin J. Johnstone
	Rev. Louise J.E. McClements
Principal Clerk:	Rev. Fiona E. Smith
Depute Clerk:	Ms Christine Paterson
Procurator:	Ms Laura Dunlop KC
Law Agent:	Miss Mary Macleod
Convener, Procedure Committee:	Rev. Donald G.B. McCorkindale
Vice-Convener, Procedure Committee:	Rev. Michael J. Mair
Precentor:	Rev. Colin C. Renwick
Chief Steward:	Mr Alexander F. Gemmill
Depute Steward:	Mr Neil Proven
Assembly Officer:	Mr William Mearns
Depute Assembly Officer:	Mrs Karen W.F. McKay

THE MODERATOR

The Right Reverend Sally Foster-Fulton BA BD

Our friend Sally has chosen as the theme of her year as Moderator, "Remember who you are."

We are beyond excited by that possibility, in particular as our Kirk journeys through a period of transition. We believe that Sally will help us all through inspirational worship and provoking reflections; through gentle encouragement and prophetic action to lift our eyes and spirits beyond the near horizon to the ongoing calling of the Church to share the love of Christ to all people and be part of life lived in all its fullness.

Sally has travelled a long way to be here, all the way from South Carolina (Beaufort, Columbia and Seneca). If she still manages to keep something of the wonderful southern drawl of the state of her birth, she describes coming to Scotland some thirty years ago as coming home. And we are glad that this is home for her and Stuart, and for their wonderful family.

Sally's early ministry in Camelon was an inspiration to young mothers who felt the stirrings of a call to serve in the Kirk. Through the warmth of her nature and ability to laugh when things didn't go quite as planned, Sally seamlessly wove motherhood into parish ministry and vice versa in a way which helped others experience a deeper awareness of God's nurturing love.

Alex and Gracie will be happy to share their Mum with others for the year, as will Nick and Katherine. We are less sure that will be the case for Oran Willow, Alex and Nick's young daughter and Stuart and Sally's granddaughter to whom they are utterly devoted. We trust the Church will be generous enough to ensure that Sally gets to spend time with her family, both in Scotland and the US, throughout her year as Moderator.

Sally is a citizen of the world and particularly committed to those citizens who are being treated unjustly. She will remind us of that regularly; and we are grateful that this will be the case.

Whilst perhaps best known to many across the Church and in wider Scottish society through her roles as Convener of the Kirk's Church & Society Council and, since 2016, the Head of Christian Aid in Scotland, these are simply some of the latest chapters in a life committed to others and to God. Whether it has been helping to establish a centre for the homeless in Seneca, helping to create the Cornton Vale Visitors' Centre, serving on the local board of Habitat for Humanity or the Scotland Board of the Disaster Emergencies Committee, Sally has spent a lifetime living out her faith.

That happens primarily not on the public stage but in the way Sally hangs out with others. Recently we spent a bit of time together. Going for a walk one afternoon we got into a conversation with a young man who had fallen on tough times. Sally's natural interest, concern and yet deep belief in that person's inherent goodness will be an attitude that she will bring to her year as Moderator.

This is a way of living that we have had the privilege of witnessing up close over many years; the ways that she has encouraged us into ministries, into faith, into doing things that we didn't believe we were capable of. The congregations that she has been a part of testify to that. Whether in her student attachments (Falkirk Erskine, Falkirk Old & St Modan's and Camelon Irving), her probationary year in Dunipace, or her ministries in Camelon Irving, Seneca and Dunblane people testify to having their faith strengthened, deepened and widened through Sally's ministry and humanity.

Her passion and compassion have also shone out in her various roles as a Christian educator in Atlanta, as a Sunday School adviser in Falkirk, as a Hospital Chaplain, and as an author and worship leader. She has brought so many of these gifts together through her time at Christian Aid, standing up fearlessly for those at the margins of our world, never afraid to speak up when others might be tempted to remain complicit.

Sally reminds us regularly that there is a spark of the divine in every human being; and that God is always present in God's wonderful creation.

In our experience Sally is naturally interested in people, and particularly interested in those others might be tempted to ignore. It might mean that getting anywhere on time will be a bit of a challenge but it's a joyous gift that she brings to the role.

Just as well that for much of her life Sally has been a runner, from her early days in school to being a member of the Stirling Triathalon Club – a club that has helped to produce a few world class athletes along the way. We are not sure how many members of the Church might be willing to join Sally for a New Year's Day swim, cycle and run.

What we do hope is that over this year the Church and wider society will be as blessed by having her as a friend as we have been.

Martin Johnstone and Louise McClements
Moderator's Chaplains

REPORT FROM THE GENERAL ASSEMBLY 2023

The Rev David Cameron, convener of the Assembly Trustees, urged the Church to display a new spirit of Reformation in the face of falling membership and ministry shortages. "Imagine Church where members are enthusiastic about doing things differently. Imagine listening to one another and dreaming bold dreams and having the energy and encouragement to experiment and learn in the process. Imagine planting new church communities where they've always been needed, breaking out of our constrained systems to do so." He acknowledged the hurt and pain caused by the Presbytery Mission Planning process, but said the time had come to "lay down burdens which have been exhausting us all."

The Assembly agreed to a proposal from the Rev Dr Doug Gay instructing the Assembly Trustees to explore alternative approaches to ministry planning which would ensure churches that can afford a minister (or be supported to afford one, in the case of deprived areas) would be permitted to call one. However, the Assembly rejected an Overture from the Presbytery of Glasgow which would have appointed a Special Commission to review the Mission Planning process. Mr Cameron said that setting up a Commission would be premature and bring delay, but assured the Assembly that review was built into the process.

During the debate of the General Trustees, some Commissioners expressed concern about the number of churches earmarked for closure under Presbytery Mission Plans. The Rev Scott Rennie, vice-chair of the Trustees, said: "There has never been a quota, in any presbytery." Buildings could either be an asset or a drain on mission: "The point of the exercise, in partnership with presbyteries, has been to try and find that middle balance, alongside affordability."

A study is to be carried out into causes of stress among ministers, after the Assembly was told there was a crisis in morale in the church. The Faith Nurture Forum convener, the Rev Rosie Frew, agreed to the work proposed by the Rev Sandy Horsburgh. Mr Horsburgh said: "Doing a survey and committing to learning from and acting on its results will be a real sign of a church caring for its ministers." Mrs Frew said that currently four per cent of ministers are off sick, 14% of those with work-related stress.

In his first letter to a General Assembly, King Charles said he had been "especially heartened" to hear of the ecumenical pilgrimage of peace to South Sudan, undertaken by Very Rev Dr Iain Greenshields with the Archbishop of Canterbury and the Pope in February. He added: "Messages of justice, peace and reconciliation made all the more powerful by their visible presence which signified both the unity and the diversity of the church." The King also said that he had been "greatly encouraged" by the signing of the Saint Margaret Declaration of friendship between the Church of Scotland and the Catholic Church.

The Lord High Commissioner, Lord Hodge, also urged the church to continue its ecumenical work, saying that by working together the Christian denominations could ensure "that the Christian voice is heard in the market of ideas in Scotland and more widely."

The Assembly was addressed by the Rev Fiona Bennett, Moderator of the General Assembly of the United Reformed Church and minister of Augustine United Church, Edinburgh, saying that her own denomination was facing similar organisational challenges, and developing similar approaches to address them. Recalling the Lund Principle, that states churches should work together at all times except where there are deep differences of conviction, she asked: "How much of the activity of our churches which we are running in parallel is really rooted in deep difference?"

The Ecumenical Relations Committee was instructed to 'initiate a conversation' across the church and with sister churches in Scotland about how they can work together in mission and service. The convener of the Committee, the Rev Ross Blackman, said some ecumenical aspects of presbytery and mission planning may have been overlooked "in our rush to meet the incredibly challenging obligations".

The Chief Rabbi, Sir Ephraim Mirvis, thanked the Church of Scotland for the 'openness, sincerity, honesty and humility' shown in conversations with the Jewish community in Scotland, as the Assembly welcomed a new Jewish-Christian Glossary, produced jointly by the two faith groups as an aid to interfaith discussions. The Glossary grew out of work to repair relationships between the Church and the Jewish community, which were damaged by the *Inheritance of Abraham?* report into the Holy Land in 2013. Chief Rabbi Mirvis said: "The relationship between the Church of Scotland and the Jewish community suffered a setback.

There was a difficulty, a crisis, a challenge. But what did we do about it? We were determined to engage in a process of healing and we achieved that."

The Faith Impact Forum was instructed to work with the Theological Forum and other groups to explore the range of theological views and opinions around the issue of assisted dying. The Forum had brought a section of its deliverance restating the Church's long-held opposition to assisted dying, but this was defeated by a countermotion from the Rev Jonathan Fleming recognising "that there exists a range of theological views and ethical opinions" on the subject. The Rev Tara Granados said: "I personally do not believe that our God wishes us to suffer, and that with appropriate safeguards society should allow people to choose to end their own suffering through assisted dying."

The Assembly commended a report which listed a number of Church ministers, elders and members who benefited from the slave trade or received compensation following the abolition of the slave trade. The report also listed nine churches (some now closed) which were at least part financed by slave owners or known to be the place of worship for merchants who benefited from the trade; and several more churches which contain memorials to people connected to slavery. The Assembly accepted a Faith Impact Forum proposal that the Forum, "in partnership with the Theological Forum and the Equality, Diversity and Inclusion Group, prepare a statement of acknowledgment and apology for the Church's involvement with and connection to historic chattel slavery, to be considered for adoption at a future General Assembly."

The General Assembly approved the creation of a Book of Confessions forming the Church's subordinate standard. The Book, to include the Westminster Confession of Faith, the Scots Confession, Nicene and Apostles Creeds, and the 1992 Statement of Faith, must now be approved by presbyteries under the Barrier Act.

The Theological Forum agreed to review the Third Article Declaratory, which commits the church to providing the 'ordinances of religion' to every parish in Scotland. Bringing the motion, the Rev Robert Allan pointed out that Scotland was now mostly secular and, given the shrinking number of ministers, asked whether it was possible to maintain that commitment. He said it was "a noble aim" but that the church should be "humble enough to reconsider".

The Assembly passed an amendment from the Rev Bryan Kerr noting "with alarm" research which suggests that black and ethnic minority ministers are being overlooked or asked not to officiate at funerals in favour of a 'Scottish minister'. Mr Kerr said: "We ought to be standing up for our ministers and calling this out for what it is. It's racist, it's xenophobic". The Assembly Trustees are to work with the Equality, Diversity and Inclusion Group to liaise with funeral directors.

The Assembly approved the merger of Argyll, Abernethy, Inverness, Lochaber, Ross, Sutherland, Caithness, Lochcarron-Skye and Uist presbyteries into a new Highlands and Hebrides presbytery, Clèir Eilean Ì. The Presbytery of Lewis has not agreed to join, but it is hoped that will happen at a later date.

The Assembly agreed the formation of an advisory Ethical Oversight Committee to help the Church of Scotland Investors Trust navigate ethical and theological issues around the church's investments, as proposed by a special commission set up following the debate in recent years on whether the church should disinvest from fossil fuels.

Laura Dunlop KC was given a lengthy ovation as she stepped down after 18 years as Procurator of the General Assembly. Jonathan Brodie KC was appointed as her successor.

A proposal to review the provision of manses for ministers, and explore allowing ministers to buy their own house if they wish, was narrowly defeated. The Rev Robert Allan said that such a review would benefit ministers struggling in unsuitable and expensive manses, and that churches could benefit financially from renting out their manses. However, concern was expressed over the tax implications, and whether ministers would be able to afford suitable accommodation.

There was a prolonged round of applause for the Rev Jean Montgomerie, the longest ordained female minister in the Church of Scotland, who celebrated 50 years in the ministry recently.

The General Assembly endorsed calls from the Social Care Council (CrossReach) for improved pay in the care sector. Convener, the Rev Thom Riddell, said that staff in the voluntary sector are now paid 19% behind "their counterparts in other agencies".

This year's Moderator, the Rt Rev Sally Foster-Fulton, closed the week saying that that the church was "the body of Christ" with "hands that aren't afraid to get dirty", "feet that walk the extra mile", and "here to hold up a sister who's struggling or sit with a brother who's afraid". And she added: "We are part of something so much bigger than any one of us and we are blessed to be. So, challenges – bring them on."

This is a summary of a report of proceedings which appeared in the July 2023 issue of Life and Work and online at www.lifeandwork.org

SECTION 5

Presbytery Lists

(1) Edinburgh and West Lothian
(2) Lothian and Borders
(3) South West
(4) Clyde
(5) Glasgow
(6) Forth Valley and Clydesdale
(7) Fife
(8) Perth
(9) North East and Northern Isles
(10) *from 1 January 2024:* Clèir Eilean Ì: Highlands and Hebrides
    Until 31 December 2023:
       (10.1) Argyll
       (10.2) Abernethy
       (10.3) Inverness
       (10.4) Lochaber
       (10.5) Ross
       (10.6) Sutherland
       (10.7) Caithness
       (10.8) Lochcarron-Skye
       (10.9) Uist
(11) Lewis
(12) England and Channel Islands
(13) International Charges
(14) Jerusalem

In each Presbytery list, the parishes/congregations ('charges') are listed in alphabetical order. In a linked charge, the names appear under the first-named. Under the name of the charge will be found the name of the minister and, where applicable, that of an associate or assistant minister, ordained local minister, auxiliary minister and member of the Diaconate. The years indicated after a name in the congregational section of each Presbytery list are the year of ordination (column 1) and the year of current appointment (column 2). Where only one year is given, it is both the year of ordination and the year of appointment. Where no other name is listed, the name of the session clerk(s) or interim moderator is given. (Some parishes have more than one church – see Section 8. For presbytery and parish boundaries, see the online map at http://arcg.is/11rSXH.)

The subsequent parts of each Presbytery list comprise:

B. ministers and deacons, members of Presbytery, in other appointments;

C. minsters and deacons, members of Presbytery, registered under the Registration of Ministries Act (Act 2, 2017, as amended) mainly as Category R (Retaining) and authorised to perform the functions of ministry outwith an appointment covered by Category O (a charge) or Category E (an employed appointment), though some of those listed who have ceased to hold an appointment may have chosen to retain Category O registration for a period of up to 3 years;

D. ministers and deacons, not members of Presbytery, in other appointments;

E. ministers and deacons, not members of Presbytery, registered as 'Retaining';

F. ministers and deacons, not members of presbytery, registered as 'Inactive'. Only those who have given consent under the (civil) General Data Protection Regulation to publication of their details are included;

G. Readers in active service; and

H. Ministries Development Staff.

In parts **B. to F.** the first year is the year of ordination, and the second is the year of appointment or retirement. If the person is retired, then the appointment last held is shown in brackets.

Abbreviations in the list of parishes:

F   A charge with a Facebook page.

GD   A charge where it is desirable that the minister should have a knowledge of Gaelic.

GE   A charge where public worship must be regularly conducted in Gaelic.

H   A hearing aid loop system has been installed.

L   A chair lift or lift has been installed.

T   A charge with a Twitter account.

W   A charge with a website.

(1) EDINBURGH AND WEST LOTHIAN (F W)

Meets at Edinburgh: Palmerston Place on Tuesdays 7 November and 5 December 2023, and in 2024 on 6 February, 30 April, 18 June, 10 September, 5 November and 3 December.

Clerk:	HAZEL HASTIE MA CQSW PhD AIWS	Postal Address: Morningside Parish Church, 2 Cluny Gardens, Edinburgh EH10 6BQ edinburghwestlothian@churchofscotland.org.uk	0131 225 9137 07827 314374
Mission Co-ordinator:	REV. KENNETH BROWN BD	Kenneth.Brown@churchofscotland.org.uk	

1 Abercorn (F H W) linked with Pardovan, Kingscavil (H) and Winchburgh (F H W)

Vacant		The Manse, West End, Winchburgh, Broxburn EH52 6TT	
Derek R. Henderson MA DipTCP DipCS	2017	45 Priory Road, Linlithgow EH49 6BP	01506 890919 01506 844787
(Ordained Local Minister)		DHenderson@churchofscotland.org.uk	07968 491441

2 Armadale (H W)

Julia C. Wiley (Ms) MA(CE) MDiv	1998	2010	70 Mount Pleasant, Armadale, Bathgate EH48 3HB	01501 730358
			JWiley@churchofscotland.org.uk	
Margaret Corrie (Miss) DCS	1989	2013	44 Sunnyside Street, Camelon, Falkirk FK1 4BH	07955 633969
			MCorrie@churchofscotland.org.uk	

3 Avonbridge (H) linked with Torphichen (F H W)

Vacant	Manse Road, Torphichen, Bathgate EH48 4LT	01506 635957
Interim Moderator: W. Richard Houston	WHouston@churchofscotland.org.uk	01506 202246

4 Bathgate: Boghall (F H W)

Vacant	1 Manse Place, Ash Grove, Bathgate EH48 1NJ	01506 652715
Interim Moderator: Hanneke I. Janse van Vuren	HJansevanVuren@churchofscotland.org.uk	

5 Bathgate: High (F H W)

Vacant	info@bathgatehigh.com	**01506 650217**
Interim Moderator: Nelu I. Balaj	NBalaj@churchofscotland.org.uk	01506 411888

6 Bathgate: St John's (H W)

Vacant	St John's Manse, Mid Street, Bathgate EH48 1QD	01506 653146
Interim Moderator: Ian D. Maxwell	IMaxwell@churchofscotland.org.uk	01506 239840

7 Blackburn and Seafield (F H W)
Sandra Boyd (Mrs) BEd BD — 2007 — 2019
The Manse, 5 MacDonald Gardens, Blackburn, Bathgate EH47 7RE
SBoyd@churchofscotland.org.uk — 07919 676242

8 Blackridge (H)
Session Clerk, Blackridge: Jean Mowitt (Mrs)
jean.mowitt@yahoo.com — 01501 750401 / 07590 901933

9 Breich Valley (F H)
Robert Craig BA BD DipRS PGCertHC — 2008 — 2020
49 Main Street, Stoneyburn, Bathgate EH47 8AU
RCraig@churchofscotland.org.uk — 01501 519085

10 Broxburn (F H W)
Vacant
Interim Moderator: Derek R. Henderson
2 Church Street, Broxburn EH52 5EL
DHenderson@churchofscotland.org.uk — 01506 337560 / 01506 844787 / 07968 491441
Session Clerk: Anne Gunn (Mrs)
anne.gunn42@gmail.com — 07833 701274

11 Edinburgh: Albany Deaf Church of Edinburgh (F H)
info@stagw.org.uk — 0131 444 2054
Albany Deaf Church is a Mission Initiative of Edinburgh: St Andrew's and St George's West

12 Edinburgh: Balerno (F H W)
Andre J. Groenewald BA BD MDiv DD CertPS DipPSRP — 1995 — 2016
bpc-admin@balernochurch.org.uk
3 Johnsburn Road, Balerno EH14 7DN
AGroenewald@churchofscotland.org.uk — 0131 449 7245 / 0131 449 3830

13 Edinburgh: Barclay Viewforth (F W)
David Clarkson BSc BA MTh — 2010 — 2020
admin@barclaychurch.org.uk
113 Meadowspot, Edinburgh EH10 5UY
DClarkson@churchofscotland.org.uk — 0131 229 6810 / 0131 478 2376

14 Edinburgh: Blackhall St Columba's (F T W)
Fergus M. Cook BD — 2020
secretary@blackhallstcolumba.org.uk
5 Blinkbonny Crescent, Edinburgh EH4 3NB
FCook@churchofscotland.org.uk — 0131 332 4431 / 0131 466 7503

15 Edinburgh: Broughton St Mary's (F H L W)
Laurene M. Lafontaine BA MDiv — 1987 — 2021
mail@bstmchurch.org.uk
78 March Road, Edinburgh EH4 3SY
LLafontaine@churchofscotland.org.uk — 0131 556 4252 / 0131 312 7440

16	**Edinburgh: Canongate (F H T W)** Neil N. Gardner CStJ MA BD DL	1991	2006	**canongatekirk@btinternet.com** The Manse of Canongate, Edinburgh EH8 8BR NGardner@churchofscotland.org.uk	**0131 556 3515** 0131 556 3515
17	**Edinburgh: Carrick Knowe (H W)** Fiona M. Mathieson (Mrs) BEd BD PGCommEd MTh	1988	2001	**ckchurch@talktalk.net** 21 Traquair Park West, Edinburgh EH12 7AN FMathieson@churchofscotland.org.uk	**0131 334 1505** 0131 334 9774
18	**Edinburgh: Colinton (F H W)** Vacant Interim Moderator: Neil N. Gardner			**church.office@colinton-parish.com** The Manse, Dell Road, Colinton, Edinburgh EH13 0JR NGardner@churchofscotland.org.uk	**0131 441 2232** 0131 466 8384 0131 556 3515
19	**Edinburgh: Corstorphine Craigsbank (F H T W)** Alan Childs BA BD MBA	2000	2019	**admin@craigsbankchurch.org.uk** 17 Craigs Bank, Edinburgh EH12 8HD AChilds@churchofscotland.org.uk	**0131 334 6365** 0131 466 5196
20	**Edinburgh: Corstorphine Old (F H W)** Moira McDonald MA BD	1997	2005	**corold@aol.com** 23 Manse Road, Edinburgh EH12 7SW MMcDonald@churchofscotland.org.uk	**0131 334 7864** 0131 476 5893
	William D. Watt BD MPhil LTCL (Assistant Minister)	2023		WWatt@churchofscotland.org.uk	07950 617560
21	**Edinburgh: Corstorphine St Anne's (F H L T W)** James J. Griggs BD MTh ALCM PGCE	2011	2013	**office@stannes.corstorphine.org.uk** 1/5 Morham Gait, Edinburgh EH10 5GH JGriggs@churchofscotland.org.uk	**0131 316 4740** 0131 447 7063
22	**Edinburgh: Corstorphine St Ninian's (F H W)** James D. Aitken BD	2002	2017	**office@st-ninians.co.uk** 17 Templeland Road, Edinburgh EH12 8RZ JAitken@churchofscotland.org.uk	**0131 539 6204** 0131 334 2978
23	**Edinburgh: Craiglockhart (F H T W)** Gordon Kennedy BSc BD MTh	1993	2012	**office@craiglockhartchurch.org** 20 Craiglockhart Quadrant, Edinburgh EH14 1HD GKennedy@churchofscotland.org.uk	**0131 455 8229** 0131 444 1615
24	**Edinburgh: Craigmillar Park (F H W)** **linked with Edinburgh: Reid Memorial (F H W)** Alexander T. McAspurren BD MTh CPS CertSMM	2002	2019	**cpkirk@btinternet.com** **reid.memorial@btinternet.com** 14 Hallhead Road, Edinburgh EH16 5QJ AMcAspurren@churchofscotland.org.uk	**0131 667 5862** **0131 662 1203** 0131 667 1623

25   Edinburgh: Currie (F H W)
V. Easter Smart BA MDiv DMin — 1996   2015
currie_kirk@btconnect.com
43 Lanark Road West, Currie EH14 5JX
ESmart@churchofscotland.org.uk
0131 451 5141
0131 449 4719

26   Edinburgh: Dalmeny and Queensferry (F H W)
Vacant
Derek B. Munn
(Ordained Local Minister) — 2022
Interim Moderator: Fiona M. Mathieson
New charge formed by the union of Edinburgh: Dalmeny and Edinburgh: Queensferry
office@qpcweb.org
1 Station Road, South Queensferry EH30 9HY
DMunn@churchofscotland.org.uk
FMathieson@churchofscotland.org.uk
0131 331 1100
0131 331 1100
07592 953261
0131 334 9774

27   Edinburgh: Davidson's Mains (F H W)
Daniel Robertson BA BD — 2009   2016
life@dmainschurch.plus.com
1 Hillpark Terrace, Edinburgh EH4 7SX
Daniel.Robertson@churchofscotland.org.uk
0131 312 6282
0131 336 3078
07909 840654

28   Edinburgh: Drylaw (F W)
Vacant
Interim Moderator: Elisabeth G.B. Spence
drylawparishchurch@btinternet.com
revspence121@gmail.com
0131 332 6863
07772 548121

29   Edinburgh: Duddingston (F H W)
James A.P. Jack
BSc BArch BD DMin RIBA ARIAS — 1989   2001
dodinskirk@aol.com
Manse of Duddingston, Old Church Lane, Edinburgh EH15 3PX
JJack@churchofscotland.org.uk
0131 661 4240
0131 661 4240

30   Edinburgh: Fairmilehead (F H W)
Cheryl S. McKellar-Young (Mrs)
BA BD MSc PGCertHC — 2013   2018
office@fhpc.org.uk
14 Margaret Rose Drive, Edinburgh EH10 7ER
CMcKellarYoung@churchofscotland.org.uk
0131 445 2374
07590 230121

31   Edinburgh: Gorgie Dalry Stenhouse (F H T W)
Vacant
Dean L. Batchelor BCom MPysch BTh — 2004   2023
(Assistant Minister)
Reuben Addis — 2023
(Ordained Local Minister)
Interim Moderator: Alex T. McAspurren
contactus@gdschurch.org.uk
90 Myreside Road, Edinburgh EH10 5BZ
DBatchelor@churchofscotland.org.uk
85 Acredales, Linlithgow EH49 6JA
Reuben.Addis@churchofscotland.org.uk
AMcAspurren@churchofscotland.org.uk
0131 337 7936
0131 337 2284
0131 337 7936
07867 915022
0131 667 1623

32 Edinburgh: Gracemount (F W) linked with Edinburgh: Liberton (F H T W) churchsecretary@libertonkirk.net
John N. Young MA BD PhD — 1996 — 7 Kirk Park, Edinburgh EH16 6HZ — **0131 664 8264**
JYoung@churchofscotland.org.uk — 0131 664 3067
Kay O. N. Haggarty BEd — 2021 — KHaggarty@churchofscotland.org.uk
(Ordained Local Minister)

33 Edinburgh: Granton (F H T W) info@granton.org.uk — **0131 552 3033**
Vacant — 8 Wardie Crescent, Edinburgh EH5 1AG
Mary A. MacLeod Rivett BA MA PhD — 2023 — MMacLeodRivett@churchofscotland.org.uk — 0131 551 2159
(Ordained Local Minister)
Interim Moderator: Fergus M. Cook — FCook@churchofscotland.org.uk — 0131 466 7503

34 Edinburgh: Greenbank (F H W) greenbankchurch@btconnect.com — **0131 447 9969**
Vacant — 112 Greenbank Crescent, Edinburgh EH10 5SZ
Julia A. Cato BA MDiv — 2022 — JCato@churchofscotland.org.uk — 0131 447 4032
(Assistant Minister)
Interim Moderator: Dorothy U. Anderson — DAnderson@churchofscotland.org.uk — 0131 226 4242 / 07926 090489

35 Edinburgh: Greenside (H W) office@greenside.org.uk — **0131 557 2124**
Guardianship of the Presbytery — 1B Royal Terrace, Edinburgh EH7 5AB
Interim Moderator: Suzie M. Stark — SStark@churchofscotland.org.uk — 0131 551 1633

36 Edinburgh: Greyfriars Kirk (F GE H T W) enquiries@greyfriarskirk.com — **0131 225 1900**
Richard E. Frazer BA BD DMin — 1986 — 2003 — 12 Tantallon Place, Edinburgh EH9 1NZ — RFrazer@churchofscotland.org.uk — 0131 667 6610

37 Edinburgh: High (St Giles') (F T W) corinne.macinnes@stgilescathedral.org.uk — **0131 225 4363**
Calum I. MacLeod BA BD — 1996 — 2014 — St Giles' Cathedral, High Street, Edinburgh EH1 1RE — Calum.MacLeod@churchofscotland.org.uk — 0131 225 4363
Sigrid Marten (Associate Minister) — 1997 — 2021 — St Giles' Cathedral, High Street, Edinburgh EH1 1RE — SMarten@churchofscotland.org.uk — 0131 225 4363

38 Edinburgh: Holy Trinity (F H W) admin@holytrinitywesterhailes.org.uk — **0131 442 3304**
Ian A. MacDonald BD MTh — 2005 — 2017 — 5 Baberton Mains Terrace, Edinburgh EH14 3DG — Ian.Angus.MacDonald@churchofscotland.org.uk — 0131 281 6153
Rita M. Welsh BA PhD — 2017 — 19 Muir Wood Road, Currie EH14 5JW — RWelsh@churchofscotland.org.uk — 0131 451 5943
(Ordained Local Minister)

39 Edinburgh: Inverleith St Serf's (F H W)
Vacant
Interim Moderator: Ian W. Alexander
IAlexander@churchofscotland.org.uk
0131 467 7185
0131 225 5722

40 Edinburgh: Juniper Green (F H W)
Vacant
Interim Moderator: Gordon Kennedy
jgpc@supanet.com
476 Lanark Road, Juniper Green, Edinburgh EH14 5BQ
GKennedy@churchofscotland.org.uk
0131 458 5147
0131 453 3494
0131 444 1615

41 Edinburgh: Kirkliston (F W)
G.F. (Erick) du Toit BTh   2016   2020
kpc.officeangels@gmail.com
43 Main Street, Kirkliston EH29 9AF
EduToit@churchofscotland.org.uk
0131 333 3298

42 Edinburgh: Leith North (F H W)
Vacant
Interim Moderator: Karen W.F. McKay
nlpc-office@btinternet.com
KarenMcKay_131241@churchofscotland.org.uk
0131 553 7378
07921 317516

43 Edinburgh: Leith St Andrew's (F H W)
A. Robert A. Mackenzie LLB BD   1993   2013
leithstandrews@yahoo.co.uk
30 Lochend Road, Edinburgh EH6 8BS
AMacKenzie@churchofscotlandorg.uk
0131 553 8839
0131 553 2122

44 Edinburgh: Leith South (H W)
John S. (Iain) May BSc MBA BD   2012
slpcoffice@gmail.com
37 Claremont Road, Edinburgh EH6 7NN
JMay@churchofscotland.org.uk
0131 554 2578
0131 555 0392

45 Edinburgh: Liberton See Edinburgh: Gracemount

46 Edinburgh: Liberton Northfield (F H W)
Vacant
Interim Moderator: Andre J. Groenewald
9 Claverhouse Drive, Edinburgh EH16 6BR
AGroenewald@churchofscotland.org.uk
0131 551 3847
0131 664 5490
0131 449 3830

47 Edinburgh: Marchmont St Giles' (F H T W)
Karen K. Campbell BD MTh DMin   1997   2002
office@marchmontstgiles.org.uk
2 Trotter Haugh, Edinburgh EH9 2GZ
KKCampbell@churchofscotland.org.uk
0131 447 4359
0131 447 2834

48 Edinburgh: Mayfield Salisbury (F W)
Alexander C. Forsyth   2009   2021
LLB DipLP BD MTh PhD
churchmanager@googlemail.com
26 Seton Place, Edinburgh EH9 2JT
AForsyth@churchofscotland.org.uk
0131 667 1522
0131 667 1286
07739 639037

49 Edinburgh: Meadowbank and Willowbrae (F H T W)
meadowbank@meadowbankchurch.com
Vacant
willowbrae@btinternet.com
Interim Moderator: John S. (Iain) May
19 Abercorn Road, Edinburgh EH8 7DP
JMay@churchofscotland.org.uk
0131 661 8259
0131 652 2938
0131 555 0392
New charge formed by the union of Edinburgh: Meadowbank and Edinburgh: Willowbrae

50 Edinburgh: Morningside (F H W)
office@morningsideparishchurch.org.uk
Derek Browning MA BD DMin   1987   2001
20 Braidburn Crescent, Edinburgh EH10 6EN
Derek.Browning@churchofscotland.org.uk
0131 447 6745
0131 447 1617

51 Edinburgh: Morningside United (F H W)
churchoffice.muc@gmail.com
Vacant
1 Midmar Avenue, Edinburgh EH10 6BS
Interim Moderator: David M. Scott (URC)
davidmscott@minister.com
0131 447 3152
0131 447 7943
0131 531 5968
Morningside United is a Local Ecumenical Partnership with the United Reformed Church

52 Edinburgh: Murrayfield (F H W)
mpchurch@btconnect.com
Keith Edwin Graham MA PGDipADS   2008   2014
45 Murrayfield Gardens, Edinburgh EH12 6DH
BD MTh
KEGraham@churchofscotland.org.uk
0131 337 1091
0131 337 1364

53 Edinburgh: Newhaven (F H W)
Peter B. Bluett BTh   1996   2007
158 Granton Road, Edinburgh EH5 3RF
PBluett@churchofscotland.org.uk
0131 476 5212

54 Edinburgh: Northwest Kirk: Cramond and Old Kirk and Muirhouse (F H T W)   cramond.kirk@blueyonder.co.uk
Vacant
martin.scott14@sky.com
Interim Moderator: Martin C. Scott
0131 336 2036
07856 165820
New charge formed by the union of Edinburgh: Cramond and Edinburgh: Old Kirk and Muirhouse

55 Edinburgh: Palmerston Place (F H T W)
admin@palmerstonplacechurch.com
Vacant
30B Cluny Gardens, Edinburgh EH10 6BJ
Douglas H. Reid LLB DipLP MDiv   2022
Douglas.Reid@churchofscotland.org.uk
(Assistant Minister)
Interim Moderator: Samuel A.R. Torrens
STorrens@churchofscotland.org.uk
0131 220 1690
0131 447 9598
0131 220 1690
0131 466 5308

56 Edinburgh: Pilrig St Paul's (F W)
mail@pilrigstpauls.org.uk
Mark M. Foster BSc BD CertCS CertTM   1998   2013
Pilrig St Paul's, 1B Pilrig Street, Edinburgh EH6 5AS
MFoster@churchofscotland.org.uk
0131 553 1876
0131 332 5736

57   Edinburgh: Polwarth (F H W)
Vacant
Interim Moderator: Karen K. Campbell

office@polwarth.org.uk
88 Craiglockhart Road, Edinburgh EH14 1EP
KKCampbell@churchofscotland.org.uk

0131 346 2711
0131 441 6105
0131 447 2834

58   Edinburgh: Portobello and Joppa (F H W)
Stewart G. Weaver BA BD PhD   2003

Lourens de Jager PgDip MDiv BTh   2013
(Associate Minister)   2015

office@portyjoppachurch.org
6 St Mary's Place, Edinburgh EH15 2QF
SWeaver@churchofscotland.org.uk
1 Brunstane Road North, Edinburgh EH15 2DL
LDeJager@churchofscotland.org.uk

0131 657 3401
0131 669 2410

07521 426644

59   Edinburgh: Priestfield (F H W)
Donald H. Scott BA BD   1983   2018

13 Lady Road, Edinburgh EH16 5PA
Donald.Scott@churchofscotland.org.uk

0131 468 3302
0131 468 1254
07720 040081

60   Edinburgh: Ratho (F W)
Vacant
Interim Moderator: Stephen Manners

2 Freelands Road, Ratho, Newbridge EH28 8NP
SManners@churchofscotland.org.uk

0131 333 1346

61   Edinburgh: Reid Memorial See Edinburgh: Craigmillar Park

62   Edinburgh: Richmond Craigmillar (F H W)
Elizabeth M. Henderson   1985   1997
OBE MA BD MTh
Kirsty C. Forsyth BD DCS   2022
New charge formed by the union of Edinburgh: Bristo Memorial Craigmillar and Edinburgh: Richmond Craigmillar

Manse of Duddingston, Old Church Lane, Edinburgh EH15 3PX
EHenderson@churchofscotland.org.uk
KForsyth@churchofscotland.org.uk

0131 661 6561
0131 661 4240

0131 661 6561

63   Edinburgh: St Andrew's and St George's West (F H L W)
Vacant
Interim Moderator: Gordon D. Jamieson MA BD

info@stagw.org.uk
25 Comely Bank, Edinburgh EH4 1AJ
gordonjamieson182@gmail.com

0131 225 3847
0131 332 5848
01506 412020

64   Edinburgh: St Andrew's Clermiston (F W)
Vacant
Interim Moderator: Andrea E. Price

87 Drum Brae South, Edinburgh EH12 8TD
APrice@churchofscotland.org.uk

0131 339 4149
0131 443 4355

65   Edinburgh: St Catherine's Argyle (F H W)
Vacant
Interim Moderator: David Clarkson

5 Palmerston Road, Edinburgh EH9 1TL
DClarkson@churchofscotland.org.uk

0131 667 7220
0131 667 9344
0131 478 2376

66	**Edinburgh: St Cuthbert's (F H L T W)** Peter R.B. Sutton BA(AKC) BD MTh PGCertCouns	2017	**office@st-cuthberts.net** St Cuthbert's Church, 5 Lothian Road, Edinburgh EH1 2EP PSutton@churchofscotland.org.uk	**0131 229 1142** 07718 311319
67	**Edinburgh: St David's Broomhouse (F H W)** Michael J. Mair MStJ BD MTh	2014	33 Traquair Park West, Edinburgh EH12 7AN MMair@churchofscotland.org.uk	**0131 443 9851** 0131 334 1730
68	**Edinburgh: St John's Colinton Mains (F W)** Peter Nelson BSc BD	2015	2 Caiystane Terrace, Edinburgh EH10 6SR PNelson@churchofscotland.org.uk	07500 057889
69	**Edinburgh: St Margaret's (F H W)** John R. Wells BD PGCE DipMin	1991	**stmpc@btconnect.com** 43 Moira Terrace, Edinburgh EH7 6TD JWells@churchofscotland.org.uk	**0131 554 7400** 0131 322 9272
70	**Edinburgh: St Martin's (F W)** William M. Wishart BD	2017	68 Milton Road West, Edinburgh EH15 1QY BWishart@churchofscotland.org.uk	0131 237 5834
71	**Edinburgh: St Michael's (H W)** Andrea E. Price (Mrs)	1997	**office@stmichaels-kirk.co.uk** 13 Dovecot Park, Edinburgh EH14 2LN APrice@churchofscotland.org.uk	**0131 478 9675** 0131 443 4355
72	**Edinburgh: St Nicholas' Sighthill (F T W)** Thomas M. Kisitu BD MTh PhD Nikki J. Kirkland BSc (Ordained Local Minister)	1993 2021	122 Sighthill Loan, Edinburgh EH11 4NT TMKisitu@churchofscotland.org.uk St Nicholas' Sighthill Church, 124 Sighthill Loan EH11 4NT NKirkland@churchofscotland.org.uk	**07306 100111** 0131 442 3978 07789 790483
73	**Edinburgh: St Stephen's Comely Bank (F W)** George Vidits BD MTh	2000	**office@comelybankchurch.com** 8 Blinkbonny Crescent, Edinburgh EH4 3NB GVidits@churchofscotland.org.uk	**0131 315 4616** 07581 449540
74	**Edinburgh: Slateford Longstone (F W)** Samuel A.R. Torrens BSc BD	1995	50 Kingsknowe Road South, Edinburgh EH14 2JW STorrens@churchofscotland.org.uk	0131 466 5308

75 Edinburgh: Stockbridge (F H T W)
Vacant
Interim Moderator: Peter B. Bluett
stockbridgechurch@btconnect.com
19 Eildon Street, Edinburgh EH3 5JU
PBluett@churchofscotland.org.uk
0131 332 0122
0131 557 6052
0131 476 5212

76 Edinburgh: Tron Kirk (Gilmerton and Moredun) (F W)
Cameron Mackenzie BSc BD — 1997
4 Fordell Road, Edinburgh EH17 8XZ
Cammy.Mackenzie@churchofscotland.org.uk
07838 912361

Janet R. McKenzie (Mrs) BA DipHS Cert CS — 2016
(Ordained Local Minister)
80C Colinton Road, Edinburgh EH14 1DD
JMcKenzie@churchofscotland.org.uk
0131 444 2054
07980 884653

Liz Crocker DipComEd DCS — 1985
77c Craigcrook Road, Edinburgh EH4 3PH
ECrocker@churchofscotland.org.uk
0131 332 0227

77 Edinburgh: Wardie (F H T W)
Dolly Purnell BD — 2003
churchoffice@wardie.org.uk
35 Lomond Road, Edinburgh EH5 3JN
DPurnell@churchofscotland.org.uk
0131 551 3847
0131 563 6495

78 Fauldhouse: St Andrew's (H)
Scott Raby LTh CertMin — 1991
7 Glebe Court, Fauldhouse, Bathgate EH47 9DX
SRaby@churchofscotland.org.uk
01501 771190

79 Harthill: St Andrew's (F H)
Vacant
Session Clerk: Alexander Kennedy
East Main Street, Harthill, Shotts ML7 5QW
alex.kend@gmail.com
01501 751239
01501 752594

80 Kirknewton (H) and East Calder (F H W)
Alistair J. Cowper BSc BD — 2011
8 Manse Court, East Calder, Livingston EH53 0HF
ACowper@churchofscotland.org.uk
01506 357083
07791 524504

81 Kirk of Calder (F H W)
Vacant
Interim Moderator: Jonanda Groenewald
19 Maryfield Park, Mid Calder, Livingston EH53 0SB
JGroenewald@churchofscotland.org.uk
01506 882495
0131 261 7977

82 Linlithgow: St Michael's (F H W)
Liam J. Fraser LLB BD MTh PhD — 2017, 2019
info@stmichaels-parish.org.uk
St Michael's Manse, Kirkgate, Linlithgow EH49 7AL
LFraser@churchofscotland.org.uk
01506 842188
01506 842195

Thomas S. Riddell BSc CEng FIChemE — 1993, 1994
(Auxiliary Minister)
4 The Maltings, Linlithgow EH49 6DS
TRiddell@churchofscotland.org.uk
01506 843251

83 Linlithgow: St Ninian's Craigmailen (H W)
W. Richard Houston BSc BD MTh   1998   2004
29 Philip Avenue, Linlithgow EH49 7BH
WHouston@churchofscotland.org.uk
01506 202246

84 Livingston: Old (F H W)
Nelu I. Balaj BD MA ThD   2010   2017
The Manse, Charlesfield Lane, Livingston EH54 7AJ
NBalaj@churchofscotland.org.uk
01506 411888

85 Livingston United (F W)
Marc B. Kenton BTh MTh   1997   2019
2 Eastcroft Court, Livingston EH54 7ET
MKenton@churchofscotland.org.uk
01506 467426

Livingston United is a Local Ecumenical Partnership with the Scottish Episcopal, Methodist and United Reformed Churches

86 Pardovan, Kingscavil and Winchburgh See Abercorn

87 Polbeth Harwood (F W) linked with West Kirk of Calder (F H W)
Jonanda Groenewald BA BD MTh DD   2000   2014
3 Johnsburn Road, Balerno EH14 7DN
JGroenewald@churchofscotland.org.uk
0131 261 7977

Alison I. Quilter DipCS   2018
(Ordained Local Minister)
27 Northfield Meadows, Longridge, Bathgate EH47 8SA
AQuilter@churchofscotland.org.uk
07741 985597

88 Strathbrock (F H T W)
Hanneke I. Janse van Vuren (Ms)   2012   2020
BTh MDiv LTh MTh
1 Manse Park, Uphall, Broxburn EH52 6NX
HJansevanVuren@churchofscotland.org.uk
01506 856433
01506 206045

89 Torphichen See Avonbridge

90 Uphall: South (F H W)
Ian D. Maxwell MA BD PhD   1977   2013
8 Fernlea, Uphall, Broxburn EH52 6DF
IMaxwell@churchofscotland.org.uk
01506 239840

91 West Kirk of Calder (H) See Polbeth Harwood

92 Whitburn: Brucefield (F H W)
Vacant
Interim Moderator: Sandra Boyd
contact@brucefieldchurch.org.uk
48 Gleneagles Court, Whitburn, Bathgate EH47 8PG
SBoyd@churchofscotland.org.uk
01501 748666
01501 229354
07919 676242

93 Whitburn: South (H W)
Vacant
Interim Moderator: Robert Craig

admin@whitburnsouthparishchurch.org.uk
5 Mansewood Crescent, Whitburn, Bathgate EH47 8HA
RCraig@churchofscotland.org.uk
01501 740333
01501 519085

B. In other appointments: members of Presbytery

Name	Dates	Appointment	Address / Email	Telephone
Alexander, Ian W. BA BD STM	1990 2020	International Partnership Development Manager, Faith Action Programme	121 George Street, Edinburgh EH2 4YN IAlexander@churchofscotland.org.uk	0131 225 5722
Ashley-Emery, Stephen BD DPS RN	2006 2019	Royal Naval Chaplain, HMS Sultan, Gosport	Holmhill, East Main Street, Chirnside, Duns TD11 3XR Stephen.Ashley-Emery100@mod.gov.uk	
Barclay, Iain C. MBE TD MA BD MTh MPhil PhD FRSA	1976 2020	Chaplain: The Robin Chapel	The Thistle Foundation, Edinburgh EH16 4EA chaplain@robinchapel.org.uk	(Home) 07882 885684 (Office) 07393 232736
Billes, Rolf H. BD	1996 2023	Learning Development Manager, Iona Community	Rolf@iona.org.uk	
Evans, Mark BSc MSc DCS	1988 2006	Head of Spiritual Care NHS Fife (for 2023 seconded to Scottish Govt.)	13 Easter Drylaw Drive, Edinburgh EH4 2QA mark.evans59@nhs.scot	(Home) 0131 343 3089 (Office) 01383 674136
Fergusson, David A.S. (Prof.) OBE MA BD DPhil DD FRSE FBA	1984 2021	Regius Professor of Divinity, University of Cambridge	19 The Eights Marina, Mariners Way, Cambridge CB4 1ZA daf52@cam.ac.uk	01223 666779
Foster, Joanne G. (Mrs) DipTMus BD AdvDipCouns MBACP(Acc)	1996 2021	Healthcare Chaplain	Western General Hospital, Crewe Road South, Edinburgh EH4 2XU joanne.foster2@nhslothian.scot.nhs.uk	0131 537 1400
Galbraith, Christopher G. BA LLB BD	2012 2022	Team Leader, Faith Service Team, HM Prison Addiewell	HM Prison Addiewell, Station Road, Addiewell, West Calder EH55 8QA chris.galbraith@sodexogov.co.uk	01506 874500
Glienecke, Urzula PhD	2022	Associate Chaplain, University of Edinburgh	Chaplaincy Centre, 1 Bristo Square, Edinburgh EH8 9AL urzula.glienecke@ed.ac.uk	0131 650 2595
Hardman Moore, Susan (Prof.) MA MAR PhD	2013 2022	Vice Principal, New College, University of Edinburgh (Ordained Local Minister)	New College, Mound Place, Edinburgh EH1 2LX SHardman-Moore@churchofscotland.org.uk	0131 650 8908 07811 345699
Howitt, Jane M. MA BD	1996 2020	Chaplain, Heriot-Watt University	The Chaplaincy, Heriot-Watt University, Edinburgh EH14 4AS j.m.howitt@hw.ac.uk	0131 451 4508
Kennedy, Fiona BA DipHE	2022	Ordained Local Minister, Edinburgh: Barclay Viewforth, Craiglockhart, Polwarth, St Michael's	20 Craiglockhart Quadrant, Edinburgh EH14 1HD FKennedy@churchofscotland.org.uk	0131 444 1615
Mathieson, Angus R. MA BD	1988 2020	Presbytery and Partnership Support Senior Manager, Faith Action Programme	21 Traquair Park West, Edinburgh EH12 7AN AMathieson@churchofscotland.org.uk	0131 334 9774
McPheat, Elspeth DCS	1985 2001	Deacon: CrossReach	53 Wood Street, Grangemouth FK3 8LS elspeth176@sky.com	01324 282406
McPherson, William BD DipEd	1994 2003	Chief Executive, The Vine Trust	83 Laburnam Road, Port Seton, Prestonpans EH32 0UD	01875 812252
Orr, Sheena BA MSc MBA BD DPT	2011 2018	Chaplaincy Adviser, Scottish Prison Service	Calton House, 5 Redheughs Rigg, South Gyle, Edinburgh EH12 9HW sheena.orr@prisons.gov.scot	0131 330 3575 07922 649160
Pennykid, Gordon J. BD DCS	2015 2018	Chaplain, HM Prison Edinburgh	8 Glenfield, Livingston EH54 7BG GPennykid@churchofscotland.org.uk	07747 652652

Stewart, Lezley J. BD ThM MTh DMin	Ministries Support Manager, Faith Action Programme	2000	2017	121 George Street, Edinburgh EH2 4YN LStewart@churchofscotland.org.uk	0131 225 5722
Swan, David BVMS BD DipTh CDRS	Chaplain, HM Prison Edinburgh	2005	2018	159 Redhall Drive, Edinburgh EH13 2LR davidswan97@gmail.com	07944 598988
Tweedie, Fiona J. BSc PhD	Ordained Local Minister: Statistician, Office of Assembly Trustees	2011	2014	121 George Street, Edinburgh EH2 4YN FTweedie@churchofscotland.org.uk	0131 225 5722
Wishart, Erica M. (Mrs) MA BD	Hospice Chaplain	2014	2020	St Columba's Hospice, 15 Boswall Road, Edinburgh EH5 3RW EWishart@churchofscotland.org.uk	0131 551 1381 07503 170173

C. Retaining: members of Presbytery

Aitchison, James W. BD	(Aberdalgie and Forteviot with Aberuthven and Dunning)	1993	2021	JAitchison@churchofscotland.org.uk	
Alexander, Helen J.R. BD DipSW CQSW	(Assistant, Edinburgh: High (St Giles'))	1981	2019	7 Polwarth Place, Edinburgh EH11 1LG HAlexander@churchofscotland.org.uk	0131 346 0685
Anderson, Dorothy U. LLB DipLP BD	(Associate, Dunblane Cathedral)	2006	2021	4GF Glencairn Crescent, Edinburgh EH12 5BS DAnderson@churchofscotland.org.uk	0131 226 4242 07926 090489
Armitage, William L. BSc BD	(Edinburgh: London Road)	1976	2006	Flat 7, 4 Papermill Wynd, Edinburgh EH7 4GJ bill@billarm.plus.com	0131 558 8534
Baird, Kenneth S. MSc PhD BD MIMarEST	(Edinburgh: Leith North)	1998	2009	3 Maule Terrace, Gullane EH31 2DB	01620 843447
Barber, Peter I. MA BD	(Edinburgh: Gorgie Dalry Stenhouse)	1984	2021	39 Roseburn Drive, Edinburgh EH12 5NR	
Bicket, Matthew S. BD	(Carnoustie: Panbride)	1989	2017	9/2 Connaught Place, Edinburgh EH6 4RQ matthew.bicket1952@gmail.com	0131 552 8781
Birnie, Carolann BD DipPSRP	(Dunfermline: St Ninian's)	2009	2022	7 Overton Court, Pitreavie Castle, Dunfermline KY11 8TY CBirnie@churchofscotland.org.uk	01383 600072
Booth, Jennifer (Mrs) LTh BD	(Associate: Edinburgh: Leith South)	1996	2005	39 Lilyhill Terrace, Edinburgh EH8 7DR	0131 661 3813
Borthwick, Kenneth S. MA BD	(Edinburgh: Holy Trinity)	1983	2016	34 Rodger Crescent, Armadale EH48 3GR kennysamuel@aol.com	07735 749594
Brown, William D. BD CQSW	(Edinburgh: Murrayfield)	1987	2013	79 Cambee Park, Edinburgh EH16 6GG wdb@talktalk.net	0131 261 7297
Cameron, David C. BD CertMin	(Edinburgh: Dalmeny with Edinburgh: Queensferry)	1993	2023	17 Morayvale, Aberdour, Burntisland KY3 0XE DavidCCameron@churchofscotland.org.uk	
Clinkenbeard, William W. BSc BD STM	(Edinburgh: Carrick Knowe)	1966	2000	3/17 Western Harbour Breakwater, Edinburgh EH6 6PA bjclinks@compuserve.com	0131 629 0519
Cowie, John A. BSc BD DMin	(Edinburgh: Stockbridge)	1983	2021	1 Liberton Place, Edinburgh EH16 6NA JCowie@churchofscotland.org.uk	0131 672 1766
Crawford, Morag (Miss) MSc DCS	(Deacon, Rosyth)	1977	2021	8 Ashbank Court, Bathgate EH4 2BL MCrawford@churchofscotland.org.uk	01506 204672 07970 982563
Davidson, D. Hugh MA	(Edinburgh: Inverleith)	1965	2009	Flat 1/2, 22 Summerside Place, Edinburgh EH6 4NZ hdavidson35@btinternet.com	0131 554 8420
Dewar, James S. MA BD	(Edinburgh: Juniper Green)	1983	2023	JDewar@churchofscotland.org.uk	
Douglas, Alexander B. BD	(Edinburgh: Blackhall St Columba's)	1979	2014	15 Inchview Gardens, Dalgety Bay, Dunfermline KY11 9SA alexandjill@douglas.net	01383 791080

Name	Ord.	Ind.	Position	Address / Email	Tel
Dunleavy, Suzanne BD DipEd	1990	2016	(Bridge of Weir: St Machar's Ranfurly)	44 Tantallon Gardens, Bellsquarry, Livingston EH54 9AT / suzanne.dunleavy@btinternet.com	0131 334 1665
Dunn, W. Iain C. DA LTh	1983	1998	(Edinburgh: Pilrig and Dalmeny Street)	10 Fox Covert Avenue, Edinburgh EH12 6UQ	07791 007158
Dunphy, Rhona B. (Mrs) BD DPTheol DrPhil	2005	2020	(Pastoral Support, Faith Nurture Forum)	92 The Vennel, Linlithgow EH49 7ET / RDunphy@churchofscotland.org.uk	01721 602157
Embleton, Brian M. BD CPS	1976	2015	(Edinburgh: Reid Memorial)	54 Edinburgh Road, Peebles EH45 8EB / bmembleton@gmail.com	01721 602157
Embleton, Sara R. (Mrs) BA BD MTh	1988	2010	(Edinburgh: Leith St Serf's)	54 Edinburgh Road, Peebles EH45 8EB / srembleton@gmail.com	0131 343 1047
Farquharson, Gordon MA BD DipEd	1998	2007	(Stonehaven: Dunnottar)	26 Learmonth Court, Edinburgh EH4 1PB / gfarqu@talktalk.net	0131 337 5646
Forrester, Margaret R. (Mrs) MA BD DD	1974	2003	(Edinburgh: St Michael's)	25 Kingsburgh Road, Edinburgh EH12 6DZ / margaret@rosskeen.org.uk	0131 347 1400
Fraser, Shirley A. (Miss) MA BD DipASS	1992	2008	(Scottish Field Director: Friends International)	6/50 Roseburn Drive, Edinburgh EH12 5NS	07712 162375
Frew, Michael W. BSc BD	1978	2017	(Edinburgh: Slateford Longstone)	37 Swanston Terrace, Edinburgh EH10 7DN	0131 443 7126
Gardner, John V.	1997	2003	(Glamis, Inverarity and Kinnettles)	75/1 Lockharton Avenue, Edinburgh EH14 1BD / jvgardner66@googlemail.com	07794 149852
Gilmour, Ian Y. BD CertMin	1985	2018	(Edinburgh: St Andrew's and St George's West)	1 Groathill Loan, Drylaw, Edinburgh EH4 2WL / iany2@gmail.com	0131 449 2554
Gordon, Margaret (Mrs) DCS	1998	2012	(Deacon, Edinburgh: Currie)	92 Lanark Road West, Currie EH14 5LA	0131 445 5763
Graham, W. Peter MA BD	1967	2008	(Presbytery Clerk: Edinburgh)	23/6 East Comiston, Edinburgh EH10 6RZ	01501 731969
Greig, Ronald G. MA BD	1987	2018	(Livingston United)	47 Mallace Avenue, Armadale EH48 2QD / rgglep@gmail.com	07787 887427
Halley, Ruth D. BEd BD PGCert	2012	2023	(Associate Minister, Edinburgh: Greyfriars)	24 Comrie Avenue, Dunbar EH42 1ZN / RHalley@churchofscotland.org.uk	07530 307413
Harkness, James KVCO CB OBE KHC MA DD	1961	1995	(Chaplain General: Army)	Lang Glen, Durisdeer, nr Thornhill DG3 5BJ	01848 500225
Harley, Elspeth S. BA MTh	1991	2020	(Caddonfoot with Galashiels: Trinity)	EHarley@churchofscotland.org.uk	07950 076528
Hay, Jared W. BA MTh DipMin DMin	1987	2017	(Edinburgh: Priestfield)	39 Netherbank, Edinburgh EH16 6YR / jaredhay3110@gmail.com	07906 662515
Herbold Ross, Kristina M.	2008	2018	(Work Place Chaplain, Edinburgh)	kristinaherboldross@gmail.com	
Holt, Jack BSc BD MTh	1985	2023	(Edinburgh: Polwarth)	3/8 Perdrixknowe, 82 Colinton Road, Edinburgh EH14 1AF / JHolt@churchofscotland.org.uk	07762 359781
Inglis, Ann (Mrs) LLB BD	1986	2015	(Langton and Lammermuir Kirk)	34 Echline View, South Queensferry EH30 9XL / revainglis@gmail.com	0131 629 0233
Irving, William D. LTh	1985	2005	(Golspie)	122 Swanston Muir, Edinburgh EH10 7HY	0131 441 3384
Jamieson, Gordon D. MA BD	1974	2012	(Head of Stewardship)	41 Goldpark Place, Livingston EH54 6LW / gordonjamieson182@gmail.com	01506 412020
Keil, Alistair H. BD DipMin	1989	2021	(Edinburgh: St Andrew's Clermiston)	14 Comiston Terrace, Edinburgh EH10 6AH / AKeil@churchofscotland.org.uk	07758 009250

Lawson, Kenneth C. MA BD	1963	1999	(Director, Ecumenical Spirituality Programme, Scottish Churches Open College)	56 Easter Drylaw View, Edinburgh EH4 2QP	0131 539 3311
Logan, Anne T. (Mrs) MA BD MTh DMin PhD	1981	2012	(Edinburgh: Stockbridge)	Sunnyside Cottage, 18 Upper Broomieknowe, Lasswade EH18 1LP / annetlogan@sky.com	0131 663 9550
Lough, Adrian J. BD AFSERT MIERE DipSW	2012	2020	(Auchtergaven and Moneydie with Redgorton and Stanley)	12 Dundrennan Cottages, Edinburgh EH16 5RG / revlough@btinternet.com	
Mackay, Kenneth J. MA BD	1971	2007	(Edinburgh: St Nicholas' Sighthill)	46 Chuckethall Road, Livingston EH54 8FB / kmth_mackay@yahoo.com	01506 410884
Mackenzie, James G. BA BD	1980	2005	(Jersey: St Columba's)	26 Drylaw Crescent, Edinburgh EH4 2AU / jgmackenzie@jerseymail.co.uk	0131 332 3720
Maclean, Ailsa G. (Mrs) BD DipCE	1979	2017	(Chaplain: George Heriot's School)	28 Swan Spring Avenue, Edinburgh EH10 6NJ	
Macmillan, Gilleasbuig I. KCVO MA BD DrHc DD FRSE HRSA FRCSEd	1969	2013	(Edinburgh: High (St Giles'))	207 Dalkeith Road, Edinburgh EH16 5DS / gmacmillan1@btinternet.com	0131 667 5732
MacMurchie, F. Lynne LLB BD	1998	2023	(Chaplain, St John's Hospital, Livingston)	101/5 Easter Warriston, Edinburgh EH7 4QZ / l.macmurchie01@btinternet.com	0131 554 2714
Manners, Stephen MA BD	1989	2022	(Kelso Country Churches)	SManners@churchofscotland.org.uk	07415 028678
Marshall, A. Scott DipComm BD	1984	2021	(Abercorn with Pardovan, Kingscavil and Winchburgh)	13 Leyland Road, Bathgate EH48 2SG	
McGregor, T. Stewart MBE MA BD	1957	1998	(Chaplain: Edinburgh Royal Infirmary)	19 Lonsdale Terrace, Edinburgh EH3 9HL / cetsm@uwclub.net	0131 229 5332
McIntosh, Kay (Mrs) DCS	1990	2023	(Deacon, Edinburgh: Mayfield Salisbury)	4 Jacklin Green, Livingston EH54 8PZ / mcintosh.kay@gmail.com	01506 440543
McPake, John M. LTh	2000	2013	(Edinburgh: Liberton Northfield)	3 Kilburn Wood Drive, Roslin EH25 9AA / john_mcpake9@yahoo.co.uk	0131 285 8386
Moir, Ian A. MA BD	1962	2000	(Adviser for Urban Priority Areas)	28/6 Comely Bank Avenue, Edinburgh EH4 1EL	0131 332 2748
Morrison, Angus MA BD PhD DD	1979	2021	(Orwell and Portmoak)	170 The Murrays, Edinburgh EH17 8UP / AMorrison@churchofscotland.org.uk	
Mulligan, Anne MA DCS	1974	2013	(Deacon: Hospital Chaplain)	27A Craigour Avenue, Edinburgh EH17 1NH / mulliganne@aol.com	0131 664 3426
Munro, John R. BD	1976	2017	(Edinburgh: Fairmilehead)	23 Braid Farm Road, Edinburgh EH10 6LE / revjohnmunro@hotmail.com	0131 446 9363
Nelson, Georgina MA BD PhD DipEd	1990	2022	(Hospital Chaplain, NHS Lothian)	63 Hawthorn Bank, Seafield, Bathgate EH47 7EB	
Nicol, Douglas A.O. MA BD	1974	2018	(Hobkirk and Southdean with Ruberslaw)	1/2 North Werber Park, Edinburgh EH4 1SY / Douglas.Nicol@churchofscotland.org.uk	07811 437075
Paterson, Douglas S. MA BD DipTP	1976	2010	(Edinburgh: St Colm's)	4 Ards Place, High Street, Aberlady EH32 0DB	01875 870192
Povey, John M. DL BD PhD	1981	2021	(Kirk of Calder)	5 Ainslie Road, East Calder, Livingston EH53 0PU / RevJPovey@aol.com	07549 525498
Ramsay, A. Malcolm BA LLB DipMin	1986	2022	(Transition Minister, Edinburgh: Willowbrae)	Ford Cottage, Ford, Pathhead EH37 5RE / amalcolmramsay@aol.com	
Rennie, Agnes M. (Miss) DCS	1974	2012	(Deacon, Edinburgh: Bristo Memorial Craigmillar)	3/1 Craigmillar Court, Edinburgh EH16 4AD	0131 661 8475

Name	Years	Role	Address / Email	Telephone
Ridland, Alistair K. MStJ MA BD PGDip MRAeS MInstLM RAFAC	1982 2022	(Chaplain: Western General Hospital)	13 Stewart Place, Kirkliston EH29 0BQ a.ridland@btinternet.com	0131 333 2711
Robertson, Charles LVO MA	1965 2005	(Edinburgh: Canongate)	3 Ross Gardens, Edinburgh EH9 3BS canongate1@aol.com	0131 662 9025
Robertson, Pauline (Mrs) DCS BA CertTheol	2003 2023	(Port Chaplain, Sailors' Society: Leith and Forth Estuary)	6 Ashville Terrace, Edinburgh EH6 8DD	0131 554 6564 07759 436303
Roger, Alexander M. BD PhD	1982 2020	(Whitburn: Brucefield)	4 Lugton Circle, South Gilmerton Brae, Edinburgh EH17 8GT amroger1951@outlook.com	0131 664 8109
Ross, Matthew Z. LLB BD MTh FSAScot	1998 2023	(Programme Executive for Diakonia and Capacity Building, World Council of Churches)	matthewzross@gmail.com	07711 706950
Scott, J. Martin C. DipMusEd RSAM BD PhD	1986 2019	(Secretary, Council of Assembly)	52 Ravenscroft Gardens, Edinburgh EH17 8RP martin.scott14@sky.com	0131 431 4195 07856 165820
Shaw, Duncan BD MTh	1975 2020	(Bathgate: St John's)	30 Meadowpark Crescent, Bathgate EH48 2SX duncan.shaw11@btinternet.com	01506 654563
Smith, Angus MA LTh	1965 2006	(Chaplain to the Oil Industry)	3/7 West Powburn, West Savile Gait, Edinburgh EH9 3EW	0131 667 1761
Smith, Graham W. BA BD FSAScot	1995 2016	(Livingston: Old)	76 Bankton Park East, Livingston EH54 9BN smithgraham824@gmail.com	01506 442917
Stark, Suzie M. BD CertMin	2013 2021	(Chaplain, St Columba's Hospice, Edinburgh)	The Lodge, 40 Warriston Gardens, Edinburgh EH3 5NE sstark1962@btinternet.com	0131 551 1633
Stevenson, John MA BD PhD HonFEIS	1963 2001	(General Secretary, Department of Education)	12 Swanston Gardens, Edinburgh EH10 7DL	0131 445 3960
Tait, John M. BSc BD	1985 2012	(Edinburgh: Pilrig St Paul's)	82 Greenend Gardens, Edinburgh EH17 7QH johnmtait@me.com	0131 258 9105
Taylor, William R. MA BD MTh	1983 2018	(Chaplaincy Adviser, Scottish Prison Service)	33 Kingsknowe Drive EH14 2JY wlretl@outlook.com	0131 443 5590 07447 258525
Teague, Yvonne (Mrs) DCS	1965 2002	(Education and Development Officer, Board of Ministry)	46 Craigcrook Avenue, Edinburgh EH4 3PX y.teague.1@blueyonder.co.uk	0131 336 3113
Watson, Nigel G. MA	1998 2012	(Associate: East Kilbride: Old/Stewartfield/West)	7 St Catherine's Place, Edinburgh EH9 1NU nigel.g.watson@gmail.com	0131 662 4191
Wells, Ian J. BD	1999 2023	(Edinburgh: Ratho)	11 Catelhock Close, Kirkliston EH29 9FF IWells@churchofscotland.org.uk	
Whyte, George J. OBE BSc BD DMin KSG	1981 2022	(Principal Clerk)	4 Baberton Mains Lea, Edinburgh EH14 3HB george.whyte@blueyonder.co.uk	07902 645109
Williams, Jenny M. BSc CQSW BD MTh	1996 2022	(Transition Minister, Edinburgh: Drylaw)	5 Kilmundy Drive, Burntisland KY3 0JN jennywilliams@gmx.co.uk	
Wynne, Alistair T.E. BA BD	1982 2009	(Nicosia Community Church, Cyprus)	Flat 6, 14 Burnbrae Drive, Edinburgh EH12 8AS awynne2@googlemail.com	0131 339 6462

D. In other appointments: not members of Presbytery

Name	Years	Appointment	Address	Telephone
Aitken, Ewan R. BA BD	1992 2014	CEO, Edinburgh Cyrenians	159 Restalrig Avenue, Edinburgh EH7 6PJ	0131 467 1660
Provan, Iain W. (Prof.) MA BA PhD	1991 1997	Professor of Biblical Studies	Regent College, 5800 University Boulevard, Vancouver BC V6T 2E4, Canada	001 604 224 3245
Storrar, William F. (Prof.) MA BD PhD	1984 2005	Director, Center of Theological Inquiry	50 Stockton Street, Princeton. NJ 08540, USA cti@ctinquiry.org	

E. Retaining: not members of Presbytery

Name	Years	Appointment	Address	Telephone
Boyd, Kenneth M. (Prof.) MA BD PhD FRCPE	1970 2011	(University of Edinburgh: Medical Ethics)	1 Doune Terrace, Edinburgh EH3 6DY k.boyd@ed.ac.uk	0131 225 6485
Crossan, William	2014 2022	(Ordained Local Minister, Campbeltown: Lorne and Lowland)	57 Caldercruix Crescent, Eliburn, Livingston EH54 7FS w.crossan@btinternet.com	07833 152345
Douglas, Colin R. MA BD STM	1969 2007	(Livingston Ecumenical)	34 West Pilton Gardens, Edinburgh EH4 4EQ colin.r.douglas@gmail.com	0131 551 3808
Drake, Wendy F. (Mrs) BD	1978 2007	(Cockpen and Carrington with Lasswade and Rosewell)	21 William Black Place, South Queensferry EH30 9QR revwdrake@hotmail.co.uk	0131 331 1520
Espie, Howard	2011 2014	(Mission Facilitator/Enabler, Edinburgh: Barclay Viewforth)	1 Sprucebank Avenue, Langbank, Port Glasgow PA14 6YX howardespie.me.com	01475 540391
Lockerbie, Caroline R. BA MDiv DMin	1978 2017	(Lerwick and Bressay: Transition Minister)	102 3300 Centenial Drive, Vernon, BC, Canada V1T 9Md5 lockerbie21@gmail.com	001 519 429 5563
MacGregor, Margaret S. (Miss) MA BD DipEd	1985 1994	(Bishop's College, Calcutta)	16 Learmonth Court, Edinburgh EH4 1PB	0131 332 1089
MacLaine, Marilyn (Mrs) LTh	1995 2009	(Inchinnan)	37 Bankton Brae, Livingston EH54 9LA marilynmaclaine@btinternet.com	01506 400619
Merrilees, Ann (Miss) DCS	1994 2006	(Deacon, Glasgow: St James' (Pollok))	7/1 Slaeside, Balerno EH14 7HL amerrilees@gmail.com	0131 449 3325
Morrison, Mary B. (Mrs) MA BD DipEd	1978 2000	(Edinburgh: Stenhouse St Aidan's)	174 Craigcrook Road, Edinburgh EH4 3PP	0131 336 4706
Newell, Alison M. (Mrs) BD 1986	1986 2021	(Associate Chaplain, University of Edinburgh)	1A Inverleith Terrace, Edinburgh EH3 5NS alinewell@aol.com	0131 556 3505
Penman, Iain D. BD DipMS	1977 2008	(Edinburgh: Kaimes Lockhart Memorial)	33/5 Carnbee Avenue, Edinburgh EH16 6GA iainpenmanklm@aol.com	0131 664 0673 07931 993427
Robson, Brenda PhD	2005 2019	(Auxiliary Minister, Kirknewton and East Calder)	22 Ratho Park Road, Ratho, Newbridge EH28 8NY BRobson@churchofscotland.org.uk	0131 281 9511
Smith, Ronald W. BA BEd BD	1979 2011	(Falkirk: St James')	1F1, 2 Middlefield, Edinburgh EH7 4PF	0131 553 1174 07900 896954
Thomson, Donald M. BD	1975 2013	(Tullibody: St Serf's)	50 Sighthill Road, Edinburgh EH11 4NY donmiethomson@tiscali.co.uk	
Torrance, Iain R. (Prof.) KCVO Kt DD FRSE	1982 2012	(President: Princeton Theological Seminary)	25 The Causeway, Duddingston Village, Edinburgh EH15 3QA irt@ptsem.edu	0131 661 3092

F. Inactive: not members of Presbytery

Name	Years	Charge / Appointment	Address & Email	Telephone
Beckett, David M. BA BD	1964 2002	(Edinburgh: Greyfriars, Tolbooth and Highland Kirk)	31/1 Sciennes Road, Edinburgh EH9 1NT davidbeckett3@aol.com	0131 667 2672
Black, David W. BSc BD	1968 2008	(Strathbrock)	66 Bridge Street, Newbridge EH28 8SH dw.black666@yahoo.co.uk	0131 333 2609
Blakey, Ronald S. MA BD MTh	1962 2000	(Secretary, Assembly Council)	24 Kimmerghame Place, Edinburgh EH4 2GE kathleen.blakey@gmail.com	0131 343 6352
Brady, Ian D. BSc ARCST BD	1967 2001	(Edinburgh: Corstorphine Old)	28 Frankfield Crescent, Dalgety Bay, Dunfermline KY11 9LW brady500@gmail.com	01383 825104
Brook, Stanley A. BD MTh CPS	1977 2016	(Newport-on-Tay)	4 Scotstoun Green, South Queensferry EH30 9YA stan_brook@btinternet.com	0131 331 4237
Buchanan, Neil BD	1991 2019	(East Kilbride: Moncrieff)	40 Links View, Port Seton, Prestonpans EH32 0EZ neil.buchanan@talk21.com	07993 720497
Chalmers, Murray MA	1965 2006	(Chaplain, Royal Edinburgh Hospital)	8 Easter Warriston, Edinburgh EH7 4QX murray.chalmers8448@gmail.com	0131 552 4211
Cuthell, Tom C. MA BD	1965 2007	(Edinburgh: St Cuthbert's)	Flat 10, 2 Kingsburgh Crescent, Waterfront, Edinburgh EH5 1JS tcuthell@gmail.com	0131 476 3864
Darroch, Richard J.G. BD MTh MA	1993 2010	(Whitburn: Brucefield)	23 Barnes Green, Livingston EH54 8PP richdar@aol.com	01506 436648
Davidson, Ian M.P. MBE MA BD	1954 1994	(Stirling: Allan Park South with Church of the Holy Rude)	13/8 Craigend Park, Edinburgh EH16 5XX ian.m.p.davidson@btinternet.com	0131 664 0074
Dickson, Graham T. MA BD	1985 2005	(Edinburgh: St Stephen's Comely Bank)	43 Hope Park Gardens, Bathgate EH48 2QT gtd194@googlemail.com	01506 237597
Lamont, Stewart J. BSc BD	1972 2015	(Arbirlot with Carmyllie)	Mas des Pins, 23 Rue du 19 mars 1962, 11500 Quillan, France lamonts@lamonts.eu	0033 9 86 56 16 78
Lithgow, Anne R. (Mrs) MA BD	1992 2009	(Dunglass)	13 Cameron Park, Edinburgh EH16 5JY anne.lithgow@btinternet.com	
McGillivray, A. Gordon MA BD STM	1951 1993	(Presbytery Clerk, Edinburgh)	36 Larchfield Neuk, Balerno EH14 7NL	0131 449 3901
Millar, Peter W. MA BD ThM PhD	1971 1998	(Warden, Iona Abbey)	6/5 Etrickdale, Edinburgh EH3 5JN ionacottage@hotmail.com	0131 557 0517
Monteith, W. Graham MA BD BPhil PhD	1974 1994	(Flotta and Fara with Hoy and Walls)	20/3 Grandfield, Edinburgh EH6 4TL	0131 552 2564
Petrie, Ian D. MA BD	1970 2008	(Dundee: St Andrew's)	27/111 West Savile Terrace, Edinburgh EH9 3DR idp-77@hotmail.com	0131 237 2857
Plate, Maria A.G. (Miss) BA LTh CQSW DSW	1983 2000	(South Ronaldsay and Burray)	Flat 29, 77 Barnton Park View, Edinburgh EH4 6EL riaplate@gmail.com	0131 339 8539
Scott, Jayne E. BA MEd MBA	1988 2019	(Secretary, Ministries Council)	52 Ravenscroft Gardens, Edinburgh EH17 8RP jayne.scott5@btinternet.com	07740 151542
Stephen, Donald M. TD MA BD ThM	1962 2001	(Edinburgh: Marchmont St Giles')	10 Hawkhead Crescent, Edinburgh EH16 6LR donaldmstephen@gmail.com	0131 658 1216
Wilson, John M. (Ian) MA	1964 1995	(Adviser, Religious Education, Highland Region)	27 Bellfield Street, Edinburgh EH15 2BR ianandshirley@talktalk.net	0131 669 5257

G. Readers (active)

Devoy, Fiona (Mrs)	196 The Murrays Brae, Edinburgh EH17 8UH	fiona.devoy@yahoo.co.uk	0131 441 9201
Drummond, Brian		BDrummond@churchofscotland.org.uk	01506 654950
Elliott, Sarah (Miss)	105 Seafield Rows, Seafield, Bathgate EH47 7AW	sarah.elliott6@btopenworld.com	0131 558 8210
Farrow, Edmund	14 Brunswick Terrace, Edinburgh EH7 5PG	edmundfarrow@blueyonder.co.uk	01506 842069
Galloway, Brenda (Dr)	16 Baron's Hill Court, Linlithgow EH49 7SP	dr.b.galloway82@gmail.com	0131 664 2366
Jackson, Kate (Ms)	3 Kedslie Road, Edinburgh EH16 6NT	katejackson1252@gmail.com	07901 501819
Kerrigan, Herbert A. (Prof.) MA LLB KC DipPTh	Airdene, 20 Edinburgh Road, Dalkeith EH22 1JY	kerrigan@kerriganqc.com	0131 660 3007 / 07725 953772
McFadzean, John	121 South Street, Armadale, Bathgate EH48 3JT	jmcfadzean2@gmail.com	01501 730260
Middleton, Alex	19 Cramond Place, Dalgety Bay KY11 9LS	alex.middleton@btinternet.com	01383 820800
Orr, Elizabeth (Mrs)	64a Marjoribanks Street, Bathgate EH48 1AL	liz-orr@hotmail.co.uk	01596 653116
Paxton, James	5 Main Street, Longridge, Bathgate EH47 8AE	jimpaxton1950@gmail.com	01501 772192
Pearce, Martin J.	4 Corbiehill Avenue, Edinburgh EH4 5DR	martin.j.pearce@blueyonder.co.uk	0131 336 4864
Tew, Helen (Mrs)	5/5 Moat Drive, Edinburgh EH14 1NU	helentew9@gmail.com	07801 717222 / 07986 170802
Wilkie, David	55 Goschen Place, Broxburn EH52 5JH	david-fmu_09@tiscali.co.uk	01506 238644

H. Ministries Development Staff

Name	Role	Email
Corrie, Margaret (Miss) DCS	Armadale – Parish Assistant	MCorrie@churchofscotland.org.uk
Crocker, Liz DipComEd DCS	Edinburgh: Tron Kirk (Gilmerton and Moredun) – Parish Assistant	ECrocker@churchofscotland.org.uk
de Jager, Lourens (Rev) PgDip MDiv BTh	Edinburgh: Portobello and Joppa – Associate Minister	LDeJager@churchofscotland.org.uk
Fejszes, Violetta (Dr)	Edinburgh: Old Kirk and Muirhouse – Parish Development Worker	VFejszes@churchofscotland.org.uk
Forsyth, Kirsty BD DCS	Edinburgh: Richmond Craigmillar – Parish Deacon	KForsyth@churchofscotland.org.uk
Hirani, Hina	Edinburgh: Old Kirk and Muirhouse – Project Development Worker	HHirani@churchofscotland.org.uk
Knott, Alice	Edinburgh: Granton – Pastoral Assistant	AKnott@churchofscotland.org.uk
Laoshe, Fadeke	Edinburgh: St Margaret's – Children, Youth and Family Worker	FLaoshe@churchofscotland.org.uk
Lawrie, Lesley	Livingston: Old – Community Outreach Worker	LLawrie@churchofscotland.org.uk
Midwinter, Alan	Edinburgh: St David's Broomhouse – Pastoral Assistant	AMidwinter@churchofscotland.org.uk
Moodie, David	Edinburgh: Granton – Parish Assistant	DMoodie@churchofscotland.org.uk
Orr, Lorraine	Linlithgow: St Michael's – Pioneer and Community Outreach Worker	LOrr@churchofscotland.org.uk
Richardson, Ian (Dr)	Edinburgh: Holy Trinity – Discipleship Team Leader	IRichardson@churchofscotland.org.uk
Robertson, Douglas S. BEng BA MTh	Edinburgh: Gracemount – Church Leader and Project Worker	Douglas.Robertson@churchofscotland.org.uk
Stark, Jennifer MA MATheol	Edinburgh: Richmond Craigmillar – Community Project Worker	JStark@churchofscotland.org.uk

EDINBURGH ADDRESSES

Church	Address
Albany	at St Andrew's and St George's West
Balerno	Johnsburn Road, Balerno
Barclay Viewforth	Barclay Place
Blackhall St Columba's	Queensferry Road
Broughton St Mary's	Bellevue Crescent
Canongate	Canongate
Carrick Knowe	North Saughton Road
Colinton	Dell Road
Corstorphine	
Craigsbank	Craigs Crescent
Old	Kirk Loan
St Anne's	Kaimes Road
St Ninian's	St John's Road
Craiglockhart	Craiglockhart Avenue
Craigmillar Park	Craigmillar Park
Currie	Kirkgate, Currie
Dalmeny and Queensferry	Main Street, Dalmeny; The Loan, S. Queensferry
Davidson's Mains	Quality Street
Drylaw	Groathill Road North
Duddingston	Old Church Lane, Duddingston
Fairmilehead	Frogston Road West, Fairmilehead
Gorgie Dalry Stenhouse	Gorgie Road
Gracemount	Gracemount Primary School
Granton	Boswall Parkway
Greenbank	Braidburn Terrace
Greenside	Royal Terrace
Greyfriars Kirk	Greyfriars Place
High (St Giles')	High Street
Holy Trinity	Hailesland Place, Wester Hailes
Inverleith St Serf's	Ferry Road
Juniper Green	Lanark Road, Juniper Green
Kirkliston	The Square, Kirkliston
Leith	
North	Madeira Street off Ferry Road
St Andrew's	Easter Road
South	Kirkgate, Leith
Liberton	Kirkgate, Liberton
Northfield	Gilmerton Road, Liberton
Marchmont St Giles'	Kilgraston Road
Mayfield Salisbury	Mayfield Road x West Mayfield
Meadowbank and Willowbrae	Dalziel Place x London Road; Willowbrae Road
Morningside	Cluny Gardens
Morningside United	Bruntsfield Place x Chamberlain Rd
Murrayfield	Abinger Gardens
Newhaven	Craighall Road
Northwest Kirk	Cramond Glebe Road; Pennywell Gardens
Palmerston Place	Palmerston Place
Pilrig St Paul's	Pilrig Street
Polwarth	Polwarth Terrace x Harrison Road
Portobello and Joppa	Abercorn Terrace
Priestfield	Dalkeith Road x Marchhall Place
Ratho	Baird Road, Ratho
Reid Memorial	West Savile Terrace
Richmond Craigmillar	Niddrie Mains Road
St Andrew's and St George's West	George Street
St Andrew's Clermiston	Clermiston View
St Catherine's Argyle	Grange Road x Chalmers Crescent
St Cuthbert's	Lothian Road
St David's Broomhouse	Broomhouse Crescent
St John's Colinton Mains	Oxgangs Road North
St Margaret's	Restalrig Road South
St Martin's	Magdalene Drive
St Michael's	Slateford Road
St Nicholas' Sighthill	Calder Road
St Stephen's Comely Bank	Comely Bank
Slateford Longstone	Kingsknowe Road North
Stockbridge	Saxe Coburg Street
Tron Kirk (Gilmerton and Moredun)	Craigour Gardens and Ravenscroft Street
Wardie	Primrosebank Road

(2) LOTHIAN AND BORDERS (W)

New presbytery formed by the union of the Presbyteries of Lothian, Melrose and Peebles, Duns, and Jedburgh.
Meets at different venues throughout the Presbytery, in 2023 on the first Saturday in November and in 2024 on the first Saturday of February, third Saturday of
June, and the first Saturdays of September and November.

Clerk:	REV. NORMAN A. SMITH MA BD		21 St Margarets Avenue, Loanhead EH20 9FH lothianandborders@churchofscotland.org.uk	07549 861770
Mission Officer:	REV. PETER J. WOOD MA BD		PWood@churchofscotland.org.uk	07776 119901

1   Aberlady and Gullane (F H W)
Vacant
Frederick Harrison CertCT   2013   2021   50 Dundas Gardens, Gorebridge EH23 4BB   01875 870777
     (Ordained Local Minister)   FHarrison@churchofscotland.org.uk   07703 527240
Interim Moderator: Jock Stein   jstein@handselpress.org.uk   01620 824896
                                                                 New charge formed by the union of Aberlady and Gullane

2   Ale and Teviot United (F H W)
Vacant   22 The Glebe, Ancrum, Jedburgh TD8 6UX   01835 830318
Interim Moderator: Derek G. Brown   kerednodrog@outlook.com   01361 810553

3   Ashkirk (W) linked with Ettrick and Yarrow (F W) linked with Selkirk (F H W)
                                                            office@selkirkparish.church   **01750 22078**
Vacant   1 Loanside, Selkirk TD7 4DJ   01750 23308
Session Clerk, Ashkirk: Fan Heafield   heafieldfan@gmail.com   01450 870425
Session Clerk, Ettrick and Yarrow: Nora Hunter   norabirks@btinternet.com   01750 52349
                                                                                           07776 343952
Session Clerk, Selkirk: Fiona Corbett   fiona.m.corbett@live.co.uk   01750 22687
                                                                                           07780 078085

4   Ayton (H) and District Churches (F)
Vacant   The Manse, Beanburn, Ayton, Eyemouth TD14 5QY   01890 781333
Interim Moderator: Susan Patterson   aspatterson1960@gmail.com   01289 386394
                                                                                           07976 902981

5   Belhaven (F H T W) linked with Spott (F W)
Vacant   secretarybelhavenchurch@outlook.com   07791 557350
Interim Moderator: Brian C. Hilsley   BHilsley@churchofscotland.org.uk

6 **Berwick-upon-Tweed: St Andrew's Wallace Green (H) and Lowick (F W)**
Adam J.J. Hood MA BD DPhil   1989   2012
3 Meadow Grange, Berwick-upon-Tweed TD15 1NW
AHood@churchofscotland.org.uk
01289 332787

7 **Bonnyrigg (F H W)**
Louise I. Purden BD   2020
officebonnyriggparishchurch@gmail.com
9 Viewbank View, Bonnyrigg EH19 2HU
LPurden@churchofscotland.org.uk
0131 654 0140
0131 258 6219

8 **Bowden (H) and Melrose (F H W)**
Rosemary Frew (Mrs) MA BD   1988   2017
bowden.melrosepc@btinternet.com
The Manse, Tweedmount Road, Melrose TD6 9ST
RFrew@churchofscotland.org.uk
01896 823339
01896 822217

9 **Caddonfoot (H W) linked with Stow: St Mary of Wedale and Heriot (W)**
Vacant
Session Clerk, Caddonfoot: Anne Grieve (Mrs)
Session Clerk, Stow and Heriot: Dianne Wilson (Mrs)
20 Wedale View, Stow, Galashiels TD1 2SJ
anneblakehope@hotmail.com
wilsond31@live.co.uk
01578 730237
07968 433547
01896 668381

10 **Carlops (W) linked with Kirkurd and Newlands (F H) linked with Upper Tweeddale (F H W) linked with West Linton: St Andrew's (F H W) (West Tweeddale Parishes)**
T.A. (Tony) Foley PhD   1992   2021
Old Joiners Croft, Skirling, Biggar ML12 6HD
TFoley@churchofscotland.org.uk
07793 294000

Upper Tweeddale formed by the union of Broughton, Glenholm and Kilbucho, Skirling, and Tweedsmuir

11 **Cavers and Kirkton (W) linked with Hawick: Trinity (H W)**
Vacant
Session Clerk, Cavers and Kirkton: Jane Cox (Mrs)
Session Clerk, Hawick: Trinity: Muriel S. Bowie (Mrs)
trinityhawick@outlook.com
Trinity Manse, Howdenburn, Hawick TD9 8PH
jane.cox2401@btinternet.com
murielbowie80@outlook.com
01450 378248
01450 379171
01450 372195
07790 689997

12 **Channelkirk and Lauder (F W)**
Lynn Brady BD DipMin   1996   2022
(Interim Minister)
The Manse, Brownsmuir Park, Lauder TD2 6QD
LBrady@churchofscotland.org.uk
01578 718996

13 **Cheviot Churches (H W)**
Colin D. Johnston MA BD   1986   2019
Cheviot Manse, Main Street, Morebattle, Kelso TD5 8QG
CDJohnston@churchofscotland.org.uk
01573 440539

14 Chirnside (F) linked with Hutton and Fishwick and Paxton
Michael A. Taylor DipTh MPhil   2006   2018
The New Manse, The Glebe, Chirnside, Duns TD11 3XE
MTaylor@churchofscotland.org.uk
01890 819947
07479 985075

15 Cockenzie and Port Seton: Chalmers Memorial (F H W)   1994   2018
contact@chalmerschurch.co.uk
Robin N. Allison BD DipMin
2 Links Road, Port Seton, Prestonpans EH32 0HA
RAllison@churchofscotland.org.uk
01875 812225

16 Cockenzie and Port Seton: Old (F H W)
Guardianship of the Presbytery
Session Clerk: Elizabeth W. Malcolm (Miss)
malcolm771@btinternet.com
01875 813659

17 Cockpen and Carrington (F H W) linked with Lasswade (H) and Rosewell (H W)
Lorna M. Souter MA BD MSc   2016
11 Pendreich Terrace, Bonnyrigg EH19 2DT
LSouter@churchofscotland.org.uk
0131 663 6392
07889 566418

18 Coldingham and St Abbs (F W) linked with Eyemouth (F W)
Andrew N. Haddow BEng BD   2012
The Manse, Victoria Road, Eyemouth TD14 5JD
AHaddow@churchofscotland.org.uk
01890 750327

19 Coldstream and District Parishes (H W) linked with Eccles and Leitholm
Vacant
Session Clerk, Coldstream: Richard Fawkes
Session Clerk, Eccles and Leitholm: Rob Cockburn
36 Bennecourt Drive, Coldstream TD12 4BY
richard@fawkes.me .uk
rob.cockburn@icloud.com
01890 883887

20 Dalkeith: St John's and Newton (F H W)
Keith L. Mack BD MTh DPS   2002
sjkpdalkeith@gmail.com
13 Weir Crescent, Dalkeith EH22 3JN
KMack@churchofscotland.org.uk
0131 660 5871
0131 454 0206

Andrew Don MBA   2006   2013
(Ordained Local Minister)
5 Eskvale Court, Penicuik EH26 8HT
ADon@churchofscotland.org.uk
01968 675766

New charge formed by the union of Dalkeith: St John's and King's Park and Newton

21 Dalkeith: St Nicholas Buccleuch (F H T W)
Alexander G. Horsburgh MA BD   1995   2004
1 Nungate Gardens, Haddington EH41 4EE
AHorsburgh@churchofscotland.org.uk
01620 824728

22 Dirleton (F H) linked with North Berwick: Abbey (F H W)
David J. Graham BSc BD PhD   1982   1998
abbeychurch@abbeychurch.co.uk
Sydserff, Old Abbey Road, North Berwick EH39 4BP
DGraham@churchofscotland.org.uk
01620 892800
01620 890800

No.	Charge / Minister	Ord.	Ind.	Address / Email	Telephone
23	**Dryburgh District Churches (F W)** Sheila W. Moir (Ms) MTheol	2008		**web4churches@gmail.com** 7 Strae Brigs, St Boswells, Melrose TD6 0DH SMoir@churchofscotland.org.uk	01835 822255
24	**Dunbar (H W)** Gordon Stevenson BSc BD	2010		The Manse, 10 Bayswell Road, Dunbar EH42 1AB revgstev@gmail.com	01368 865482
25	**Dunglass (W)** Suzanne G. Fletcher BA MDiv MA DMin	2001	2011	The Manse, Cockburnspath TD13 5XZ SFletcher@churchofscotland.org.uk	01368 830713 07973 960544
26	**Duns and District Parishes (F W)** Andrew J. Robertson BD	2008	2019	**admin@dunsanddistrict.org.uk** The Manse, Castle Street, Duns TD11 3DG ARobertson@churchofscotland.org.uk	**01361 884502** 01361 883496
27	**Earlston (F W)** Vacant Session Clerk: Robert Turnbull			rgtapoth@btinternet.com	01896 848515
28	**Eccles and Leitholm** See Coldstream				
29	**Eddleston (F H) linked with Peebles: Old (F H W) linked with Stobo and Drumelzier (F W)** Aftab Gohar MA MDiv PgDip	1996	2021	**admin@topcop.org.uk** 7 Clement Gunn Square, Peebles EH45 8LW AGohar@churchofscotland.org.uk	**01721 723986** 07528 143784
30	**Ettrick and Yarrow** See Ashkirk				
31	**Eyemouth** See Coldingham and St Abbs				
32	**Fogo (F W)** H. Dane Sherrard BD DMin (Non-Stipendiary)	1971	2019	Mount Pleasant Granary, Mount Pleasant Farm, Duns TD11 3HU dane@mountpleasantgranary.net	01361 882254 07582 468468
33	**Galashiels (H W)** Graeme M. Glover MA MBA MSc	2017	2022	**office@galashielschurchofscotland.org.uk** Woodlea, Abbotsview Drive, Galashiels TD1 3SL GGlover@churchofscotland.org.uk	**01896 752967** 01896 209455

34 Garvald and Morham (W) linked with Haddington: West (H W)

		hwcofs@hotmail.com	
John D. Vischer	1993	2011	15 West Road, Haddington EH41 3RD	01620 822213
			JVischer@churchofscotland.org.uk	

35 Gladsmuir linked with Longniddry (F H W)

Robin E. Hill LLB BD PhD	2004	The Manse, 8a Elcho Road, Longniddry EH32 0LB	01875 853195
		RHill@churchofscotland.org.uk	

36 Gordon: St Michael's (F)
Guardianship of the Presbytery
Session Clerk: Janice Cossigny (Mrs)   gordonkirktd3@gmail.com   01573 410518

37 Gorebridge (F H W)

		office@gorepc.com	**01875 820387**
Mark S. Nicholas MA BD	1999	100 Hunterfield Road, Gorebridge EH23 4TT	01875 820387
		MNicholas@churchofscotland.org.uk	07816 047493

38 Greenlaw (H)

Susan M. Brown (Mrs) BD DipMin DUniv	1985	2021	The Manse, Todholes, Greenlaw, Duns TD10 6XD	01361 810553
			Susan.Brown@churchofscotland.org.uk	07747 825755

39 Haddington: St Mary's (F H T W)

				01620 829354
Alison P. McDonald MA BD	1991	2019	1 Nungate Gardens, Haddington EH41 4EE	01620 823109
			Alison.McDonald@churchofscotland.org.uk	

40 Haddington: West See Garvald and Morham

41 Hawick: Burnfoot (F T W)

Vacant		29 Wilton Hill, Hawick TD9 8BA	01450 373181
Session Clerk: Marlynn Kerr (Miss)		marlynn.kerr231@btinternet.com	01450 375724

42 Hawick: St Mary's and Old (F H W) linked with Hawick: Teviot (H) and Roberton (F W)   info@smop-tero.org

Alistair W. Cook BSc CA BD	2008	2017	4 Heronhill Close, Hawick TD9 9RA	01450 378175
			ACook@churchofscotland.org.uk	07802 616352

43 Hawick: Teviot and Roberton See Hawick: St Mary's and Old
44 Hawick: Trinity See Cavers and Kirkton

45 Hawick: Wilton linked with Teviothead
Lisa-Jane Rankin BD CPS   2003
4 Wilton Hill Terrace, Hawick TD9 8BE
LRankin@churchofscotland.org.uk
01450 370744

46 Hobkirk and Southdean (F W) linked with Ruberslaw (F W)
Rachel Wilson BA MTh   2018
The Manse, Leydens Road, Denholm, Hawick TD9 8NB
RWilson@churchofscotland.org.uk
01450 870874

47 Humbie (F W) linked with Yester, Bolton and Saltoun (F W)
Anikó Schütz Bradwell BA MA BD   2015
The Manse, Tweeddale Avenue, Gifford, Haddington EH41 4QN
ASchuetzBradwell@churchofscotland.org.uk
01620 811193

48 Hutton and Fishwick and Paxton See Chirnside

49 Innerleithen (H), Traquair and Walkerburn (W)
Fraser Edwards BSc BA   2021
Pamela Kennedy BA PGCE MEd MSc BA   2022
(Pioneer Minister, Cardrona Village)
The Manse, 1 Millwell Park, Innerleithen, Peebles EH44 6JF
FEdwards@churchofscotland.org.uk
PKennedy@churchofscotland.org.uk
01896 490742
07812 994424

50 Jedburgh: Old and Trinity (F W)
Vacant
Session Clerk: Richard Gordon
The Manse, Honeyfield Drive, Jedburgh TD8 6LQ
r.j.gordon@talk21.com
01835 863417
01835 864365
07971 298541

51 Kelso Country Churches (W)
Vacant
Session Clerk: Jim Smith
Meadow View, Greenlaw, Duns TD10 6UW
jamessmith484@btinternet.com
01573 470250

52 Kelso: North (H) and Ednam (F H W)
Anna S. Rodwell BD DipMin   1998   2016
office@kelsonorthandednam.org.uk
The Manse, 20 Forestfield, Kelso TD5 7BX
ARodwell@churchofscotland.org.uk
01573 224154
01573 224248
07508 810237

53 Kelso: Old and Sprouston (F)
Vacant
Session Clerk: Frances Gordon
The Manse, Glebe Lane, Kelso TD5 7AU
francesgordon38@btinternet.com
01573 348749
07966 435484

54 Kirkurd and Newlands See Carlops

55   Lasswade and Rosewell See Cockpen and Carrington

56   Legerwood
Guardianship of the Presbytery
Interim Moderator: Susan M. Brown   Susan.Brown@churchofscotland.org.uk

01361 810553
07747 825755

57   Loanhead and Bilston (F T W)
Graham L. Duffin BSc BD DipEd   1989   2001   120 The Loan, Loanhead EH20 9AJ   0131 448 2459
                                                                 GDuffin@churchofscotland.org.uk
New charge formed by the union of Bilston and Loanhead

58   Longniddry See Gladsmuir

59   Lyne and Manor (W) linked with Peebles: St Andrew's Leckie (F H W)
                                                                 office@standrewsleckie.co.uk   **01721 723121**
Malcolm S. Jefferson   2012   Mansefield, Innerleithen Road, Peebles EH45 8BE   01721 725148
                                                                 MJefferson@churchofscotland.org.uk

60   Musselburgh: Northesk (F H W)
Hayley L. Cohen BA MDiv   2020   34 Battlefield Drive, Musselburgh EH21 7DF   0131 665 8688
                                                                 HCohen@churchofscotland.org.uk

61   Musselburgh: St Andrew's High (H W)   **0131 665 7239**
A. Leslie Milton MA BD PhD   1996   2019   8 Ferguson Drive, Musselburgh EH21 6XA   0131 665 1124
                                                                 AMilton@churchofscotland.org.uk

62   Musselburgh: St Clement's and St Ninian's
Guardianship of the Presbytery
Session Clerk: Ivor A. Highley   110 Inveresk Road, Musselburgh EH21 7AY   0131 665 5674

63   Musselburgh: St Michael's Inveresk (F W)
Malcolm M. Lyon BD   2007   2017   5 Crookston Ct., Crookston Rd., Inveresk, Musselburgh EH21 7TR   0131 653 2411
                                                                 MLyon@churchofscotland.org.uk

64   Newbattle (F H W)   **0131 663 3245**
Gayle J.A. Taylor MA BD PGDipCouns 1999 2019   Parish Office, Mayfield and Easthouses Church, Bogwood Court,
   (Transition Minister)   Easthouses EH22 5DG   0131 663 3245
                                                                 GTaylor@churchofscotland.org.uk

65 North Berwick: Abbey See Dirleton

66 North Berwick: St Andrew Blackadder (F H W) 1991
Neil J. Dougall BD DipMin DMin 2003
admin@standrewblackadder.org.uk
7 Marine Parade, North Berwick EH39 4LD
NDougall@churchofscotland.org.uk
01620 892132

67 Ormiston (W) linked with Pencaitland (F W) 1993
David J. Torrance BD DipMin 2009
The Manse, Pencaitland, Tranent EH34 5DL
DTorrance@churchofscotland.org.uk
01875 340963

68 Oxnam
Guardianship of the Presbytery
Session Clerk: Morag McKeand (Mrs)
mh.mckeand@gmail.com
01835 840284

69 Peebles: Old See Eddleston
70 Peebles: St Andrew's Leckie See Lyne and Manor
71 Pencaitland See Ormiston

72 Penicuik: North (F H W) 2007
Graham D. Astles BD MSc 2019
35 Esk Bridge, Penicuik EH26 8QR
GAstles@churchofscotland.org.uk
07906 290568

73 Penicuik: Trinity (F H W) 2010
John C.C. Urquhart MA MA BD 2017
10 Fletcher Grove, Penicuik EH26 0JT
JCUrquhart@churchofscotland.org.uk
01968 382116
07821 402901

74 Prestonpans: Prestongrange (F W) 1982
Kenneth W. Donald BA BD 2014
The Manse, East Loan, Prestonpans EH32 9ED
KDonald@churchofscotland.org.uk
01875 813643
07392 069957

75 Roslin (H)
Guardianship of the Presbytery
Session Clerk: Kathleen Taylor (Mrs)
kathtaylor1212@gmail.com

76 Ruberslaw See Hobkirk and Southdean
77 Selkirk See Ashkirk
78 Spott See Belhaven

79 **Stobo and Drumelzier** See Eddleston
80 **Stow: St Mary of Wedale and Heriot** See Caddonfoot
81 **Teviothead** See Hawick: Wilton

82 **Tranent (F W)**
Katherine A. Taylor LLB MDiv — 2021
1 Toll House Gardens, Tranent EH33 2QQ
KTaylor@churchofscotland.org.uk
01875 880011

83 **Traprain (W)**
Douglas Hamilton LLB MSc MDiv — 2022
5 The Glebe, East Linton EH40 3EF
dhamilton@churchofscotland.org.uk
07831 657854

Michael D. Watson CertCS — 2013 2019
(Ordained Local Minister)
2/1 Stanton Marches, Haddington EH41 3FB
MWatson@churchofscotland.org.uk
01620 614009

84 **Tyne Valley (F H W)**
Dale K. London BTh FSAScot — 2011 2018
Cranstoun Cottage, Ford, Pathhead EH37 5RE
DLondon@churchofscotland.org.uk
01875 321329

85 **Upper Tweeddale** See Carlops
86 **West Linton: St Andrew's** See Carlops
87 **Yester, Bolton and Saltoun** See Humbie

B. In other appointments: members of Presbytery

Berry, Geoff T. BSc BD — 2009 2011 — Army Chaplain
3 SCOTS, Fort George, Ardersier, Inverness IV2 7TE
revgeoffberry@gmail.com

Cobain, Alan R. BD — 2000 2017 — Army Chaplain
HQ SW, Building 56, Jellabad Barracks, Tidworth SP9 7BQ
Alan.Cobain100@mod.gov.uk

Kellock, Chris N. MA BD — 1998 2012 — Army Chaplain
Permanent Joint Headquarters, Sandy Lane, Northwood HA6 3HP
nicandchris@hotmail.co.uk

Linford, Victoria J. (Mrs) LLB BD — 2010 2023 — Presbytery Resource Adviser, Office of the General Assembly
121 George Street, Edinburgh EH2 4YN
VLinford@churchofscotland.org.uk
0131 225 5722

Magee, Rosemary E. BSc MDiv DMin — 2009 2023 — Healthcare Chaplain
Royal Infirmary of Edinburgh, 51 Little France Crescent, Edinburgh EH16 4SA
rosie.magee@nhslothian.scot.nhs.uk
0131 242 1997

Smith, Norman A. MA BD — 1997 2022 — Presbytery Clerk: Lothian and Borders
21 St Margarets Avenue, Loanhead EH20 9FH
NSmith@churchofscotland.org.uk
07549 861770

Wood, Peter J. MA BD — 1993 2023 — Presbytery Mission Officer, Lothian and Borders
49 Oxgangs Farm Drive, Edinburgh EH13 9PT
PWood@churchofscotland.org.uk
07776 119901

C. Retaining: members of Presbytery

Name	Ord.	Ind.	(Charge)	Address / Email	Telephone
Allison, Ann BSc PhD BD	2000	2017	(Crail with Kingsbarns)	99 Coalgate Avenue, Tranent EH33 1JW revam@sky.com	01875 571778 07857 525439
Arnott, A. David K. MA BD	1971	2010	(St Andrews: Hope Park with Strathkinness)	53 Whitehaugh Park, Peebles EH45 9DB adka53@btinternet.com	01721 725979 07759 709205
Atkins, Yvonne E.S. (Mrs) BD	1997	2018	(Musselburgh: St Andrew's High)	6 Robert de Quincy Place, Prestonpans EH32 9NS yveatkins@yahoo.com	01875 819858
Brown, Derek G. BD DipMin DMin	1989	2021	(Lead Chaplain: NHS Highland)	The Manse, Todholes, Greenlaw, Duns TD10 6XD kerednodrog@outlook.com	01361 810553
Burt, Thomas W. BD	1982	2013	(Carlops with Kirkurd and Newlands with West Linton: St Andrew's)	7 Arkwright Court, North Berwick EH39 4RT tomburt@westlinton.com	01620 895494
Campbell, Thomas R.	1986	1993	(Paisley: St James)	The White House, Nairns Mains, Haddington EH41 4HF tom@trcampbell.co.uk	07778 183830
Cartwright, Alan C.D. BSc BD	1976	2016	(Fogo and Swinton with Ladykirk and Whitsome with Leitholm)	Drumgray, Edrom, Duns TD11 3PX alan@cartwright-family.org.uk	01890 819191
Coltart, Ian O. CA BD	1988	2010	(Arbirlot with Carmyllie)	25 Bothwell Gardens, Dunbar EH42 1PZ	01368 860064
Dick, Andrew B. BD DipMin	1986	2015	(Musselburgh: St Michael's Inveresk)	4 Kirkhill Court, Gorebridge EH23 4TW dixbit@aol.com	07540 099480
Dobie, Rachel J.W. (Mrs) LTh	1991	2008	(Broughton, Glenholm and Kilbucho with Skirling with Stobo and Drumelzier with Tweedsmuir)	20 Moss Side Crescent, Biggar ML12 6GE revracheldobie@gmail.com	01899 229244
Dodd, Marion E. (Miss) MA BD LRAM	1988	2010	(Kelso: Old and Sprouston)	Esdaile, Tweedmount Road, Melrose TD6 9ST mariondodd@btinternet.com	01896 822446
Donaldson, David MA BD DMin	1969	2018	(Manish-Scarista)	13 Rose Park, Peebles EH45 8HP davidandjeandonaldson@gmail.com	07817 479866
Duncan, Maureen M. (Mrs) BD	1996	2018	(Lochend and New Abbey)	2 Chalybeate, Haddington EH41 4NX revmo43@gmail.com	01620 248559 07443 501738
Duncan, Rosslyn P. BD MTh	2007	2018	(Stonehaven: Dunnottar with Stonehaven: South)	Four Oaks, Broomdykes, Duns TD1 3LZ rosslynpduncan@gmail.com	07899 878427
Glover, Robert L. BMus BD MTh ARCO	1971	2010	(Cockenzie and Port Seton: Chalmers Memorial)	12 Seton Wynd, Port Seton, Prestonpans EH32 0TY rlglover@btinternet.com	01875 818759
Gordon, Thomas J. MA BD	1974	2009	(Chaplain, Marie Curie Hospice, Edinburgh)	22 Gosford Road, Port Seton, Prestonpans EH32 0HF tom.swallowsnest@gmail.com	01875 812262
Guy, Scott C. BD	1989	2020	(Aberdeen: Northfield)	41 Jenny Moore's Road, St Boswells TD6 0AN scguy55@gmail.com	07805 711148
Hilsley, Brian L. LLB BD	1990	2020	(Aberlady with Gullane)	15 Letham Place, Dunbar EH42 1AJ BHilsley@churchofscotland.org.uk	07791 557350
Hogg, Thomas M. BD	1986	2007	(Tranent)	22 Douglas Place, Galashiels TD1 3BT	01896 759381
Hope, Geraldine H. (Mrs) MA BD	1986	2007	(Foulden and Mordington with Hutton and Fishwick and Paxton)	4 Well Court, Chirnside, Duns TD11 3UD geraldine.hope@virgin.net	01890 818134
Johnston, June E. BSc MEd BD	2013	2023	(Ordained Local Minister, Bilston with Roslin)	21 Caberston Road, Walkerburn EH43 6AT June.Johnston@churchofscotland.org.uk	01896 870754 07754 448889

Name	Years	Charge / Role	Address	Telephone
Kellet, John M. MA	1962 1995	(Edinburgh: Leith South)	1 Dyers Close, Innerleithen EH44 6QF	01896 830201
Landale, William S.	2005 2016	(Auxiliary Minister, Chirnside with Hutton and Fishwick and Paxton)	Green Hope Guest House, Ellemford, Duns TD11 3SG WLandale@churchofscotland.org.uk	01361 890242
Levison, Chris L. MA BD	1972 2010	(Health Care Chaplaincy Training and Development Officer)	Gardenfield, Nine Mile Burn, Penicuik EH26 9LT chrislevison@hotmail.com	01968 674566
Macdougall, Malcolm M. BD MTh DipCE	1981 2019	(Eddleston with Peebles: Old)	2 Woodilee, Broughton, Biggar ML12 6GB calum.macdougall@btopenworld.com	01899 830615
McLarty, R. Russell MA BD DipArch	1985 2022	(Transition Minister, Edinburgh: Meadowbank)	9 Sanderson's Wynd, Tranent EH33 1DA RussellMcLarty@churchofscotland.org.uk	01875 614496 07751 755986
McNab, Douglas G. BA BD	1999 2021	(New Machar)	17 Wester Kippielaw Park, Dalkeith EH22 2GE dougie.mcnab@btinternet.com	0131 563 8034 0766 042033
Mitchell, John LTh CertMin	1991 2018	(Bonnyrigg)	28 Shiel Hall Crescent, Rosewell EH24 9DD JMitchell@churchofscotland.org.uk	0131 448 2676
Moore, W. Haisley MA	1966 1996	(Secretary: The Boys' Brigade)	37 Wilkie Gardens, White Rose Place, Galashiels TD1 2FF haisley37@outlook.com	01896 829809
Munson, Winnie (Ms) BD DipTh	1996 2006	(Delting with Northmavine)	6 St Cuthbert's Drive, St Boswells, Melrose TD6 0DF wabsmith@btinternet.com	01835 823375
Neill, Bruce F. MA BD	1966 2007	(Maxton and Mertoun with Newtown with St Boswells)	18 Brierydean, St Abbs, Eyemouth TD14 5PQ bneill@phonecoop.coop	01890 771569
Norman, Nancy M. (Miss) BA MDiv MTh	1988 2012	(Lyne and Manor)	25 March Street, Peebles EH45 8EP nancy.norman1@googlemail.com	01721 721699
Rennie, John D. MA	1962 1996	(Broughton, Glenholm and Kilbucho with Skirling with Stobo and Drumelzier with Tweedsmuir)	29/1 Rosetta Road, Peebles EH45 8HJ tworennies@btinternet.com	01721 720963
Riddell, John A. MA BD	1967 2006	(Jedburgh: Trinity)	Orchid Cottage, Gingham Row, Earlston TD4 6ET	01896 848784
Scott, Ian G. BSc BD STM	1965 2006	(Edinburgh: Greenbank)	50 Forthview Walk, Tranent EH33 1FE igscott50@btinternet.com	01875 612907
Shand, George C. MA BD	1981 2021	(Cairngryffe with Libberton and Quothquan with Symington)	15 Kittlegairy Place, Peebles EH45 9LW George.Shand@churchofscotland.org.uk	07765 987163
Shields, John M. MBE LTh	1972 2007	(Channelkirk and Lauder)	12 Eden Park, Ednam, Kelso TD5 7RG john.shields118@btinternet.com	01573 229015
Simpson, Robert R. BA BD	1994 2014	(Callander)	19 Cadwell Walk, Gorebridge EH23 4LF robert@pansmanse.co.uk	01875 823180
Sinclair, Colin A.M. BA BD	1981 2022	(Edinburgh: Palmerston Place)	18 Dukehaugh, Peebles EH45 9DN camsinclair90@gmail.com	07752 538954
Spence, Elisabeth G.B. BD DipEd	1995 2021	(Pioneer Minister, Hopefield Connections)	18 Castell Maynes Avenue, Bonnyrigg EH19 3RW revspence121@gmail.com	07772 548121
Steele, Leslie M. MA BD	1973 2013	(Galashiels: Old Parish and St Paul's)	23 Mayburn Avenue, Loanhead EH20 9EY lmslms@hotmail.co.uk	
Steele, Margaret D.J. (Miss) BSc BD	2000 2022	(Ashkirk with Ettrick and Yarrow with Selkirk)	33 Anderson Drive, Perth PH1 1JX MSteele@churchofscotland.org.uk	07801 365068
Steele, Marilynn J. (Mrs) BD DCS	1999 2012	(Deacon, Edinburgh: Granton)	2 Northfield Gardens, Prestonpans EH32 9LQ marilynnsteele@aol.com	01875 811497

Stein, Jock MA BD PhD	1973 2008	(Tulliallan and Kincardine)	35 Dunbar Road, Haddington EH41 3PJ jstein@handselpress.org.uk	01620 824896
Stein, Margaret E. (Mrs) DA BD DipRE	1984 2008	(Tulliallan and Kincardine)	35 Dunbar Road, Haddington EH41 3PJ margaretestein@hotmail.com	01620 824896
Strachan, Pamela D. (Lady)	2015 2021	(Ordained Local Minister, Broughton, Glenholm and Kilbucho with Carlops with Kirkurd and Newlands with Skirling with Tweedsmuir with West Linton: St Andrew's)	Glenhighton, Broughton, Biggar ML12 6JF PStrachan@churchofscotland.org.uk	01899 830423 07837 873688
Taverner, David J. MCIBS ACIS BD	1996 2023	(Coldstream and District Parishes with Eccles and Leitholm)	Woodcot, Waverley Road, Innerleithen, Peebleshire TD12 4BY DTaverner@churchofscotlans.org.uk	01896 829289
Thornthwaite, Anthony P. MTh	1995 2019	(Dundee: Coldside)	19 Dovecote Way, Haddington EH41 4HY tony.thornthwaite@sky.com	07706 761841
Walker, Kenneth D.F. MA BD PhD	1976 2008	(Athelstaneford with Whitekirk and Tyninghame)	Allanbank Kothi, Allanton, Duns TD11 3PY walkerkenneth49@gmail.com	01890 817102
Walker, Veronica (Mrs) BSc BD		(Licentiate)	Allanbank Kothi, Allanton, Duns TD11 3PY walkerkenneth49@gmail.com	01890 817102
Wallace, James H. MA BD	1973 2011	(Peebles: St Andrew's Leckie)	52 Waverley Mills, Innerleithen EH44 6RH jimwallace121@btinternet.com	01896 831637
Watson, James B. BSc	1969 2009	(Coldstream with Eccles)	20 Randolph Crescent, Dunbar EH42 1GL jimwatson007@hotmail.com	01368 865045 07419 759451

D. In other appointments: not members of Presbytery

Scouler, Michael D. MBE BSc BD	1988 2018	Head of Spiritual Care, NHS Borders	Chaplaincy Centre, Borders General Hospital, Melrose TD6 9BS michael.scouler@borders.scot.nhs.uk	01896 826565

E. Retaining: not members of Presbytery

Black, James S.	1976 1978	(Associate, Paisley: St Ninian's Ferguslie)	7 Breck Terrace, Penicuik EH26 0RJ jsb.black@btopenworld.com	01968 677559
Cairns, John B. KCVO LTh LLB LLD DD	1974 2009	(Aberlady with Gullane)	Bell House, Roxburghe Park, Dunbar EH42 1LR johncairns@mail.com	01368 862501
Haslett, Howard J. BA BD	1972 2010	(Traprain)	26 The Maltings, Haddington EH41 4EF howard.haslett@btinternet.com	01620 481208
Macaulay, Glendon D. BD ALCM	1999 2012	(Falkirk: Erskine) '	43 Gavin's Lee, Tranent EH33 2AP gd.macaulay@btinternet.com	01875 615851
McHaffie, Robin D. BD	1979 2016	(Cheviot Churches)	Shepherd's Cottage, Castle Heaton, Cornhill-on-Tweed TD12 4XQ robinmchaffie@btinternet.com	01890 885946
McKay, Johnston R. MA BA PhD	1969 2002	(Editor, BBC Scotland, Religious Programmes)	40 Sinton Park, Dunbar EH42 1ZP johnston.mckay@btinternet.com	07938 438391

Milloy, A. Miller DipPE LTh DipTrMan LHD	1979	2011	(General Secretary: United Bible Societies)	18 Kittlegairy Crescent, Peebles EH45 9NJ ammilloy@aol.com	01721 723380
Paterson, William BD	1977	2001	(Bonkyl and Preston with Chirnside with Edrom Allanton)	Benachie, Gavinton, Duns TD11 3QT billdm.paterson@btinternet.com	01361 882727
Stewart, Una B. (Ms) BD DipEd	1995	2014	(Law)	10 Inch Park, Kelso TD5 7BQ rev.ubs@virgin.net	01573 219231
Turnbull, Julian S. BSc BD MSc CEng MBCS	1980	1986	(Dumfries: Lochside with Terregles)	39 Suthren Yett, Prestonpans EH32 9GL jules@turnbull25.plus.com	01875 818305
Young, Alexander W. BD ThM DipMin	1988	2017	(Kelso: Old and Sprouston)	9 Towerburn, Denholm, Hawick TD9 8TB sandy.young45@yahoo.com	07489 241344

F. Inactive: not members of Presbytery

Auld, A. Graeme (Prof.) MA BD PhD DLitt FSAScot FRSE	1973	2008	(Principal, New College, University of Edinburgh)	Nether Swanshiel, Hobkirk, Bonchester Bridge, Hawick TD9 8JU a.g.auld@ed.ac.uk	01450 860636
Brown, Ronald H.	1974	1998	(Musselburgh: Northesk)	6 Monktonhall Farm Cottages, Musselburgh EH21 6RZ	0131 653 2531
Buchanan, Marion (Mrs) MA DCS	1983	2019	(Deacon, Glasgow: Garthamlock and Craigend East; Glasgow: Ruchazie)	40 Links View, Port Seton, Prestonpans EH32 0EZ	01875 814632
Cowie, James M. BD CCE	1977	2016	(Paris: The Scots Kirk)	24 Cowdrait, Burnmouth, Eyemouth TD14 5SW jimcowie@europe.com	01890 781394
Dick, J. Ronald BD	1973	2012	(Spiritual Care Manager, NHS Borders)	1 Viewfield Terrace, Leet Street, Coldstream TD12 4BL ron.dick180@yahoo.co.uk	01890 882206
Dutton, David W. BA MTh MPhil	1973	2008	(Stranraer: High Kirk)	13 Acredales, Haddington, East Lothian, EH41 4NT duttondw@gmail.com	01620 825999
Finlay, Quintin BA BD	1975	1996	(North Bute)	Ivy Cottage, Greenlees Farm, Kelso TD5 8BT	07901 981171
Fraser, John W. MA BD	1974	2011	(Penicuik: North)	66 Camus Avenue, Edinburgh EH10 6QX jjjjj2005@hotmail.co.uk	07469 704091
Jones, Anne M. (Mrs) BD	1998	2011	(Hospital Chaplain, NHS Lothian)	7 North Elphinstone Farm, Tranent EH33 2ND revamjones@aol.com	01875 614442
Kenny, Celia G. BA MTh MPhil LLM PhD	1994	2004	(Bonkyl and Preston with Chirnside with Edrom Allanton)	37 Grosvenor Road, Dublin, Ireland cgkenny@tcd.ie	
Kingston, David V.F. BD DipPTh	1993	2015	(Chaplain: Army)	2 Cleuch Avenue, North Middleton, Gorebridge EH23 4RP	01875 822026
Lawrie, Bruce B. BD DPSS	1974	2012	(Duffus, Spynie and Hopeman)	5 Thorncroft House, Scotts Place, Selkirk TD7 4LN thorncroft54@gmail.com	01750 725427
Ledgard, J. Christopher BA CertTh	1969	1998	(Upper Donside)	Streonshalh, 8 David Hume View, Chirnside, Duns TD11 3SX	01890 817124
Lyall, David BSc BD STM PhD	1965	2002	(Lecturer and Principal, New College, University of Edinburgh)	Flat 2, 9 Bayswell Road, Dunbar EH42 1AB lyall13@gmail.com	01368 864079
Macdonald, Finlay A.J. MA BD PhD DD	1971	2010	(Principal Clerk)	8 St Ronan's Way, Innerleithen EH44 6RG finlaymacdonald5@gmail.com	01896 831631
Spowart, Mary G. (Mrs) BD	1978	1991	(Papa Westray with Westray)	Aldersyde, St Abbs Road, Coldingham, Eyemouth TD14 5NR	01890 771697
Steven, Gordon R. BD DCS	2000	2012	(Deacon, Newbattle)	51 Nantwich Drive, Edinburgh EH7 6RB grsteven@btinternet.com	0131 669 2054 / 07904 385256

| Torrance, David W. MA BD | 1955 1991 | (Earlston) | 38 Forth Street, North Berwick EH39 4JQ
torrance103@btinternet.com | 01620 895109 |

G. Readers (active)

Findlay, Elizabeth (Mrs)	7e Rose Lane, Kelso TD5 7AP	findlay290@gmail.com	01573 226641
Hogg, David MA	82 Eskhill, Penicuik EH26 8DQ	hogg-d2@sky.com	01968 676350 07821 693946
Johnston, Alan C.	36 Foster Road, Penicuik EH26 0FL	alanacj2@gmail.com	01968 664860 07901 501819
Knox, Dagmar (Mrs)	3 Stichill Road, Ednam, Kelso TD5 7QQ	dagmar.knox.riding@btinternet.com	01573 224883
Landale, Alison (Mrs)	Green Hope Guest House, Ellemford, Duns TD11 3SG	alison@greenhope.co.uk	01361 890242
Millan, Mary (Mrs)	33 Polton Vale, Loanhead EH20 9DF	marymillan@gmail.com	0131 440 1624 07814 466104
Selkirk, Frances (Mrs)	21 Park Crescent, Newtown St Boswells, Melrose TD6 0QR	f.selkirk@hillview2selkirk.plus.com	01835 823669
Waugh, Jacqueline (Mrs)	15 Garleton Drive, Haddington EH41 3BL	jacqueline.waugh@yahoo.com	01620 825007 0131 653 2291
Yeoman, Edward T.N. FSAScot	75 Newhailes Crescent, Musselburgh EH21 6EF	edwardyeoman6@aol.com	07896 517666

H. Ministries Development Staff

Name	Role	Email
Billes, Shirley	Tranent – Youth and Families Worker	SBilles@churchofscotland.org.uk
MacDonald, Catriona MTh	Newbattle – Congregational Support Worker	Catriona.MacDonald @churchofscotland.org.uk
McKenzie, Susan	Newton – Mission and Discipleship Outreach Worker	SMcKenzie@churchofscotland.org.uk
Pryde, Erika	Newton – Mission and Outreach Co-ordinator	EPryde@churchofscotland.org

HAWICK ADDRESSES

Burnfoot	Fraser Avenue
St Mary's and Old	Kirk Wynd
Teviot	St George's Lane
Trinity	Central Square
Wilton	Princes Street

(3) SOUTH WEST (W)

Meets at 10.30am on the second Saturday in June and September and the first Tuesday in March and December.

Clerk: MRS CHRISTINE M. MURRAY LLB   southwestscotland@churchofscotland.org.uk   07526 892228
Presbytery Office: 50 Main Street, Prestwick KA9 1NX   01292 678556
SCaldwell@churchofscotland.org.uk

1   Alloway (F H W)   secretary.allowaypc@gmail.com   **01292 442083**
Neil A. McNaught BD MA   1987   1999   1A Parkview, Alloway, Ayr KA7 4QG   01292 441252
NMcNaught@churchofscotland.org.uk

David Hume MSc PhD CertHE   2020   8 Finlaggan Place, Kilmarnock KA3 1UY   07858 966367
(Ordained Local Minister)   DHume@churchofscotland.org.uk

2   Annan: Old (F H W) linked with Dornock (F)
David Whiteman BD   1998   2018   12 Plumdon Park Avenue, Annan DG12 6EY   01461 392048
DWhiteman@churchofscotland.org.uk

3   Annan: St Andrew's (H W) linked with Brydekirk (W)
John G. Pickles BD MTh MSc   2011   1 Annerley Road, Annan DG12 6HE   01461 202626
JPickles@churchofscotland.org.uk

4   Annbank (H W) linked with Tarbolton (F W)
Mandy R. H. Ralph RGN CertCS BTh   2013   2019   The Manse, Tarbolton, Mauchline KA5 5QJ   01292 541452
MRalph@churchofscotland.org.uk

5   Applegarth, Sibbaldbie (H) and Johnstone (F) linked with Lochmaben (H W)
Vacant   The Manse, Barrashead, Lochmaben, Lockerbie DG11 1QF   01387 810640
Interim Moderator: David Whiteman   DWhiteman@churchofscotland.org.uk   01461 392048
Session Clerk, Lochmaben: Winifred B. Dickie (Mrs)   michael.dickie44@btinternet.com   01387 810713

6   Ardrossan: Park (W)
Vacant   35 Ardneil Court, Ardrossan KA22 7NQ   **01294 463711**
Interim Moderator: Alan H. Ward   alanhward@hotmail.co.uk   01294 822244

7   Ardrossan and Saltcoats: Kirkgate (F H W)   **01294 472001**
T. Nigel Chikanya BTh BA MTh   2014   2020   10 Seafield Drive, Ardrossan KA22 8NU   07566 278132
NChikanya@churchofscotland.org.uk

8 **Arnsheen Barrhill and Colmonell: St Colmon (W) linked with Ballantrae (H W)** 2006 2019
Theodore L. Corney BA MTh GDipTh
The Manse, 1 The Vennel, Ballantrae, Girvan KA26 0NH
TCorney@churchofscotland.org.uk
01465 831252

9 **Auchinleck (F H) linked with Catrine (F)**
Stephen F. Clipston MA BD 1982 2006
28 Mauchline Road, Auchinleck KA18 2BN
SClipston@churchofscotland.org.uk
01290 424776

10 **Ayr: Auld Kirk of Ayr (St John the Baptist) (H L W)** 1991 1999
David R. Gemmell MA BD
auldkirkayr@hotmail.co.uk
20 Seafield Drive, Ayr KA7 4BQ
DGemmell@churchofscotland.org.uk
01292 262938
01292 864140

11 **Ayr: Castlehill (F H W)** 1984 2019
Paul R. Russell MA BD
castlehillchurch44@gmail.com
3 Old Hillfoot Road, Ayr KA7 3LW
PRussell@churchofscotland.org.uk
01292 267520
01292 261464

12 **Ayr: Newton Wallacetown (F H W)**
Vacant
Interim Moderator: Rona M. Young
9 Nursery Grove, Ayr KA7 3PH
revronyoung@hotmail.com
01292 611371
01292 264251
01292 471982

13 **Ayr: St Andrew's (F H W)** 2012 2020
Stanley Okeke BA BD MSc
ayrstandrews@gmail.com
17 Whiteford View, Ayr KA7 3LL
SOkeke@churchofscotland.org.uk
01292 268164

14 **Ayr: St Columba (F H W)** 1994 2019
Scott S. McKenna BA BD MTh MPhil PhD
irene@ayrstcolumba.co.uk
3 Upper Crofts, Alloway, Ayr KA7 4QX
SMcKenna@churchofscotland.org.uk
01292 265794
01292 226075

15 **Ayr: St James' (F H W)**
Barbara V. Suchanek-Seitz CertMin DTh 2016
admin@stjamesayr.plus.com
1 Prestwick Road, Ayr KA8 8LD
BSuchanek-Seitz@churchofscotland.org.uk
01292 266993
01292 262420

16 **Ayr: St Leonard's (F H W) linked with Dalrymple (F)** 1992 2015
Brian R. Hendrie BD CertMin
st_leonards@btinternet.com
35 Roman Road, Ayr KA7 3SZ
BHendrie@churchofscotland.org.uk
01292 611117
01292 283825

17 Ayr: St Quivox (F H W)
John McCutcheon BA BD(Min) 2014 2019 11 Springfield Avenue, Prestwick KA9 2HA
JMcCutcheon@churchofscotland.org.uk
01292 861641

18 Ayrshire Mission to the Deaf, Kilmarnock
Vacant

19 Ballantrae See Arnsheen Barrhill and Colmonell: St Colmon

20 Balmaclellan, Kells (H) and Dalry (H) linked with Carsphairn (H)
Vacant The Manse, Dalry, Castle Douglas DG7 3PJ 01644 430380
Pamela A. Bellis BA DipTheol 2004 2022 12 Woodlands Avenue, Kirkcudbright DG6 4BP 07751 379249
(Ordained Local Minister) PBellis@churchofscotland.org.uk
Interim Moderator: Mark R.S. Smith Mark.Smith@churchofscotland.org.uk 01387 820475

21 Barr (F) linked with Dailly (F W) linked with Girvan: South (F)
Vacant 30 Henrietta Street, Girvan KA26 9AL 01465 713370
Interim Moderator: Theodore L. Corney TCorney@churchofscotland.org.uk 01465 831252

22 Beith (F H W)
Vacant **beithchurch@btinternet.com** **01505 502686**
Fiona Blair DCS 1994 2015 2 Glebe Court, Beith KA15 1ET 01505 503858
9 Powgree Crescent, Beith KA15 1ES 07368 696550
FBlair@churchofscotland.org.uk
Interim Moderator: Jean C.Q. Hunter (Mrs) j.hunter744@btinternet.com 01770 810218

23 Bengairn Parishes (W) linked with Castle Douglas (H W)
Alison H. Burnside (Mrs) MA BD 1990 2018 1 Castle View, Castle Douglas DG7 1BG 01556 505983
ABurnside@churchofscotland.org.uk

24 Border Kirk (F W)
Wesley C. Brandon BA MDiv 2003 2022 **Chapel Street, Carlisle CA1 1JA** **01228 591757**
95 Pinecroft, Carlisle CA3 0DB 01228 599572
WBrandon@churchofscotland.org.uk

25 Brodick (W) linked with Corrie linked with Lochranza and Pirnmill (W) linked with Shiskine (F H W)
Vacant **brodickchurch@gmail.com;**
info@lochranzachurch.org.uk; stmolios@gmail.com
Session Clerk, Brodick: Shona Hume (Mrs) 4 Manse Crescent, Brodick, Isle of Arran KA27 8AS
shonah14@yahoo.co.uk
Session Clerk, Corrie: Anne Pringle (Mrs) anne.m.pringle@btinternet.com 01770 830304
Session Clerk, Lochranza and Pirnmill: Bill Scott bill.ornsay@btinternet.com 01770 860498
Session Clerk, Shiskine: John Kerr jmkhmk@gmail.com

26   Brydekirk See Annan: St Andrew's

27   Caerlaverock (F) linked with Dumfries: St Mary's-Greyfriars' (F H W)
Vacant
Session Clerk, Caerlaverock: Sheila Wilson   4 Georgetown Crescent, Dumfries DG1 4EQ
   wilson.glencaple@btopenworld.com   01387 270128
Interim Moderator: Fiona A. Wilson
   FWilson@churchofscotland.org.uk   01387 770327
                                       01556 610708

28   Caldwell (F W) linked with Dunlop (F W)
Alison J.S. McBrier MA BD   2011   2017   4 Dampark, Dunlop, Kilmarnock KA3 4BZ
   AMcBrier@churchofscotland.org.uk   01560 673686

29   Canonbie United (F H W) linked with Liddesdale (F H W)
Morag Crossan BA   2016   2020
   churchoffice@liddesdalechurch.org.uk   Liddesdale: **01387 375488**
   23 Langholm Street, Newcastleton TD9 0QX   01387 375603
   MCrossan@churchofscotland.org.uk   07861 736071
Canonbie United is a Local Ecumenical Partnership with the United Free Church

30   Carsphairn See Balmaclellan, Kells and Dalry
31   Castle Douglas See Bengairn Parishes
32   Catrine See Auchinleck

33   Closeburn linked with Kirkmahoe
Vacant
Session Clerk, Closeburn: Jack Tait   The Manse, Kirkmahoe, Dumfries DG1 1ST
   jacktait1941@gmail.com   01387 710572
                              01848 331700
Session Clerk, Kirkmahoe: Bob McBride
   rjmcbride91@hotmail.com   07717 247092

34   Colvend, Southwick and Kirkbean (W)
John A.H. Murdoch BA BD DPSS   1979   2022   The Manse, Colvend, Dalbeattie DG5 4QN
   JMurdoch@churchofscotland.org.uk   01556 630255
                                        07578 558978

35   Corrie See Brodick

36   Corsock and Kirkpatrick Durham (W) linked with Crossmichael, Parton and Balmaghie (W)
Vacant
Session Clerk, Corsock and Kirkpatrick Durham: Knockdrocket, Clarebrand, Castle Douglas DG7 3AH
   Mary Burney   maryburney1@btinternet.com   01556 503645
                                                  01556 650503
Session Clerk, Crossmichael, Parton and Balmaghie:
   Anne Carstairs   annegcarstairs@gmail.com   01556 670279

37 Coylton (F W) linked with Drongan: The Schaw Kirk (W)
Alwyn Landman BTh MDiv MTh DMin 2005 2019
4 Hamilton Place, Coylton, Ayr KA6 6JQ
ALandman@churchofscotland.org.uk — 01292 571287

38 Craigie Symington (W) linked with Prestwick South (H W)
Kenneth C. Elliott BD BA Cert Min 1989
office.pwksouth@gmail.com — **01292 678556**
68 St Quivox Road, Prestwick KA9 1JF — 01292 478788
KElliott@churchofscotland.org.uk

Tom McLeod 2014 2015
3 Martnaham Drive, Coylton KA6 6JE — 01292 570100
TMcleod@churchofscotland.org.uk
(Ordained Local Minister)

39 Crosshill (H) linked with Maybole (F W)
Vacant
74A Culzean Road, Maybole KA19 8AH — 01655 889454
Interim Moderator: Paul R. Russell
PRussell@churchofscotland.org.uk — 01292 261464

40 Crosshouse (F H W)
Vacant
Interim Moderator: John A. Urquhart
John.Urquhart@churchofscotland.org.uk — 01563 538289

41 Crossmichael, Parton and Balmaghie See Corsock and Kirkpatrick Durham

42 Cumbrae (F W) linked with Largs: St John's (F H W)
Vacant
Session Clerk, Cumbrae: Eleanor Browne (Mrs)
Cumbrae: **01475 531198** St John's: **01475 674468**
1 Newhaven Grove, Largs KA30 8NS — 01475 329933
langeron@btinternet.com
Session Clerk, Largs: St John's: Jim Welsh
jimwelsh@ssky.com

43 Cummertrees, Mouswald and Ruthwell (H W)
Vacant
The Manse, Ruthwell, Dumfries DG1 4NP — 01387 870217
Interim Moderator: Gary J. Peacock
GPeacock@churchofscotland.org.uk — 01387 730759

44 Dailly See Barr

45 Dalbeattie and Kirkgunzeon (F H W) linked with Urr (H W)
Fiona A. Wilson (Mrs) BD 2008 2014
36 Mill Street, Dalbeattie DG5 4HE — 01556 610708
FWilson@churchofscotland.org.uk

46 Dalmellington (F) linked with Patna Waterside (F)
Vacant
4 Carsphairn Road, Dalmellington, Ayr KA6 7RE — 01292 551503
Interim Moderator: Allan S. Vint
AVint@churchofscotland.org.uk — 01290 518528

47 Dalry: St Margaret's (F W)
David A. Albon BA MCS
1991 2019
stmargaret@talktalk.net
33 Templand Crescent, Dalry KA24 5EZ
DAlbon@churchofscotland.org.uk
01294 **832264**
01294 832747

48 Dalry: Trinity (F H W)
Martin Thomson BSc DipEd BD
1988 2004
Trinity Manse, 3 West Kilbride Road, Dalry KA24 5DX
MThomson@churchofscotland.org.uk
01294 832363

49 Dalrymple See Ayr: St Leonard's

50 Dalton and Hightae (F) linked with St Mungo (F)
Vacant
Interim Moderator: Andrew Morton (Mr)
The Manse, Hightae, Lockerbie DG11 1JL
andrew.morton@mac.com
01387 811499
01576 203164

51 Darvel (F W)
Vacant
Session Clerk: John Grier
Interim Moderator: Margaret A. Hamilton (Mrs)
46 West Main Street, Darvel KA17 0AQ
johngrier46@btinternet.com
mahamilton1@outlook.com
01560 **322924**
01560 322924
01560 321355
01563 534431

52 Dornock See Annan: Old

53 Dreghorn and Springside (F T W)
Jamie W. Milliken BD PGCertADS
2005 2020
7 Sycamore Wynd, Perceton, Irvine KA11 2FA
JMilliken@churchofscotland.org.uk
01294 211893

54 Drongan: The Schaw Kirk See Coylton

55 Dumfries: Maxwelltown West (H W)
Johannes Wildner MTh
2006 2021
Maxwelltown West Manse, 11 Laurieknowe, Dumfries DG2 7AH
JWildner@churchofscotland.org.uk
01387 **255900**
01387 257238

56 Dumfries: Northwest (F T)
Vacant
Session Clerk: Clara Jackson
c/o Church Office, Dumfries Northwest Church, Lochside Road, Dumfries DG2 0DZ
sessionclerk.dumfriesnorthwest@gmail.com
01387 249964
01387 249964

57	**Dumfries: St George's (F H W)**		
	Donald Campbell BD	1997	office@saint-georges.org.uk 9 Nunholm Park, Dumfries DG1 1JP DCampbell@churchofscotland.org.uk	**01387 267072** 01387 252965
58	**Dumfries: St Mary's-Greyfriars'** See Caerlaverock		
59	**Dumfries: St Michael's and South (W)**		
	Vacant		39 Cardoness Street, Dumfries DG1 3AL	01387 253849
	Session Clerk: Esther Preston		prestoncraigavon@supanet.com	01387 263402
60	**Dumfries: Troqueer (F H W)**		
	Vacant		secretary@troqueerparishchurch.com Troqueer Manse, Troqueer Road, Dumfries DG2 7DF	01387 253043
61	**Dundonald (H W)**		
	Lynsey J. Brennan BSc MSc BA	2019	64 Main Street, Dundonald, Kilmarnock KA2 9HG LBrennan@churchofscotland.org.uk	01563 850243
62	**Dunlop** See Caldwell		
63	**Dunscore (F W) linked with Glencairn and Moniaive (F W)**	1990 2020	
	Mark R.S. Smith BSc CertMin		The Manse, Wallaceton, Auldgirth, Dumfries DG2 0TJ Mark.Smith@churchofscotland.org.uk	01387 820475
64	**Durisdeer linked with Penpont, Keir and Tynron linked with Thornhill (H)**		
	Vacant		The Manse, Manse Park, Thornhill DG3 5ER	01848 331191
	Interim Moderator: David Gibson (Mr)		gibson186@btinternet.com	01387 250318
65	**Ervie Kirkcolm (H W) linked with Leswalt (W)**		
	Guardianship of the Presbytery		randglynn@btinternet.com	01776 860665
	Interim Moderator: Gillian Lynn (Mrs)			
66	**Fairlie (F H W) linked with Largs: St Columba's (F W)**	2005 2019	
	Graham McWilliams BSc BD DMin		secretary@largscolumba.org 14 Fairlieburne Gardens, Fairlie, Largs KA29 0ER GMcWilliams@churchofscotland.org.uk	**01475 686212** 01475 568515
67	**Fenwick (F H W)**		
	Vacant		KWatt@churchofscotland.org.uk	07881 680982
	Interim Moderator: Kim Watt			

68 Fisherton (H) linked with Kirkoswald (H W)
Vacant
Interim Moderator: Jeanette Whitecross
The Manse, Kirkoswald, Maybole KA19 8HZ
jeanettewx@yahoo.com
01655 760532
07803 181150

69 Galston (F H W)
Kristina I. Hine BS MDiv   2011   2016
19 Manse Gardens, Galston KA4 8DJ
KHine@churchofscotland.org.uk
01563 820136
01563 257172

70 Gatehouse and Borgue linked with Tarff and Twynholm
Valerie J. Ott (Mrs) BA BD DipARSM   2002
The Manse, Planetree Park, Gatehouse of Fleet, Castle Douglas DG7 2EQ
VOtt@churchofscotland.org.uk
01557 814233

71 Girvan: North (F H W)
Vacant
Interim Moderator: James Anderson (Dr)
churchoffice12@btconnect.com
38 The Avenue, Girvan KA26 9DS
jc.anderson2@talktalk.net
01465 712672
01465 713203
01465 710059

72 Girvan: South See Barr

73 Glasserton and Isle of Whithorn linked with Whithorn: St Ninian's Priory (F W)
Alexander I. Currie BD CPS   1990
The Manse, St Ninian's Grove, Whithorn, Newton Stewart DG8 8PT
ACurrie@churchofscotland.org.uk
01988 500267

74 Glencairn and Moniaive See Dunscore

75 Gretna: Old (H), Gretna: St Andrew's (H), Half Morton and Kirkpatrick Fleming (F)
Vacant

76 Hoddom, Kirtle-Eaglesfield and Middlebie (F W)
Vacant
Interim Moderator: John Bicket
The Manse, Main Road, Ecclefechan, Lockerbie DG11 3BU
johnbicket46@gmail.com
01576 300108
07517 169847

77 Hurlford (F H W)
Vacant
Session Clerk: Elizabeth F.G. Lauchlan
Interim Moderator: Colin G.F. Brockie
12 Main Road, Crookedholm, Kilmarnock KA3 6JT
elizabeth.lauchlan@btinternet.com
revcolin@uwclub.net
01563 539739
01563 537381
01563 559960

78 Inch linked with Luce Valley (F W)
Stephen Ogston MPhys MSc BD   2009   2017   Ladyburn Manse, Main Street, Glenluce, Newton Stewart   DG8 0PU   01581 300316
SOgston@churchofscotland.org.uk

79 Irongray, Lochrutton and Terregles
Gary J. Peacock MA BD MTh   2015   The Manse, Shawhead, Dumfries   DG2 9SJ   01387 730759
GPeacock@churchofscotland.org.uk

80 Irvine: Fullarton (F H T W)
Neil Urquhart BD DipMin DipSC   1989   secretary@fullartonchurch.co.uk   01294 273741
48 Waterside, Irvine KA12 8QJ   01294 279909
NUrquhart@churchofscotland.org.uk

81 Irvine: Girdle Toll (F H) linked with Irvine: St Andrew's (F H)
Vacant   WHHewitt@churchofscotland.org.uk   01294 276051
Interim Moderator: William C. Hewitt   01563 533312

82 Irvine: Mure Relief (F H)
Vacant   9 West Road, Irvine KA12 8RE   01294 279916
Interim Moderator: Jamie W. Milliken   JMilliken@churchofscotland.org.uk   01294 211893

83 Irvine: Old (F H)
Vacant   22 Kirk Vennel, Irvine KA12 0DQ   01294 273503
Interim Moderator: Alexander C. Wark   alecwark@yahoo.co.uk   01294 279265
01563 559581

84 Irvine: St Andrew's See Irvine: Girdle Toll

85 Kilbirnie: Auld Kirk (F H W)
Vacant   49 Holmhead, Kilbirnie KA25 6BS   01505 682342
Session Clerk: Archie Currie   archiecurrie@yahoo.co.uk   01505 681474

86 Kilbirnie: St Columba's (F H)
Fiona C. Ross (Miss) BD DipMin   1996   2004   Manse of St Columba's, Dipple Road, Kilbirnie KA25 7JU   01505 683342
FRoss@churchofscotland.org.uk

87 Kilmarnock: Kay Park (F H W)
Fiona E. Maxwell BA BD   2004   2018   chrchdmnstr@outlook.com   01563 574106
1 Glebe Court, Kilmarnock KA1 3BD   01563 521762
FMaxwell@churchofscotland.org.uk

88 Kilmarnock: New Laigh Kirk (F H W)
David S. Cameron BD — 2001
newlaighkirkchurch@hotmail.com
1 Holmes Farm Road, Kilmarnock KA1 1TP
David.Cameron@churchofscotland.org.uk
01563 573307
01563 525416

89 Kilmarnock: St John's Onthank (F H W)
Vacant
Interim Moderator: Fiona E. Maxwell
84 Wardneuk Drive, Kilmarnock KA3 2EX
FMaxwell@churchofscotland.org.uk
07716 162380
01563 521762

90 Kilmarnock: St Kentigern's (F W)
Vacant
Interim Moderator: George K. Lind
hub@stkentigern.org.uk
gklind@talktalk.net
01560 428732

91 Kilmarnock: St Marnock's (F W)
James McNaughtan BD DipMin — 1983 1989
35 South Gargieston Drive, Kilmarnock KA1 1TB
JMcNaughtan@churchofscotland.org.uk
01563 521665

92 Kilmaurs: St Maur's Glencairn (F H)
John A. Urquhart BD — 1993
9 Standalane, Kilmaurs, Kilmarnock KA3 2NB
John.Urquhart@churchofscotland.org.uk
01563 538289

93 Kilmory (F W) linked with Lamlash (W)
Vacant
Session Clerk, Kilmory: Mairi Duff (Mrs)
Session Clerk, Lamlash: Lilias Nicholls (Mrs)
The Manse, Margnaheglish Road, Lamlash, Isle of Arran KA27 8LL
mairid67@gmail.com
lnicholls21@hotmail.com
01770 600074

94 Kilwinning: Abbey (F W)
Vacant
Isobel Beck BD DCS — 2014 2016
Interim Moderator: James J. McNay
54 Dalry Road, Kilwinning KA13 7HE
16 Patrick Avenue, Stevenston KA20 4AW
IBeck@churchofscotland.org.uk
JMcNay@churchofscotland.org.uk
01294 552606
01294 552606
07919 193425
01294 823186

95 Kilwinning: Mansefield Trinity (F W)
Hilary J. Beresford BD PGCertCS — 2000 2018
Mansefield Trinity Church, West Doura Way, Kilwinning KA13 6DY
HBeresford@churchofscotland.org.uk
01294 550746
01294 550746

96 Kirkconnel (H) linked with Sanquhar: St Bride's (F H W)
Vacant
Session Clerk, Kirkconnel: Fay Rafferty
Session Clerk, Sanquhar: Robert Hughes
fayrafferty1957@gmail.com
mackiehughes@hotmail.com
01659 67650
01659 50553

97 Kirkcowan (H) linked with Wigtown (F H W)
Eric Boyle BA MTh   2006
Seaview Manse, Church Lane, Wigtown, Newton Stewart DG8 9HT   01988 402314
EBoyle@churchofscotland.org.uk

98 Kirkcudbright (H W)
James F. Gatherer BD   1984   2020
church@kirkcudbrightparishchurch.org.uk
6 Bourtree Avenue, Kirkcudbright DG6 4AU   01557 339108
JGatherer@churchofscotland.org.uk

99 Kirkinner linked with Mochrum linked with Sorbie (H)
Vacant
Session Clerk, Kirkinner: John W. MacDonald (Dr)   jwamacdonald1@gmail.com   01988 402329
Session Clerk, Mochrum: Jenni Gray (Mrs)   j.saunders201@btinternet.com   01988 700948
Session Clerk, Sorbie: Morag Donnan (Mrs)   morag.donnan1@btinternet.com   01988 850288

100 Kirkmabreck (W) linked with Monigaff (H W)
Vacant
Session Clerk, Kirkmabreck: Robert McQuistan   Monigaff Manse, Creebridge, Newton Stewart DG8 6NR
mcquistan@mcquistan.plus.com   01671 403361
   01671 820327
Session Clerk, Monigaff: Margaret McDowall (Mrs)   monigaffsessionclerk@gmail.com   01671 403847

101 Kirkmahoe See Closeburn

102 Kirkmaiden (H)
Guardianship of the Presbytery
Session Clerk: Maureen Graham (Mrs)   maureen.grahamm@btinternet.com   01776 840209

103 Kirkmichael linked with Straiton: St Cuthbert's (W)
W. Gerald Jones MA BD ThM   1984   1985
straitonchurchayr@gmail.com
The Manse, Patna Road, Kirkmichael, Maybole KA19 7PJ   01655 750286
WJones@churchofscotland.org.uk

104 Kirkmichael, Tinwald and Torthorwald (W)
Vacant
Mhairi Wallace   2013   2017
(Ordained Local Minister)
Manse of Tinwald, 6 Sundew Lane, Dumfries DG1 3TW
5 Dee Road, Kirkcudbright DG 4HQ   07701 375064
MWallace@churchofscotland.org.uk

105 Kirkoswald See Fisherton

106 Kirkpatrick Juxta (F) linked with Moffat: St Andrew's (F H W) linked with Wamphray (F)   standrewsmoffat@gmail.com
Elsie Macrae BA   2020
The Manse, 1 Meadow Bank, Moffat DG10 9LR   01683 225146
Elsie.Macrae@churchofscotland.org.uk

107 **Lamlash** See Kilmory

108 **Langholm, Eskdalemuir, Ewes and Westerkirk (W)** 1984 2019
Robert G. D. W. Pickles BD MPhil PhD
leewparishchurch@outlook.com
The Manse, Thomas Telford Road, Langholm DG13 0BL
RPickles@churchofscotland.org.uk
01387 380252

109 **Largs: Clark Memorial (H W)** 1988 2014
T. David Watson BSc BD
31 Douglas Street, Largs KA30 8PT
DWatson@churchofscotland.org.uk
01475 675186
01475 672370

110 **Largs: St Columba's** See Fairlie
111 **Largs: St John's** See Cumbrae
112 **Leswalt** See Ervie Kirkcolm
113 **Liddesdale** See Canonbie United

114 **Lochend and New Abbey**
Vacant
Elizabeth A. Mack (Miss) DipPE 1994 2018
(Auxiliary Minster)
New Abbey Manse, 32 Main Street, New Abbey, Dumfries DG2 8BY 01387 850490
24 Roberts Crescent, Dumfries DG2 7RS 01387 264847
mackliz@btinternet.com

115 **Lochmaben** See Applegarth, Sibbaldbie and Johnstone
116 **Lochranza and Pirnmill** See Brodick

117 **Lockerbie: Dryfesdale, Hutton and Corrie (F W)**
Vacant
Dryfesdale Manse, 5 Carlisle Road, Lockerbie DG11 2DW
01576 204188

118 **Luce Valley** See Inch

119 **Lugar (W) linked with Old Cumnock: Old (H)** 1994
John W. Paterson BSc BD DipEd
33 Barrhill Road, Cumnock KA18 1PJ
paterson-j6@sky.com
01290 420769

120 **Mauchline (H W) linked with Sorn** 1989 2021
Allan S. Vint BSc BD MTh PhD
mauchlineparish@yahoo.com
4 Westside Gardens, Mauchline KA5 5DJ
AVint@churchofscotland.org.uk
01290 518528
07795 483070

121 **Maybole** See Crosshill
122 **Mochrum** See Kirkinner

123 Moffat: St Andrew's See Kirkpatrick Juxta
124 Monigaff See Kirkmabreck

125 Monkton and Prestwick: North (F H T W)
Vacant
Interim Moderator: Brian R. Hendrie
office@mpnchurch.org.uk
40 Monkton Road, Prestwick KA9 1AR
BHendrie@churchofscotland.org.uk
01292 **678810**
01292 471379
01292 283825

126 Muirkirk (H W) linked with Old Cumnock: Trinity (F W)
Vacant
Interim Moderator: Alwyn Landman
46 Ayr Road, Cumnock KA18 1DW
ALandman@churchofscotland.org.uk
01290 422145
01292 571287

127 New Cumnock (F H W)
Vacant
Interim Moderator: Kenneth B. Yorke
37 Castle, New Cumnock, Cumnock KA18 4AG
kenyorke@yahoo.com
01290 338296
01292 670476

128 Newmilns: Loudoun (F H T W)
Vacant
Interim Moderator: Gavin A. Niven
Loudoun Manse, 116A Loudoun Road, Newmilns KA16 9HH
GNiven@churchofscotland.org.uk
01560 320174
01560 482418

129 Ochiltree (W) linked with Stair (F W)
Vacant
Interim Moderator: George R. Fiddes
10 Mauchline Road, Ochiltree KA18 2PZ
grfiddes@outlook.com
01290 700365
01292 737512

130 Old Cumnock: Old See Lugar
131 Old Cumnock: Trinity See Muirkirk
132 Patna Waterside See Dalmellington

133 Penninghame (F H)
Edward D. Lyons BD MTh   2007
The Manse, 1A Corvisel Road, Newton Stewart DG8 6LW
ELyons@churchofscotland.org.uk
01671 404425

134 Penpont, Keir and Tynron See Durisdeer

135 Portpatrick linked with Stoneykirk
Vacant
Session Clerk, Portpatrick: David Maxwell
Session Clerk, Stoneykirk: Gillian Lynn (Mrs)
Church Road, Sandhead, Stranraer DG9 9JJ
maxwell@supanet.com
randglynn@btinternet.com
01776 830757
01776 704045
01776 860665

136 Prestwick: Kingcase (F H W)
Ian Wiseman BTh DipHSW   1993   2015
office@kingcase.co.uk
15 Bellrock Avenue, Prestwick KA9 1SQ
IWiseman@churchofscotland.org.uk
01292 **470755**
01292 479571

137 Prestwick: St Nicholas' (H W)
Vacant
Interim Moderator: David R. Gemmell
office@stnicholasprestwick.org.uk
3 Bellevue Road, Prestwick KA9 1NW
DGemmell@churchofscotland.org.uk
01292 **671547**
01292 864140

138 Prestwick: South See Craigie Symington
139 St Mungo See Dalton and Hightae

140 Saltcoats: North (W)
Vacant
Session Clerk: Rosann McLean (Mrs)
25 Longfield Avenue, Saltcoats KA21 6DR
01294 **464679**
01294 604923
01294 467106

141 Saltcoats: St Cuthbert's (H W)
Vacant
webmaster@saltcoats-stcuthberts.org.uk
10 Kennedy Road, Saltcoats KA21 5SF
01294 605109

142 Sanquhar: St Bride's See Kirkconnel
143 Shiskine See Brodick
144 Sorbie See Kirkinner
145 Sorn See Mauchline
146 Stair See Ochiltree

147 Stevenston: Ardeer (F) linked with Stevenston: Livingstone (F H W)
Vacant
Session Clerk, Livingstone: Alexander Hershaw
27 Cuninghame Drive, Stevenston KA20 4AB
gavsandor@aol.com
01294 608993
01294 466293

148 Stevenston: High (F H W)
M. Scott Cameron MA BD   2002
High Kirk Manse, Stevenston KA20 3DL
Scott.Cameron@churchofscotland.org.uk
01294 463356

149 Stevenston: Livingstone See Stevenston: Ardeer

150 Stewarton: John Knox (F T W)
Gavin A. Niven BSc MSc BD   2010
getconnected@johnknox.org.uk
27 Avenue Street, Stewarton, Kilmarnock KA3 5AP
GNiven@churchofscotland.org.uk
01560 **484560**
01560 482418

151 Stewarton: St Columba's (H W)
Vacant
Interim Moderator: Robert A. Anderson
stewartonstcolumbas@gmail.com
1 Kirk Glebe, Stewarton, Kilmarnock KA3 5BJ
robertanderson307@btinternet.com
01560 485113
01563 850554

152 Stoneykirk See Portpatrick
153 Straiton: St Cuthbert's See Kirkmichael

154 Stranraer (F H W) 2022
Andy Muir BA
Birchgrove, Whitehouse Road, Stranraer DG9 0JB
AMuir@churchofscotland.org.uk
01776 700867

155 Tarbolton See Annbank
156 Tarff and Twynholm See Gatehouse and Borgue
157 Thornhill See Durisdeer

158 Troon: Old (F H W)
Vacant
Gillean S.M. Richmond BDS BA 2022
(Assistant Minister)
Session Clerk: Andrew Fell
office@troonold.org.uk
85 Bentinck Drive, Troon KA10 6HZ
GRichmond@churchofscotland.org.uk
sessionclerk@troonold.org.uk
01292 313520
01292 313644
07811 835197
01292 313520

159 Troon: Portland (F H W)
Vacant
Interim Moderator: Bill Duncan
office@troonportlandchurch.org.uk
89 South Beach, Troon KA10 6EQ
bill.jan.duncan@gmail.com
01292 317929
01292 318929
01292 440560

160 Troon: St Meddan's (F H T W)
Vacant
Interim Moderator: Neil A. McNaught
stmeddanschurch@gmail.com
27 Bentinck Drive, Troon KA10 6HX
NMcNaught@churchofscotland.org.uk
01292 317750
01292 441252

161 Tundergarth
Guardianship of the Presbytery
Session Clerk: David Paterson
jilljoe@tiscali.co.uk
07982 037029

162 Urr See Dalbeattie and Kirkgunzeon
163 Wamphray See Kirkpatrick Juxta

164 West Kilbride (F H T W) 2008
James J. McNay MA BD
office@westkilbrideparishchurch.org.uk
The Manse, Goldenberry Avenue, West Kilbride KA23 9LJ
JMcNay@churchofscotland.org.uk
01294 829902
01294 823186

165 Whithorn: St Ninian's Priory See Glasserton and Isle of Whithorn

166 Whiting Bay and Kildonan
Vacant
Session Clerk: Sharon MacLeod (Mrs)

The Manse, Whiting Bay, Brodick, Isle of Arran KA27 8RE
macleodsharon@hotmail.com

01770 700289

167 Wigtown See Kirkcowan

B. In other appointments: members of Presbytery

Blackshaw, Christopher J. BA(Theol)	2015	2017	Pioneer Minister, Farming Community	Ellwood Croft, Gamblesby, Penrith CA10 1HY	07980 975062
Chris Blackshaw is a Methodist Minister				CBlackshaw@churchofscotland.org.uk	
Campbell, Neil G. BA BD	1988	2018	Chaplain, HM Prison Dumfries	12 Charles Street, Annan DG12 5AJ	
				neil.campbell2@prisons.gov.scot	
Clancy, P. Jill (Mrs) BD DipMin	2000	2017	Chaplain, HM Prison Barlinnie	27 Cross Street, Galston KA4 8AA	07956 557087
				JClancy@churchofscotland.org.uk	
Harvey, P. Ruth (Ms) MA BD	2007	2020	Leader, Iona Community	Croslands, Beacon Street, Penrith CA11 7TZ	01768 840749
				ruth@iona.org.uk	07403 638339
Hogg, James	2018		Ordained Local Minister	JHogg@churchofscotland.org.uk	07974 576295
Kelly, Ewan R. BSc MB ChB BD PhD	1994	2020	Lecturer in Healthcare Chaplaincy, University of Glasgow	ewan.kelly@glasgow.ac.uk	
Steenbergen, Pauline (Ms) MA BD	1996	2022	Cumbria Fresh Expression Team Leader, Diocese of Carlisle	p.steenbergen1@gmail.com	07743 927182
Watt, Kim CertThS	2015		Ordained Local Minister, Presbytery	Reddans Park Gate, The Crescent, Stewarton, Kilmarnock KA3 5AY	01560 482267
				KWatt@churchofscotland.org.uk	

C. Retaining: members of Presbytery

Adamson, R. Angus BD	2006	2020	(Brodick with Corrie with Lochranza and Pirnmill with Shiskine)	Otterburn, Corriecravie, Isle of Arran KA27 8PD	01770 870228
				RAdamson@churchofscotland.org.uk	
Aitken, Fraser R. GCSJ MA BD	1978	2019	(Ayr: St Columba)	Sandringham, 38 Coylebank, Prestwick KA9 2DH	01292 225087
				sandringham381@outlook.com	
Anderson, Robert A. MA BD DPhil	1984	2017	(Blackburn and Seafield)	Aiona, 8 Old Auchans View, Dundonald KA2 9EX	01563 850554
				robertanderson307@btinternet.com	07484 206190
Baker, Carolyn M. (Mrs) BD	1997	2008	(Ochiltree with Stair)	Clanary, 1 Maxwell Drive, Newton Stewart DG8 6EL	01671 404292
				cncbaker@btinternet.com	
Becker, Allison E. BA MDiv	2015	2022	(Kilmarnock: St John's Onthank)	ABecker@churchofscotland.org.uk	
Black, Andrew R. BD CertMin	1987	2018	(Irvine: Relief Bourtreehill)	4 Nursery Wynd, Kilwinning KA13 6ER	01294 673090
				andrewblack@tiscali.co.uk	
Bogle, Thomas C. BD CPS HDipRE	1983	2003	(Fisherton with Maybole: West)	38 McEwan Crescent, Mossblown, Ayr KA6 5DR	01292 521215

Name	(Charge)			Address	Tel
Bond, Maurice S. BA DipEd MTh PhD	(Dumfries: St Michael's and South)	1983	2019	15 Pleasance Avenue, Dumfries DG2 7JJ	01563 559960
Brockie, Colin G.F. BSc(Eng) BD SOSc	(Kilmarnock: Grange)	1967	2007	36 Braehead Court, Kilmarnock KA3 7AB / colin@brockie.org.uk	
Brown, H. Taylor BD CertMin FRAI	(Kilmarnock: St Marnock's)	1997	2022	HBrown@churchofscotland.org.uk	07596 111310
Brown, Jack M. BSc BD	(Applegarth, Sibbaldbie and Johnstone with Lochmaben)	1977	2012	69 Berelands Road, Prestwick KA9 1ER / jackmbrown47@gmail.com	01292 477151
Buck, Maxine SRN ONC CertMgS	(Auxiliary Minister, Presbytery of Forth Valley and Clydesdale)	2007	2023	Kirkgate, 92 Main Street, Dunlop, Kilmarnock KA3 4AG / MBuck@churchofscotland.org.uk	07812 712197
Burgess, Paul C.J. MA	(World Mission Partner, Gujranwala Theological Seminary, Pakistan)	1970	2003	Springvale, Halket Road, Lugton, Kilmarnock KA4 3EE / paulandcathie@gmail.com	01505 850254
Burns, John H. BSc BD	(Inch with Portpatrick with Stranraer: Trinity)	1985	2019	The Cabin, Dundeugh, Dalry DG7 3SY	01644 460553
Cairns, Alexander B. MA	(Turin)	1957	2009	Beechwood, Main Street, Sandhead, Stranraer DG9 9JG / dorothycairns@aol.com	01776 830389
Cant, Thomas M. MA BD	(Paisley: Laigh Kirk)	1964	2004	3 Meikle Cutstraw, Stewarton, Kilmarnock KA3 5HU / revtmcant@aol.com	01560 480566
Crichton, James MA BD MTh	(Crosshill with Dalrymple)	1969	2010	60 Kyle Court, Ayr KA7 3AW / crichton.james@btinternet.com	07549 988643
Cruickshank, Norman BA BD	(West Kilbride: Overton)	1983	2006	24D Faulds Wynd, Seamill, West Kilbride KA23 9FA	01294 822239
Cuthbert, Helen E. MA MSc BD	(New Cumnock)	2009	2021	63 Haining Avenue, Bellfield, Kilmarnock KA1 3QN / helenncuthbertk21@hotmail.co.uk	07941 027480
Dee, Oonagh	(Ordained Local Minister, Bengairn Parishes with Castle Douglas)	2014	2019	Kendoon, Merse Way, Kippford, Dalbeattie DG5 4LL / ODee@churchofscotland.org.uk	01556 620001
Dempster, Eric T. MBA	(Ordained Local Minister, Lockerbie: Dryfesdale, Hutton and Corrie)	2016	2021	Annanside, Wamphray, Moffat DG10 9LZ	01576 470496
Dickie, Michael M. BSc	(Ayr: Castlehill)	1955	1993	8 Noltmire Road, Ayr KA8 9ES	01292 618512
Falconer, Alan D. MA BD DLitt DD	(Aberdeen: St Machar's Cathedral)	1972	2011	18 North Crescent Road, Ardrossan KA22 8NA / alanfalconer@gmx.com	07491 484800
Faris, Janice M. (Mrs) BSc BD	(Innerleithen, Traquair and Walkerburn)	1991	2018	Overdale Cottage, Grange Park Road, Orton Grange, Carlisle CA5 6LT / revjfaris@gmail.com	07427 371239
Fiddes, George R. BD	(Prestwick: St Nicholas')	1979	2019	4 St Cuthbert's Crescent, Prestwick KA9 2EG / grfiddes@outlook.com	01292 737512 / 07925 004062
Finch, Graham S. MA BD	(Cadder)	1977	2015	32a St Mary Street, Kirkcudbright DG6 4DN / gsf231@gmail.com	01557 620123
Ford, Alan A. BD	(Glasgow: Springburn)	1977	2013	14 Corsankell Wynd, Saltcoats KA21 6HY / alan.andy@btinternet.com	01294 465740
Frail, Nicola R. BLE MBA MDiv	(Army Chaplain)	2000	2012	Chaplains Office, DM (SW), Whittington Barracks, Lichfield WS14 9PY / Nicola.Frail188@mod.gov.uk	
Garrity, T. Alan W. BSc BD MTh	(Bermuda: Christ Church, Warwick)	1969	2008	17 Solomon's View, Dunlop, Kilmarnock KA3 4ES / alangarrity@btinternet.com	01560 486879
Gillon, C. Blair BD	(Glasgow: Ibrox)	1975	2007	East Muirshiel Farmhouse, Dunlop, Kilmarnock KA3 4EJ / charlesgillon21@gmail.com	01560 483778
Glencross, William M. LTh	(Bellshill: Macdonald Memorial)	1968	1999	1 Lochay Place, Troon KA10 7HH	01292 317097

Godfrey, Linda BSc BD	2012	2014	(Ayr: St Leonard's with Dalrymple)	9 Taybank Drive, Ayr KA7 4RL / godfreykayak@aol.com	07825 663866
Guthrie, James A.	1969	2005	(Corsock and Kirkpatrick Durham with Crossmichael and Parton)	2 Barrhill Road, Pinwherry, Girvan KA26 0QE / p.h.m.guthrie@btinternet.com	01465 841236
Hall, William M. BD	1972	2010	(Kilmarnock: Old High Kirk)	33 Cairns Terrace, Kilmarnock KA1 2JG / revwillie@talktalk.net	01563 525080
Hammond, Richard J. BA BD	1993	2007	(Kirkmahoe)	3 Marchfield Mount, Marchfield, Dumfries DG1 1SE / libby.hammond@virgin.net	07764 465783
Harper, David L. BSc BD	1972	2012	(Troon: St Meddan's)	19 Calder Avenue, Troon KA10 7JT / d.l.harper@btinternet.com	01292 312626
Hewitt, William C. BD DipPS	1977	2017	(Presbytery Clerk: Glasgow)	60 Woodlands Grove, Kilmarnock KA3 1TZ / WHewitt@churchofscotland.org.uk	01563 533312
Hogg, William T. MA BD	1979	2018	(Kirkconnel with Sanquhar: St Bride's)	30 Castle Street, Kirkcudbright DG6 4JD / WHogg@churchofscotland.org.uk	07515 102776
Holland, William MA	1967	2009	(Lochend and New Abbey)	Ardshean, 55 Georgetown Road, Dumfries DG1 4DD / billholland55@btinternet.com	01387 256131 / 07766 531732
Horsburgh, Gary E. BA	1977	2015	(Dreghorn and Springside)	1 Woodlands Grove, Kilmarnock KA3 1TY / garyhorsburgh@hotmail.co.uk	01563 624508
Howie, Marion L.K. (Mrs) MA ARCS	1992	2019	(Auxiliary Minister, Dalry: St Margaret's)	51 High Road, Stevenston KA20 3DY / MHowie@churchofscotland.org.uk	01294 466571
Huggett, Judith A. (Miss) BA BD	1990	2020	(Lead Chaplain, NHS Ayrshire and Arran)	3 Black Morrow Close, Kirkcudbright DG6 4DF	01557 330931
Hutcheson, Norman M. MA BD	1973	2013	(Dalbeattie with Urr)	66 Maxwell Park, Dalbeattie DG5 4LS / norman.hutcheson@gmail.com	01556 610102
Irving, Douglas R. LLB BD WS	1984	2016	(Kirkcudbright)	17 Galla Crescent, Dalbeattie DG5 4JY / douglas.irving@outlook.com	01556 610156
Jackson, Nancy M. CertThRS CertChS	2009	2015	(Auxiliary Minister, Crosshill with Maybole)	35 Auchentrae Crescent, Ayr KA7 4BD / nancyjaxon@btinternet.com	01292 262034
Keating, Glenda K. (Mrs) MTheol	1996	2015	(Craigie Symington)	8 Wardlaw Gardens, Irvine KA11 2EW / kirkglen@btinternet.com	01294 218820
Kelly, William W. BSc BD	1994	2014	(Dumfries: Troqueer)	8 Talia Drive, Stirling, WA 6021 Australia / wwkelly@yahoo.com	04 11 104890
Kyle, Caryl A.E. BD DipEd	2008	2021	(Holytown with New Stevenston: Wrangholm Kirk)	58 Kelvin Walk, Netherhall, Largs KA30 8SJ / caryl_kyle@hotmail.com	01475 310390
Lacy, David W. DL BA BD DLitt	1976	2017	(Kilmarnock: Kay Park)	4 Cairns Terrace, Kilmarnock KA1 2JG / DLacy@churchofscotland.org.uk	01563 624034 / 07974 760272
Lamarti, Samuel H. BD MTh PhD	1979	2006	(Stewarton: John Knox)	7 Dalwhinnie Crescent, Kilmarnock KA3 1QS / samlamar@pobroadband.co.uk	01563 529632
Lennox, Lawrie I. MA BD DipEd	1991	2006	(Cromar)	7 Carwinshoch View, Ayr KA7 4AY / lennox127@btinternet.com	01292 288658
Lind, George K. BD MCIBS	1998	2017	(Stewarton: St. Columba's)	Endrig, 98 Loudoun Road, Newmilns KA16 9HQ / gklind@talktalk.net	01560 428732
Lines, Charles M.D. BA	2010	2022	(Carnock and Oakley)	CLines@churchofscotland.org.uk	07909 762257

Lochrie, John S. BSc BD MTh PhD	1967	2008	(Amsheen Barrhill and Colmonell: St Colmon)	Cosyglen, Kilkerran, Maybole KA19 8LS revjslochrie@btinternet.com	01465 811262
MacDonald, Roderick I.T. BD CertMin	1992	2022	(Beith)	27 Holmston Crescent, Ayr KA7 3JJ RMacDonald@churchofscotland.org.uk	
Macintyre, Thomas MA BD	1972	2011	(Sandsting and Aithsting with Walls and Sandness)	the2macs.macintyre@btinternet.com	
Mackay, Marjory H. (Mrs) BD DipEd CCE	1998	2008	(Cumbrae)	4 Golf Road, Millport, Isle of Cumbrae KA28 0HB marjory.mackay@gmail.com	01475 530388
MacLeod, Ian LTh BA MTh PhD	1969	2006	(Brodick with Corrie)	Cromla Cottage, Corrie, Isle of Arran KA27 8JB i.macleod829@btinternet.com	01770 810237
MacPherson, Gordon C. MA BD MTh	1963	1988	(Associate, Kilmarnock: Henderson)	6 Crosbie Place, Troon KA10 6EY ggmacpherson@btinternet.com	01292 679146
Matthews, John C. OBE MA BD MTh	1992	2010	(Glasgow: Ruchill Kelvinside)	12 Arrol Drive, Ayr KA7 4AF mejohnmatthews@gmail.com	01292 264382
Mayes, Robert BD CertMin	1982	2017	(Dundonald)	Garfield Cottage, Sorn Road, Mauchline KA5 6HQ bobmayes3@gmail.com	01290 519869
McAllister, Anne C. BSc DipEd CCS	2013	2021	(Ordained Local Minister, Kilmarnock: St Kentigern's)	39 Bowes Rigg, Stewarton, Kilmarnock KA3 5EN AMcAllister@churchofscotland.org.uk	01560 483191
McCallum, Alexander D. BD	1987	2005	(Saltcoats: New Trinity)	59 Woodcroft Avenue, Largs KA30 9EW sandyandjose@madasafish.com	01475 670133
McCulloch, James D. BD MIOP MIP3 FSAScot	1996	2016	(Hurlford)	18 Edradour Place, Dunsmuir Park, Kilmarnock KA3 1US mcculloch mansel@btinternet.com	01563 535833
McGurk, Andrew F. BD	1983	2011	(Largs: St John's)	15 Fraser Avenue, Troon KA10 6XF afmcg.largs@talk21.com	01292 676008
McKay, David M. MA BD	1979	2007	(Kirkpatrick Juxta with Moffat: St Andrew's with Wamphray)	20 Auld Brig View, Auldgirth, Dumfries DG2 0XE davidmckay20@tiscali.co.uk	01387 740013
McKenzie, William M. DA	1958	1993	(Dumfries: Troqueer)	41 Kingholm Road, Dumfries DG1 4SR mckenzie.dumfries@btinternet.com	01387 253688
McKinnon, Lily F. H. (Mrs) MA BD PGCE	1993	2021	(Kilmory with Lamlash)	Rowan Cottage, 6 Sheean Drive, Brodick, Isle of Arran KA27 8DH lily.mackinnon@yahoo.co.uk	07917 548357
McLauchlan, Mary C. (Mrs) LTh	1997	2013	(Mochrum)	3 Ayr Street, Moniaive, Thornhill DG3 4HP mary@revmother.co.uk	01848 200786
McLeod, David C. BSc MEng BD	1969	2001	(Dundee: Fairmuir)	76 Ayr Road, Prestwick KA9 1RR	
McNidder, Roderick H. BD DipCE	1987	2007	(Chaplain: NHS Ayrshire and Arran Trust)	6 Hollow Park, Alloway, Ayr KA7 4SR roddymcnidder@sky.com	01292 442554
McPhail, Andrew M. BA	1968	2002	(Ayr: Wallacetown)	25 Maybole Road, Ayr KA7 2QA	01292 282108
Mitchell, D. Ross BA BD	1972	2007	(West Kilbride: St Andrew's)	11 Dunbar Gardens, Saltcoats KA21 6GJ ross.mitchell@virgin.net	01294 474375
Moore, Douglas T.	2003	2019	(Auxiliary Minister, Coylton with Drongan: The Schaw Kirk)	9 Midton Avenue, Prestwick KA9 1PU douglastmoore@hotmail.com	01292 671352
Morrison, Alistair H. BTh DipYCS	1985	2004	(Paisley: St Mark's Oldhall)	92 St Leonard's Road, Ayr KA7 2PU alistairhmorrison@gmail.com	01292 266021
Ness, David T. LTh	1972	2008	(Ayr: St Quivox)	17 Winston Avenue, Prestwick KA9 2EZ davidtness@gmail.com	01292 471625

Ogston, Edgar J. BSc BD	1976	2017	(North West Lochaber)	14 North Park Avenue, Girvan KA26 9DH edgar.ogston@macfish.com	01465 713081
Owen, John J.C. LTh	1967	2001	(Applegarth and Sibbaldbie with Lochmaben)	5 Galla Avenue, Dalbeattie DG5 4JZ jj.owen@onetel.net	01556 612125
Paterson, John L. MA BD STM	1964	2003	(Linlithgow: St Michael's)	9 The Pines, Murdoch's Lane, Alloway, Ayr KA7 4WD lip38rev@gmail.com	01292 443615
Rae, Scott M. MBE BD CPS	1976	2016	(Muirkirk with Old Cumnock: Trinity)	2 Primrose Place, Kilmarnock KA1 2RR scottrae1@btopenworld.com	01563 532711
Roy, Iain M. MA BD	1960	1997	(Stevenston: Livingstone)	2 The Fieldings, Dunlop, Kilmarnock KA3 4AU	01560 483072
Sanderson, Alastair M. LTh BA	1971	2007	(Craigie with Symington)	26 Main Street, Monkton, Prestwick KA9 2QL aesanderson2@gmail.com	01292 475819
Shaw, Catherine A.M. MA DipCE BA	1998	2005	(Auxiliary Minister, Kilmarnock: St. John's Onthank)	40 Merrygreen Place, Stewarton, Kilmarnock KA3 5EP catherine.shaw@tesco.net	01560 483352
Sheppard, Michael J. BD	1997	2016	(Ervie Kirkcolm with Leswalt)	4 Mill Street, Drummore, Stranraer DG9 9PS michaelsheppard00@gmail.com	01776 840369
Simpson, Edward V. BSc BD	1972	2009	(Glasgow: Giffnock South)	7 Whitehill Grove, Newton Mearns, Glasgow G77 5DH eddie.simpson3@talktalk.net	0141 237 4048 07896 013605
Sorensen, Alan K. DL BD MTh DipMin FSAScot	1983	2022	(Greenock: Wellpark Mid Kirk)	51A Castlepark Drive, Fairlie KA29 0DG ASorensen@churchofscotland.org.uk	01475 568314
Steele, Hugh D. LTh DipMin	1994	2020	(Kelty)	23 Mossgiel Avenue, Troon KA10 7DQ hugdebra@btinternet.com	07449 974940
Stewart, David MA DipEd BD MTh	1977	2013	(Howwood)	72 Glen Avenue, Largs KA30 8QQ revdavidst@aol.com	01475 675159
Stirling, Ian R. BSc BD MTh MSc DPT	1990	2021	(Fisherton with Kirkoswald)	71 Caulstran Road, Dumfries DG2 9FJ colin.csutherland@btinternet.com	01387 279954
Sutherland, Colin A. LTh	1995	2007	(Blantyre: Livingstone Memorial)		
Taylor, Andrew S. BTh FPhS	1959	1992	(Greenock: The Union)	9 Raillies Avenue, Largs KA30 8QY andrew.taylor_123@btinternet.com	01294 674709
Telfer, Alan B. BA CQSW BD	1983	2021	(Strathaven: Avendale Old and Drumclog)	22 Crawford Avenue, Prestwick KA9 2BN ATelfer@churchofscotland.org.uk	01292 474041
Urquhart, Barbara (Mrs) DCS	1986	2017	(Deacon, Kilmarnock: New Laigh Kirk)	9 Standalane, Kilmaurs, Kilmarnock KA3 2NB barbaraurquhart1@gmail.com	01563 538289
Ward, Alan H. MA BD	1978	2015	(Interim Minister, Kilwinning: Mansfield Trinity)	47 Meadowfoot Road, West Kilbride KA23 9BU alanhward@hotmail.co.uk	01294 822244 07709 906130
Wark, Alexander C. MA BD STM	1982	2017	(Mid Deeside)	43 Mure Avenue, Kilmarnock KA 3 1TT alecwark@yahoo.co.uk	01563 559581
Watson, Elizabeth R.L. (Miss) BA BD	1981	2021	(Whiting Bay and Kildonan)	3 Fernside, Brisbane Street, Largs KA30 8QG revewatson@btinternet.com	01475 673548
Welsh, Alex M. MA BD	1979	2019	(Hospital Chaplain, NHS Ayrshire and Arran)	8 Greenside Avenue, Prestwick KA9 2HB alexandevelyn@hotmail.com	01292 475341
Whitecross, Jeanette BD	2002	2019	(Kilwinning: Old)	4 Fir Bank, Ayr KA7 3SX jeanettewx@yahoo.com	07803 181150

Name	Dates	Charge	Address	Telephone
Whyte, Norman R. BD MTh DipMin	1982 2022	(Ayton and District Churches)	34 Hollywood, Largs KA 30 8SP burraman@msn.com	07387 229806
Wilson, Muriel (Miss) MA BD DCS	1997 2011	(Deacon, Dalmellington with Patna Waterside)	28 Bellevue Crescent, Ayr KA7 2DR me.wilson28@btinternet.com	01292 264039
Yorke, Kenneth B. BD DipEd	1982 2009	(Dalmellington with Patna Waterside)	13 Annfield Terrace, Prestwick KA9 1PS kenyorke@yahoo.com	01292 670476
Young, Rona M. (Mrs) BD DipEd	1991 2015	(Ayr: St Quivox)	16 Macintyre Road, Prestwick KA9 1BE revronyoung@hotmail.com	01292 471982

D. In other appointments: not members of Presbytery
Nil

E. Retaining: not members of Presbytery

Name	Dates	Charge	Address	Telephone
Bartholomew, David S. BSc MSc PhD BD	1994 2022	(Balmaclellan, Kells and Dalry with Carsphairn)	Craigend Cottage, Broughton, Biggar ML12 6HH dhbart99@gmail.com	
Christie, Robert S. MA BD ThM	1964 2000	(Kilmarnock: West High)	24 Homeroyal House, 2 Chalmers Crescent, Edinburgh EH9 1TP	
Cox, Lesley Paton BD	1994 2013	(Saline and Blairingone)		
Davidson, Amelia (Mrs) BD	2004 2011	(Coatbridge: Calder)	11 St Mary's Place, Saltcoats KA21 5NY	07468 852376
Finlay, William P. MA BD	1969 2000	(Glasgow: Townhead Blochairn)	High Corrie, Brodick, Isle of Arran KA27 8JB	01770 810689
Jackson, William BD CertMin	1994 2020	(Airdrie: New Monkland with Greengairs)	15 Dalwhinnie Crescent, Kilmarnock KA3 1QS	01294 279265
Travers, Robert BA BD	1993 2015	(Irvine: Old)	74 Caledonian Road, Stevenston KA20 3LF roberttravers@live.co.uk	
Webster, John G. BSc	1964 1998	(Glasgow: St John's Renfield)	Plane Tree, King's Cross, Brodick, Isle of Arran KA27 8RG	01770 700747
Wotherspoon, Robert D. LTh	1976 1998	(Corsock and Kirkpatrick Durham with Crossmichael and Parton)	5 Goddards Green Cottages, Goddards Green, Beneden, Cranbrook TN17 4AW	01580 243091

F. Inactive: not members of Presbytery

Name	Dates	Charge	Address	Telephone
Gillon, D. Ritchie M. BD DipMin	1994 2017	(Paisley: St Luke's)	12 Fellhill Street, Ayr KA7 3JF revgillon@hotmail.com	01292 270018
Harris, Samuel McC. OStJ BA BD	1974 2010	(Rothesay: Trinity)	56 Rowland Street, Skipton, North Yorkshire BD23 2DU mhar10@hotmail.com	01756 794505
Logan, Thomas M. LTh	1971 1995	(Clydebank: Abbotsford)	3 Duncan Court, Kilmarnock KA3 7TF thomasmlogan8@gmail.com	01563 524398
MacKinnon, Ronald M. DCS	1996 2012	(Deacon, Cumbernauld: St Mungo's)	32 Strathclyde House, Shore Road, Skelmorlie PA17 5AN ronnie@ronniemac-plus.com	01475 521333 07594 427960
McIntyre, Allan G. BD	1985 2017	(Greenock: St Ninian's)	9a Templehill, Troon KA10 6BQ agmcintyre@lineone.net	07876 445626

G. Readers (active)

Anderson, James PhD DVM FRCPath	67 Henrietta Street, Girvan KA26 9AN jc.anderson2@talktalk.net	01465 710059 07952 512720

Name	Address	Email	Phone
Brown, S. Jeffrey BA	Skara Brae, Holm Park, 8 Ballplay Road, Moffat DG10 9JU	sjbrown@btinternet.com	01683 220475
Bruce, Andrew J.	57 Dockers Gardens, Ardrossan KA22 8GB	andrew_bruce2@sky.com	01294 605113
Cash, Marlane (Mrs)	5 Maxwell Drive, Newton Stewart DG8 6EL	marlanegf690@btinternet.com	01671 401375
Clarke, Elizabeth (Mrs)	Swallowbrae, Torbeg, Isle of Arran KA27 8HE	lizahclarke@gmail.com	01770 860219
			07780 574367
Corson, Gwen (Mrs)	7 Sunnybrae, Borgue, Kirkcudbright DG46 4SJ	gwendolyn@hotmail.com	01557 870328
Currie, Archie BD	55 Central Avenue, Kilbirnie KA25 6JP	Archie.Currie@churchofscotland.org.uk	01505 681474
			07881 452115
Dodds, Alan	Trinco, Battlehill, Annan DG12 6SN	alanandjen46@talktalk.net	01461 201235
Graham, Barbara (Miss) MA MLitt MPhil CertChSt	42 Annanhill Avenue, Kilmarnock KA1 2LQ	barbara.graham74@btinternet.com	01563 522108
Hunter, Jean C.Q. (Mrs) BD	Leucheram, Corrie, Isle of Arran KA27 8JB	j.hunter744@btinternet.com	01770 810218
Jackson, Susan (Mrs)	48 Springbells Road, Annan DG12 6LQ	peter-jackson24@sky.com	07498 714675
Jamieson, Ian A.	2 Whinfield Avenue, Prestwick KA9 2BH	ian4189_jamieson@gmail.com	01242 476898
MacLeod, Sharon (Mrs)	Creag Dhubh, Golf Course Road, Whiting Bay, Isle of Arran KA27 8QT	macleodsharon@hotmail.com	01770 700353
Matheson, David	44 Auchenkeld Avenue, Heathhall, Dumfries DG1 3QY	davidb.matheson-44@btinternet.com	01387 252042
McCool, Robert	17 McGregor Avenue, Stevenston KA20 4BA		01294 466548
McGeever, Gerard	23 Kinloch Avenue, Stewarton, Kilmarnock KA3 3HQ	mcgeege1@gmail.com	01560 484331
Mills, Catherine (Mrs)	59 Crossdene Road, Crosshouse, Kilmarnock KA2 0JU	cfmills5lib@hotmail.com	01563 535305
Monk, Geoffrey	Hibre Cottage, Laurieston, Castle Douglas DG7 2PW		01644 450679
Morrison, James	27 Monkton Road, Prestwick KA9 1AP	jamessmorrisonprestwick@gmail.com	01292 479313
			07773 287852
Morton, Andrew A. BSc	19 Sherwood Park, Lockerbie DG11 2DX	andrew_morton@mac.com	01576 203164
Murphy, Ian	56 Lamont Crescent, Netherthird, Cumnock KA18 3DU	ianm_cumnock@yahoo.co.uk	01290 423675
Murray, Brian	19 Snowdon Terrace, Seamill KA23 9HN	brian.murray100@btinternet.com	01294 822272
Ogston, Jean (Mrs)	14 North Park Avenue, Girvan KA26 9DH	jeanogston@gmail.com	01465 713081
Robertson, William	1 Archers Avenue, Irvine KA11 2GB	willie.robert@yahoo.co.uk	01294 203577
Ronald, Glenn	188 Prestwick Road, Ayr KA8 8NP	glennronald@btinternet.com	01292 286861
Ross, Magnus M.B. BA MEd	39 Beachway, Largs KA30 8QH	m.b.ross@btinternet.com	01475 689572
Savill, Hilda		qjhnic@gmail.com	01683 222854
Stewart, Christine (Mrs)	52 Kilnford Drive, Dundonald KA2 9ET	christistewart@btinternet.com	01563 850486
Whitelaw, David	9 Kirkhill, Kilwinning KA13 6NB	whitelawfam@talktalk.net	01294 551695

H. Ministries Development Staff

Algeo, Paul	North Ayr Parish Grouping – Family/Development Worker	PAlgeo@churchofscotland.org.uk
Anderson, Peter	Stewarton 20s-40s Initiative – Mission Pioneer	PAnderson@churchofscotland.org.uk
Beck, Isobel BD DCS	Kilwinning Abbey – Deacon	IBeck@churchofscotland.org.uk
Blair, Fiona DCS	Beith – Parish Assistant	FBlair@churchofscotland.org.uk
Devlin, Brian	Stevenston: Ardeer linked with Livingstone – Community Mission Worker	BDevlin@churchofscotland.org.uk

Forsyth, Stuart — Irvine Virtual Church Initiative – Mission Pioneer — SForsyth@churchofscotland.org.uk
Hendry, Jill — Kilmarnock South Area – Growing Together with God – Mission Pioneer — JHendry@churchofscotland.org.uk
Jenkinson, Barbara (Dr) — Dalmellington linked with Patna Waterside – Parish Assistant — BJenkinson@churchofscotland.org.uk
McKay, Angus BA — Cumbrae linked with Largs: St John's – Parish Assistant — AMcKay@churchofscotland.org.uk
McTernan, Margaret (Rev) LLB MSW CertCP CertSWM — Presbytery Mission Pioneer Team Leader — MMcTernan@churchofscotland.org.uk

Muir, Alison — Irvine Towerlands Church Plant Initiative – Mission Pioneer — Alison.Muir@churchofscotland.org.uk
Templeton, Katrona — Irvine Open Door (Disability Inclusion) Initiative – Mission Pioneer — KTempleton@churchofscotland.org.uk
Thomson, Robert — Irvine Sports Development Initiative – Mission Pioneer — RThomson@churchofscotland.org.uk
Wardrop, Elaine — Kilmarnock: St Marnock's: Mission Development Worker — EWardrop@churchofscotland.org.uk

TOWN ADDRESSES

Ayr
Auld Kirk — Kirkport (116 High Street)
Castlehill — Castlehill Road x Hillfoot Road
Newton Wallacetown — Main Street
St Andrew's — Park Circus
St Columba — Midton Road x Carrick Park
St James' — Prestwick Road x Falkland Park Road
St Leonard's — St Leonard's Road x Monument Road

Dumfries
Maxwelltown West — Laurieknowe
Northwest — Lochside Road
St George's — George Street
St Mary's-Greyfriars — St Mary's Street
St Michael's and South — St Michael's Street
Troqueer — Troqueer Road

Girvan
North — Montgomery Street
South — Stair Park

Irvine
Fullarton — Marress Road x Church Street
Girdle Toll — Bryce Knox Court
Mure Relief — West Road
Old — Kirkgate
St Andrew's — Caldon Road x Oaklands Ave

Kilmarnock
Ayrshire Mission to the Deaf — 10 Clark Street
Kay Park — London Road
New Laigh Kirk — John Dickie Street
St John's Onthank — 84 Wardneuk Street
St Marnock's — St Marnock Street
St Kentigern's — Dunbar Drive

Prestwick
Kingcase — Waterloo Road
Monkton and Prestwick North — Monkton Road
St Nicholas — Main Street
South — Main Street

Troon
Old — Ayr Street
Portland — St Meddan's Street
St Meddan's — St Meddan's Street

(4) CLYDE (W)

Meets for ordinary business on 14 September 2023, and 13 February and 18 June 2024.

Clerk: REV. PETER McENHILL BD PhD	07837 729333
Presbytery Office:	01505 615033

The Presbytery Office (see below)
clyde@churchofscotland.org.uk
'Homelea', Faith Avenue, Quarrier's Village, Bridge of Weir
PA11 3SX

1 Arrochar (F W) linked with Luss (F W)
Vacant
Interim Moderator: David Nicolson
DNicolson@churchofscotland.org.uk   0141 570 8103

2 Baldernock (H) linked with Milngavie: St Paul's (F H W)
Vacant
Interim Moderator: Barbara A. O'Donnell
stpauls@btconnect.com   **0141 956 4405**
8 Buchanan Street, Milngavie, Glasgow G62 8DD   0141 956 1043
revbarb1@gmail.com   01389 752356

3 Barrhead: Bourock (F H W)   2006   2014
Pamela Gordon BD
14 Maxton Avenue, Barrhead, Glasgow G78 1DY   **0141 881 9813**
PGordon@churchofscotland.org.uk   0141 881 8736

4 Barrhead: St Andrew's (F H W)   2020
Timothy Mineard BA BD
10 Arthurlie Avenue, Barrhead, Glasgow   G78 2BU   **0141 881 8442**
TMineard@churchofscotland.org.uk   0141 587 7913

5 Bearsden: Baljaffray (F H W)
Vacant
Interim Moderator: Alan J. Hamilton
5 Fintry Gardens, Bearsden, Glasgow   G61 4RJ   **0141 942 5304**
AHamilton@churchofscotland.org.uk   0141 942 0366
    0141 942 0021

6 Bearsden: Cross (F H W)   2006   2013
Graeme R. Wilson MCIBS BD ThM DMin
secretary@bearsdencross.org   **0141 942 0507**
61 Drymen Road, Bearsden, Glasgow   G61 2SU   0141 942 0507
GWilson@churchofscotland.org.uk

7 Bearsden: Killermont (F H W)   2003
Alan J. Hamilton LLB BD PhD
8 Clathic Avenue, Bearsden, Glasgow   G61 2HF   0141 942 0021
AHamilton@churchofscotland.org.uk

8 Bearsden: New Kilpatrick (F H W)
Roderick G. Hamilton MA BD   1992   2011
51 Manse Road, Bearsden, Glasgow G61 3PN
mail@nkchurch.org.uk
Roddy.Hamilton@churchofscotland.org.uk
0141 942 8827
0141 942 0035

9 Bearsden: Westerton Fairlie Memorial (H W)
Christine M. Goldie LLB BD MTh DMin   1984   2008
3 Canniesburn Road, Bearsden, Glasgow G61 1PW
westertonchurch@talktalk.net
CGoldie@churchofscotland.org.uk
0141 942 6960
0141 942 2672

10 Bishopton (F H W)
Yvonne Smith BSc BD   2017
The Manse, Newton Road, Bishopton PA7 5JP
office@bishoptonkirk.org.uk
YSmith@churchofscotland.org.uk
01505 862583
01505 862161

11 Bonhill (F H W) linked with Renton: Trinity (F H)
Vacant
Interim Moderator: Graeme R. Wilson
1 Glebe Gardens, Bonhill G83 9NZ
bonhillchurchoffice@gmail.com
GWilson@churchofscotland.org.uk
Bonhill: 01389 756516
01389 609329
0141 942 0507

12 Bridge of Weir: Freeland (F H W)
Kenneth N. Gray BA BD   1988
15 Lawmarnock Crescent, Bridge of Weir PA11 3AS
aandkgray@btinternet.com
01505 612610
01505 690918

13 Bridge of Weir: St Machar's Ranfurly (F W)
Hanneke A.S. Marshall (Mrs) MTh MA   2017
PGCE CertMin
9 St Andrew's Drive, Bridge of Weir PA11 3HS
Hanneke.Marshall@churchofscotland.org.uk
01505 612975
01505 612975

14 Cardross (F H W)
Margaret McArthur BD DipMin   1995   2015
16 Bainfield Road, Cardross G82 5JQ
MMcArthur@churchofscotland.org.uk
01389 841322
01389 849329
07799 556367

15 Clydebank: Faifley (F W)
Gregor McIntyre BSc BD   1991
Kirklea, Cochno Road, Hardgate, Clydebank G81 6PT
Gregor.McIntyre@churchofscotland.org.uk
01389 876836

16 Clydebank: Kilbowie St Andrew's (F) linked with Clydebank: Radnor Park (H)
Vacant
Interim Moderator: Robert Kinloch (Mr)
11 Tiree Gardens, Old Kilpatrick, Glasgow G60 5AT
rkinloch@blueyonder.co.uk
01389 875599
01389 750544

17 Clydebank: Radnor Park See Clydebank: Kilbowie St Andrew's

18 Clydebank: Waterfront (F W) linked with Dalmuir: Barclay (F W)   **Dalmuir Barclay: 0141 941 3988**
0141 941 3317
Vacant   **lifeatwaterfront@virginmedia.com**
Interim Moderator: Gregor McIntyre   16 Parkhall Road, Dalmuir, Clydebank G81 3RJ   01389 876836
Gregor.McIntyre@churchofscotland.org.uk

19 Craigrownie (F W) linked with Garelochhead (F W) linked with Rosneath: St Modan's (F H W)   **Garelochhead: 01436 810589**
Christine M. Murdoch BD   1999   2015   The Manse, Argyll Road, Kilcreggan, Helensburgh G84 0JW   01436 842274
CMurdoch@churchofscotland.org.uk   07973 331890

20 Dalmuir: Barclay See Clydebank: Waterfront

21 Dumbarton: Riverside (F H W) linked with Dumbarton: St Andrew's (H W) linked with Dumbarton: West Kirk (F H W)   **Riverside: 01389 742551**
office@dumbartonriverside.org.uk
administration@standrewsdumbarton.co.uk
Vacant   18 Castle Road, Dumbarton G82 1JF   01389 726685
Mark Boshoff AB BTh   2006   2022   mboshoff@churchofscotland.org.uk   07541 604255
(Assistant Minister)
Ian J. Millar BA   2020   2022   Lochfada House, Succoth, Arrochar G83 7AL   01301 702133
(Ordained Local Minister; Interim Moderator)   IMillar@churchofscotland.org.uk

22 Dumbarton: St Andrew's See Dumbarton: Riverside
23 Dumbarton: West Kirk See Dumbarton: Riverside

24 Duntocher: Trinity (F H L T W)   **info@duntochertrinitychurch.co.uk**
Vacant   The Manse, Roman Road, Duntocher, Clydebank G81 6BT   01389 380038
Session Clerk: Colin G. Dow   colin.g.dow@ntlworld.com

25 Elderslie Kirk (F H W)   **01505 323348**
G. Gray Fletcher BSc BD   1989   2019   282 Main Road, Elderslie, Johnstone PA5 9EF   01505 321767
GFletcher@churchofscotland.org.uk

26 Erskine (F T W)   **0141 812 4620**
David Nicolson BA   2019   The Manse, 7 Leven Place, Linburn, Erskine PA8 6AS   0141 570 8103
DNicolson@churchofscotland.org.uk

27 Garelochhead See Craigrownie

28 Gourock: Old Gourock and Ashton (H W) linked wth Greenock: St Ninian's
David W.G. Burt BD DipMin MTh   1989   2014
secretary@ogachurch.org.uk
331 Eldon Street, Greenock PA16 7QN
DBurt@churchofscotland.org.uk
01475 633914

29 Gourock: St John's (F H T W)
Teri C. Peterson BMus MDiv   2006   2018
office@stjohns-gourock.org.uk
6 Barrhill Road, Greenock PA19 1JX
TPeterson@churchofscotland.org.uk
01475 632143

30 Greenock: East End (F) linked with Greenock: Mount Kirk (F W)
Francis E. Murphy BEng DipDSE BD   2006
info@themountkirk.org.uk
76 Finnart Street, Greenock PA16 8HJ
FMurphy@churchofscotland.org.uk
01475 722338

31 Greenock: Lyle Kirk (F T W)
Jonathan C. Fleming MA BD   2012   2021
office@lylekirk.org
333 Eldon Street, Greenock PA16 7QN
JFleming@churchofscotland.org.uk
01475 722694
07393 995397

32 Greenock: Mount Kirk See Greenock: East End

33 Greenock: St Margaret's (F W)
Guardianship of the Presbytery
Interim Moderator: Teri C. Peterson
TPeterson@churchofscotland.org.uk
01475 781953
01475 632143

34 Greenock: St Ninian's See Gourock: Old Gourock and Ashton

35 Greenock: Wellpark Mid Kirk (F)
Vacant
Interim Moderator: Ian W. Bell
101 Brisbane Street, Greenock PA16 8PA
revianbell@gmail.com
01475 721741
01475 529312

36 Greenock: Westburn (F W)
Karen E. Harbison (Mrs) MA BD   1991   2014
50 Ardgowan Street, Greenock PA16 8EP
KHarbison@churchofscotland.org.uk
01475 720257
01475 721048

37 Helensburgh (F W) linked with Rhu and Shandon (F W)
Vacant
Interim Moderator: Ann J. Cameron
hello@helensburghcos.org
35 East Argyle Street, Helensburgh G84 7EL
anncameron2@googlemail.com
Helensburgh: 01436 676880
Rhu and Shandon: 01436 820605
01436 673365
01436 831800

38 Houston and Killellan (F H W)
Gary D. Noonan BA   2018
The Manse of Houston, Main Street, Houston, Johnstone PA6 7EL
GNoonan@churchofscotland.org.uk
01505 612569

39 Howwood (W) linked with Johnstone: St Paul's (F H W)   1982   2003
Alistair N. Shaw MA BD MTh PhD
9 Stanley Drive, Brookfield, Johnstone PA5 8UF
Alistair.Shaw@churchofscotland.org.uk
St Paul's: **01505 321632**
01505 320060

40 Inchinnan (F H W)   2017
Ann Knox BD Cert.Healthc.Chap
51 Old Greenock Road, Inchinnan, Renfrew PA4 9PH
AKnox@churchofscotland.org.uk
0141 812 1263
0141 389 1724
07534 900065

41 Inverkip (H W) linked with Skelmorlie and Wemyss Bay (W)
Vacant
Interim Moderator: Karen E. Harbison
admin@inverkip.org.uk
3a Montgomerie Terrace, Skelmorlie PA17 5DT
KHarbison@churchofscotland.org.uk
01475 529320
01475 721048

42 Johnstone: High (F H W)   2001
Ann C. McCool (Mrs) BD DSD IPA ALCM 1989
76 North Road, Johnstone PA5 8NF
AMcCool@churchofscotland.org.uk
01505 336303
01505 320006

43 Johnstone: St Andrew's Trinity (W)
Vacant
Interim Moderator: Stephen J. Smith
45 Woodlands Crescent, Johnstone PA5 0AZ
SSmith@churchofscotland.org.uk
01505 337827
01505 672908
01505 702621

44 Johnstone: St Paul's   See Howwood

45 Kilbarchan (F T W)   1993   2015
Stephen J. Smith BSc BD
41 Shuttle Street, Kilbarchan PA10 2JR
SSmith@churchofscotland.org.uk
01505 702621

46 Kilmacolm: Old (F H W)
Vacant
Interim Moderator: A. Sonia Blakesley
The Old Kirk Manse, Glencairn Road, Kilmacolm PA13 4NJ
SBlakesley@churchofscotland.org.uk
01505 873911
01505 873174
0141 258 1161

47 Kilmacolm: St Columba (F H)
Vacant
Interim Moderator: Ann Knox
6 Churchill Road, Kilmacolm PA13 4LH
AKnox@churchofscotland.org.uk
01505 873271
0141 389 1724

48 Kilmaronock Gartocharn linked with Lomond (F W)
Vacant
Session Clerk, Kilmaronock Gartocharn: Mark Smith
kilgartoch@gmail.com
01389 830785
07796 938318
Session Clerks, Lomond: Linda Cust (Miss)
lindaccust@btinternet.com
01389 754502
Robert M. Kinloch
rkinloch@blueyonder.co.uk
07760 276505

49 Langbank (F T W) Guardianship of the Presbytery Interim Moderator: Stuart C. Steell			**info@langbankparishchurch.co.uk** SSteell@churchofscotland.org.uk	0141 387 2464
50 Linwood (F H) Vacant Interim Moderator: Ann C. McCool			1 John Neilson Avenue, Paisley PA1 2SX AMcCool@churchofscotland.org.uk	0141 887 2801 01505 320006
51 Lomond See Kilmaronock Gartocharn				
52 Luss See Arrochar				
53 Milngavie: Cairns (H W) Andrew Frater BA BD MTh	1987	1994	**office@cairnschurch.org.uk** 4 Cairns Drive, Milngavie, Glasgow G62 8AJ AFrater@churchofscotland.org.uk	**0141 956 4868** 0141 956 1717
54 Milngavie: St Luke's (W) Ramsay B. Shields BA BD	1990	1997	70 Hunter Road, Milngavie, Glasgow G62 7BY RShields@churchofscotland.org.uk	**0141 956 4226** 0141 577 9171 Fax 0141 577 9181
55 Milngavie: St Paul's See Baldernock				
56 Neilston (F W) Matthew D. Ritchie BA	2020		The Church Hall, 45 High Street, Neilston, Glasgow G78 3HJ Matthew.Ritchie@churchofscotland.org.uk	**0141 881 9445** 07548 342672
57 Old Kilpatrick Bowling (F W) Vacant Interim Moderator: Christine M. Goldie			The Manse, 175 Dumbarton Road, Old Kilpatrick, Glasgow G60 5JQ CGoldie@churchofscotland.org.uk	08005 668242 0141 942 2672
58 Paisley: Abbey (F H W) Vacant Interim Moderator: James M. Gibson			**info@paisleyabbey.org.uk** 1 Carriagehall Drive, Paisley PA2 6JG jamesmgibson@msn.com	**0141 889 7654; Fax 0141 887 3929** 01698 854907
59 Paisley: North (F W) Vacant Stuart Davidson BD (Pioneer Minister)	2008	2017	**wallneuknorthchurch@gmail.com** 5 Glenvilla Crescent, Paisley PA2 8TL 25H Cross Road, Paisley PA2 9QJ SDavidson@churchofscotland.org.uk	**0141 889 9265** 0141 884 4429 07717 503059

60 Paisley: Oakshaw Trinity (F H W)
Gordon B. Armstrong BD FIAB BRC CertCS 1998 2012
The Manse, 52 Balgonie Drive, Paisley PA2 9LP
GArmstrong@churchofscotland.org.uk
0141 887 4647; Fax 0141 848 5139
0141 587 3124

Oakshaw Trinity is a Local Ecumenical Partnership with the United Reformed Church

61 Paisley: St George's (F W T)
Vacant
Mhairi M. Breingan BSc CertCS 2011 2019
(Ordained Local Minister)
6 Park Road, Inchinnan, Renfrew PA4 4QJ
mhairi.b@btinternet.com
0141 812 1425

62 Paisley: St Mark's Oldhall (F H L W)
A. Sonia Blakesley MB ChB BD 2020
office@stmarksoldhall.org.uk
36 Newtyle Road, Paisley PA1 3JX
SBlakesley@churchofscotland.org.uk
0141 882 2755
0141 258 1161

63 Paisley: Sherwood Greenlaw (F H W)
John Murning BD CPS 1988 2014
5 Greenlaw Drive, Paisley PA1 3RX
JMurning@churchofscotland.org.uk
0141 889 7060
0141 316 2678

64 Paisley: South (F H W)
David P. Hood BD CertMin IOB(Scot) 1997 2020
6 Southfield Avenue, Paisley PA2 8BY
DHood@churchofscotland.org.uk
0141 561 7139
0141 587 9374

65 Paisley: West
Vacant
Interim Moderator: G. Gray Fletcher
GFletcher@churchofscotland.org.uk
01505   321767

66 Port Glasgow: Hamilton Bardrainney (F)
Guardianship of the Presbytery
Interim Moderator: Francis E. Murphy
80 Bardrainney Avenue, Port Glasgow PA14 6HD
FMurphy@churchofscotland.org.uk
01475 701213
01475 722338

67 Port Glasgow: New (F H W)
William A. Boyle BA 2020
New Parish Church Manse, Barr's Brae Lane, Port Glasgow PA14 5QA
WBoyle@churchofscotland.org.uk
01475 745407

68 Renfrew: North (F T W)
Philip D. Wallace BSc BTh DTS 1998 2018
contact@renfrewnorth.org.uk
1 Alexandra Drive, Renfrew PA4 8UB
PWallace@churchofscotland.org.uk
0141 530 1308
0141 570 3502

G. Douglas Adam BD BA 2023
(Assistant Minister)
132 Castle Gardens, Paisley PA2 9RD
DAdam@churchofscotland.org.uk
07895 593660

69 Renfrew: Trinity (F H W)

Stuart C. Steell BD CertMin	1992	2015	25 Paisley Road, Renfrew PA4 8JH SSteell@churchofscotland.org.uk	0141 885 2129 0141 387 2464

70 Renton: Trinity See Bonhill
71 Rhu and Shandon See Helensburgh
72 Roseneath: St Modan's See Craigrownie
73 Skelmorlie and Wemyss Bay See Inverkip

B. In other appointments: members of Presbytery

Dalton, Mark F. BD DipMin RN	2002		Chaplain: Royal Navy	The Chaplaincy, HMS Neptune, HM Naval Base Clyde, Faslane, Helensburgh G84 8HL. Mark.Dalton242@mod.gov.uk	
McEnhill, Peter BD PhD	1992	2021	Presbytery Clerk: Clyde	Flat 3/1, 112 Cloch Road, Gourock PA19 1FN PMcEnhill@churchofscotland.org.uk	07837 729333
McMahon, Eleanor J. BEd BD	1994	2022	Ministries Recruitment and Training Manager, Faith Action Programme	81 Moorpark Square, Renfrew PA4 8DB EMcMahon@churchofscotland.org.uk	07974 116539
Peel, Jeanette L. BA BD MTh	2020		Healthcare Chaplain	Inverclyde Royal Hospital, Larkfield Road, Greenock PA16 0XN Jeanette.Peel@churchofscotland.org.uk	01475 504759 07903 681003
Stevenson, Stuart CertCE	2011		Ordained Local Minister	143 Springfield Park, Johnstone PA5 8JT SStevenson@churchofscotland.org.uk	0141 886 2131

C. Retaining; members of Presbytery

Armstrong, William R. BD	1979	2008	(Skelmorlie and Wemyss Bay)	25A The Lane, Skelmorlie PA17 5AR w.armstrong@btinternet.com	01475 520891
Bell, Ian W. LTh	1990	2011	(Erskine)	40 Brueacre Drive, Wemyss Bay PA18 6HA revianbell@gmail.com	01475 529312
Bell, May (Mrs) LTh	1998	2012	(Johnstone: St Andrew's Trinity)	40 Brueacre Drive, Wemyss Bay PA18 6HA revmaybell122@gmail.com	01475 529312
Buchanan, Fergus C. MA BD MTh	1982	2022	(Baldernock with Milngavie: St Paul's)	114 Moorpark Square, Renfrew PA4 8JF Fergus.Buchanan@churchofscotland.org.uk	07760 138960
Cameron, Ann J. (Mrs) CertCS	2005	2019	(Auxiliary Minister, Craigrownie with Garelochhead with Rosneath: St Modan's)	Water's Edge, Ferry Road, Rosneath, Helensburgh G84 0RS anncameron2@googlemail.com	01436 831800
Cameron, Charles M. BA BD PhD	1980	2021	(Johnstone: St Andrew's Trinity)	5 Weavers Road, Paisley PA2 9DP charlescameron@hotmail.co.uk	07469 198443
Clark, David W. MA BD	1975	2014	(Helensburgh: St Andrew's Kirk with Rhu and Shandon)	3 Ritchie Avenue, Cardross, Dumbarton G82 5LL clarkdw@talktalk.net	01389 849319
Coull, Morris C. BD	1974	2018	(Greenock St Margaret's)	14 Kelvin Gardens, Largs KA30 8SY	01475 338674
Cowie, Marian (Mrs) MA BD MTh	1990	2012	(Aberdeen: Midstocket)	2 Glenmore Avenue, Alexandria, Glasgow G83 0QA mcowieou@aol.com	07740 174969
Geddes, Elizabeth (Mrs)	2013	2021	(Ordained Local Minister, Langbank)	9 Shillingworth Place, Bridge of Weir PA11 3DY gedds_liz@hotmail.com	01505 612639

Gray, Greta (Miss) DCS	1992	2014	(Deacon, Paisley: Lylesland)	67 Crags Avenue, Paisley PA3 6SG greta.gray@ntlworld.com	0141 884 6178
Hamilton, David G. MA BD	1971	2004	(Braes of Rannoch with Foss and Rannoch)	79 Finlay Rise, Milngavie, Glasgow G62 6QL davidhamilton40@googlemail.com	0141 956 4202
Hood, E. Lorna OBE MA BD DD	1978	2016	(Renfrew: North)	4 Thornly Park Drive, Paisley PA2 7RR revlornahood@gmail.com	0141 384 9516
Houston, Elizabeth W. MA BD DipEd	1985	2018	(Alexandria)	Croftengea, 25 Honeysuckle Lane, Jamestown, Alexandria G83 8PL Cleric2@hotmail.com	01389 721165
Kay, David BA BD MTh	1974	2008	(Paisley: Sandyford: Thread Street)	36 Donaldswood Park, Paisley PA2 8RS david.kay500@o2.co.uk	0141 884 2080
Kemp, Tina MA	2005	2021	(Auxiliary Minister, Helensburgh with Rhu and Shandon)	12 Oaktree Gardens, Dumbarton G82 1EU TKemp@churchofscotland.org.uk	01389 730477
Lees, Andrew P. BD	1984	2017	(Baldernock)	58 Lindores Street, Stepps G33 6PD andrew.lees@yahoo.co.uk	0141 389 5840
Leitch, Maureen (Mrs) BA BD DipPhysEd	1995	2011	(Barrhead: Bourock)	Rockfield, 92 Paisley Road, Barrhead G78 1NW maureen.leitch@ntlworld.com	0141 580 2927
Macdonald, Alexander MA BD	1966	2006	(Neilston)	35 Lochore Avenue, Paisley PA3 4BY alexsmacdonald42@aol.com	0141 889 0066
Manson, Eileen (Mrs) DipCE	1994	2021	(Auxiliary Minister, Greenock: St Ninian's)	1 Cambridge Avenue, Gourock PA19 1XT EManson@churchofscotland.org.uk	01475 632401
Marshall, T. Edward BD CertMin	1987	2020	(Crosshouse)	20 Alloway Drive, Paisley PA2 7DS	
McFarlane, Robert G. BD	2001	2018	(Paisley St Mark's Oldhall)	990 Crookston Road, Glasgow G53 7DY	
Miller, Ian H. BD BA	1975	2012	(Bonhill)	Derand, Queen Street, Alexandria G83 0AS revianmiller@btinternet.com	01389 753039
Moore, Norma MA BD	1995	2017	(Jamestown)	25 Miller Street, Dumbarton G82 2JA norma-moore@sky.com	
Nutter, Margaret A.E. BA BD MFPh	2014	2021	(Ordained Local Minister, Presbytery-wide)	Kilmorich, 14 Balloch Road, Balloch, Alexandria G83 8SR MNutter@churchofscotland.org.uk	01389 754505
O'Donnell, Barbara A. BD PGSE	2007	2022	(Bonhill with Renton: Trinity)	Ashbank, 258 Main Street, Alexandria G83 0NU revbarb1@gmail.com	01389 752356
Read, Paul R. BSc DipEd MA(Th)	2000	2021	(Applegarth, Sibbaldbie and Johnstone with Lochmaben)	21 Brechanshaw, Erskine PA8 7EZ prr747@icloud.com	0141 560 0561 07791 724162
Robertson, Ishbel A. R. MA BD	2013	2018	(Ordained Local Minister)	Oakdene, 81 Bonhill Road, Dumbarton G82 2DU	01389 763436
Whyte, Margaret A. (Mrs) BA BD	1988	2011	(Glasgow: Pollokshaws)	4 Springhill Road, Barrhead G78 2AA mawhyte@hotmail.co.uk	0141 881 4942
Wilson, John BD CPS	1985	2010	(Glasgow: Temple Anniesland)	4 Carron Crescent, Bearsden, Glasgow G61 1HJ revjwilson@btinternet.com	0141 931 5609

D. In other appointments: not members of Presbytery

Davidson, Mark R. MA BD STM PhD PhD RN	2005	2011	Chaplain: Royal Navy	The Manse, Main Street, Kippen FK8 3DN Mark.Davidson122@mod.gov.uk	01786 871249

E. Retaining; not members of Presbytery

Christie, John C. BSc BD CBiol MRSB | 1990 2012 | (Interim Minister, Paisley: Oakshaw Trinity) | 10 Cumberland Avenue, Helensburgh   G84 8QG | JChristie@churchofscotland.org.uk | 01436 674078

McCrum, Scott BD | 2015 2022 | (Old Kilpatrick Bowling) | SMcCrum@churchofscotland.org.uk | 07711 336392

McEwan, Ian K. BSc PhD BD FRSE FRAE | 2008 2022 | (Bearsden: Baljaffray) | IMcEwan@churchofscotland.org.uk

Reid, A. Gordon BSc BD | 1982 2008 | (Dunfermline: Gillespie Memorial) | 7 Arkleston Crescent, Paisley   PA3 4TG | reid501@fsmail.com | 0141 842 1542 / 07773 300989

Speirs, Archibald BD | 1995 2021 | (Inverkip with Skelmorlie and Wemyss Bay) | 27 Annochie Road, Paisley   PA2 0LB | archiespeirs1@aol.com | 01505 815327

Stewart, Charles E. BSc BD MTh PhD | 1976 2010 | (Chaplain, Royal Hospital School, Holbrook) | 105 Sinclair Street, Helensburgh   G84 9HY | c.e.stewart@btinternet.com | 01436 678113

F. Inactive: not members of Presbytery

Alexander, Douglas N. MA BD | 1961 1999 | (Bishopton) | West Morningside, Main Road, Langbank, Port Glasgow   PA4 6XP | 01475 540249

Black, Janette M.K. (Mrs) BD | 1993 2006 | (Assistant: Paisley: Oakshaw Trinity) | 5 Craigiehall Avenue, Erskine   PA8 7DB | 0141 812 0794

Fraser, Ian C. BA BD | 1982 2008 | (Glasgow: St Luke's and St Andrew's) | 62 Kingston Avenue, Neilston, Glasgow   G78 3JG | ianandlindafraser@gmail.com | 0141 563 6794

Harris, John W.F. MA | 1967 2012 | (Bearsden: Cross) | 21 Strathmore Court, 20 Abbey Drive, Jordanhill, Glasgow   G14 9JX | jwfh@sky.com | 0141 463 1046 / 07740 982079

Johnston, Mary (Miss) DCS | 1988 2003 | (Deacon, Paisley: St Columba Foxbar) | 19 Lounsdale Drive, Paisley   PA2 9ED | jamcintyre@hotmail.com | 0141 849 1615

Lawrie, Robert M. BD MSc DipMin LLCM(TD) MCMI FCMI | 1994 1998 | (Fyvie with Rothienorman) | West Benview, Main Road, Langbank   PA14 6XP | revrmlawrie@gmail.com | 01475 540240 / 07789 824479

McCully, M. Isobel (Miss) DCS | 1974 1999 | (Deacon, Greenock: Old West Kirk) | 10 Broadstone Avenue, Port Glasgow   PA14 5BB | mi.mccully@btinternet.com | 01475 742240

McIntyre, J. Ainslie MA BD | 1963 1984 | (Lecturer, New Testament, University of Glasgow) | 60 Bonnaughton Road, Bearsden, Glasgow   G61 4DB | jamcintyre@hotmail.com | 0141 942 5143

Nicol, Joyce (Mrs) BA DCS | 1974 2001 | (Deacon, Greenock: St Ninian's) | 93 Brisbane Street, Greenock   PA16 8NY | joycenicol@hotmail.co.uk | 01475 723235 / 07957 642709

Prentice, George BA BTh | 1964 1997 | (Paisley: Martyrs') | 46 Victoria Gardens, Corsebar Road, Paisley   PA2 9AQ | g.prentice04@talktalk.net | 0141 842 1585

Steven, Harold A.M. OStJ LTh FSAScot | 1970 2001 | (Baldernock) | 9 Cairnhill Road, Bearsden, Glasgow   G61 1AT | harold.allison.steven@gmail.com | 0141 942 1598

Taylor, Jane C. BD DipMin | 1990 2013 | (Insch-Leslie-Premnay-Oyne) | Timbers, Argyll Road, Kilcreggan   G84 0JW | jane.c.taylor@btinternet.com | 01436 842336

Watson, Valerie G.C. MA BD STM | 1987 2018 | (North and West Islay) | 11 Roxburgh Street, Greenock   PA5 4PU | vgcwatson@btinternet.com

Webster, Brian G. BD BSc CEng MIEE | 1988 2011 | (Cambusbarron: The Bruce Memorial) | 3/1 Cloch Court, 57 Albert Road, Gourock   PA19 1NJ | revwebby@aol.com | 01475 787116

G. Readers (active)

Banks, Russell	18 Aboyne Drive, Paisley PA2 7SJ	margaret.banks2@ntlworld.com	0141 884 6925
Bird, Mary Jane (Miss)	Greenhill Farm, Barochan Road, Houston PA6 7HS	mjbird55@gmail.com	01475 720125
Boag, Jennifer (Miss)	11 Madeira Street, Greenock PA16 7UJ	jenniferboag@hotmail.com	01475 631544
Davey, Charles L.	16 Divert Road, Gourock PA19 1DT	charlesdavey16@hotmail.co.uk	01505 704208
Hood, Eleanor (Mrs)	12 Clochoderick Avenue, Kilbarchan, Johnstone PA10 2AY	eleanor.hood.kilbarchan@ntlworld.com	01505 355779
MacDonald, Christine (Ms)	33 Collier Street, Johnstone PA5 8AG	christine.macdonald10@ntlworld.com	01505 872417
Marshall, Leon M.	Glenisla, Gryffe Road, Kilmacolm PA13 4BA	lm@stevenson-kyles.co.uk	0141 884 3710
Maxwell, Margaret A. (Sandra) (Mrs) BD	2 Grants Avenue, Paisley PA2 6AZ	sandra@maxwellmail.co.uk	
McFarlan, Elizabeth (Miss)	20 Fauldswood Crescent, Paisley PA2 9PA	elizabeth.mcfarlan@ntlworld.com	01505 358411
McHugh, Jack	Earlshaugh, Earl Place, Bridge of Weir PA11 3HA	jackmchugh1@btinternet.com	01505 612789
Morgan, Richard	Annandale, School Road, Rhu, Helensburgh G84 8RS	themorgans@hotmail.co.uk	01436 821269
Rankin, Kenneth	20 Bruntsfield Gardens, Glasgow G53 7QJ	krankin@hotmail.co.uk	0141 880 7474
Spooner, John R. BSc PGC(Mgt)	Onslow, Uplawmoor Road, Neilston, Glasgow G78 3LB	jrspooner@btopenworld.com	0141 881 5182 / 07481 008033
Theaker, Philip D. (Dr)	17 Kilmory Gardens, Skelmorlie PA17 5EX	ptheaker48@gmail.com	07904 919776

H. Ministries Development Staff

Name	Role	Email
Dungavell, Marie Claire	Dumbarton: Riverside linked with West – Development Worker	MCDungavell@churchofscotland.org.uk
Graham, Gillian	Clydebank: Waterfront linked with Dalmuir: Barclay – Children, Young People and Family Worker	GGraham@churchofscotland.org.uk
Wilson, Lorraine	Clydebank: Waterfront linked with Dalmuir: Barclay – Pastoral Assistant	LWilson@churchofscotland.org.uk

TOWN ADDRESSES

Bearsden
Baljaffray	Grampian Way
Cross	Drymen Road
Killermont	Rannoch Drive
New Kilpatrick	Manse Road
Westerton	Crarae Avenue

Clydebank
Faifley	Faifley Road
Kilbowie St Andrew's	Kilbowie Road
Radnor Park	Radnor Street
Waterfront	Town Centre

Dumbarton
Riverside	High Street
St Andrew's	Aitkenbar Circle
West Kirk	West Bridgend

Gourock
Old Gourock and Ashton	41 Royal Street
St John's	Bath Street x St John's Road

Greenock
East End	49–51 Belleville Street
Lyle Kirk	31 Union Street
Mount Kirk	Dempster Street at Murdieston Park
St Margaret's	Finch Road x Kestrel Crescent
St Ninian's	Warwick Road, Larkfield
Wellpark Mid Kirk	Cathcart Square
Westburn	9 Nelson Street

Helensburgh
	Colquhoun Square

Milngavie
Cairns	Buchanan Street
St Luke's	Kirk Street

St Paul's	Strathblane Road

Paisley
Abbey	Cotton Street
North	off Renfrew Road
Oakshaw Trinity	Churchill
St George's	Causeyside Street, and Nethercraigs Drive
St Mark's Oldhall	Glasgow Road, Ralston
Sherwood Greenlaw	Glasgow Road
South	Rowan Street off Neilston Road
West	King Street

Port Glasgow
Hamilton Bardrainney	Bardrainney Avenue x Auchenbothie Road
New	Princes Street

(5) GLASGOW (F W)

Meets at 7pm on the second Tuesday of every month apart from June when it is the third Tuesday and July, August and January when it does not meet. Details of the venue are displayed on the Presbytery website.

Clerk:	REV. S. GRANT BARCLAY LLB DipLP BD MSc PhD	260 Bath Street, Glasgow G2 4JP	0141 332 6606
		glasgow@churchofscotland.org.uk	07743 779929
Depute Clerk:	REV. HILARY N. McDOUGALL MA PGCE BD	HMcDougall@churchofscotland.org.uk	
Treasurer:	MRS ALISON WHITELAW	treasurer@presbyteryofglasgow.org.uk	

1 Bishopbriggs: Kenmure (F W) — 0141 762 4242
Vacant
Kaye Gardiner BD (Assistant Minister) 2023 — KGardiner@churchofscotland.org.uk
Session Clerk: Jim Wright — jim@auchendavie.co.uk — 07808 365845

2 Bishopbriggs: Springfield Cambridge (F W) — 0141 772 1596
Ian Taylor BD ThM DipPSRP 1995 2006 — springfieldcamb@btconnect.com — 0141 772 1540
64 Miller Drive, Bishopbriggs, Glasgow G64 1FB
ITaylor@churchofscotland.org.uk

3 Broom (F W) — 0141 639 3528
James A.S. Boag BD CertMin 1992 2007 — office@broomchurch.org.uk — Tel 0141 639 2916
3 Laigh Road, Newton Mearns, Glasgow G77 5EX — Fax 0141 639 3528
JBoag@churchofscotland.org.uk

4 Burnside Blairbeth (F W) — 0141 634 7383
William T.S. Wilson BSc BD 1999 2006 — theoffice@burnsideblairbeth.church — 0141 583 6470
59 Blairbeth Road, Burnside, Glasgow G73 4JD
WWilson@churchofscotland.org.uk

5 Busby (F W) — 0141 644 2073
Jeremy C. Eve BSc BD 1995 1998 — 17A Carmunnock Road, Busby, Glasgow G76 8SZ — 0141 644 3670
JEve@churchofscotland.org.uk

6 Cadder (F W) — 0141 772 7436
John B. MacGregor BD 1999 2017 — 231 Kirkintilloch Road, Bishopbriggs, Glasgow G64 2JB — 0141 576 7127
JMacGregor@churchofscotland.org.uk

7 Cambuslang (F W)
Peter W. Nimmo BD ThM 1996 2020
office@churchofscotland.org.uk
74 Stewarton Drive, Cambuslang, Glasgow G72 8DG
PNimmo@churchofscotland.org.uk
0141 642 9271
0141 586 2126

Karen M. Hamilton (Mrs) DCS 1995 2014
6 Beckfield Gate, Glasgow G33 1SW
KHamilton@churchofscotland.org.uk
0141 558 3195
07514 402612

8 Cambuslang: Flemington Hallside (F W)
Ian A. Cathcart BSc BD 1994 2018
59 Hay Crescent, Cambuslang, Glasgow G72 6QA
ICathcart@churchofscotland.org.uk
0141 641 1049
07588 441895

9 Campsie (F W)
Jane M. Denniston MA BD MTh 2002 2016
DPT DipPSRP
campsieparishchurch@gmail.com
Campsie Parish Church, 130 Main Street, Lennoxtown,
Glasgow G66 7DA
Jane.Denniston@churchofscotland.org.uk
01360 310939
07738 123101

10 Chryston (H T W)
Mark Malcolm MA BD 1999 2008
chrystonchurch@hotmail.com
The Manse, 109 Main Street, Chryston, Glasgow G69 9LA
MMalcolm@churchofscotland.org.uk
0141 779 4188
0141 779 1436
07731 737377

11 Cumbernauld: Abronhill (H W)
Joyce A. Keyes (Mrs) BD 1996 2003
26 Ash Road, Cumbernauld, Glasgow G67 3ED
JKeyes@churchofscotland.org.uk
01236 723833

12 Cumbernauld: Condorrat (H W)
Vacant
11 Rosehill Drive, Cumbernauld, Glasgow G67 4EQ
g8dross@gmail.com
Session Clerk: Gordon Ross
01236 452090
07979 911647

13 Cumbernauld: Kildrum and St Mungo's (W)
Vacant
Fiona M.E. Crawford BA BD 2022
(Assistant Minister)
FCrawford@churchofscotland.org.uk
07801 855314

James R. Gemmell MA BD 2022
(Assistant Minister)
James.Gemmell@churchofscotland.org.uk
07577 907824

New charge formed by the union of Cumbernauld: Kildrum and Cumbernauld: St Mungo's

14 Cumbernauld: Old (H W)
Vacant
Valerie S. Cuthbertson (Miss) DipTMus DCS — 2003
Fiona M.E. Crawford BA BD (Assistant Minister) — 2022
James R. Gemmell MA BD (Assistant Minister) — 2022

2 Muirhill Court, Hamilton ML3 6DR
VCuthbertson@churchofscotland.org.uk
FCrawford@churchofscotland.org.uk
James.Gemmell@churchofscotland.org.uk

01698 429232
07801 855314
07577 907824

15 Eaglesham (F W)
Jade M. Ableitner BA — 2021
office@eagleshamparishchurch.co.uk
2 West Glebe, Cheapside Street, Eaglesham, Glasgow G76 0NS
Jade.Ableitner@churchofscotland.org.uk

01355 302087
07470 046982

16 Fernhill and Cathkin (F W)
Aquila R. Singh BA PGCE BD — 2017
20 Glenlyon Place, Rutherglen, Glasgow G73 5PL
ASingh@churchofscotland.org.uk

0141 389 3599

17 Gartcosh (F H T W) linked with Glenboig (F T W)
David G. Slater BSc BA DipThRS — 2011
26 Inchnock Avenue, Gartcosh, Glasgow G69 8EA
DSlater@churchofscotland.org.uk

Gartcosh: **01236 872274**
07722 876616

18 Giffnock: Orchardhill (F W)
Gillian Rooney BA — 2021
23 Huntly Avenue, Giffnock, Glasgow G46 6LW
GRooney@churchofscotland.org.uk

0141 638 3604
0141 387 8254

19 Giffnock: South (F W)
Catherine J. Beattie (Mrs) BD — 2008, 2011
giffnocksouth@gmail.com
164 Ayr Road, Newton Mearns, Glasgow G77 6EE
CBeattie@churchofscotland.org.uk

0141 638 2599
0141 258 7804

20 Giffnock: The Park (F W)
Calum D. Macdonald BD CertMin — 1993, 2001
contact@parkchurch.org.uk
41 Rouken Glen Road, Thornliebank, Glasgow G46 7JD
CMacdonald@churchofscotland.org.uk

0141 620 2204
0141 638 3023

21 Glenboig See Gartcosh

22 Greenbank (F H W)
Jeanne N. Roddick BD — 2003
greenbankoffice@tiscali.co.uk
Greenbank Manse, 38 Eaglesham Road, Clarkston, Glasgow G76 7DJ
JRoddick@churchofscotland.org.uk

0141 644 1841
0141 644 1395

23 Kilsyth: Anderson (F T W)
Vacant
Session Clerk: Christine Johnston
johnstonchristine@hotmail.co.uk
01236 821060

24 Kilsyth: Burns and Old (F W)
Robert Johnston BD MSc FSAScot 2017
boldchurch@hotmail.com
The Grange, 17 Glasgow Road, Kilsyth G65 9AE
RJohnston@churchofscotland.org.uk
07810 377582

25 Kirkintilloch: St Columba's Hillhead (H W)
Philip A. Wright BSc MSc PhD BTh 2017
stcolumbassecretary@outlook.com
14 Crossdykes, Kirkintilloch G66 3EU
PWright@churchofscotland.org.uk
0141 578 0016
07427 623393

26 Kirkintilloch: St David's Memorial Park (F H W)
Vacant
Session Clerk: David S. Forsyth
sdmp2@outlook.com
forsyth12@btinternet.com
0141 776 4989
07715 971397

27 Kirkintilloch: St Mary's (W)
Ruth H.B. Morrison MA BD PhD 2009 2021
office.stmarys@btconnect.com
23 Braes o' Yetts, Kirkintilloch, Glasgow G66 3FF
RMorrison@churchofscotland.org.uk
0141 775 1166
07557 657079

28 Lenzie: Old (H W)
Vacant
Contact: Eleanor Yates
eyates321@aol.com
07893 985263

29 Lenzie: Union (F H W)
Daniel J.M. Carmichael MA BD 1994 2003
office@lenzieunion.org
1 Larch Avenue, Lenzie, Glasgow G66 4HX
DCarmichael@churchofscotland.org.uk
0141 776 1046
0141 776 3831

30 Maxwell Mearns Castle (W)
Scott R.M. Kirkland BD MAR DMin 1996 2011
office@maxwellmearns.org.uk Tel/Fax
122 Broomfield Avenue, Newton Mearns, Glasgow G77 5JR
SKirkland@churchofscotland.org.uk
0141 639 5169
0141 560 5603

31 Mearns (F H W)
Vacant
office@mearnskirk.church
0141 639 6555

32 Milton of Campsie (F H W)
Julie H.C. Moody BA BD PGCE 2006
16 Cannerton Park, Milton of Campsie, Glasgow G66 8HR
JMoody@churchofscotland.org.uk
01360 310548

No.	Charge / Minister	Year	Year	Contact	Telephone
33	**Moodiesburn (F W)** Mark W.J. McKeown MEng MDiv DipMin	2013	2020	**info@moodiesburn.church** 6 Glenapp Place, Moodiesburn, Glasgow G69 0HS MMcKeown@churchofscotland.org.uk	**01236 870515** 01236 263406 07761 097633
34	**Netherlee and Stamperland (F H W)** Scott Blythe BSc BD MBA	1997	2017	**nethandstamchurch@gmail.com** 25 Ormonde Avenue, Netherlee, Glasgow G44 3QY SBlythe@churchofscotland.org.uk	**0141 637 2503** 0141 533 7147 07504 692046
35	**Newton Mearns (F H W)** Stuart J. Crawford BD MTh	2017		**office@churchatthecross.org.uk** 28 Waterside Avenue, Newton Mearns, Glasgow G77 6TJ SCrawford@churchofscotland.org.uk	**0141 639 7373** 07305 239128
36	**Rutherglen: Old (F H T W)** Jean J. de Villiers BATheol BTh HonPsych	2003	2021	31 Highburgh Drive, Rutherglen, Glasgow G73 3RR JdeVilliers@churchofscotland.org.uk	07960 312218
37	**Rutherglen: Stonelaw (F T W)** Neil H. Watson BD	2017	2021	**info@stonelawchurch.org** 12 Hawthorn Way, Cambuslang, Glasgow G72 7AF NWatson@churchofscotland.org.uk	**0141 647 5113** 07871 615840
38	**Rutherglen: West and Wardlawhill (F W)** Vacant Session Clerk: Alistair K. McInnes			**info@westandwardlawhill.org** 12 Albert Drive, Rutherglen, Glasgow G73 3RT sessionclerk@westandwardlawhill.org.	**0844 736 1470** 07971 079600
39	**Stepps (F H W)** Vacant Session Clerk: Lorraine Robertson			sessionclerkspc2020@gmail.com	07952 490036
40	**Thornliebank (F H W)** Mike R. Gargrave BD	2008	2014	12 Parkholm Quadrant, Thornliebank, Glasgow G53 7ZH MGargrave@churchofscotland.org.uk	0141 880 5532
41	**Torrance (F T W)** Stuart D. Irvin BD	2013	2021	**office@tpc.org.uk** 1 Atholl Avenue, Torrance, Glasgow G64 4JA SIrvin@churchofscotland.org.uk	**01360 620970** 07421 352 893

42 Williamwood (F W)
Janet S. Mathieson MA BD   2003   2015   125 Greenwood Road, Clarkston, Glasgow G76 7LL   **0141 638 2091**
ALCM PGSE   JMathieson@churchofscotland.org.uk   0141 579 9997

43 Glasgow: Baillieston Mure Memorial (F W) linked with Glasgow: Baillieston St Andrew's (F W)   Mure Memorial: **0141 773 1216**
Vacant   aborthwick93@gmail.com   07928 567680
Session Clerk, Mure Memorial: Alastair Borthwick

44 Glasgow: Baillieston St Andrew's See Glasgow: Baillieston Mure Memorial

45 Glasgow: Barlanark Greyfriars (W)   enquiries@barlanark-greyfriars.co.uk   **0141 771 6477**
Vacant
Session Clerk: Janette McMaster   janettemcmaster@yahoo.co.uk   07956 579799

46 Glasgow: Blawarthill (F T W) linked with Glasgow: St Columba (F GE W)
G. Melvyn Wood MA BD   1982   2009   46 Earlbank Avenue, Glasgow G14 9HL   0141 579 6521
                                                                                      GMelvynWood@churchofscotland.org.uk

47 Glasgow: Bridgeton St Francis in the East (F H L W)   bridgetonstfrancis@gmail.com   **0141 556 2830**
                                                                                                                                                     (Church House: **0141 554 8045**)
Vacant
Session Clerk: Barbara Jennings (Mrs)   barbara.jennings1@ntlworld.com   07856 912267

48 Glasgow: Broomhill Hyndland (F W)   info@broomhillhyndlandchurch.org   **0141 334 2540**
George C. Mackay   1994   2014   27 St Kilda Drive, Glasgow G14 9LN   0141 959 8697
BD CertMin CertEd DipPC   GMackay@churchofscotland.org.uk   07711 569127

49 Glasgow: Calton Parkhead
Alison E.S. Davidge MA BD   1990   2008   98 Drumover Drive, Glasgow G31 5RP   **0141 554 3866**
                                                                                      ADavidge@churchofscotland.org.uk   07843 625059

50 Glasgow: Cardonald (F W)   **0141 882 6264**
Gavin McFadyen BEng BD   2006   2018   133 Newtyle Road, Paisley PA1 3LB   0141 576 6818
                                                                                      GMcFadyen@churchofscotland.org.uk   07960 212106

51 Glasgow: Carmunnock (F)   **0141 644 0655**
Vacant
Session Clerk: George Dow   george.dow2019@outlook.com   0141 644 0689
                                                                                                                                                      07801 613 127

52 Glasgow: Carmyle (W) linked with Glasgow: Kenmuir Mount Vernon (F W)

Murdo MacLean BD CertMin	1997	1999	3 Meryon Road, Glasgow G32 9NW Murdo.MacLean@churchofscotland.org.uk	0141 778 2625
Roland Hunt BSc PhD CertEd (Ordained Local Minister)		2016	4 Flora Gardens, Bishopbriggs, Glasgow G64 1DS RHunt@churchofscotland.org.uk	0141 563 3257

53 Glasgow: Carntyne and Cranhill (W)

Vacant — 163 Lethamhill Road, Glasgow G33 2SQ
mayfawns@sky.com — 0141 778 4186 / 0141 770 9247 / 0141 774 4250

Session Clerk: May Fawns

New charge formed by the union of Glasgow: Carntyne and Glasgow: Cranhill

54 Glasgow: Carnwadric (F L W)

James Gemmell BD MTh	1999	2020	62 Loganswell Road, Thornliebank, Glasgow G46 8AX JGemmell@churchofscotland.org.uk	0141 638 9575 07577 907824
Mary S. Gargrave (Mrs) DCS	1989	2007	12 Parkholm Quadrant, Thornliebank, Glasgow G53 7ZH Mary.Gargrave@churchofscotland.org.uk	0141 880 5532 07896 866618

55 Glasgow: Castlemilk (F H W)

Vacant — 0141 634 7113

Session Clerk: David Fraser — david.fraser1959@gmail.com — 07803 825116

56 Glasgow: Cathcart Old (F)

Vacant — 0141 637 4168

Session Clerk: Anne Neilson — aneilson@btinternet.com — 07307 865530

57 Glasgow: Cathcart Trinity (F H W)

Alasdair R. MacMillan LLB BD	2015	office@cathcarttrinity.org.uk 21 Muirhill Avenue, Glasgow G44 3HP Alasdair.MacMillan@churchofscotland.org.uk	0141 637 6658 0141 391 9102

58 Glasgow: Cathedral (High or St Mungo's) (F W)

Mark E. Johnstone DL MA BD	1993	2019	41 Springfield Road, Bishopbriggs, Glasgow G64 1PL Mark.Johnstone@churchofscotland.org.uk — 0141 552 8198 / 07515 285374

59 Glasgow: Causeway (Tollcross) (F)

Monica Michelin-Salomon BD	1999	2007	228 Hamilton Road, Glasgow G32 9QU MMichelin-Salomon@churchofscotland.org.uk — 0141 778 2413

60	**Glasgow: Clincarthill (F H W)** Stuart Love BA MTh	2016		90 Mount Annan Drive, Glasgow G44 4RZ SLove@churchofscotland.org.uk	**0141 632 4206** 0141 632 2985
61	**Glasgow: Colston Milton** Christopher J. Rowe BA BD	2008		118 Birsay Road, Milton, Glasgow G22 7QP CRowe@churchofscotland.org.uk	**0141 772 1922** 0141 564 1138
62	**Glasgow: Colston Wellpark (F H W)** Guardianship of the Presbytery Leslie E.T. Grieve BSc BA (Ordained Local Minister)	2014		23 Hertford Avenue, Kelvindale, Glasgow G12 0LG LGrieve@churchofscotland.org.uk	**0141 772 8672** 07813 255052
63	**Glasgow: Croftfoot (F H W)** Robert M. Silver BA BD	1995	2011	4 Inchmurrin Gardens, High Burnside, Rutherglen, Glasgow G73 5RU RSilver@churchofscotland.org.uk	**0141 637 3913** 0141 258 7268
64	**Glasgow: Dennistoun New (F H W)** Ian M.S. McInnes BD DipMin	1995	2008	31 Pencaitland Drive, Glasgow G32 8RL IMcInnes@churchofscotland.org.uk	**0141 554 1350** 0141 564 6498
65	**Glasgow: Drumchapel St Andrew's (F W)** Vacant Session Clerks: Steven and Gillian Hay			sessionclerkdrumchapel@gmail.com	**0141 944 3758** 07816 261296
66	**Glasgow: Drumchapel St Mark's (F)** Audrey J. Jamieson BD MTh	2004	2007	146 Garscadden Road, Glasgow G15 6PR AJamieson@churchofscotland.org.uk	0141 944 5440
67	**Glasgow: Easterhouse (F W)** Derek W. Hughes BSc BD DipEd	1990	2018	3 Barony Gardens, Springhill, Glasgow G69 6TS DHughes@churchofscotland.org.uk	07723 578573
68	**Glasgow: Eastwood (F W)** James R. Teasdale BA BD	2009	2016	54 Mansewood Road, Eastwood, Glasgow G43 1TL JTeasdale@churchofscotland.org.uk	0141 571 7648
69	**Glasgow: Gairbraid (F H W)** Donald Michael MacInnes BD	2002	2011	4 Blackhill Gardens, Summerston, Glasgow G23 5NE DMacInnes@churchofscotland.org.uk	0141 946 0604

70 Glasgow: Gallowgate
Peter L. V. Davidge BD MTh   2003   2009
98 Drumover Drive, Glasgow G31 5RP
PDavidge@churchofscotland.org.uk
07765 096599

71 Glasgow: Garthamlock and Craigend (F W)
I. Scott McCarthy BD   2010   2018
9 Craigievar Court, Garthamlock, Glasgow G33 5DJ
ISMcCarthy@churchofscotland.org.uk
07725 037394

72 Glasgow: Gorbals
Vacant
Session Clerk: Douglas Ellis
6 Stirlingfauld Place, Gorbals, Glasgow G5 9QF
dandvellis@btinternet.com
07786 678783

73 Glasgow: Govan and Linthouse (F T W)
David T. Gray BArch BD   2010   2020
glpcglasgow@googlemail.com
44 Forfar Avenue, Glasgow G52 3JQ
DGray@churchofscotland.org.uk
0141 445 2010
07789 718622

74 Glasgow: Hillington Park (F H W)
David A. Sutherland BD   2001   2022
81 Raeswood Road, Glasgow G53 7HH
DSutherland@churchofscotland.org.uk
0141 883 5897

75 Glasgow: Ibrox (F H W)
Tara P. Granados (Ms) BA MDiv   2018
ibroxparishchurch@gmail.com
Ibrox Parish Church, 67 Clifford Street, Glasgow G51 1QH
TGranados@churchofscotland.org.uk
07380 830030
07380 830030

76 Glasgow: Jordanhill (F W)
Bruce H. Sinclair BA BD   2009   2015
jordchurch@btconnect.com
12 Priorwood Gardens, Academy Park, Glasgow G13 1GD
BSinclair@churchofscotland.org.uk
0141 959 2496
0141 959 1310

77 Glasgow: Kelvinbridge (F W)
Gordon Kirkwood BSc BD MTh MPhil PGCE   1987   2003
Flat 2/2, 94 Hyndland Road, Glasgow G12 9PZ
GKirkwood@churchofscotland.org.uk
0141 339 1750
0141 334 5352

78 Glasgow: Kelvinside Hillhead (F W)
Vacant
Roger D. Sturrock (Prof.) BD MD FCRP   2014
(Ordained Local Minister)
36 Thomson Drive, Bearsden, Glasgow G61 3PA
RSturrock@churchofscotland.org.uk
0141 334 2788
0141 286 8130

No.	Charge / Minister	Ordained	Inducted	Address / Email	Telephone
79	**Glasgow: Kenmuir Mount Vernon** See Glasgow: Carmyle				
80	**Glasgow: King's Park (F H W)** Vacant Session Clerks: Ian and Eunice Black			office@kingspark.church.co.uk office@kingsparkchurch.co.uk	**0141 636 8688**
81	**Glasgow: Kinning Park (W)** Margaret H. Johnston BD DipPEd	1988	2000	168 Arbroath Avenue, Cardonald, Glasgow G52 3HH MHJohnston@churchofscotland.org.uk	0141 810 3782
82	**Glasgow: Knightswood Anniesland Trinity (F H W)** Fiona M.E. Gardner (Mrs) MA MLitt BD	1997	2011	info@tachurch.org.uk 76 Victoria Park Drive North, Glasgow G14 9PJ FGardner@churchofscotland.org.uk	**0141 530 9745** 0141 959 5647
	Ruth Forsythe (Mrs) DipRS MCS (Ordained Local Minister)	2017	2018	28 Gardenside Avenue, Carmyle, Glasgow G32 8DY RForsythe@churchofscotland.org.uk	07824 641212
83	**Glasgow: Langside (F T W)** Vacant Session Clerk: Douglas McCulloch			langsidechurch@gmail.com 36 Madison Avenue, Glasgow G44 5AQ d.mcculloch3@btinternet.com	**0141 632 7520** 0141 637 0797 07770 928130
84	**Glasgow: Maryhill Ruchill (F H W)** Stuart C. Matthews BD MA	2006	2010	251 Milngavie Road, Bearsden, Glasgow G61 3DQ SMatthews@churchofscotland.org.uk	**0141 946 3512** 0141 942 0804
	James Hamilton DCS	1997	2000	6 Beckfield Gate, Glasgow G33 1SW James.Hamilton@churchofscotland.org.uk	0141 558 3195 07584 137314
	New charge formed by the union of Glasgow: Maryhill and Glasgow: Ruchill Kelvinside				
85	**Glasgow: Merrylea (F W)** Vacant Session Clerk: Ralph P. Boettcher			4 Pilmuir Avenue, Glasgow G44 3HX merryleasessionclerk@outlook.com	**0141 637 2009** 07806 453724
86	**Glasgow: Newlands South (H T W)** Vacant Session Clerk: Catherine Taylor			secretary@newlandschurch.org.uk 24 Monreith Road, Glasgow G43 2NY catherine.taylor10@ntlworld.com	**0141 632 3055** 0141 632 2588 07929 292479
87	**Glasgow: Partick Trinity (F H T W)** Timothy D. Sinclair MA MDiv		2018	enquiry@particktrinity.org.uk 99 Balshagray Avenue, Glasgow G11 7EQ TSinclair@churchofscotland.org.uk	0141 563 6424

88 Glasgow: Partick Victoria Park (F H W)
James Andrew McIntyre BD   2010
3 Branklyn Crescent, Glasgow G13 1GJ
Andy.McIntyre@churchofscotland.org.uk
0141 339 8816
0141 959 3732
New charge formed by the union of Glasgow: Balshagray Victoria Park and Glasgow: Partick South

89 Glasgow: Pollokshaws (F)
Roy J.M. Henderson MA BD DipMin   1987   2013
33 Mannering Road, Glasgow G41 3SW
RHenderson@churchofscotland.org.uk
0141 649 1879
0141 632 8768

90 Glasgow: Pollokshields (F H T W)
David R. Black MA BD   1986   1997
36 Glencairn Drive, Glasgow G41 4PW
DBlack@churchofscotland.org.uk
0141 423 4000

91 Glasgow: Possilpark (F)
Vacant
Session Clerk: Edward Hyde
1262 Balmuildy Road, Glasgow G23 5HE
wee.eddy@ntlword.com
0141 336 8028
07493 261202

92 Glasgow: Queen's Park Govanhill (F W)
Vacant
Session Clerk: Jonathan Gibb
officeQPG@btinternet.com
jogibb60@gmail.com
0141 423 3654
07522 997748
Incorporating Glasgow: John Ross Memorial Deaf Local Mission Church (W)
New charge formed by the union of Glasgow: John Ross Memorial Church for Deaf People and Glasgow: Queen's Park Govanhill

93 Glasgow: Robroyston (F W)
Jonathan A. Keefe BSc BD   2009
info@robroystonchurch.org.uk
7 Beckfield Drive, Glasgow G33 1SR
JKeefe@churchofscotland.org.uk
0141 558 8414
0141 558 2952

94 Glasgow: Ruchazie (F)
Guardianship of the Presbytery
Session Clerk: Margaret Dott
info@ruchaziechurch.org
0141 774 2759
0141 572 0451

95 Glasgow: St Andrew and St Nicholas (F W)
Vacant
Session Clerk: Stewart Boyle
80 Tweedsmuir Road, Glasgow G52 2RX
stewartmboyle@gmail.com
0141 882 3601
0141 883 9873
0141 427 2666

96 Glasgow: St Andrew's East (F W)
Vacant
Session Clerk: Elizabeth McIvor
43 Broompark Drive, Glasgow G31 2JB
emcivor@talktalk.net
0141 554 1485
0141 556 4838

97 Glasgow: St Andrew's West (F W)
Kleber Machado BD MTh   1998   2019
BTh MSc PhD
info@rsscentre.org.uk
101 Hill Street, Glasgow G3 6TY
KMachado@churchofscotland.org.uk
0141 332 4293
0141 353 6551

98 Glasgow: St Christopher's Priesthill and Nitshill (W)
Vacant
Session Clerk: Douglas MacLaren
douglas_maclaren@hotmail.co.uk
0141 881 6541
07948 193783

99 Glasgow: St Columba See Glasgow: Blawarthill

100 Glasgow: St David's Knightswood (F)   1988   1999
Graham M. Thain LLB BD
60 Southbrae Drive, Glasgow G13 1QD
GThain@churchofscotland.org.uk
0141 954 1081
0141 959 2904

101 Glasgow: St Enoch's Hogganfield (F H W)
Vacant
church@st-enoch.org.uk
0141 770 5694

102 Glasgow: St George's Tron (F W)   1989   2013
Alastair S. Duncan MA BD
info@sgt.church
29 Hertford Avenue, Glasgow G12 0LG
ADuncan@churchofscotland.org.uk
0141 229 5746
07968 852083

103 Glasgow: St James' (Pollok)
Vacant
Session Clerk: David T. Arbuckle
davidtarbuckle@outlook.com
0141 882 4984
07469 878303

104 Glasgow: St John's Renfield (F W)
Vacant
Interim Moderator: Kleber Machado
office@sjrchurch.com
26 Leicester Avenue, Glasgow G12 0LU
KMachado@churchofscotland.org.uk
0141 334 0782
0141 339 4637
0141 353 6551

105 Glasgow: St Paul's (F T W)
Vacant
Session Clerk: Scott Stewart
38 Lochview Drive, Glasgow G33 1QF
scottstewart@live.co.uk
0141 770 8559
0141 770 1561
07999 007900

106 Glasgow: St Rollox (F W)
Vacant
inbox@strollox.co.uk
42 Melville Gardens, Bishopbriggs, Glasgow G64 3DE
0141 558 1809
0141 581 0050

107 Glasgow: Sandyford Henderson Memorial (F H L T W)   2021
Benjamin Thorp BD

enquiries@sandyfordhenderson.net   **0141 226 3696**
66 Woodend Drive, Glasgow G13 1TG   07707 608562
BThorp@churchofscotland.org.uk

108 Glasgow: Sandyhills (W)   2018
Norman A. Afrin BA MRes

60 Wester Road, Glasgow G32 9JJ   **0141 778 3415**
NAfrin@churchofscotland.org.uk   0141 778 1213

109 Glasgow: Scotstoun (W)   2000
Richard Cameron BD DipMin

15 Northland Drive, Glasgow G14 9BE   0141 959 4637
RCameron@churchofscotland.org.uk

110 Glasgow: Shawlands Trinity (F W)
Vacant
Interim Moderator: Stuart J. Crawford

SCrawford@churchofscotland.org.uk   **0141 649 0266**
     07912 534280

111 Glasgow: Sherbrooke Mosspark (F H W)   2003   2021
Adam J. Dillon BD ThM

sherbrooke-inii@btconnect.com   **0141 427 1968**
114 Springkell Avenue, Glasgow G41 4EW   0141 737 7299
ADillon@churchofscotland.org.uk

112 Glasgow: Shettleston New (F W)   2017
W. Louis T. Reddick MA BD

211 Sandyhills Road, Glasgow G32 9NB   **0141 778 4769**
LReddick@churchofscotland.org.uk   0141 230 7365
     07843 083548

113 Glasgow: Springburn (F H T W)   2014
Brian M. Casey MA BD

springburnparishchurch@btconnect.com   **0141 557 2345**
c/o Springburn Parish Church, 180 Springburn Way, Glasgow G21 1TU   07703 166772
BCasey@churchofscotland.org.uk

114 Glasgow: Toryglen (F H T W)
Guardianship of the Presbytery

toryglenparish@gmail.com   **07587 207981**

115 Glasgow: Trinity Possil and Henry Drummond (W)   1990   1995
Richard G. Buckley BD MTh DMin

tphdcofs@yahoo.com
50 Highfield Drive, Glasgow G12 0HL   0141 339 2870
RBuckley@churchofscotland.org.uk

116 Glasgow: Tron St Mary's (F)
Rhona E. McDonald BA BD — 2015 — 30 Louden Hill Road, Robroyston, Glasgow G33 1GA / RMcDonald@churchofscotland.org.uk — **0141 558 1011** / 0141 389 8816

117 Glasgow: Wallacewell (New Charge Development) (F T W)
Vacant — **info@wallacewell.org** — **0141 558 4466** / 0141 585 0283
Kaye Gardiner BD (Assistant Minister) — 2023 — 8 Streamfield Gate, Glasgow G33 1SJ / KGardiner@churchofscotland.org.uk
Team Member: Marysia Roberts — marysia1@hotmail.com — 07572 153019

118 Glasgow: Wellington (F H T W)
Richard Baxter MA BD (Transition Minister) — 1997 2022 — 31 Hughenden Gardens, Glasgow G12 9YH / RBaxter@churchofscotland.org.uk — **wellingtonchurch@btinternet.com** / **0141 339 0454** / 07958 541418
Roger D. Sturrock (Prof.) BD MD FCRP (Ordained Local Minister) — 2014 — 36 Thomson Drive, Bearsden, Glasgow G61 3PA / RSturrock@churchofscotland.org.uk — 0141 286 8130

119 Glasgow: Whiteinch (F W)
Laura Digan — 2021 — 65 Victoria Park Drive South, Glasgow G14 9NX / LDigan@churchofscotland.org.uk — **0141 959 9317** / 0141 576 9020

120 Glasgow: Yoker (F T)
Karen E. Hendry BSc BD — 2005 — 15 Coldingham Avenue, Glasgow G14 0PX / KHendry@churchofscotland.org.uk — 0141 952 3620

B. In other appointments: members of Presbytery

Barclay, S. Grant LLB DipLP BD MSc PhD	1995	2021	Presbytery Clerk: Glasgow	Presbytery Office, 260 Bath Street, Glasgow G2 4JP / GBarclay@churchofscotland.org.uk	0141 332 6606
Cathcart, John Paul DCS	2000	2023	Presbytery Vacant Charge Enabler	9 Glen More, East Kilbride, Glasgow G74 2AP / John.Cathcart@churchofscotland.org.uk	01355 243970 / 07708 396074 / 07903 926727
Denniston, David W. BD DipMin	1981	2022	Presbytery Post Probation Support Officer	c/o Campsie Parish Church, 130 Main Street, Lennoxtown, Glasgow G66 7DA / David.Denniston@churchofscotland.org.uk	
Forrest, Martin R. BA MA BD	1988	2012	Chaplain: HM Prison Low Moss	4/1, 7 Blochairn Place, Glasgow G21 2EB / martinrforrest@gmail.com	0141 552 1132
Foster-Fulton, Sally BA BD	1999	2016	Head of Christian Aid Scotland (on sabbatical while Moderator)	2 Rothesay Terrace, Edinburgh EH3 7RY / sfoster-fulton@churchofscotland.org	07850 937226
Gardner, Peter M. MA BD	1988	2016	Pioneer Minister, Glasgow Arts Community	Flat 3/2, 10 Haggswood Avenue, Glasgow G41 4RE / PGardner@churchofscotland.org.uk	07743 539654
Gay, Douglas C. MA BD PhD	1998	2005	University of Glasgow: Trinity College	4 Copland Place, Glasgow G51 2RS / douggay@mac.com	0141 330 2073 / 07971 321452

Name	Year	Year	Role	Address / Email	Telephone
Herbert, Claire DCS	2019		Chaplain, Lodging House Mission, Glasgow	35 East Campbell Street, Glasgow G51 5DT CHerbert@churchofscotland.org.uk	0141 552 0285
Johnston, Mark G. BSc BD DMin	1998	2020	Tutor in Pastoral Studies, Trinity College, University of Glasgow	4 Professors' Square, Glasgow G12 8QQ mark.johnston.2@glasgow.ac.uk	0141 330 6526
Kelly, Carolyn PhD	2015	2020	Chaplain, University of Glasgow	West Quadrangle, University Avenue, Glasgow G12 8QQ chaplaincy@glasgow.ac.uk	0141 331 4160
Love, Joanna R. (Ms) BSc DCS	1992	2009	Iona Community: Wild Goose Resource Group	92 Everard Drive, Glasgow G21 1XQ jo@wildgoose.scot	(Office) 0141 429 7281
McDougall, Hilary N. (Mrs) MA PGCE BD	2004	2013	Depute Clerk & Congregational Facilitator: Presbytery of Glasgow	Presbytery Office, 260 Bath Street, Glasgow G2 4JP HMcdougall@churchofscotland.org.uk	0141 332 6606
McPake, John L. BA BD PhD	1987	2017	Ecumenical Officer, Church of Scotland	121 George Street, Edinburgh EH2 4YN JMcPake@churchofscotland.org.uk	0131 225 5722
Shackleton, Scott J.S. KCVS BA BD PhD	1993	2021	Head of Faith Action Programme	121 George Street, Edinburgh EH2 4YN SShackleton@churchofscotland.org.uk	0131 225 5722

C. Retaining: members of Presbytery

Name	Year	Year	Role	Address / Email	Telephone
Beaton, Margaret S. (Miss) DCS	1989	2015	(Deacon: Leader, Church House, Bridgeton)	64 Gardenside Grove, Carmyle, Glasgow G32 8EZ margaretbeaton54@hotmail.com	0141 646 2297
Bell, John L. MA BD FRSCM DUniv	1978	2022	(Iona Community: Wild Goose Resource Group)	148 West Princes Street, Glasgow G4 9DA jlb31@tiscali.co.uk	07796 642382 0141 387 7628
Birch, James PgDip FRSA FIOC	2001	2007	(Auxiliary Minister, Cambuslang: St Andrew's)	1 Kirkhill Grove, Cambuslang, Glasgow G72 8EH	0141 583 1722
Black, Ian W. MA BD	1976	2013	(Grangemouth: Zetland)	Flat 1R, 2 Carrickvale Court, Carrickstone, Cumbernauld, Glasgow G68 0LA iwblack@hotmail.com	01236 453370
Black, William B. MA BD	1970	2011	(Stornoway: High)	33 Tankerland Road, Glasgow G44 4EN revwillieblack@gmail.com	0141 637 4717
Blount, A. Sheila (Mrs) BD BA	1978	2010	(Cupar: St John's and Dairsie United)	28 Alcaig Road, Mosspark, Glasgow G52 1NH asheilablount@gmail.com	0141 419 0746
Campbell, John LTh BA MA BSc	1973	2009	(Caldwell)	96 Boghead Road, Lenzie, Glasgow G66 4EN johncampbell.lenzie@gmail.com	0141 776 0874
Cartledge, Graham R.G. MA BD STM	1977	2015	(Glasgow: Eastwood)	5 Briar Grove, Newlands, Glasgow G43 2TG	0141 637 3228
Christie, Helen F. (Mrs) BD	1998	2015	(Haggs)	4B Glencairn Road, Cumbernauld G67 2EN andychristie747@yahoo.com	01236 611583
Clark, Douglas W. LTh	1993	2015	(Lenzie: Old)	2 Poplar Drive, Lenzie, Glasgow G66 4DN douglaswclark@hotmail.com	0141 776 1298
Cunningham, Alexander MA BD	1961	2002	(Presbytery Clerk: Glasgow)	18 Lady Jane Gate, Bothwell, Glasgow G71 8BW	01698 811051
Cuthbertson, Malcolm BA BD	1984	2023	(Rutherglen: West and Wardlawhill)	375 New Edinburgh Road, Bellshill ML4 3HH	07864 820612
Drummond, John W. MA BD	1971	2011	(Rutherglen: West and Wardlawhill)	25 Kingsburn Drive, Rutherglen, Glasgow G73 2AN	0141 571 6002
Duff, T. Malcolm F. MA BD MTh	1985	2009	(Glasgow: Queen's Park)	54 Hawkhead Road, Paisley PA1 3NB	0141 570 0614 07846 926584

Dutch, Morris M. BD BA Dip BTI	1998	2013	(Costa del Sol)	41 Baronald Drive, Glasgow G12 OHN; mmdutch@yahoo.co.uk	0141 357 2286
Easton, David J.C. MA BD	1965	2005	(Burnside Blairbeth)	6 Peveril Court, Burnside, Glasgow G73 4RE; deaston@btinternet.com	0141 634 9775
Farrington, Alexandra L Th	2003	2015	(Campsie)	'Glenburn', High Banton, Kilsyth G65 0RA; revsfarrington@aol.co.uk	01236 824516
Ferguson, James B. L Th.	1972	2002	(Lenzie: Union)	3 Bridgeway Place, Kirkintilloch, Glasgow G66 3HW	0141 588 5868
Finnie, Bill H. BA DipSW CertCRS	2015	2022	(Ordained Local Minister, Kirkintilloch: Hillhead)	27 Hallside Crescent, Cambuslang, Glasgow G72 7DY; BFinnie@churchofscotland.org.uk	07518 357138
Fraser, Alexander M. BD DipMin	1985	2019	(Glasgow: Knightswood St Margaret's)		
Fulton, R. Stuart M. BA BD PGCE	1991	2022	(Glasgow: Newlands South)	2 Rothesay Terrace, Edinburgh EH3 7RY; SFulton@churchofscotland.org.uk	07850 066104
Galbraith, Neil W. BD CertMin	1987	2023	(Glasgow: Cathcart Old)	20 Limdale Oval, Glasgow G45 9QT	0141 579 9948
Galloway, Ian F. BA BD	1977	2021	(Glasgow: Gorbals)	39 McConnell Road, Lochwinnoch PA12 4EB; IGalloway@churchofscotland.org.uk	07753 686603
Haley, Derek BD DPS	1960	1999	(Chaplain: Gartnavel Royal Hospital)	9 Kinnaird Crescent, Bearsden, Glasgow G61 2BN	0141 942 9281
Hope, Evelyn P. (Miss) BA BD	1990	1998	(Wishaw: Thornlie)	Flat 0/1, 48 Moss Side Road, Glasgow G41 3UA	0141 649 1522
Hudson, Howard R. MA BD	1982	2021	(Glasgow: Bridgeton St Francis in the East)	4 Larch Square, Cambuslang, Glasgow G72 7BQ	
Hughes, Helen (Miss) DCS	1977	2008	(Deacon, Glasgow: Springburn)	2/2, 43 Burnbank Terrace, Glasgow G20 6UQ; helhug35@gmail.com	0141 333 9459 / 07752 604817
Hunter, Alastair G. BSc MSc BD	1976	2009	(University of Glasgow: Biblical Studies)		
Johnson, C. Ian W. MA BD	1997	2022	(Dumbarton: Riverside with Dumbarton: St Andrew's with Dumbarton: West)	6 Whittingehame Court, 1350 Great Western Road, Glasgow G12 0BG; ian.ciw.johnson@btinternet.com	07484 256472
Johnston, Robert W.M. MA BD STM MThPh	1964	1999	(Glasgow: Temple Anniesland)	Flat 0/2, 68 Strathblane Gardens, Glasgow G13 1BX	0141 230 7287
Johnstone, H. Martin J. MA BD MTh PhD	1989	2020	(Secretary: Church and Society Council)	3/1, 952 Pollokshaws Road, Glasgow G41 2ET; MJohnstone@churchofscotland.org.uk	0141 636 5819
Kavanagh, Joseph A. BD DipPTh MTh MTh	1992	2023	(Mearns)	JKavanagh@churchofscotland.org.uk	
Lunan, David W. MA BD DLitt DD	1970	2009	(Presbytery Clerk: Glasgow)	30 Mill Road, Banton, Glasgow G65 0RD; DLunan@churchofscotland.org.uk	01236 824110
Lyall, Ann DCS	1980	2022	(Deacon, Glasgow: Baillieston Mure Memorial with St Andrew's; Glasgow: Govan and Linthouse)	117 Barlia Drive, Glasgow G45 0AY; ALyall@churchofscotland.org.uk	0141 631 3643
MacDonald, Anne (Miss) BA DCS	1980	2023	(Chaplain, Glasgow Royal Infirmary)	annie.anne502@gmail.com	07976 786174
MacDonald, Kenneth D. MA BA	2001	2006	(Auxiliary Minister, Glasgow: Sandyford Henderson Memorial; Glasgow: Yoker)	5 Henderland Road, Bearsden, Glasgow G61 1AH	0141 943 1103
MacFadyen, Anne M. (Mrs) BSc BD FSAScot	1995	2003	(Auxiliary Minister, Glasgow: Pollokshaws)	295 Mearns Road, Glasgow G77 5LT	0141 639 3605
Mackenzie, Gordon R. BScAgr BD	1977	2014	(Chapelhall)	16 Crowhill Road, Bishopbriggs, Glasgow G64 1QY; rev.g.mackenzie@btopenworld.com	0141 772 6052
Mackinnon, Campbell BSc BD	1982	2019	(Glasgow: Balshagray Victoria Park)	campbellbvp@live.com	
MacKinnon, Charles M. BD CertMin	1989	2009	(Kilsyth: Anderson)	36 Hilton Terrace, Bishopbriggs, Glasgow G64 3HB; cm.ccmackinnon@gmail.com	0141 772 3811

Macleod, Donald BD LRAM DRSAM	1987	2008	(Blairgowrie)	9 Millersneuk Avenue, Lenzie G66 5HJ / donmac2@sky.com	0141 776 6235
MacQuarrie, Stuart D. JP BD BSc MBA MPhil	1984	2020	(Chaplain: University of Glasgow)		
MacRae, Elaine H. (Mrs) BD	1985	2021	(Glasgow: St Enoch's Hogganfield)	21 Lakeview Grove, Stepps G33 1FU / EMacRae@churchofscotland.org.uk	07834 269487
MacRae, Gordon BD MTh	1985	2023	(Stepps)	21 Lakeview Grove, Stepps G33 1FU / GMacRae@churchofscotland.org.uk	07703 163206
Manastireanu, Daniel BA MTh AdvDipTCouns	2010	2020	(Glasgow: St Paul's)	61 Vancouver Walk, Glasgow G40 4TP / DManastireanu@churchofscotland.org.uk	
Maxwell, David	2014	2020	(Ordained Local Minister, Cambuslang)	248 Old Castle Road, Glasgow G44 5EZ / DMaxwell@churchofscotland.org.uk	0141 569 6379 / 07561 427802 / 07846 168170
McClements, Louise J.E. RGN BD	2008	2023	(Lenzie: Old)	21 Gray Buchanan Court, Polmont, Falkirk FK2 0XR / LMcClements@churchofscotland.org.uk	
McLachlan, David N. BD	1985	2021	(Glasgow: Langside)	7A Glenlyon Place, Glasgow G73 5PL	0141 482 9704
McLachlan, Eric BD MTh CPS	1978	2005	(Glasgow: Cardonald)	16 Kinpurnie Road, Paisley PA1 3HH / eric.janis@btinternet.com	0141 810 5789
McLachlan, T. Alastair BSc	1972	2009	(Craignish with Kilbrandon and Kilchattan with Kilninver and Kilmelford)	9 Alder Road, Milton of Campsie, Glasgow G66 8HH / talastair@btinternet.com	01360 319861
McLaren, D. Muir BA BD MTh PhD	1971	2001	(Glasgow: Mosspark)	House 44, 145 Shawhill Road, Glasgow G43 1SX / muir44@yahoo.co.uk	07931 155779
McLellan, Margaret DCS	1986	2018	(Deacon, Glasgow: Merrylea)	18 Broom Road East, Newton Mearns, Glasgow G77 5SD / margaretdmclellan@outlook.com	0141 639 6853
McWilliam, Alan BD MTh	1993	2019	(Glasgow: Whiteinch)	1 Springbank Gardens, Glasgow G31 4QD / AMcWilliam@churchofscotland.org.uk	
Miller, John D. BA BD STM DD	1971	2007	(Glasgow: Castlemilk East)	98 Kirkcaldy Road, Glasgow G41 4LD / rev.john.miller@btinternet.com	0141 423 0221
Moffat, Thomas BSc BD	1976	2008	(Culross and Torryburn)	Flat 8/1, 8 Cranston Street, Glasgow G3 8GG / tom@gallus.org.uk	0141 248 1886
Nelson, Thomas BSc BD	1992	2002	(Netherlee)	11a Crosshill Drive, Rutherglen, Glasgow G73 3QU	0141 534 7834
Nicholson, David DCS	1994	2020	(Deacon, Cumbernauld: Kildrum with Cumbernauld: St Mungo's)	2D Doonside, Kildrum, Cumbernauld, Glasgow G67 2HX	01236 732260
Nicol, Douglas M. CA BD	1987	2021	(Glasgow: St Christopher's Priesthill and Nitshill)	19 Rockmount Avenue, Thornliebank, Glasgow G46 7BU / DNicol@churchofscotland.org.uk	0141 569 7848
Ninian, Esther J. (Miss) MA BD DipLib	1993	2015	(Newton Mearns)	21 St Ronan's Drive, Burnside, Rutherglen G73 3SR / estherninian5914@btinternet.com	
Paciti, Stephen A. MA	1963	2003	(Black Mount with Culter with Libberton and Quothquan)	157 Nithsdale Road, Glasgow G41 5RD	0141 647 9720 / 0141 423 5792
Pearson, Wilma (Mrs) BD	2004	2018	(Associate, Glasgow: Cathcart Trinity)	90 Newlands Road, Glasgow G43 2JR / WPearson@churchofscotland.org.uk	0141 632 2491
Peat, Derek A. BA BD MTh	2013	2022	(Strategy Officer: Presbytery of Glasgow)	DPeat@churchofscotland.org.uk	

Pollock, Thomas L. BA BD MTh FSAScot JP	1982	2021	(Glasgow: Sherbrooke Mosspark)	27 Dorchester Court, Monmouth Avenue, Glasgow G12 0BT / TPollock@churchofscotland.org.uk	
Purves, John S. LLB BD	1983	2022	(Glasgow: Drumchapel St Andrew's)	28 Cloberhill Road, Glasgow G13 2JL / johnpurves278@btinternet.com	0141 286 0917
Reid, Iain M.A. BD CQSW DipSW	1990	2017	(Paisley: Glenburn)	16 Walker Court, Glasgow G16 6QP / ireid@churchofscotland.org.uk	0141 577 1200
Ross, Donald M. MA	1953	1993	(Industrial Mission Organiser)	14 Cartsbridge Road, Busby, Glasgow G76 8DH	
Ross, Joan BSc BD PhD	1999	2022	(Glasgow: Carntyne)	4 Moncrieff Gardens, Lenzie G66 4NN / rossjoan261@gmail.com	0141 644 2220
Spencer, John MA BD	1962	2001	(Dumfries: Lincluden with Holywood)	10 Kinkell Gardens, Kirkintilloch, Glasgow G66 2HJ	0141 777 8935
Stewart, Norma D. (Miss) MA MEd BD MTh	1977	2000	(Glasgow: Strathbungo Queen's Park)	127 Nether Auldhouse Road, Glasgow G43 2YS	0141 637 6956
Thomson, Andrew BA	1976	2007	(Airdrie: Broomknoll)	3 Laurel Wynd, Drumsagard Village, Cambuslang, Glasgow G72 7BH / AThomson@churchofscotland.org.uk	0141 641 2936 / 07772 502774
Tuton, Robert M. MA	1957	1995	(Glasgow: Shettleston Old)	6 Holmwood Gardens, Uddingston, Glasgow G71 7BH	01698 321108
White, C. Peter BVMS BD	1974	2011	(Glasgow: Sandyford Henderson Memorial)	2 Hawthorn Place, Torrance, Glasgow G64 4EA / revcpw@gmail.com	01360 622680
White, David M. BA BD DMin	1988	2016	(Kirkintilloch: St Columba's)	9 Lapwing Avenue, Lenzie, Glasgow G66 3DJ / drdavidmwhite@btinternet.com	0141 578 4357
Whyte, James BD	1981	2011	(Fairlie)	32 Torburn Avenue, Giffnock, Glasgow G46 7RB / jameswhyte89@btinternet.com	0141 620 3043
Wilson, Phyllis M. (Mrs) DipCom DipRE CertMin	1985	2006	(Motherwell: South Dalziel)	Glasgow / thomas.wilson38@btinternet.com	
Younger, Adah (Mrs) BD LLB	1978	2004	(Glasgow: Dennistoun Central)	Flat 2/3, 53 Barloch Street, Glasgow G22 5BX	07947 580924

D. In other appointments: not members of Presbytery
Nil

E. Retaining: not members of Presbytery

Anderson, Susan M. (Mrs) BD GRSM ARMCM	1997	2014	(Kilmarnock: St John's Onthank)	32 Murrayfield, Bishopbriggs, Glasgow G64 3DS / susanbbriggs32@gmail.com	0141 772 6338
Blount, Graham K. LLB BD PhD	1976	2017	(Presbytery Clerk: Glasgow)	28 Alcaig Road, Mosspark, Glasgow G52 1NH / Graham.Blount@churchofscotland.org.uk	0141 419 0746
Bradley, Andrew W. BD	1975	2007	(Paisley: Lylesland)	Flat 1/1, 38 Cairnhill View, Bearsden, Glasgow G61 1RP / andrewwbradley@hotmail.com	0141 931 5344
Duff, Valerie J. (Miss) DMin	1993	2021	(Glasgow: Shawlands Trinity)	Flat 25, 2 Melrose Avenue, Rutherglen, Glasgow G73 3BU	
McNaughton, Janette (Miss) DCS	1982	2007	(Deacon, Cumbernauld: Condorrat)	4 Clelland Avenue, Moodiesburn, Glasgow G69 0GB	01236 870180
Murray, George M. LTh	1995	2011	(Glasgow: St Margaret's Tollcross Park)	6 Mayfield, Lesmahagow ML11 0FH / george.murray7@gmail.com	01555 895216
Saunders, Keith BD MSc CertPS	1983	2015	(Chaplain, Glasgow Western Infirmary)	1/2, 10 Rutherford Drive, Lenzie G66 3US / revchap53@hotmail.com	0141 558 4338

Name	Ord	Ind	Charge	Address	Telephone
Shanks, Norman J. MA BD DD	1983	2007	(Glasgow: Govan Old)	1 Marchmont Terrace, Glasgow G12 9LT rufuski@btinternet.com	0141 339 4421
Spiers, John M. LTh MTh	1972	2004	(Giffnock: Orchardhill)	58 Woodlands Road, Thornliebank, Glasgow G46 7JQ j.spiers@icloud.com	0141 638 0632

F. Inactive: not members of Presbytery

Name	Ord	Ind	Charge	Address	Telephone
Campbell, A. Iain MA DipEd	1961	1997	(Bushy)	430 Clarkston Road, Glasgow G44 3QF iaingillian@talktalk.net	0141 637 7460
Cherry, Alastair J. BD BA FPLD	1982	2009	(Glasgow: Penilee St Andrew)	8 Coruisk Drive, Clarkston, Glasgow G76 7NG ajcherry133@gmail.com	07483 221141
Cullen, William T. BA LTh	1984	1996	(Kilmarnock: St John's Onthank)	6 Laurel Wynd, Cambuslang, Glasgow G72 7BA	0141 641 4337
Cunningham, J.S.A. MA BD BLitt PhD	1992	2000	(Glasgow: Barlanark Greyfriars)	Kirkland, 5 Inveresk Place, Coatbridge ML5 2DA	01236 421541
Fleming, Alexander F. MA BD	1966	1995	(Strathblane)	11 Bankwood Drive, Kilsyth, Glaagow G65 0GZ alex@koror99.com	01236 820915
Galloway, Kathy J. (Mrs) BD DD DipPS	1977	2020	(Co-Leader, Iona Community)	20 Hamilton Park Avenue, Glasgow G12 8UU kathygalloway200@btinternet.com	0141 357 4079
Grant, David I.M. MA BD	1969	2003	(Dalry: Trinity)	8 Mossbank Drive, Glasgow G33 1LS	0141 770 7186
Gray, Christine M. (Mrs) DCS	1969	2003	(Deacon, Glasgow: Carnwadric)	11 Woodside Avenue, Thornliebank, Glasgow G46 7HR	0141 571 1008
Green, Alex H. MA BD	1986	2010	(Strathblane)	44 Laburnum Drive, Milton of Campsie, Glasgow G66 8HY lesvert@btinternet.com	01360 313001
Harvey, W. John BA BD DD	1965	2002	(Interim Minister, Edinburgh: Corstorphine Craigsbank)	501A Shields Road, Glasgow G41 2RF jonmol@phonecoop.coop	0141 429 3774 07709 651335
Kerr, Hugh F. MA BD	1968	2006	(Aberdeen: Ruthrieston South)	33 Strathmore Court, 20 Abbey Drive, Glasgow G14 9JX	0141 959 8143
Lindsay, W. Douglas BD CPS	1978	2004	(Eaglesham)	3 Drummond Place, Calderwood, East Kilbride, Glasgow G74 3AD	01355 234169
Macdonald, William J. BD CPS	1976	2002	(Board of National Mission: New Charge Development)	21 Muirfield Court, 20 Muirend Road, Glasgow G44 3QP williejohnmac@gmail.com	0141 384 3014
MacKay, Alan H. BD DipPS	1974	2010	(Glasgow: Mosspark)	Flat 1/1, 18 Newburgh Street, Glasgow G43 2XR alanhmackay@aol.com	07910 167690
McKenzie, Mary O. CPS	1976	1996	(Edinburgh: Richmond Craigmillar)	4 Dunellan Avenue, Moodiesburn, Glasgow G69 0GB maemck@btinternet.com	01236 870180
McLachlan, Fergus C. BD	1982	1988	(Dunbarney with Forgandenny)	46 Queen Square, Glasgow G41 2AZ whitegoldfm@gmail.com	07544 721032
Miller, Elsie M. (Miss) DCS	1974	2001	(Deacon, Cumbernauld: St Mungo's)	30 Swinton Avenue, Rowanbank, Baillieston, Glasgow G69 6JR	0141 771 0857
Raeburn, Alan C. MA BD	1971	2010	(Glasgow: Battlefield East)	3 Orchard Gardens, Strathaven ML10 6UN acraeburn@hotmail.com	01357 522924
Reid, Janette G. BD CertMin	1991	2009	(Glasgow: St Andrew's East)	c/o Presbytery Office, 260 Bath Street, Glasgow G2 4JP	0141 424 0493
Turner, Angus BD	1976	1998	(Industrial Chaplain)	46 Keir Street, Glasgow G41 2LA	

G. Readers (active)

Allan, Phillip — 34 Muirhead Way, Bishopbriggs, Glasgow G64 1YG — hampdenhorror@gmail.com — 07954 497930

Fullarton, Andrew — Flat 2/2, 2263 Paisley Road West, Glasgow G52 3QA — drewf225@gmail.com — 0141 883 9518

Kelly, George — 25 Westerton, Lennoxtown G66 7LR — geojkelly@btinternet.com — 01360 311739

Kilpatrick, Joan (Mrs) — 39 Brent Road, Regent's Park, Glasgow G46 8JG — je-kilpatrick@sky.com — 0141 621 1809

McFarlane, Robert — 25 Avenel Road, Glasgow G13 2PB — robertmcfrin@yahoo.co.uk — 0141 954 5540

McInally, Gordon — 10 Melville Gardens, Bishopbriggs, Glasgow G64 3DF — gmcinally@sky.com — 0141 563 2685

Millar, Kathleen (Mrs) — 18 Greenwood Grove West, Stewarton Road, Glasgow G77 6ZF — 07793 203045

Morrison, Graham — 1/1, 40 Gardner Street, Glasgow G11 5DF — 0141 579 4772

Morrison, Katie (Miss) — 3b Lennox Court, 16 Stockiemuir Avenue, Bearsden G61 3JL — katiemorrison2003@hotmail.co.uk — 0141 942 3024

Nicolson, John C. — 2 Lindsaybeg Court, Chryston, Glasgow G69 9DD — john.c.nicolson@btinternet.com — 07852 373840

Robertson, Lynne M. (Mrs) MA MEd — 2 Greenhill, Bishopbriggs, Glasgow G64 1LE — emrobertsonmed@btinternet.com — 0141 779 2447 / 0141 772 1323

Smith, Ann — 52 Robslee Road, Thornliebank, Glasgow G46 7BX — 07720 053981

Stead, May (Mrs) — 9A Carrick Drive, Mount Vernon, Glasgow G32 0RW — maystead@hotmail.co.uk — 0141 621 0638

Struthers, Ivar — 7 McVean Place, Longcroft, Bonnybridge FK4 1QZ — ivar.struthers@btinternet.com — 07917 785109 / 01324 841145

Tindall, Mararget (Mrs) — 23 Ashcroft Avenue, Lennoxtown, Glasgow G65 7EN — margarettindall@aol.com — 01360 310911

H. Ministries Development Staff

Black, Karen — Glasgow: Garthamlock and Craigend – Family and Community Worker — KBlack@churchofscotland.org.uk

Boland, Susan (Mrs) DipHE(Theol) — Cumbernauld: Abronhill and Cumbernauld: Condorrat – Family Development Worker — SBoland@churchofscotland.org.uk

Cameron, Lisa — Glasgow: Castlemilk – Development Worker — LCameron@churchofscotland.org.uk

Carroll, Helen — Glasgow: Springburn – Church and Community Development Worker — HCarroll@churchofscotland.org.uk

Cathcart, John Paul DCS — Presbytery – Vacant Charge Enabler — John.Cathcart@churchofscotland.org.uk

Cooke, Marie (Dr) — Presbytery – MDS Ministry Support Officer — MCooke@churchofscotland.org.uk

Cuthbertson, Valerie S. (Miss) DCS — Cumbernauld: Old – Deacon — VCuthbertson@churchofscotland.org.uk

Denniston, David W. (Rev) BD DipMin — Presbytery – Post Probation Support Co-ordinator — David.Denniston@churchofscotland.org.uk

Gargrave, Mary S. (Mrs) DCS — Glasgow: Carnwadric – Deacon — Mary.Gargrave@churchofscotland.org.uk

Goodwin, Jamie — Glasgow: Govan and Linthouse – Arts and Worship Development Worker — JGoodwin@churchofscotland.org.uk

Graham, Susan — Glasgow: Sherbrooke Mosspark – Church and Community Outreach Worker — SGraham@churchofscotland.org.uk

Hamilton, James DCS — Glasgow: Maryhill Ruchill – Deacon — James.Hamilton@churchofscotland.org.uk

Hamilton, Karen (Mrs) DCS — Cambuslang – Deacon — KHamilton@churchofscotland.org.uk

Herbert, Claire BD DCS — Lodging House Mission, Glasgow – Chaplain — CHerbert@churchofscotland.org.uk

Howie, Lamont — Glasgow: Drumchapel St Mark's – Community Outreach Worker — LHowie@churchofscotland.org.uk

Hyndman, Graham — Church House, Bridgeton – Youth Worker — GHyndman@churchofscotland.org.uk

Johnstone, Susan — Glasgow: Castlemilk – Community Development Worker — SJohnstone@churchofscotland.org.uk

Macdonald-Haak, Aileen D. — Glasgow: Carntyne – Development Worker, Older People — AMacdonald-Haak@churchofscotland.org.uk

Mackay, Shona BA MSc — Presbytery – Strategy Officer — Shona.Mackay@churchofscotland.org.uk

McDougall, Hilary N. (Rev) MA PGCE BD — Presbytery – Depute Clerk and Congregational Facilitator — HMcDougall@churchofscotland.org.uk

McKinlay, Naomi — Glasgow: Ruchazie – Congregational Leader — NMcKinlay@churchofscotland.org.uk

McMahon, Deborah	Glasgow: Easterhouse – Children's and Development Worker Team Leader	DMcMahon@churchofscotland.org.uk
McWilliam, David	Glasgow: Ruchazie – Project Support Worker	DMcWilliam@churchofscotland.org.uk
Milligan, Catriona	Glasgow: Gorbals – Community Development Worker	CMilligan@churchofscotland.org.uk
Morrison, Iain J.	Glasgow: Colston Milton – Community Arts Worker	IMorrison@churchofscotland.org.uk
Morrow, Angela	Glasgow: Drumchapel St Andrew's – Parish Assistant	AMorrow@churchofscotland.org.uk
Robertson, Douglas J.	Glasgow: Shettleston New – Discipleship Facilitator	DJRobertson@churchofscotland.org.uk
Thomas, Jay MA BA	Glasgow: St James' (Pollok) – Youth and Children's Worker	JThomas@churchofscotland.org.uk
Thorp, Heather	Presbytery – Pioneering and Planting Co-ordinator	HThorp@churchofscotland.org.uk
Usher, Eileen	Glasgow: Garthamlock and Craigend, and Ruchazie Parish Grouping – Family Worker	EUsher@churchofscotland.org.uk
Wilson, Marie	Netherlee and Stamperland – Pastoral Assistant	Marie.Wilson@churchofscotland.org.uk
Young, Neil J.	Glasgow: St Paul's – Youth Team Leader	NYoung@churchofscotland.org.uk

ADDRESSES

Bishopbriggs		
Kenmure		Viewfield Road, Bishopbriggs
Springfield Cambridge		The Leys, off Springfield Road
Broom		Mearns Road, Newton Mearns
Burnside Blairbeth		Church Avenue, Burnside / Kirkriggs Avenue, Blairbeth
Busby		Church Road, Busby
Cadder		Cadder Road, Bishopbriggs
Cambuslang		
Flemington Hallside		Armott Way / Hutchinson Place
Campsie		Main Street, Lennoxtown
Chryston		Main Street, Chryston
Cumbernauld		
Abronhill		Larch Road
Condorrat		Main Road
Kildrum and St Mungo's		St Mungo's Road
Old		Baronhill
Eaglesham		Montgomery Street, Eaglesham
Fernhill and Cathkin		Neilvaig Drive
Gartcosh		113 Lochend Road, Gartcosh
Giffnock		
Orchardhill		Church Road
South		Eastwood Toll
The Park		Ravenscliffe Drive

Glenboig		Main Street, Glenboig
Greenbank		Eaglesham Road, Clarkston
Kilsyth		
Anderson		Kingston Road, Kilsyth
Burns and Old		Church Street, Kilsyth
Kirkintilloch		
St Columba's Hillhead		Newdyke Road and Waterside Road nr Auld Aisle Road
St David's Mem Pk		Alexandra Street
St Mary's		Cowgate
Lenzie		
Old		Kirkintilloch Road x Gamgaber Ave
Union		65 Kirkintilloch Road
Maxwell		
Mearns Castle		Waterfoot Road
Mearns		Mearns Road, Newton Mearns
Milton of Campsie		Locheil Drive, Milton of Campsie
Moodiesburn		20 Blackwoods Crescent, Moodiesburn
Netherlee and Stamperland		Ormonde Drive x Ormonde Avenue
Newton Mearns		Ayr Road, Newton Mearns
Rutherglen		
Old		Main Street at Queen Street
Stonelaw		Stonelaw Road x Dryburgh Avenue

West and Wardlawhill	3 Western Avenue
Stepps	Whitehill Avenue
Thornliebank	61 Spiersbridge Road
Torrance	School Road, Torrance
Williamwood	4 Vardar Avenue, Clarkston
Glasgow	
Baillieston	
Mure Memorial	Maxwell Drive, Garrowhill
St Andrew's	Bredisholm Road
Barlanark Greyfriars	Edinburgh Rd x Hallhill Rd (365)
Blawarthill	Millbrix Avenue
Bridgeton St Francis in the East	26 Queen Mary Street
Broomhill Hyndland	64–66 Randolph Rd (x Marlborough Ave)
Calton Parkhead	122 Helenvale Street
Cardonald	2155 Paisley Road West
Carmunnock	Kirk Road, Carmunnock
Carmyle	155 Carmyle Avenue
Carntyne and Cranhill	358 Carntynehall Road
Carnwadric	556 Boydstone Road, Thornliebank
Castlemilk	1 Dougrie Road

Cathcart Old	119 Carmunnock Road
Trinity	90 Clarkston Road
Cathedral	Cathedral Square, 2 Castle Street
Causeway, Tollcross	1134 Tollcross Road
Clincarthill	1216 Cathcart Road
Colston Milton	Egilsay Crescent
Colston Wellpark	1378 Springburn Road
Croftfoot	Croftpark Ave x Crofthill Road
Dennistoun New	9 Armadale Street
Drumchapel St Andrew's	153 Garscadden Road
St Mark's	281 Kinfauns Drive
Easterhouse	Boyndie Street
Eastwood	Mansewood Road
Gairbraid	1517 Maryhill Road
Gallowgate	Calton Parkhead halls
	122 Helenvale Street
Garthamlock and Craigend	46 Porchester Street
Gorbals	1 Errol Gardens
Govan and Linthouse	Govan Cross
Hillington Park	24 Berryknowes Road
Ibrox	Carillon Road x Clifford Street
Jordanhill	28 Woodend Drive (x Munro Road)

Kelvinbridge	Belmont Street at Belmont Bridge
Kelvinside Hillhead	Observatory Road
Kenmuir Mount Vernon	2405 London Road, Mount Vernon
King's Park	242 Castlemilk Road
Kinning Park	Eaglesham Place
Knightswood Anniesland Trinity	2000 Great Western Road
	869 Crow Road
Langside	167–169 Ledard Road (x Lochleven Road)
Maryhill Ruchill	1990 Maryhill Road
Merrylea	78 Merrylee Road
Newlands South	Riverside Road x Langside Drive
Partick Trinity	20 Lawrence Street x Elie Street
Partick Victoria Park	259 Dumbarton Road
Pollokshaws	223 Shawbridge Street
Pollokshields	Albert Drive x Shields Road
Possilpark	124 Saracen Street
Queen's Park Govanhill	170 Queen's Drive
Robroyston	34 Saughs Road
Ruchazie	4 Elibank Street (x Milncroft Road)
St Andrew and St Nicholas	224 Hartlaw Crescent
St Andrew's East	681 Alexandra Parade
St Andrew's West	260 Bath Street
St Christopher's Priesthill	100 Priesthill Rd (x Muirshiel Cr)

and Nitshill	at Blawarthill Church
St Columba	66 Boreland Drive (nr Lincoln Avenue)
St David's Knightswood	860 Cumbernauld Road
St Enoch's Hogganfield	163 Buchanan Street
St George's Tron	Lyoncross Road x Byrebush Road
St James' (Pollok)	22 Beaconsfield Road
St John's Renfield	30 Langdale St (x Greenrig St)
St Paul's	70 Fountainwell Road
St Rollox	
Sandyford Henderson Memorial	Kelvinhaugh Street at Argyle Street
Sandyhills	28 Baillieston Rd nr Sandyhills Rd
Scotstoun	Earlbank Ave x Ormiston Ave
Shawlands Trinity	Shawlands Cross (1114 Pollokshaws Road)
Sherbrooke Mosspark	Nithsdale Rd x Sherbrooke Avenue
Shettleston New	679 Old Shettleston Road
Springburn	180 Springburn Way
Toryglen	Glenmore Ave nr Prospecthill Road
Trinity Possil and Henry Drummond	2 Crowhill Street (x Broadholm Street)
Tron St Mary's	128 Red Road
Wallacewell	57 Northgate Rd, Balornock
Wellington	University Ave x Southpark Ave
Whiteinch	1a Northinch Court
Yoker	10 Hawick Street

(6) FORTH VALLEY AND CLYDESDALE (F W)

Meets in 2023 on the last Saturday of November and in 2024 on the first Saturday of March, June and September at Motherwell: Dalziel St Andrew's Church.

Presbytery Office: Rex House, 103 Bothwell Road, Hamilton ML3 0DW
fvandc@churchofscotland.org.uk — **01698 285672**

Clerk:	REV. JULIE M. RENNICK BTh c/o The Presbytery Office; jrennick@churchofscotland.org.uk
Depute Clerk:	REV. BRYAN KERR BA BD c/o The Presbytery Office; bkerr@churchofscotland.org.uk — **01698 662537**
Treasurer:	MR DAVID J. WATT BAcc CA CPFA c/o The Presbytery Office; david.j.watt@btinternet.com

1 Airdrie: Cairnlea (F H W) linked with Calderbank (F T)
Peter H. Donald MA PhD BD   1991   2018
31 Victoria Place, Airdrie ML6 9BU
PDonald@churchofscotland.org.uk
Cairnlea: 01236 762101
01236 753159

2 Airdrie: Clarkston (F W)
Hanna I. Rankine BA BD   2018
enquiries@airdrieclarkstonparishchurch.org.uk
66 Wellhall Road, Hamilton ML3 9BY
HRankine@churchofscotland.org.uk
01236 756862

3 Airdrie: High (W) linked with Caldercruix and Longriggend (H)
Ian R.W. McDonald BSc BD PhD   2007
17 Etive Drive, Airdrie ML6 9QL
IMcDonald@churchofscotland.org.uk
High: 01236 779620
01236 760023

4 Airdrie: Jackson (F H W)
Kay Gilchrist (Miss) BD CertMin DipPC   1996   2008
48 Dunrobin Road, Airdrie ML6 8LR
KGilchrist@churchofscotland.org.uk
01236 597649

5 Airdrie: New Monkland (F H W) linked with Greengairs (F W)
Vacant
Session Clerk, Airdrie: New Monkland: Helene Marshall
Session Clerk, Greengairs: Sheena Walker
3 Dykehead Crescent, Airdrie ML6 6PU
helenemarshall@blueyonder.co.uk
sheena.walker4@icloud.com
01236 761723
01236 751945
01236 830347

6 Airdrie: New Wellwynd (W)
Robert A. Hamilton BA BD   1995   2001
72 Inverlochy Road, Airdrie ML6 9DJ
RHamilton@churchofscotland.org.uk
01236 748646
01236 763022

7 Airdrie: St Columba's (F)
Margaret F. Currie BEd BD — 1980 — 1987
52 Kennedy Drive, Airdrie ML6 9AW
MCurrie@churchofscotland.org.uk
01236 763173

8 Airth (F H)
James F. Todd BD CPS — 1984 — 2012
The Manse, Airth, Falkirk FK2 8LS
JTodd@churchofscotland.org.uk
01324 831120

9 Bellshill: Central (F T W)
Kevin M. de Beer BTh — 1995 — 2016
32 Adamson Street, Bellshill ML4 1DT
KdeBeer@churchofscotland.org.uk
01698 841176
07555 265609

10 Bellshill: West (F H W)
Vacant
Session Clerk: Annabel Leitch
16 Croftpark Street, Bellshill ML4 1EY
leitch.a@sky.com
01698 747581
01698 842877
01698 810143

11 Biggar (F H W) linked with Black Mount
Mike D. Fucella BD MTh — 1997 — 2013
biggarkirk09@gmail.com
'Candlemas', 6C Leafield Road, Biggar ML12 6AY
MFucella@churchofscotland.org.uk
01889 229291
01899 229291

12 Black Mount See Biggar

13 Blackbraes and Shieldhill (W) linked with Muiravonside (F W)
Vacant
Interim Moderator: Scott W. Burton
Scott.Burton@churchofscotland.org.uk
01324 341590

14 Blantyre: Livingstone Memorial (F W) linked with Blantyre St Andrew's (F) — 2002 — 2017
Murdo C. Macdonald MA BD
info@livingstonechurch.org.uk
332 Glasgow Road, Blantyre, Glasgow G72 9LQ
Murdo.Macdonald@churchofscotland.org.uk
01698 769699

15 Blantyre: Old (F H T W)
Vacant
Session Clerk: Mary Gallacher
The Manse, Craigmuir Road, High Blantyre, Glasgow G72 9UA
mary.gallacherclerk@yahoo.com
01698 769046
01698 821958

16 Blantyre: St Andrew's See Blantyre: Livingstone Memorial

17 Bo'ness: Old (F H T W)
Amanda J. MacQuarrie MA PGCE MTh — 2014 — 2016
10 Dundas Street, Bo'ness EH51 0DG
A.MacQuarrie@churchofscotland.org.uk
01506 828504

18 Bo'ness: St Andrew's (F W)
Vacant
Interim Moderator: F. Derek Gunn
St Andrew's Manse, 11 Erngath Road, Bo'ness EH51 9DP
RevDerekGunn@hotmail.com
01506 825803
01506 822195
01324 624938

19 Bonnybridge: St Helen's (F H W)
Vacant
Interim Moderator: Ronald Matandakufa
The Manse, 32 Reilly Gardens, High Bonnybridge FK4 2BB
RMatandakufa@churchofscotland.org.uk
01324 874807
01324 337885

20 Bothkennar and Carronshore (W)
Andrew J. Moore   BSc BD   2007
11 Hunter Place, Greenmount Park, Carronshore, Falkirk FK2 8QS
AMoore@churchofscotland.org.uk
01324 570525

21 Bothwell (F H W)
Iain M.T. Majcher   BD   2020
office@bothwellparishchurch.org.uk
Bothwell Parish Church, Main Street, Bothwell, Glasgow G71 8EX
IMajcher@churchofscotland.org.uk
01698 854903
01698 600933

22 Brightons (F H T W)
Scott W. Burton   BA BA   2019
info@brightonschurch.org.uk
77 Wallace Brae Drive, Reddingmuirhead, Falkirk FK2 0FB
Scott.Burton@churchofscotland.org.uk
01324 713855
01324 341590

23 Cairngryffe (F W) linked with Libberton and Quothquan (F H W) linked with Symington (F W) (The Tinto Parishes)
Vacant
Session Clerk, Cairngryffe: Rosmairi J. Galloway (Dr)
Session Clerk, Libberton and Quothquan: Paul J. Dobie

Session Clerk, Symington: Robert Carson
contactus@symingtonkirk.com
16 Abington Road, Symington, Biggar ML12 6JX
pepperknowes@btinternet.com
paul.dobie@hebrides.net

robertdcarson@yahoo.com
01899 309400
07733 446567
01899 308248
07717 847446
01899 309061

24 Calderbank   See Airdrie: Cairnlea
25 Caldercruix and Longriggend   See Airdrie: High

26 Carluke: Kirkton (H W)
Vacant
Session Clerk: Valerie MacSween
office@kirktonchurch.com
9 Station Road, Carluke ML8 5AA
sessionclerk.kirktonchurch@gmail.com
01555 750778
01555 771262

27 Carluke: St Andrew's (H W)
Helen E. Jamieson (Mrs)   BD DipEd   1989
standrewscarluke@btinternet.com
120 Clyde Street, Carluke ML8 5BG
HJamieson@churchofscotland.org.uk
01555 771218

28 Carluke: St John's (F H W)
Elijah O. Obinna BA MTh PhD   2002   2016
18 Old Bridgend, Carluke ML8 4HN
EObinna@churchofscotland.org.uk
01555 751730
01555 752389

29 Carnwath (H) linked with Carstairs (W)
Sumit Harrison BA DipTh BTh   2013   2020
11 Range View, Cleghorn, Carstairs, Lanark ML11 8TF
SHarrison@churchofscotland.org.uk
01555 668868

30 Carriden (H W)
Vacant
David C. Wandrum   1993   2017
(Auxiliary Minister)
The Spires, Foredale Terrace, Carriden, Bo'ness EH51 9LW
5 Cawder View, Carrickstone Meadows, Cumbernauld,
Glasgow G68 0BN
DWandrum@churchofscotland.org.uk
01506 822141
01236 723288

31 Carstairs See Carnwath

32 Chapelhall (F H W) linked with Kirk o' Shotts (F H W)
Vacant
The Manse, Russell Street, Chapelhall, Airdrie ML6 8SG
bettymc1175@btinternet.com
rossdrumduff@gmail.com
01236 763439
01236 765249
07450 275307
Session Clerk, Chapelhall: Betty McLean
Session Clerk, Kirk o' Shotts: Eileen Ross

33 Cleland (F H) linked with Wishaw: St Mark's (F)
Vacant
3 Laburnum Crescent, Wishaw ML2 7EH
craig.mains@yahoo.co.uk
barbaracurtin47@gmail.com
01698 384596
01698 814875
07939 102784
Session Clerk, Cleland: Craig Mains
Session Clerk, Wishaw: St Mark's: Barbara Curtin

34 Coalburn and Lesmahagow (F H W)
Morag V. Garrett (Mrs) BD   2011   2021
candle.church2@gmail.com
9 Elmbank, Lesmahagow ML11 0EA
MGarrett@churchofscotland.org.uk
01555 892425
01555 890460

35 Coatbridge: Blairhill Dundyvan (H W) linked with Coatbridge: Middle (W)
Vacant   **Blairhill Dundyvan: 01236 435198**
1 Nelson Terrace, East Kilbride, Glasgow G74 2EY
myrafraser@hotmail.co.uk
01355 520093
01236 421728
Session Clerk, Blairhill Dundyvan: Myra Fraser

36 Coatbridge: Calder (F H W) linked with Coatbridge: Old Monkland (F W)
Vacant
alisonrobertsonmcgowan@gmail.com
07798 644253
Session Clerk, Old Monkland: Alison McGowan (Mrs)

37 Coatbridge: Middle See Coatbridge: Blairhill Dundyvan

#	Congregation / Minister	Ordained	Address / Email	Phone
38	**Coatbridge: New St Andrew's (W)** Fiona M. Nicolson BA BD CQSW	1996 2005	77 Eglinton Street, Coatbridge ML5 3JF FNicolson@churchofscotland.org.uk	01236 437271
39	**Coatbridge: Old Monkland** See Coatbridge: Calder			
40	**Coatbridge: Townhead (F H)** Ecilo Selemani LTh MTh	1993 2004	The Manse, Crinan Crescent, Coatbridge ML5 2LH ESelemani@churchofscotland.org.uk	01236 702914
41	**Crossford (H) linked with Kirkfieldbank** Steven Reid BAcc CA BD	1989 1997	74 Lanark Road, Crossford, Carluke ML8 5RE SReid@churchofscotland.org.uk	01555 860415
42	**Dalserf (F H)** Vacant Fiona Anderson DipHE BA (Ordained Local Minister; Interim Moderator) Session Clerk: Joan Pollok	2020 2023	Manse Brae, Dalserf, Larkhall ML9 3BN 52 Cooper Crescent, Ferniegair, Hamilton ML3 7FT FAnderson@churchofscotland.org.uk joan.pollok@btinternet.com	01698 882195 07913 153608 07728 337212
43	**Denny: Old (W) linked with Haggs (H W)** Raheel Arif MSc MEd BA	2019	haggschurch1@yahoo.co.uk 57 Singers Place, Dennyloanhead FK4 1FD RArif@churchofscotland.org.uk	01324 819149
44	**Denny: Westpark (F H W)** Kipchumba Too BTh MTh MSc	2017	13 Baxter Crescent, Denny FK6 5EZ KToo@churchofscotland.org.uk	01324 882220
45	**Douglas Valley (F W)** Guardianship of the Presbytery Session Clerk: Andy Robinson		office.tdvc@yahoo.co.uk The Manse, Douglas, Lanark ML11 0RB gavdrewandjoe@aol.com	**01555 850000** 01555 851246
46	**Dunipace (F H W)** Jean W. Gallacher BD CertMin CertTheol DMin	1989	The Manse, 239 Stirling Street, Dunipace, Denny FK6 6QJ JGallacher@churchofscotland.org.uk	01324 824540

47	**East Kilbride: Claremont (F H W)**		office@claremontparishchurch.co.uk	**01355 238088**
	Vacant		17 Deveron Road, East Kilbride, Glasgow G74 2HR	01355 248526
	Session Clerk: Moraig Drumgold		mogie.drumgold@btinternet.com	01355 231815

48	**East Kilbride: Greenhills**			**01355 221746**
	Vacant			01355 224469
	Interim Moderator: Mahboob Masih		MMasih@churchofscotland.org.uk	

49	**East Kilbride: Moncrieff (F H W)**		theoffice@moncrieffparishchurch.co.uk	**01355 223328**
	Sarah L. Ross BD MTh PGDipCS	2004 2020	16 Almond Drive, East Kilbride, Glasgow G74 2HX	01355 715735
			SRoss@churchofscotland.org.uk	

50	**East Kilbride: Mossneuk (F)**		30 Eden Grove, Mossneuk, East Kilbride, Glasgow G75 8XU	**01355 260954**
	Vacant			01355 234196
	George Sneddon BD	2022	26 Dormiston Road, Kirkmuirhill ML11 9SL	07496 023443
	(Assistant Minister)		GSneddon@churchofscotland.org.uk	
	Session Clerk: Mhairi MacLeod		sessionclerk@mossneuk.church	

51	**East Kilbride: Old (H W)**		ekopc.office@btconnect.com	**01355 279004**
	Anne S. Paton BA BD	2001	40 Maxwell Drive, East Kilbride, Glasgow G74 4HJ	01355 220732
			APaton@churchofscotland.org.uk	

52	**East Kilbride: South (F H W)**		7 Clamps Wood, St Leonard's, East Kilbride, Glasgow G74 2HB	01355 902758
	Vacant		CStark@churchofscotland.org.uk	01357 523031
	Interim Moderator: Calum M. Stark			

53	**East Kilbride: Stewartfield (F)**			01555 759993
	Vacant			
	Interim Moderator: Colin Russell		russellc56@gmail.com	

| 54 | **East Kilbride: West (F H W)** | | 4 East Milton Grove, East Kilbride, Glasgow G75 8SN | 01355 224469 |
| | Mahboob Masih BA MDiv MTh | 1999 2008 | MMasih@churchofscotland.org.uk | |

| 55 | **East Kilbride: Westwood (H W)** | | 16 Inglewood Crescent, East Kilbride, Glasgow G75 8QD | **01355 245657** |
| | Kevin Mackenzie BD DipPS | 1989 1996 | Kevin.Mackenzie@churchofscotland.org.uk | 01355 223992 |

56 Falkirk: Bainsford (F H T W)
Vacant
Andrew Sarle BSc BD   2013   1 Valleyview Place, Newcarron Village, Falkirk FK2 7JB
  (Ordained Local Minister)
Interim Moderator: Alastair M. Horne   114 High Station Road, Falkirk FK1 5LN
  ASarle@churchofscotland.org.uk   07743 726013
  AHorne@churchofscotland.org.uk   01324 623308

57 Falkirk: Camelon (F W)   **01324 870011**
Vacant   01324 623631
Interim Moderator: Jean W. Gallacher   30 Cotland Drive, Falkirk FK2 7GE   01324 824450
  JGallacher@churchofscotland.org.uk

58 Falkirk: Grahamston United (F H T W)
Hilda M. Warwick (Methodist Minister)   2017   2022   13 Wallace Place, Falkirk FK2 7EN
  warwickhilda@gmail.com
Anne W. White BA CQSW DipHE   2018   94 Craigleith Road, Grangemouth FK3 0BA   01324 880864
  (Ordained Local Minister)   Anne.White@churchofscotland.org.uk
Grahamston United is a Local Ecumenical Partnership with the Methodist and United Reformed Churches

59 Falkirk: Laurieston (W) linked with Redding and Westquarter (W)
Vacant   11 Polmont Road, Laurieston, Falkirk FK2 9QQ   01324 621196
Interim Moderator: Deborah L. van Welie   DLVanWelie@churchofscotland.org.uk   01324 713427

60 Falkirk: St Andrew's West (H W)
Alastair M. Horne BSc BD   1989   1997   1 Maggiewood's Loan, Falkirk FK1 5SJ   **01324 622091**
  AHorne@churchofscotland.org.uk   01324 623308

61 Falkirk: Trinity (F H T W)   **office@falkirktrinity.org.uk**   **01324 611017**
Robert S.T. Allan LLB DipLP BD   1991   2003   9 Major's Loan, Falkirk FK1 5QF   01324 625124
  RAllan@churchofscotland.org.uk

62 Forth: St Paul's (F H W)
Vacant   22 Lea Rig, Forth, Lanark ML11 8EA   01555 728837
Eckhardt Bosch BTh MTh   2022   The Manse, 9 Kirk Road, Shotts ML7 5ET   07871 959996
  (Assistant Minister)   EBosch@churchofscotland.org.uk
Session Clerk: Margaret Hunter   sclerkforthstpauls@outlook.com

63 Grangemouth: Abbotsgrange (F T W)
Vacant   8 Naismith Court, Grangemouth FK3 9BQ   01324 482109
Interim Moderator: Andrew Sarle   ASarle@churchofscotland.org.uk   07743 726013

64	**Grangemouth: Kirk of the Holy Rood (F W)** Ronald Matandakufa BTh MA	2014	2019	The Manse, Bowhouse Road, Grangemouth FK3 0EX RMatandakufa@churchofscotland.org.uk	01324 337885
65	**Grangemouth: Zetland (F H W)** Alison A. Meikle (Mrs) BD	1999	2014	Ronaldshay Crescent, Grangemouth FK3 9JH AMeikle@churchofscotland.org.uk	01324 336729
66 67	**Greengairs** See Airdrie: New Monkland **Haggs** See Denny: Old				
68	**Hamilton: Cadzow (F H W)** W. John Carswell BS MDiv DPT	1996	2009	contact@cadzowchurch.org.uk 3 Carlisle Road, Hamilton ML3 7BZ JCarswell@churchofscotland.org.uk	**01698 428695** 01698 426682
69	**Hamilton: Gilmour and Whitehill (H W) linked with Hamilton: West (H W)** Vacant Session Clerk, Gilmour: Ann Paul Session Clerk, West: Ian Hindle			annepaul_gandw@gmail.com ianmarilyn.hindle@googlemail.com	West: **01698 284670** 01698 284670 01698 421697 01698 429080
70	**Hamilton: Hillhouse (F W)** Christopher A. Rankine MA MTh PgDE	2016		66 Wellhall Road, Hamilton ML3 9BY CRankine@churchofscotland.org.uk	01698 327579
71	**Hamilton: Old (F H W)** I. Ross Blackman BSc MBA BD CertTh	2015		office@hamiltonold.co.uk 1 Chateau Grove, Hamilton ML3 7DS RBlackman@churchofscotland.org.uk	**01698 281905** 01698 640185
72	**Hamilton: St John's (H W)** Joanne C. Hood (Miss) MA BD	2003	2012	9 Shearer Avenue, Ferniegair, Hamilton ML3 7FX JHood@churchofscotland.org.uk	**01698 283492** 01698 425002
73	**Hamilton: South (F H) linked with Quarter (F)** Andrew (Drew) Gebbie BTh	2021		70 Huntly Gardens, Blantyre G72 0GW DGebbie@churchofscotland.org.uk	South: **01698 281014** 07729 128818
74	**Hamilton: Trinity** Vacant Session Clerk: Catherine Hamilton			69 Buchan Street, Hamilton ML3 8JY cathiehamilton@hotmail.com	**01698 284254** 01698 284919

75 Hamilton: West See Hamilton: Gilmour and Whitehill

76 Holytown (W) linked with New Stevenston: Wrangholm Kirk (W)
Vacant
Session Clerk, Holytown: Stewart McNeil
Session Clerk, New Stevenston: Wrangholm Kirk: Netta Lithgow

The Manse, 260 Edinburgh Road, Holytown, Motherwell ML1 5RU
asmcneil@aol.com
n.lithgow@btinternet.com

01698 832622
01698 831269
01698 833743

77 Kirkfieldbank See Crossford

78 Kirkmuirhill (F H W)
Andrew D. Rooney BSc BD   2019

kirkmuirhillchurch@btinternet.com
The Manse, 82 Vere Road, Kirkmuirhill, Lanark ML11 9RP
ARooney@churchofscotland.org.uk

01555 895593
01555 892409

79 Kirk o' Shotts (H) See Chapelhall

80 Lanark: Greyfriars (F H T W)
Bryan Kerr BA BD   2002   2007

office@lanarkgreyfriars.com
Greyfriars Manse, 3 Bellefield Way, Lanark ML11 7NW
BKerr@churchofscotland.org.uk

01555 437050
01555 663363

81 Lanark: St Nicholas' (F H W)
Louise E. Mackay BSc BD   2017

lanarkstnicholas@outlook.com
2 Kairnhill Court, Lanark ML11 9HU

01555 666220
01555 661936

82 Larbert: East (F W)
Vacant
Session Clerk: Margaret Tooth

1 Cortachy Avenue, Carron, Falkirk FK2 8DH
margaret.tooth@larberteast.church

01324 562402

83 Larbert: Old (F H W)
Guardianship of the Presbytery
Session Clerk: Eric Appelbe

The Manse, 38 South Broomage Avenue, Larbert FK5 3ED
larbertoldcontact@gmail.com

01324 872760
01324 556551

84 Larbert: West (F H W)
Vacant
Mhairi M. Gilchrist BD   2023
(Assistant Minister)

29 Drysdale Avenue, Kinnaird, Larbert FK2 8RE
MGilchrist@churchofscotland.org.uk

07519 364059

85 **Larkhall: New (F H W)**
Alastair G. McKillop BD DipMin   1995   2004   2 Orchard Gate, Larkhall ML9 1HA
AMcKillop@churchofscotland.org.uk   01698 321976

86 **Larkhall: Trinity**
Vacant
Session Clerk: Wilma Gilmour (Miss)   13 Machan Avenue, Larkhall ML9 2HE
gilmourgilmour@btinternet.com   01698 881401
01698 883002

87 **Law (F W)**
Vacant   **info@lawparishchurch.org**
A. Kwame Ahaligah MA STM PhD   2004   2023   3 Shawgill Court, Law, Carluke ML8 5SJ
DipTh FHEA (Assistant Minister)   KAhaligah@churchofscotland.org.uk   01698 373180
01698 591961

88 **Libberton and Quothquan** See Cairngryffe

89 **Motherwell: Crosshill (F H W) linked with Motherwell: St Margaret's (F W)**   **info@crosshillparishchurch.org.uk**
Vacant
Session Clerk, Motherwell: Crosshill: Willie Talbot   talbottally@aol.com   01698 269598

90 **Motherwell: Dalziel St Andrew's (F H T W)**
Alistair S. May LLB BD PhD   2002   2020   4 Pollock Street, Motherwell ML1 1LP
AMay@churchofscotland.org.uk   **01698 264097**
01698 263414

91 **Motherwell: North (F W) linked with Wishaw: Craigneuk and Belhaven (H)**
Derek H.N. Pope BD DipYCW   1987   1995   35 Birrens Road, Motherwell ML1 3NS
DPope@churchofscotland.org.uk   01698 266716

92 **Motherwell: St Margaret's** See Motherwell: Crosshill

93 **Motherwell: St Mary's (F H T W)**   **office@stmarysmotherwell.org.uk**
Bryce Calder MA BD   1995   2017   19 Orchard Street, Motherwell ML1 3JE
BCalder@churchofscotland.org.uk   **01698 268554**
07986 144834

94 **Motherwell: South (H T W)**
Alan W. Gibson BA BD   2001   2016   62 Manse Road, Motherwell ML1 2PT
Alan.Gibson@churchofscotland.org.uk   01698 239279

95 **Muiravonside** See Blackbraes and Shieldhill

96 Newarthill and Carfin (F H T W)
Elaine W. McKinnon MA BA BD   1988   2014
Church Street, Newarthill, Motherwell ML1 5HS
EMcKinnon@churchofscotland.org.uk
01698 296850

97 Newmains: Bonkle (F H W) linked with Newmains: Coltness Memorial (F H W)
Sandra Black BSc BD   1988   2023
(Interim Minister)
36 Glencairn Drive, Glasgow G41 4PW
SBlack@churchofscotland.org.uk
01698 344001
07703 827057

98 Newmains: Coltness Memorial See Newmains: Bonkle
99 New Stevenston: Wrangholm Kirk See Holytown

100 Overtown (F W)
Lorna I. MacDougall MA DipGC BD   2003   2017
The Manse, 146 Main Street, Overtown, Wishaw ML2 0QP
LMacDougall@churchofscotland.org.uk
01698 358727
01698 352090

101 Polmont: Old (F W)
Deborah L. van Welie (Ms) MTheol   2015
3 Orchard Grove, Polmont, Falkirk FK2 0XE
DLVanWelie@churchofscotland.org.uk
01324 715995
01324 713427

102 Quarter See Hamilton: South
103 Redding and Westquarter See Falkirk: Laurieston

104 Shotts: Calderhead Erskine
Vacant
Session Clerk: Liam T. Haggart SSC
The Manse, 9 Kirk Road, Shotts ML7 5ET
a2lth@hotmail.com
01501 823204
07896 557687

105 Slamannan
Vacant
Monica J. MacDonald (Mrs)   2014
(Ordained Local Minister)
60 Kennedy Way, Airth FK2 8GG
Monica.MacDonald@churchofscotland.org.uk
01324 832782

106 Stenhouse and Carron (F H)
Vacant
Interim Moderator: Alison A. Meikle
The Manse, 21 Tipperary Place, Stenhousemuir, Larbert FK5 4SX
AMeikle@churchofscotland.org.uk
01324 416628
01324 336729

107 Stonehouse: St Ninian's (F H T W)
Stewart J. Cutler BA MSc DipHE 2017
info@st-ninians-stonehouse.org.uk
4 Hamilton Way, Stonehouse, Larkhall ML9 3PU
revstewartcutler@gmail.com
01698 791508

Stonehouse: St Ninian's is a Local Ecumenical Partnership with the United Reformed Church

108 Strathaven: Avendale Old and Drumclog (F H W)
Calum M. Stark LLB BD 2011 2021
info@avendale-drumclog.org.uk
4 Fortrose Gardens, Strathaven ML10 6FH
CStark@churchofscotland.org.uk
01357 671557
01357 523031

109 Strathaven: Trinity (F H W)
Shaw J. Paterson BSc BD MSc DPT 1991
15 Lethame Road, Strathaven ML10 6AD
SPaterson@churchofscotland.org.uk
Tel 01357 520019
Fax 01357 529316

110 Symington See Cairngryffe

111 Uddingston: Burnhead (F H W)
Les N. Brunger BD 2010
90 Laburnum Road, Uddingston, Glasgow G71 5DB
LBrunger@churchofscotland.org.uk
01698 813716

112 Uddingston: Old (F H W)
Fiona L.J. McKibbin (Mrs) MA BD 2011
1 Belmont Avenue, Uddingston, Glasgow G71 7AX
FMcKibbin@churchofscotland.org.uk
01698 814015
01698 814757

113 Uddingston: Viewpark (F H W)
Michael G. Lyall BD CertMin 1993 2001
enquiries@viewparkparishchurch.org.uk
14 Holmbrae Road, Uddingston, Glasgow G71 6AP
MLyall@churchofscotland.org.uk
01698 810478
01698 813113

114 Upper Clyde (F W)
Nikki M. Macdonald BD MTh PhD 2014
31 Carlisle Road, Crawford, Biggar ML12 6TP
NMacdonald@churchofscotland.org.uk
01864 502139

115 Wishaw: Cambusnethan North (F H W)
Vacant
Session Clerk: Tom McIvor
350 Kirk Road, Wishaw ML2 8LH
tommcivor13@yahoo.co.uk
01698 381305
01698 383815

116 Wishaw: Cambusnethan Old and Morningside
Vacant
Session Clerk: Graeme Vincent
22 Coronation Street, Wishaw ML2 8LF
gvincent@theiet.org
01698 384235
01555 752166

117 Wishaw: Craigneuk and Belhaven See Motherwell: North

118 Wishaw: Old (F H)
Vacant
Session Clerk: Thomas W. Donaldson

130 Glen Road, Wishaw ML2 7NP
tomdonaldson@talktalk.net

01698 376080
01698 375134
01698 357605

119 Wishaw: St Mark's See Cleland

120 Wishaw: South Wishaw (F H W)
Terence C. Moran BD CertMin　1995　2015

southwishaw@tiscali.co.uk
3 Walter Street, Wishaw ML2 8LQ
TMoran@churchofscotland.org.uk

01698 375306
01698 767459

B. In other appointments: members of Presbytery

Name	Ord.	Appt.	Appointment	Address / Email	Telephone
Bogle, Albert O. BD MTh	1981	2016	Pioneer Minister, Sanctuary First	49a Kenilworth Road, Bridge of Allan FK9 4RS AlbertBogle@churchofscotland.org.uk	07715 374557
Chestnutt, Deborah A. BSc PGCE BD(Min)		2022	Chaplain, Divine Healing Fellowship (Scotland)	Braehead House Christian Healing and Retreat Centre, Braidwood Road, Crossford, Carluke ML8 5NQ DChestnutt@churchofscotland.org.uk	01555 860716
Fyfe, Lorna K. BD		2020	Ordained Local Minister	20 Kennoway Crescent, Hamilton ML3 7WQ LFyfe@churchofscotland.org.uk	01698 633304
Grant, Paul G.R. BD MTh	2003	2022	Healthcare Chaplain	Glasgow Royal Infirmary, 84 Castle Street, Glasgow G4 0SF PGrant@churchofscotland.org.uk	0141 201 6300
Hacking, Philip R.		2021	Ordained Local Minister; Chaplain, HM Prison Glenochil	101 Craig's Crescent, Falkirk FK2 0ET PHacking@churchofscotland.org.uk	01324 337936
Macpherson, Duncan J. BSc BD	1993	2022	Deputy Assistant Chaplain General: Army	177 Station Road, Shotts ML7 4BA padredjm@btinternet.com	01501 821484
Murphy, Jim		2014	Ordained Local Minister	10 Hillview Crescent, Bellshill ML4 1NX JMurphy@churchofscotland.org.uk	01698 740189
Rennick, Julie M. (Mrs) BTh	2005	2022	Presbytery Clerk: Forth Valley and Clydesdale	Presbytery Office, Rex House, 103 Bothwell Road, Hamilton ML3 0DW JRennick@churchofscotland.org.uk	01698 662537
Wilson, Angela DCS	2015	2021	Community Outreach Worker, Southern Ministry Cluster	52 Victoria Park, Lockerbie DG11 2AY Angela.Wilson@churchofscotland.org.uk	07543 796820

C. Retaining: members of Presbytery

Name	Ord.	Appt.	Former charge	Address / Email	Telephone
Barrie, Arthur P. LTh	1973	2007	(Hamilton: Cadzow)	30 Airbles Crescent, Motherwell ML1 3AR	01698 261147
Baxendale, Georgina M. DipEd BD DMin	1981	2014	(Motherwell: South)	32 Meadowhead Road, Plains, Airdrie ML6 7HG georgiebaxendale@btinternet.com	01236 842752

Campbell, James W. BD	1995	2020	(Ceres, Kemback and Springfield)	145 Mungalhead Road, Falkirk FK2 7JH	01324 638686 / 07975 976024
Colvin, Sharon E.F. (Mrs) BD LRAM LTCL.	1985	2008	(Airdrie: Jackson)	25 Balblair Road, Airdrie ML6 6GQ / dibleycol@hotmail.com	01236 590796
Cook, J. Stanley BD DipPSS DipPC	1974	2001	(Hamilton: West)	Mansend, 137A Old Manse Road, Netherton, Wishaw ML2 0EW / stancook@blueyonder.co.uk	01698 299600
Cowan, James S.A. BD DipMin	1986	2019	(Barrhead: St Andrew's)	30 Redding Road, Falkirk FK2 9XJ / jim_cowan@ntlworld.com	07966 489609
Crosthwaite, Melville D. BD DipEd DipMin	1984	2021	(Larbert: East)	16 Southend Drive, Strathaven ML10 6QT / revcrosthwaite@gmail.com	
Cunningham, Iain D. MA BD	1979	2022	(Carluke: Kirkton)	6 Twister Crescent, Stonehouse, Larkhall ML9 3FU	01698 263472
Doyle, David W. MA BD	1977	2015	(Motherwell: St Mary's)	76 Kethers Street, Motherwell ML1 3HN	01698 748244
Fuller, Agnes A. (Mrs) BD	1987	2014	(Bellshill: West)	14 Croftpark Street, Bellshill ML14 1EY / revamoore2@tiscali.co.uk	
Gibson, James M. TD LTh LRAM	1978	2019	(Bothwell)	22 Kirklands Crescent, Bothwell, Glasgow G71 8HU / jamesmgibson@msn.com	01698 854907
Gilroy, Lorraine (Mrs) DCS	1988	1994	(Deacon, Uddingston: Burnhead)	68 Clement Drive, Airdrie ML16 7FB / lorraine.gilroy@sky.com	07923 540602
Gunn, F. Derek BD	1986	2017	(Airdrie: Clarkston)	6 Yardley Place, Falkirk FK2 7FH / RevDerekGunn@hotmail.com	01324 624938
Jones, Robert BSc BD	1990	2017	(Rosskeen)	3 Grantown Avenue, Airdrie ML6 8HH / rob2jones@btinternet.com	07761 782714
Kent, Robert M. MA BD	1973	2011	(Hamilton: St John's)	48 Fyne Crescent, Larkhall ML9 2UX / robertmkent@talktalk.net	01698 769244
Kerr, Angus BD CertMin ThM DMin	1983	2019	(Whitburn: South)	27 Pelham Court, Jackton, East Kilbride G74 5PZ	01355 570962
Macdonald, Mhorag (Ms) MA BD	1989	2021	(Wishaw: Cambusnethan North)	90 Dumbuck Road, Dumbarton G82 3NA / Mhorag.Macdonald@churchofscotland.org.uk	
MacKenzie, Ian C. MA BD	1970	2011	(Interim Minister, Carnwath)	21 Wilson Street, Motherwell ML1 1NP / iancmac@blueyonder.co.uk	01698 301230
Mathers, Alexena (Sandra)	2015	2018	(Ordained Local Minister, Denny: Old with Haggs)	10 Ercall Road, Brightons, Falkirk FK2 0RS / SMathers@churchofscotland.org.uk	01324 872253
McKee, Norman B. BD	1987	2010	(Uddingston: Old)	148 Station Road, Blantyre, Glasgow G72 9BW / normanmckee946@btinternet.com	01698 827358
Murdoch, Iain C. MA LLB DipEd BD	1995	2017	(Wishaw: Cambusnethan Old and Morningside)	2 Pegasus Avenue, Carluke ML8 5TN / iaincmurdoch@btopenworld.com	01555 773891
Ogilvie, Colin BA DCS	1998	2015	(Deacon, Kilmarnock: New Laigh Kirk)	21 Neilsland Drive, Motherwell ML1 3DZ / colinogilvie2@gmail.com	01698 321836
Palmer, Gordon R. MA BD STM	1986	2022	(East Kilbride: Claremont)	128 Boyd Street, Glasgow G42 8TP / gkrspalmer@blueyonder.co.uk	07837 287804 / 07804 817522
Ross, Eileen M. (Mrs) BD MTh	2005	2022	(Linwood)	2 Millburn Way, East Kilbride, Glasgow G75 8EB	
Ross, Keith W. MA BD MTh	1984	2015	(Congregational Development Officer, Presbytery of Hamilton)	Easter Bavelaw House, Pentland Hills Regional Park, Balerno EH14 7JS / keithwross@outlook.com	07855 163449
Salmond, James S. BA BD MTh ThD	1979	2003	(Holytown)	165 Torbothie Road, Shotts ML7 5NE	

Smith, G. Stewart MA BD STM	1966	2006	(Glasgow: King's Park)	33 Brent Road, Stewartfield, East Kilbride, Glasgow G74 4RA; stewartandmary@googlemail.com	Tel/Fax 01355 226718
Stevenson, John LTh	1998	2006	(Cambuslang: St Andrew's)	20 Knowehead Gardens, Uddingston, Glasgow G71 7PY; therev20@sky.com	01698 817582
Stewart, William T. BD DipPS	1980	2018	(Glassford with Strathaven: East)	8 Cot Castle Grove, Stonehouse ML9 3RQ	01698 793979
Taylor, Terry Ann BA MTh	2005	2023	(East Kilbride: South)	TTaylor@churchofscotland.org.uk; 8 Skylands Place, Hamilton ML3 8SB	01698 422511
Thomson, John M.A. TD JP BD ThM	1978	2014	(Hamilton: Old)	jt@john1949.plus.com	
Turnbull, S. Lindsay A. BSc BD	2014	2021	(Hamilton: Trinity)		
Waddell, Elizabeth A. (Mrs) BD	1999	2014	(Hamilton: West)	114 Branchalfield, Wishaw ML2 8QD; elizabethwaddell@tiscali.co.uk	01698 382909
Wallace, Douglas W. MA BD	1981	2019	(East Kilbride: Stewartfield)	11 Cromalt Avenue, East Kilbride, Glasgow G75 GQ; DWallace@churchofscotland.org.uk	01355 260879
Zambonini, James LlADip	1997	2015	(Auxiliary Minister, Coatbridge: Calder)	100 Old Manse Road, Netherton, Wishaw ML2 0EP	01698 350889

D. In other appointments: not members of Presbytery
Nil

E. Retaining: not members of Presbytery

Brown, Kathryn I. (Mrs)	2014	2019	(Ordained Local Minister, Falkirk: Trinity)	1 Callendar Park Walk, Callendar Grange, Falkirk FK1 1TA; kaybrown1cpw@talktalk.net	01324 617352
Brown, T. John MA BD	1995	2006	(Tullibody: St Serf's)	1 Callendar Park Walk, Callendar Grange, Falkirk FK1 1TA; johnbrown1cpw@talktalk.net	01324 617352
Buchan, William BD DipTheol	1987	2001	(Kilwinning: Abbey)	9 Leafield Road, Biggar ML12 6AY; billbuchan3@btinternet.com	01899 229253
Collard, John K. MA BD	1986	2019	(Interim Minister, Kirkcudbright)	1 Nelson Terrace, East Kilbride G74 2EY; JCollard@churchofscotland.org.uk	01355 520093
Cowell, Susan G. (Miss) BA BD	1986	1998	(Budapest: St Columba's)	3 Gavel Lane, Regency Gardens, Lanark ML11 9FB	01555 665509
Currie, David E.P. BSc BD	1983	2011	(Emerging Church Development Officer, Mission and Discipleship Council)	42 Onslow Gardens, Muswell Hill, London N10 3JX; davidepcurrie@gmail.com	01355 248510
Cutler, James S.H. BD CEng MIStructE	1986	2011	(Black Mount with Cutler with Libberton and Quothquan)	Grainstore, 11 Cuthill Towers Farm, Milnathort, Kinross KY13 9SE; revjimc@outlook.com	07809 484812
Donaghy, Leslie G. BD DipMin PGDipPsych PhD FSAScot AVCM	1990	2004	(Dumbarton: St Andrew's)	53 Oak Avenue, East Kilbride G75 9ED; les@donaghy.ie	
Donaldson, George M. MA BD	1984	2015	(Caldercruix and Longriggend)	4 Toul Gardens, Motherwell ML1 2FE; g.donaldson505@btinternet.com	01698 239477
Findlay, Henry J.W. MA BD	1965	2005	(Wishaw: St Mark's)	2 Alba Gardens, Carluke ML8 5US; henryfindlay@btinternet.com	01555 759995
Gauld, Beverly G.D.D. MA BD	1972	2009	(Carnwath)	7 Rowan View, Lanark ML11 9FQ	01555 665765
Jessamine, Alistair L. MA BD	1979	2011	(Dunfermline: Abbey)	11 Gallowhill Farm Cottages, Strathaven ML10 6BZ	01357 520934

Job, Anne J. BSc BD	1993	2010	(Kirkcaldy: Viewforth with Thornton)	5 Carse View, Airth, Falkirk FK2 8NY / aj@ajob.co.uk	01324 832094
Lusk, Alastair S. BD DipPS	1974	2010	(East Kilbride: Moncrieff)	9 MacFie Place, Stewartfield, East Kilbride G74 4TY	01324 832782
MacDonald, George BTh	1996	2021	(Bonnybridge: St Helen's)	60 Kennedy Way, Airth, Falkirk FK2 8GG / gmd1946@gmail.com	
Mailer, Colin M.	1996	2005	(Auxiliary Minister, Grangemouth: Zetland)	25 Saltcoats Drive, Grangemouth FK3 9JP / colinmailer@blueyonder.co.uk	01324 712401
McCracken, Gordon A. BD CertMin	1988	2021	(Presbytery Clerk: Hamilton)	1 Kenilworth Road, Lanark ML11 7BL / GMcCracken@churchofscotland.org.uk	07918 600720
Wyllie, Hugh R. MA DD FCIBS	1962	2000	(Hamilton: Old)	18 Chantinghall Road, Hamilton ML3 8NP / hrwyllie@gmail.com	01698 420002

F. Inactive: not members of Presbytery

Barclay, Neil W. BSc BEd BD	1986	2006	(Falkirk: Grahamston United)	4 Gibsongray Street, Falkirk FK2 7LN / neil.barclay@virginmedia.com	01324 874681
Chalmers, George A. MA BD MLitt	1962	2002	(Catrine with Sorn)	3 Cricket Place, Brightons, Falkirk FK2 0HZ	01324 712030
Grier, James BD	1991	2005	(Coatbridge: Middle)	14 Love Drive, Bellshill ML4 1BY	01698 742545
McAlpine, John BSc PGCE	1988	2004	(Auxiliary Minister, Newmains: Bonkle with Newmains: Coltness Memorial)	Braeside, 201 Bonkle Road, Newmains, Wishaw ML2 9AA / jonedmcalpine@aol.com	01698 384610
McDonald, John A. MA BD	1978	1997	(Cumbernauld: Condorrat)	1 John Murray Court, Motherwell ML1 2QW	01324 871947
McDowall, Ronald J. BD	1980	2001	(Falkirk: Laurieston with Redding and Westquarter)	'Kailas', Windsor Road, Falkirk FK1 5EJ	
McKenzie, Raymond D. DipTh BD	1978	2012	(Hamilton: Burnbank with Hamilton: South)	25 Austine Drive, Hamilton ML3 7YE	
Morrison, Iain C. BA BD	1990	2003	(Linlithgow: St Ninian's Craigmailen)	Whaligoe, 53 Eastcroft Drive, Polmont, Falkirk FK2 0SU / iain@kirkweb.org	01324 713249
Munton, James G. BA	1969	2002	(Coatbridge: Old Monkland)	2 Moorcroft Drive, Airdrie ML6 8ES	01236 754848
Price, Peter O. CBE KHC BA FPhS	1957	1996	(Blantyre: Old)	22 Old Bothwell Road, Bothwell, Glasgow G71 8AW / peteroprice@sky.com	01698 854032
Robertson, John M. BSc BD	1975	1992	(Campsie)	8 North Green Drive, Airth, Falkirk FK2 8RA	01324 832244
Ross, Evan J. LTh	1986	1998	(Cowdenbeath: West with Mossgreen and Crossgates)	5 Arneil Place, Brightons, Falkirk FK2 0NJ	01324 719936
Smith, Richard BD	1976	2002	(Denny: Old)	Easter Wayside, 46 Kennedy Way, Airth, Falkirk FK2 8GB / richards@uklinex.net	01324 831386
Spence, Sheila M. (Mrs) MA BD	1979	2010	(Kirk o' Shotts)	12 Machan Avenue, Larkhall ML9 2HE	01698 310370

G. Readers (active)

Allan, Angus J.	Blackburn Mill, Chapelton, Strathaven ML10 6RR / angus.allan@hotmail.com	01357 300916
Beattie, Richard	4 Bent Road, Hamilton ML3 6QB / richardbeattie1958@hotmail.com	01698 420806
Codona, Joy (Mrs)	Dykehead Farm, 300 Dykehead Road, Airdrie ML6 7SR / jcodona772@btinternet.com	01236 767063 / 07810 770609

Name	Address	Email	Phone
Douglas, Ian	24 Abbotsford Crescent, Strathaven ML10 6EQ	IDouglas@churchofscotland.org.uk	07742 022423
Duncan, Lorna M. (Mrs) BA	28 Solway Drive, Head of Muir, Denny FK6 5NS	ell.dee@blueyonder.co.uk	01324 813020
Grant, Alan	25 Moss-side Avenue, Carluke ML8 5UG	amgrant25@aol.com	01555 771419
Hastings, William Paul	186 Glen More, East Kilbride, Glasgow G74 2AN	wphastings@hotmail.co.uk	01355 521228 / 07954 167158
Henderson, William D.	48 Watson Street, High Blantyre G72 9SJ	bill_henderson@icloud.com	01698 829938
Hislop, Eric	1 Castlegait, Strathaven ML10 6FF	eric.hislop@tiscali.co.uk	01357 520003
Jardine, Lynette	1 Hume Drive, Uddingston, Glasgow G71 4DW	lpjardine@blueyonder.co.uk	01698 812404
Love, William	30 Barmore Avenue, Carluke ML8 4PE	janbill30@tiscali.co.uk	01555 751243
McCleary, Isaac	719 Coatbridge Road, Bargeddie, Glasgow G69 7PH	isaacmccleary@gmail.com	07908 547040
McMillan, Isabelle (Mrs)	17 Castle Avenue, Airth, Falkirk FK2 8GA		07896 433314
Preston, Steven J.	24 Glen Prosen, East Kilbride, Glasgow G74 3TA	steven.preston1@btinternet.com	01355 237359 / 07752 120536
Scoular, Iain W.	15 Bonnyside Road, Bonnybridge FK4 2AD	scoulariain@gmail.com	01324 812395 / 07717 131596
Stevenson, Thomas	34 Castle Wynd, Quarter, Hamilton ML3 7XD	weetamgtr@gmail.com	01698 282263 / 07860 477344
Stewart, Arthur MA	51 Bonnymuir Crescent, Bonnybridge FK4 1GD	arthur.stewart1@btinternet.com	01324 812667
White, Ian T.	4 Gilchrist Walk, Lesmahagow ML11 0FQ	iantwhite@aol.com	01555 890704

H. Ministries Development Staff

Name	Role	Email
Robertson, Julie	Strathaven: Trinity – Children and Youth Development Worker	JRobertson@churchofscotland.org.uk
Wilson, Angela	Southern Ministry Cluster – Community Outreach Worker	Angela.Wilson@churchofscotland.org.uk

TOWN ADDRESSES

Airdrie
Cairnlea	89 Graham Street
Clarkston	Forrest Street
High	North Bridge Street
Jackson	Glen Road
New Monkland	Glenmavis
New Wellwynd	Wellwynd
St Columba's	Thrashbush Road

Bo'ness
Old	Panbrae Road
St Andrew's	Grahamsdyke Avenue
Carriden	Carriden Brae

Carluke
Kirkton	Station Road

St Andrew's	Mount Stewart Street
St John's	Hamilton Street

Coatbridge
Blairhill Dundyvan	Blairhill Street
Calder	Calder Street
Middle	Bank Street
New St Andrew's	Church Street
Old Monkland	Woodside Street
Townhead	Crinan Crescent

Denny
Old	Denny Cross
Westpark	Duke Street
Dunipace	Stirling Street

East Kilbride
Claremont	High Common Road, St Leonard's
Greenhills	Greenhills Centre
Moncreiff	Calderwood Road
Mossneuk	Eden Drive
Old	Montgomery Street
South	Baird Hill, Murray
Stewartfield	Stewartfield Community Centre
West	Kittoch Street
Westwood	Belmont Drive, Westwood

Falkirk
Bainsford	Hendry Street, Bainsford
Camelon	Dorrator Road
Grahamston United	Bute Street
Laurieston	Polmont Road
St Andrew's West	Newmarket Street
Trinity	Kirk Wynd

Grangemouth
Abbotsgrange — Abbot's Road
Kirk of the Holy Rood — Bowhouse Road
Zetland — Ronaldshay Crescent

Hamilton
Cadzow — Woodside Walk
Gilmour and Whitehill — Glasgow Road, Burnbank
Hillhouse — Clerkwell Road
Old — Leechlee Road
St John's — Duke Street
South — Strathaven Road
Trinity — Neilsland Square off Neilsland Road
West — Burnbank Road

Larbert
East — Kirk Avenue
Old — Denny Road x Stirling Road
West — Main Street

Motherwell
Crosshill — Windmillhill Street x Airbles Street
Dalziel St Andrew's — Merry Street x Muir Street
North — Chesters Crescent
St Margaret's — Shields Road
St Mary's — Avon Street
South — Gavin Street

Uddingston
Burnhead — Laburnum Road
Old — Old Glasgow Road
Viewpark — Old Edinburgh Road

Wishaw
Cambusnethan North — Kirk Road
Old — Kirk Road
Craigneuk and Belhaven — Craigneuk Street
Old — Main Street
St Mark's — Coltness Road
South Wishaw — East Academy Street

(7) FIFE (F W)

Meets in varying locations on the third Saturday in February, June, September and November.

| Clerk: | REV. DAVID G. COULTER CB OStJ KHC BA BD MDA PhD | Presbytery Office, Wellesley Centre, Wellesley Parish Church, Wellesley Road, Methil KY8 3PD fife@churchofscotland.org.uk | 07340 461921 |

1   Aberdour: St Fillan's (H W)
Vacant
Session Clerk: Bill Henderson

St Fillan's Manse, 36 Bellhouse Road, Aberdour, Fife KY3 0TL
billhenderson2306@hotmail.co.uk

01383 861522
01383 432851

2   Anstruther and Cellardyke: St Ayle (H W) linked with Crail (F)
Vacant

16 Taeping Close, Cellardyke, Anstruther KY10 3YL

01333 311630

3   Auchterderran Kinglassie (F W)
Donald R. Lawrie MA BD DipCouns   1991   2018

7 Woodend Road, Cardenden, Lochgelly KY5 0NE
DLawrie@churchofscotland.org.uk

01592 720508

4   Auchtertool (W) linked with Kirkcaldy: Linktown (F H W)
Vacant
Session Clerk, Auchtertool
Session Clerk, Kirkcaldy: Linktown: J. Stewart Milne

16 Raith Crescent, Kirkcaldy KY2 5NN

jstewartmilne@blueyonder.co.uk

01592 641080
01592 265536

01592 266018

5   Balmerino (H W) linked with Wormit (F H W)
Vacant
Session Clerk, Balmerino: Christopher Hill
Session Clerk, Wormit: Kimberley Falconer

5 Westwater Place, Newport-on-Tay DD6 8NS
christopherhill566@btinternet.com
kimberleywatt1960@gmail.com

01382 542626
01382 330459
01334 838827

6   Beath and Cowdenbeath: North (F H W)
Deborah J. Dobby (Mrs)   2014   2018
BA BD PGCE RGN RSCN

10 Stuart Place, Cowdenbeath KY4 9BN
DDobby@churchofscotland.org.uk

01383 325520

7   Boarhills and Dunino linked with St Andrews: Holy Trinity (F W) holytrinitystandrews@gmail.com
Guardianship of the Presbytery
Session Clerk, Boarhills and Dunino: Kenneth S. Morris
Session Clerk, Holy Trinity: Michael Stewart (Dr)

kensm48@gmail.com
htsessionclerk@gmail.com

01334 478317

01334 474468
01334 461270

8 Buckhaven and Wemyss (F)
Vacant
Jacqueline Thomson (Mrs) MTh DCS   2004   2008
16 Aitken Place, Coaltown of Wemyss, Kirkcaldy KY1 4PA
Jacqueline.Thomson@churchofscotland.org.uk

01592 **715577**

07806 776560

9 Burntisland (F H)
Vacant
Session Clerk: William Sweenie
21 Ramsay Crescent, Burntisland KY3 9JL
billsweenie01@gmail.com

01592 873567

10 Cairneyhill (F H W) linked with Limekilns (F H W)

office@limekilnschurch.org

Norman M. Grant BD DipMin   1990
The Manse, 10 Church Street, Limekilns, Dunfermline KY11 3HT
NGrant@churchofscotland.org.uk

Cairneyhill: 01383 **882352**
Limekilns: **01383** **873337**
01383 872341

11 Cameron (F W) linked with St Andrews: St Leonard's (F H W)   1993   2017   **stlencam@btconnect.com**
Graeme W. Beebee BD
1 Cairnhill Gardens, St Andrews KY16 8QY
GBeebee@churchofscotland.org.uk

01334 478702
01334 472793

12 Carnbee linked with Pittenweem
Vacant
Session Clerk, Carnbee: Henry Watson
Session Clerk, Pittenweem: to be appointed
29 Milton Road, Pittenweem, Anstruther KY10 2LN

01333 312838
01333 313796

13 Carnock and Oakley (F H W)
Vacant
Session Clerk: Sandy Muirhead
sandy_muirhead@hotmail.com

01383 850077

14 Ceres, Kemback and Springfield (W)   1999   2021   **info@ckschurch.org**
Jane L. Barron (Mrs) BA DipEd BD
Denhead Old Farm, St Andrews KY16 8PA
JBarron@churchofscotland.org.uk

01334 850135
07545 904541

15 Cowdenbeath: Trinity (F H W)
Vacant
Session Clerk: John Bain
2 Glenfield Road, Cowdenbeath KY4 9EL
johnbain1@btinternet.com

01383 510696
01383 512779

16 Crail See Anstruther and Cellardyke: St Ayle

17 Creich, Flisk and Kilmany (W)
Guardianship of the Presbytery
Session Clerk: Patricia Pearce
p.pearce@tiscali.co.uk
01334 655799

18 Culross and Torryburn (H)
Vacant
Contact via Presbytery Office

19 Cupar: Old and St Michael of Tarvit (H W) linked with Monimail
Jeffrey A. Martin BA MDiv   1991
76 Hogarth Drive, Cupar KY15 5YU
JMartin@churchofscotland.org.uk
01334 656181

20 Cupar: St John's and Dairsie United (F W)
Gavin W.G. Black BD   2006
The Manse, 23 Hogarth Drive, Cupar KY15 5YH
GBlack@churchofscotland.org.uk
01334 650751

21 Dalgety (H W)
Vacant
office@dalgety-church.co.uk
9 St Colme Drive, Dalgety Bay, Dunfermline KY11 9LQ
01383 824092
01383 822316

Andrea Fraser BSc PGCert MDiv   2023
(Assistant Minister)
Andrea.Fraser@churchofscotland.org.uk
Session Clerk: Elma Doig (Mrs)
elmadoig@yahoo.co.uk
01383 249845

22 Dunfermline: Abbey (F H T W)
Mary-Ann R. Rennie (Mrs) BD   1998
MTh CPS
dunfermline.abbey.church@gmail.com
3 Perdieus Mount, Dunfermline KY12 7XE
MARennie@churchofscotland.org.uk
01383 724586
01383 727311

23 Dunfermline: East (F W)
Andrew A. Morrice MA BD   1999
71 Swift Street, Dunfermline KY11 8SN
AMorrice@churchofscotland.org.uk
01383 223144
07815 719301

24 Dunfermline: Gillespie Memorial (F H W)
Michael A. Weaver BSc BD   2017
office@gillespiechurch.org
4 Killin Court, Dunfermline KY12 7XF
MWeaver@churchofscotland.org.uk
01383 621253
01383 724347

25 Dunfermline: North
Guardianship of the Presbytery
Session Clerk: Graham Primrose
sessionclerk@dunfermlinenorthparishchurch.co.uk
07920 445669

26 Dunfermline: St Andrew's Erskine (F W) 2006
Muriel F. Willoughby (Mrs) MA BD
2013
staechurch@standrewserskine.org.uk
71A Townhill Road, Dunfermline KY12 0BN
MWilloughby@churchofscotland.org.uk
01383 841660
01383 738487

27 Dunfermline: St Leonard's (F W)
Vacant
Margaret B. Mateos 2018
(Ordained Local Minister)
office@slpc.org
12 Torvean Place, Dunfermline KY11 4YY
43 South Street, Lochgelly KY5 9LJ
MMateos@churchofscotland.org.uk
01383 620106
01383 300092
01592 780073

28 Dunfermline: St Margaret's (F W) 1985
Iain M. Greenshields
BD CertMin DipRS ACMA MSc MTh DD
2007
38 Garvock Hill, Dunfermline KY12 7UU
IGreenshields@churchofscotland.org.uk
01383 723955
07427 477575

29 Dunfermline: St Ninian's (F W)
Vacant
Session Clerk: John Thomson
51 St John's Drive, Dunfermline KY12 7TL
johncthomson@btinternet.com
01383 271548
01383 730074

30 Dunfermline: Townhill and Kingseat (F H W)
Vacant
Session Clerk: David Henderson
info@townhillandkingseatchurchofscotland.org
7 Lochwood Park, Kingseat, Dunfermline KY12 0UX
davidw-henderson@sky.com
01383 723691
01383 737679

31 Dysart: St Clair (F H W)
Vacant
Session Clerk: Raymond Domin
42 Craigfoot Walk, Kirkcaldy KY1 1GA
raymonddomin@blueyonder.co.uk
01592 561967
01592 203620

32 East Neuk Trinity (F H W) 2020
Douglas R. Creighton BSc BTh
eastneuktrinityoffice@btconnect.com
6 Reaper Lane, Anstruther KY10 3FR
DCreighton@churchofscotland.org.uk
01333 311045

33 Edenshead (F W)
Vacant
Session Clerk: Liz Slattery
The Manse, Kirk Wynd, Strathmiglo, Cupar KY14 7QS
halhill14@gmail.com
01337 860256
07719 724730

34 Falkland (F W) linked with Freuchie (H W)
Guardianship of the Presbytery
Session Clerk, Falkland: Marion Baldie
Session Clerk, Freuchie: Margaret Cuthbert
1 Newton Road, Falkland, Cupar KY15 7AQ
sessionclerk.falkland@gmail.com
cuthbertmargaret@yahoo.co.uk
01337 858557
07951 824488
01337 830940

35   Freuchie See Falkland

36   Glenrothes: Christ's Kirk (H W)
Vacant — christskirkglenrothes@yahoo.com — 01592 745938
Session Clerk: Ruth Anderson — ruthp.anderson@yahoo.com — 07970 594033

37   Glenrothes: St Columba's (F W)   2013
Alan W.D. Kimmitt BSc BD — info@st-columbas.com — 01592 752539
40 Liberton Drive, Glenrothes KY6 3PB — 01592 742233
Alan.Kimmitt@churchofscotland.org.uk

38   Glenrothes: St Margaret's (F H W)   2014
Vacant — office@stmargaretschurch.org.uk — 01592 328162
8 Alburne Park, Glenrothes KY7 5RB — 01592 752241
Session Clerk: Catriona Reidpath — catriona.reidpath@outlook.com — 01592 753534

39   Glenrothes: St Ninian's (F H W)   1992   2017
David J. Smith BD DipMin — office@stninians.co.uk — 01592 610560
1 Cawdor Drive, Glenrothes KY6 2HN — 01592 611963
David.Smith@churchofscotland.org.uk

40   Howe of Fife (F W)
Vacant — The Manse, 83 Church Street, Ladybank, Cupar KY15 7ND — 01337 832717
Session Clerk: Anne Jeffcoat (Mrs) — annejeffcoat02@gmail.com — 01337 832508

41   Inverkeithing (F W) linked with North Queensferry (W)
Vacant
Andrea Fraser BSc PGCert MDiv   2023 — Andrea.Fraser@churchofscotland.org.uk
(Assistant Minister)
Session Clerk, Inverkeithing: Moira Lamont (Mrs) — moiralamont@aol.com — 01383 415859
Session Clerk, North Queensferry: Douglas Short — douglas.short@sky.com — 01383 416492

42   Kelty (W)
Vacant — info@keltychurch.co.uk — 01383 831219
15 Arlick Road, Kelty KY4 0BH — 01383 831362
Session Clerk: Veronica Forrest — forveronica2@gmail.com — 01383 830130

43   Kennoway, Windygates and Balgonie: St Kenneth's (F W)   2018
Allan P. Morton MA BD PGDip — stkennethsparish@gmail.com — 01333 351372
2 Fernhill Gardens, Windygates, Leven KY8 5DZ — 01333 350240
AMorton@churchofscotland.org.uk

44 Kilrenny (W)
Guardianship of the Presbytery
Session Clerk: Corinne Peddie
corinne@peddies.com

01333 311408

45 Kinghorn (F W)   1985   1997
James Reid BD
17 Myre Crescent, Kinghorn, Burntisland KY3 9UB
JReid@churchofscotland.org.uk

01592 890269

46 Kingsbarns (F H)
Guardianship of the Presbytery
Sarah Whittle BA MA PhD PGDipPsych   2023
PGCertCBT FHEA
(Ordained Local Minister)
Session Clerk: Elizabeth Spittal
SWhittle@churchofscotland.org.uk
elibby.t21@btinternet.com

07801 492158
01334 880387

47 Kirkcaldy: Abbotshall (F H T W)
Vacant
Session Clerk: Morag Michael
83 Milton Road, Kirkcaldy KY1 1TP
msmichael@icloud.com

01592 267915
01592 263087

48 Kirkcaldy: Bennochy (F W)
Vacant
Session Clerk: George Drummond
25 Bennochy Avenue, Kirkcaldy KY2 5QE
gdrummond@btinternet.com

01592 201723
01592 643518
01592 200179

49 Kirkcaldy: Linktown See Auchtertool

50 Kirkcaldy: Pathhead (F H W)   1992   2005
Andrew C. Donald BD DPS
pathheadchurch@btconnect.com
73 Loughborough Road, Kirkcaldy KY1 3DB
ADonald@churchofscotland.org.uk

01592 204635
01592 652215

51 Kirkcaldy: St Bryce Kirk (F H T W)
Vacant
Session Clerk: Margaret Hunter
office@stbrycekirk.org.uk
mannehunter@hotmail.com

01592 640016

01592 265927

52 Kirkcaldy: Templehall and Torbain United (F W)
Joshua Z. Milton BA BA DipCSE   2022
27 Stocks Street, Kirkcaldy KY2 6ND
JMilton@churchofscotland.org.uk

01592 375148

53 Largo (F W)
Vacant
Session Clerk: Andrew Gilmour

infolargochurches@gmail.com
1 Castaway Lane, Lower Largo KY8 6FA
andrew.gilmour@montrave.net

01333 320850
01333 350209

54 Largoward (H W)
Guardianship of the Presbytery
Session Clerk: Robert Scott

bobandandge@gmail.com

55 Leslie: Trinity
Guardianship of the Presbytery
Session Clerk: Alec Redpath

sessionclerk@leslietrinitychurch.co.uk

01592 742636

56 Leuchars: St Athernase and Tayport (F)
Vacant
Session Clerk: Richard Trewern

7 David Wilson Park, Balmullo, St Andrews   KY16 0NP
rrit_lucklaw@btinternet.com
New charge formed by the union of Leuchars: St Athernase and Tayport

01334 870038
07702 160769

57 Leven (F)
Vacant
Session Clerk: Linda Archer

levenparish@tiscali.co.uk
lindaarcher847@ymail.com

01333 423969
01333 329850

58 Limekilns See Cairneyhill

59 Lindores (F H)
Guardianship of Presbytery
Session Clerk: Elizabeth Lee

2 Guthrie Court, Cupar Road, Newburgh, Cupar KY14 6HA
elee1963.el@gmail.com

01337 842228
07761 342131

60 Lochgelly and Benarty: St Serf's (F W)
Zoltán Sáfrány BD   2000   2020
Pamela Scott (Mrs) BD DCS   2017

82 Main Street, Lochgelly KY5 9AA
ZSafrany@churchofscotland.org.uk
177 Primrose Avenue, Rosyth KY11 2TZ
PScott@churchofscotland.org.uk

01592 780435
07411 444743
01383 410530
07548 819334

61 Markinch and Thornton (F W)
Conor Fegan MA MTh PhD   2022

7 Guthrie Crescent, Markinch, Glenrothes KY7 6AY
CFegan@churchofscotland.org.uk

01592 758264

62 Methil: Wellesley (F H W)
Gillian Paterson (Mrs) BD — 2010 — 10 Vettriano Vale, Leven KY8 4GD
GPaterson@churchofscotland.org.uk — 01333 423147

63 Methilhill and Denbeath (F)
Elisabeth F. Cranfield (Ms) MA BD — 1988 — 9 Chemiss Road, Methilhill, Leven KY8 2BS
ECranfield@churchofscotland.org.uk — 01592 713142

64 Monimail See Cupar: Old and St Michael of Tarvit

65 Newport-on-Tay (F H W)
Amos B. Chewachong BTh MTh PhD — 2005 — 2017 — 17 East Station Place, Newport-on-Tay DD6 8EG
AChewachong@churchofscotland.org.uk — 01382 542893

66 North Queensferry See Inverkeithing
67 Pittenweem See Carnbee

68 Rosyth (F W)
Vacant
Session Clerk: Margaret Miller (Mrs) — **rpc@cos82a.plus.com** — **01383 412534**
magmiller119@btinternet.com — 01383 414299

69 St Andrews: Holy Trinity See Boarhills and Dunino
70 St Andrews: St Leonard's See Cameron

71 St Andrews: St Mark's (F H W)
Allan McCafferty BSc BD — 1993 — 2011 — **admin@hpmchurch.org.uk** — **01334 478144**
20 Priory Gardens, St Andrews KY16 8XX — Tel/Fax 01334 478287
AMcCafferty@churchofscotland.org.uk

72 St Monans (F H W)
Vacant
Session Clerk: Fiona Keay (Mrs) — **info@stmonanschurch.org.uk** — 01333 730009
fionakeay@hotmail.co.uk

73 Saline and Blairingone (F W) linked with Tulliallan and Kincardine (F W) **tulliallanandkincardine@gmail.com**
Alexander J. Shuttleworth MA BD — 2004 — 2013 — 62 Toll Road, Kincardine, Alloa FK10 4QZ — 01259 731002
AShuttleworth@churchofscotland.org.uk

74 Tulliallan and Kincardine See Saline and Blairingone
75 Wormit See Balmerino

B. In other appointments: members of Presbytery

Coulter, David G. CB OStJ KHC BA BD MDA PhD	1989	2021	Presbytery Clerk: Fife	62B Buchanan Gardens, St Andrews KY16 9LX DCoulter@churchofscotland.org.uk	01334 473836
MacEwan, Donald G. MA BD PhD	2001	2011	Chaplain: University of St Andrews	Chaplaincy Centre, 3A St Mary's Place, St Andrews KY16 9UY dgm21@st-andrews.ac.uk	01334 462865 07713 322036
McPherson, Marjory (Mrs) LLB BD MTh	1990	2023	Chaplain, Royal Infirmary of Edinburgh	41 Woodlands Bank, Dalgety Bay KY11 9SX MMcPherson@churchofscotland.org.uk	07968 670765
McPherson, Stewart M. BD CertMin	1991	2023	Interim Minister, Presbytery of Fife	41 Woodlands Bank, Dalgety Bay KY11 9SX SMcPherson@churchofscotland.org.uk	07814 901429
Miller, Eileen A. BD DipComEd AdvDipCouns MBCAP(Snr Accred.)	2014	2022	Chaplain, Queen Margaret Hospital, Dunfermline	9 Car Craig View, Burntisland KY3 0DS EMiller@churchofscotland.org.uk	07923 033933
Smith, Fiona E. (Mrs) LLB BD	2010	2022	Principal Clerk	11 Bridge Street, Saline, Dunfermline KY12 9TS FSmith@churchofscotland.org.uk	07824 037271
Strang, Gordon I. BSc BD	2014	2021	Chaplain, NHS Fife	Department of Spiritual Care, Victoria Hospital, Kirkcaldy KY2 5AH GStrang@churchofscotland.org.uk	01592 648158

C. Retaining: members of Presbytery

Adams, David G. BD	1991	2011	(Cowdenbeath: Trinity)	13 Fernhill Gardens, Windygates, Leven KY8 5DZ adams.69@btinternet.com	01333 351214
Allardice, Michael MA MPhil DipTheol FHEA	2014	2020	(Ordained Local Minister)	2 Station Road, Kingskettle, Cupar KY15 7PR MAllardice@churchofscotland.org.uk	01337 597073 07936 203465
Alston, Colin M. BMus BD BN RN	1975	2023	(Inverkeithing with North Queensferry)	32c Townhill Road, Dunfermline KY12 0QX CAlston@churchofscotland.org.uk	01383 621050
Barr, G. Russell BA BD MTh DMin	1979	2020	(Edinburgh: Cramond)	4 Balone Steading, St Andrews KY16 8NS GBarr@churchofscotland.org.uk	01334 781142
Boswell, Gavin B. BTheol	1993	2023	(Largo)	51 St John's Drive, Dunfermline KY12 7TL GBoswell@churchofscotland.org.uk	01383 271548
Boyle, Robert P. LTh CPS	1990	2010	(Saline and Blairingone)	23 Farnell Way, Dunfermline KY12 0SR boab.boyle@btinternet.com	01383 729568
Bradley, Ian C. (Prof.) MA BD DPhil	1990	2018	(University of St Andrews: Cultural and Spiritual History)	4 Donaldson Gardens, St Andrews KY16 9DN icb@st-andrews.ac.uk	
Brewster, John MA BD DipEd	1988	2021	(East Kilbride: Greenhills)	82 Harcourt Road, Kirkcaldy KY2 5HF johnbrewster@blueyonder.co.uk	07917 333812
Burton, Scott E. BD DipMin	1999	2021	(Gigha and Cara with Kilcalmonell with Killean and Kilchenzie)	SBurton@churchofscotland.org.uk	
Campbell, Reginald F. BSc BD DipChEd	1979	2015	(Daviot and Dunlichity with Moy, Dalarossie and Tomatin)	12 Alloway Drive, Kirkcaldy KY2 6DX campbell578@talktalk.net	
Chalmers, John P. BD CPS DD	1979	2017	(Principal Clerk)	10 Liggars Place, Dunfermline KY12 7XZ JChalmers@churchofscotland.org.uk	01383 739130
Christie, Arthur A. BD	1997	2018	(Anstruther and Cellardyke: St Ayle with Kilrenny)	194 Foulford Road, Cowdenbeath KY4 9AX revacc@btinternet.com	01383 511326

Name			(Charge)	Address	Tel
Clark, David M. MA BD	1989	2013	(Dundee: The Steeple)	2b Rose Street, St Monans, Anstruther KY10 2BQ dmclark72@gmail.com	01333 739034
Collins, Catherine E.E. (Mrs) MA BD	1993	2021	(Dundee: Broughty Ferry New Kirk)	Eden Cottage, 16 Melville Road, Ladybank, Cupar KY15 7LU revccollins@btinternet.com	01337 830707
Collins, David A. BSc BD	1993	2016	(Auchterhouse with Monikie and Newbigging and Murroes and Tealing)	Eden Cottage, 16 Melville Road, Ladybank, Cupar KY15 7LU revdacollins@btinternet.com	01337 830707
Conkey, Hugh BSc BD	1987	2023	(Newtonhill)	15 Calender Park, Kirkcaldy KY1 2HG HConkey@churchofscotland.org.uk	07476 943330
Connolly, Daniel BD DipTh DipMin	1983	2015	(Army Chaplain)	2 Cairngreen, Cupar KY15 2SY damyconnolly@hotmail.co.uk	07951 078478
Deans, Graham D.S. MA BD MTh MLitt DMin	1978	2017	(Aberdeen: Queen Street)	38 Sir Thomas Elder Way, Kirkcaldy KY2 6ZS graham.deans@btopenworld.com	01592 641429
Dick, John H.A. (Ian) MA MSc BD	1982	2012	(Aberdeen: Ferryhill)	18 Fairfield Road, Kelty KY4 0BY	07889 411158
Dobby, D. Brian BA MA	1999	2023	(Rosyth)	10 Stuart Place, Cowdenbeath KY4 9BN	01383 325520
Elston, Ian J. BD MTh	1999	2019	(Kirkcaldy: Torbain)	65 Longbrae Gardens, Kirkcaldy KY2 5YJ IElston@churchofscotland.org.uk	01592 592393
Fairlie, George BD BVMS MRCVS	1971	2002	(Crail with Kingsbarns)	12 Dunnydeer Place, Insch AB52 6HP	
Farquhar, William E. BA BD	1987	2006	(Dunfermline: Townhill and Kingseat)	29 Queens Drive, Middlewich, Cheshire CW10 0DG	01606 835097
Fisk, Elizabeth A. BD	1996	2022	(Culross and Torryburn)	30 Masterton Road, Dunfermline KY11 8RB elizabethfisk10@hotmail.com	01383 730039
Foggie, Janet P. MA BD PhD	2003	2021	(Pioneer Minister, University of Stirling)	Old Schoolhouse, Dunbog, Newburgh KY14 6JF	07899 349246
Forrester, Ian L. MA	1964	1996	(Friockheim Kinnell with Inverkeilor and Lunan)	8 Bennochy Avenue, Kirkcaldy KY2 5QE	01592 260251
Forsyth, Alexander R. TD BA MTh	1973	2014	(Markinch)	49 Scaraben Crescent, Formonthills, Glenrothes KY6 3HL arforsyth516@gmail.com	07483 232581
Fraser, Ann G. BD CertMin	1990	2007	(Auchtermuchty)	24 Irvine Crescent, St Andrews KY16 8LG	01334 461329
Froude, J. Kenneth (Ken) MA BD	1979	2020	(Kirkcaldy: St Bryce Kirk)	44 Templars Crescent, Kinghorn KY3 9XS JFroude@churchofscotland.org.uk	01592 892512
Galbraith, D. Douglas MA BD BMus MPhil ARSCM PhD	1965	2005	(Office for Worship, Doctrine and Artistic Matters)	34 Balbirnie Street, Markinch, Glenrothes KY7 6DA dgalbraith@churchofscotland.org.uk	01592 752403
Gerbrandy-Baird, Peter S. MA BD MSc FRSA FRGS	2004	2023	(Aberdour: St Fillan's)		
Gordon, Ian D. LTh	1972	2001	(Markinch)	2 Somerville Way, Glenrothes KY7 5GE	01592 742487
Hamilton, Ian W.F. BD LTh ALCM AVCM	1978	2012	(Nairn: Old)	Mossneuk, 5 Windsor Gardens, St Andrews KY16 8XL reviwfh@btinternet.com	01334 477745
Harrison, Cameron BSc MEd	2006	2010	(Auxiliary Minister, St Andrews: Holy Trinity)	Woodfield House, Priormuir, St Andrews KY16 8LP cameron@harrisonleimon.co.uk	01334 478067
Henderson, J. Mary MA BD DipEd PhD	1990	2020	(Falkirk: Laurieston with Redding and Westquarter)	8 Miller Terrace, St Monans KY10 2BB jmary.henderson1@gmail.com	01333 730138
Jenkins, Gordon F.C. MA BD PhD	1968	2006	(Dunfermline: North)	2 Balrymonth Court, St Andrews KY16 8XT jenkinsgordon1@sky.com	01335 477194
Johnston, Thomas N. LTh	1972	2008	(Edinburgh: Priestfield)	71 Main Street, Newmills, Dunfermline KY12 8ST tomjohnston@blueyonder.co.uk	01383 889240

Name	(Parish/Role)			Address / Email	Telephone
Kenny, Elizabeth S.S. BD RGN SCM	(Carnock and Oakley)	1989	2010	5 Cobden Court, Crossgates, Cowdenbeath KY4 8AU / esskenny@btinternet.com	07831 763494
Kesting, Sheilagh M. BA BD DD DSG	(Ecumenical Officer, Church of Scotland)	1980	2016	Restalrig, Chance Inn, Cupar KY15 5QJ / smkesting@btinternet.com	01334 829485
Laidlaw, Victor W.N. BD CertCE	(Edinburgh: St Catherine's Argyle)	1975	2008	9 Tern Road, Dunfermline KY11 8GA / v9wintern@hotmail.co.uk	01383 620134
Lane, Margaret R. (Mrs) BA BD MTh	(Edinburgh: Kirkliston)	2009	2019	6 Overhaven, Limekilns KY11 3JH / margaretlane@btinternet.com	01383 873328
Leitch, D. Graham MA BD	(Tyne Valley)	1974	2012	9 St Margaret Wynd, Dunfermline KY12 0UT / dgrahamleitch@gmail.com	01383 249245
McAlpine, Robin J. BDS BD MTh	(Kirkcaldy: Bennochy)	1988	2022	1 Branxton Wynd, Kirkcaldy KY1 1SF / RMcAlpine@churchofscotland.org.uk	
McCulloch, William B. BD	(Rome: St Andrew's)	1997	2016	81 Meldrum Court, Dunfermline KY11 4XR / revwbmcculloch@hotmail.com	01383 730305
McDonald, Tom BD	(Kelso: North and Ednam)	1994	2015	12 Woodmill Grove, Dunfermline KY11 4JR / revtomparadise12@gmail.com	01383 695365
McKay, Violet C.C. BD	(Rosyth)	1988	2017	20B Blane Crescent, Dunfermline KY11 8ZF / violetcm@gmail.com	01383 727255
McKimmon, Eric G. BA BD MTh PhD	(Cargill Burrelton with Collace)	1983	2014	1 Dolan Grove, Saline KY12 9UP / ericmckimmon@gmail.com	07835 069115
McLean, John P. BSc BPhil BD	(Glenrothes: St Margaret's)	1994	2013	72 Lawmill Gardens, St Andrews KY16 8QS / jpmclean72@gmail.com	01334 470803
McLellan, Andrew R.C. CBE MA BD STM DD	(HM Chief Inspector of Prisons for Scotland)	1970	2009	4 Liggars Place, Dunfermline KY12 7XZ / iamclellan4@gmail.com	01383 725959
McLeod, Alistair G.	(Glenrothes: St Columba's)	1988	2005	13 Greenmantle Way, Glenrothes KY6 3QG / alistairmcleod1936@gmail.com	01592 744558
McNaught, Samuel M. MA BD MTh	(Kirkcaldy: St John's)	1968	2002	6 Munro Court, Glenrothes KY7 5GD / sjmcnaught@btinternet.com	01592 742352
Meager, Peter MA BD CertMgmt(Open)	(Elie with Kilconquhar and Colinsburgh)	1970	1998	7 Lorraine Drive, Cupar KY15 5DY / meager52@btinternet.com	01334 656991 / 07777 657414
Melville, David D. BD	(Kirkconnel)	1989	2008	28 Porterfield, Comrie, Dunfermline KY12 9HJ / revddm@gmail.com	01383 850075
Munro, Andrew MA BD PhD	(Glencaple with Lowther)	1972	2000	7 Dunvegan Avenue, Kirkcaldy KY2 5SG / am.smm@blueyonder.co.uk	01592 566129
Murray, John W. LLB BA	(Anstruther and Cellardyke: St Ayle with Crail)	2001	2022	JMurray@churchofscotland.org.uk	
Neilson, Peter MA BD MTh	(Mission Consultant)	1975	2016	Linne Bheag, 2 School Green, Anstruther KY10 3HF / neilson.peter@btinternet.com	01333 310477 / 07818 418608
Nicol, George G. BD DPhil	(Falkland with Freuchie)	1982	2013	48 Fidra Avenue, Burntisland KY3 0AZ / ggnicol@totalise.co.uk	01592 873258
Nicol, Sarah E.C. (Mrs) BSc BD MTh	(Saltcoats: St Cuthbert's)	1985	2023	13 Hawthorn Grove, Dunfermline KY12 0DZ / Sarabecn1008@gmail.com	

Name	Year	Year	Role	Address / Email	Phone
Nisbet, Gilbert C. CA BD	1993	2019	(Leven)	Upper Flat, 2 Temple Crescent, Crail KY10 3RS gcn@insprint.co.uk	01333 450929
Paterson, Andrew E. JP	1994	2020	(Auxiliary Minister, Presbytery-wide)	6 The Willows, Kelty KY4 0FQ	01383 830998
Paterson, Maureen (Mrs) BSc	1992	2010	(Auxiliary Minister, Kennoway, Windygates and Balgonie: St Kenneth's)	91 Dalmahoy Crescent, Kirkcaldy KY2 6TA m.e.paterson@blueyonder.co.uk	01592 262300
Paton, Marion J. (Miss) MA BMus BD	1991	2017	(Dundee: St David's High Kirk)	18 Winram Place, St Andrews KY16 8XH mjpdht@gmail.com	01334 208743
Porteous, Brian W. BSc DipRM DipCS CertCounsS	2018	2023	(Ordained Local Minister, Kirkcaldy Templehall and Torbain United)	Kildene, Westfield Road, Cupar KY15 5DS BPorteous@churchofscotland.org.uk	01334 653561
Redmayne, David W. BSc BD	2001	2017	(Beath and Cowdenbeath: North)	10 Hawthorn Park, Dunfermline KY12 0DY	01383 738137
Robb, Nigel J. FCP MA BD ThM MTh	1981	2014	(Associate Secretary, Mission and Discipleship Council)		07966 286958
Rose, Margaret E.S. BD	2007	2022	(Carnbee with Pittenweem)	10a Dunlop Street, Strathaven ML10 6LA MRose@churchofscotland.org.uk	
Roy, Allistair D. BD DipSW PgDip	2007	2016	(Glenrothes: St Ninian's)	39 Ravenswood Drive, Glenrothes KY6 2PA minister@revroy.co.uk	
Scott, David D. BSc BD	1981	2019	(Traprain)	259 Lamond Drive, St Andrews KY16 8RR revdd.scott@gmail.com	01334 473460
Sharp, Alan BSc BD	1980	2019	(Burntisland)	29 Cromwell Road, Burntisland KY3 9EH alansharp03@aol.com	
Sime, Christine M. (Miss) BSc BD	1994	2023	(Dalgety)	3 St Mary's Place, Kinross KY13 8BZ CSime@churchofscotland.org.uk	
Sinclair, David I. BSc BD PhD DipSW CQSW	1990	2020	(Ecumenical and International Officer, Evangelical Church of the Czech Brethren)	42 South Road, Cupar KY15 5JF davidsinclair@btinternet.com	01334 659171
Symington, Alastair H. MA BD	1972	2012	(Troon: Old)	70 The Walled Garden, Abbey Park Avenue, St Andrews KY16 9JW revdahs@virginmedia.com	07703 176717
Templeton, James L. BSc BD	1975	2012	(Innerleven: East)	29 Coldstream Avenue, Leven KY8 5TN jamietempleton@btinternet.com	01333 427102
Thom, Ian G. BSc PhD BD	1990	2020	(Dunfermline: North)	4 Calaiswood Crescent, Dunfermline KY11 8ZR ianthom58@btinternet.com	01383 733471
Thomson, John D. BD	1985	2005	(Kirkcaldy: Pathhead)	3 Tottenham Court, Hill Street, Dysart, Kirkcaldy KY1 2XY j.thomson10@sky.com	01592 655313 / 07885 414979
Tomlinson, Bryan L. TD	1969	2003	(Kirkcaldy: Abbotshall)	2 Duddingston Drive, Kirkcaldy KY2 6JP abbkirk@blueyonder.co.uk	01592 564843
Torrance, Alan J. (Prof.) MA BD DrTheol ARCM	1984	2020	(University of St Andrews: Systematic Theology)	Kincaple House, Kincaple, St Andrews KY16 9SH	01334 850755
Unsworth, Ruth BA BD CertMHS PgDipCBP BABCP	1984	1987	(Glasgow: Pollokshaws)	5 Lindsay Gardens, St Andrews KY16 8XB RUnsworth@churchofscotland.org.uk	07894 802119
Walker, James B. MA BD DPhil	1975	2011	(Chaplain: University of St Andrews)	5 Priestden Park, St Andrews KY16 8DL	01334 472839
Wallace, Hugh M. MA BD	1980	2018	(Newhills)	15 West End, St Monans KY10 2BX	07707 539991 / 01333 730607
Watt, Robert J. BD	1994	2009	(Dumbarton: Riverside)	101 Birrell Drive, Dunfermline KY11 8FA robertwatt101@gmail.com	01383 735417 / 07753 683717

Wilson, Tilly (Miss) MTh	1990	2012	(Dysart)	6 Citron Glebe, Kirkcaldy KY1 2NF
				tillywilson1@sky.com
Wotherspoon, Ian G. BA LTh	1967	2004	(Coatbridge: St Andrew's)	12 Cherry Lane, Cupar KY15 5DA
				wotherspoonrg@aol.com
Wright, Lynda BEd DCS	1979	2021	Community Chaplaincy Listening Co-ordinator, NHS Fife	1 Union Street, Kirkcaldy KY1 3DN
				lyndawright20@gmail.com

01592 263134

01334 650710
07711 706634
07835 303395

D. In other appointments: not members of Presbytery
Nil

E. Retaining: not members of Presbytery

Pieterse, Ben BA BTh LTh	1968	2014	(Auchterderran Kinglassie)	15 Bakeoven Close, Seaforth Sound, Simon's Town, 7975, South Africa
				benhpl@gmail.com
Thrower, Charles D. BSc	1965	2002	(Carnbee with Pittenweem)	Grange House, Wester Grangemuir, Pittenweem, Anstruther KY10 2RB 01333 312631
				charlesandsteph@btinternet.com

F. Inactive: not members of Presbytery

Bjarnason, Sven S. CandTheol CPS	1973	2011	(Tomintoul, Glenlivet and Inveraven)	14 Edward Street, Dunfermline KY12 0JW
				sven@bjarnason.org.uk
Campbell, J. Ewen R. MA BD	1967	2005	(Auchterderran St Fothad's with Kinglassie)	20 St Margaret's Road, North Berwick EH39 4PJ
Collins, Mitchell BD CPS	1996	2005	(Creich, Flisk and Kilmany with Monimail)	6 Netherby Park, Glenrothes KY6 3PL
Donaldson, Colin V.	1982	1998	(Ormiston with Pencaitland)	3A Playfair Terrace, St Andrews KY16 9HX
				colinmarion80@gmail.com
Whyte, Iain A. BA BD STM PhD	1968	2005	(Community Mental Health Chaplain)	14 Carlingnose Point, North Queensferry, Inverkeithing KY11 1ER
				iainwhyte67@gmail.com

01383 724625

01620 890835

01592 742915

01334 472889

01383 410732

G. Readers (active)

Brown, Gordon	Nowell, Fossoway, Kinross KY13 0UW	brown.nowell@hotmail.co.uk
Cunningham, Martin	5 Livingstone Place, St Andrews KY16 3JH	martincunninghamteacher@gmail.com
Elder, Morag Anne (Ms)	5 Provost Road, Tayport DD6 9JE	benuardin@btinternet.com
Grant, Allan	6 Normandy Place, Rosyth KY11 2HJ	allan75@talktalk.net
Mitchell, Ian G. KC	17 Carlingnose Point, North Queensferry, Inverkeithing KY11 1ER	igmitchell@easynet.co.uk
Monk, Alan	36 North Road, Saline KY12 9UQ	salinemonks@gmail.com

01577 840248

01382 552218
01383 428760
07449 278378
01383 416240

01383 851283

Muirhead, Sandy	7 Westpark Gate, Saline KY12 9US	sandy_muirhead@hotmail.com	01383 850077
Peacock, Graham	6 Balgove Avenue, Gauldry, Newport-on-Tay DD6 8SQ	grahampeacock6@btinternet.com	01382 330124
Smith, Elspeth (Mrs)	Glentarkie Cottage, Glentarkie, Strathmiglo, Cupar KY14 7RU	elspeth.smith@btinternet.com	01337 860824

H. Ministries Development Staff

Christie, Aileen	Lochgelly and Benarty: St Serf's – Outreach Worker	Aileen.Christie@churchofscotland.org.uk
Davie, Sandra	Glenrothes: St Margaret's – Children Youth and Family Worker	SDavie@churchofscotland.org.uk
Hutchison, John BA	Rothes Trinity Parish Grouping – Families Worker and Parish Assistant	JHutchison@churchofscotland.org.uk
Jones, Lauren	Kirkcaldy: Templehall and Torbain United – Community Outreach Worker	LJones@churchofscotland.org.uk
Kerr, Fiona	Methil: Wellesley – Parish Assistant	FKerr@churchofscotland.org.uk
Pringle, Iona M. BD	Kennoway, Windygates and Balgonie: St Kenneth's – Parish Assistant	IPringle@churchofscotland.org.uk
Scott, Pamela (Mrs) DCS	Lochgelly and Benarty: St Serf's – Parish Assistant	PScott@churchofscotland.org.uk
Thomson, Jacqueline (Mrs) MTh DCS	Buckhaven and Wemyss – Deacon	Jaqueline.Thomson@churchofscotland.org.uk
Thorburn, Susan (Rev) MTh	Eden Tay Cluster – Mission Development Worker	SThorburn@churchofscotland.org.uk
Ure, Irene	Glenrothes Area Partnership Development Co-ordinator	IUre@churchofscotland.org.uk

TOWN ADDRESSES

Cupar
Old and St Michael of Tarvit — Kirkgate
St John's and Dairsie United — Bonnygate / Main Street, Dairsie

Dunfermline
Abbey — St Catherine's Wynd
East — Nightingale Place
Gillespie Memorial — Chapel Street
North — Goldrum Street
St Andrew's Erskine — Robertson Road
St Leonard's — Brucefield Avenue

St Margaret's — Abel Place
St Ninian's — Allan Crescent
Townhill and Kingseat — Main Street, Townhill / Church Street, Kingseat

Glenrothes
Christ's Kirk — Pitcoudie Avenue
St Columba's — Church Street
St Margaret's — Woodside Road
St Ninian's — Durris Drive

Kirkcaldy
Abbotshall — Abbotshall Road

Bennochy — Elgin Street
Linktown — Nicol Street x High Street
Pathhead — Harriet Street x Church Street
St Bryce Kirk — St Brycedale Avenue x Kirk Wynd
Templehall and Torbain United — Beauly Place / Carron Place

St Andrews
Holy Trinity — South Street
St Leonard's — Donaldson Gardens
St Mark's — St Mary's Place

(8) PERTH (F W)

Meets at various locations on the first Tuesday in November 2023 and in 2024 on the first Tuesday in February, the third Saturday in June, the first Saturday in September and the first Tuesday in November.

Clerk:	REV. JOHN A. FERGUSON BD DipMin DMin	07596 868064
Presbytery Office:	Suite F3, Riverview House, Friarton Road, Perth PH2 8DF	07596 868064
	perth@churchofscotland.org.uk	

1 Aberdalgie and Forteviot (F H W) linked with Aberuthven and Dunning (F H W)
Vacant
Interim Moderator: Allan J. Wilson
awilson@churchofscotland.org.uk   01738 812211

2 Aberfeldy (F H W) linked with Dull and Weem (H W) linked with Grantully, Logierait and Strathtay (F W)
Neil M. Glover BSc BD   2005   2017
The Manse, Taybridge Terrace, Aberfeldy PH15 2BS
NGlover@churchofscotland.org.uk   01887 820819
                                     07779 280074

3 Aberfoyle (H W) linked with Port of Menteith (H W)
Vacant
Interim Moderator: Dan Gunn
degunn@hotmail.co.uk   01786 823798

4 Aberlemno (H W) linked with Guthrie and Rescobie (W)
Vacant
Interim Moderator: Margaret J. Hunt
The Manse, Guthrie, Forfar DD8 2TP
MHunt@churchofscotland.org.uk   01241 828243
                                   01307 462044

5 Abernethy and Dron and Arngask (F W)
Vacant
Interim Moderator: Elizabeth M. Stenhouse
EStenhouse@churchofscotland.org.uk   01577 842128

6 Abernyte (W) linked with Inchture and Kinnaird (F W) linked with Longforgan (F H W)
Catriona M. Morrison MA BD   1995   2021
2 Boniface Place, Invergowrie, Dundee DD2 5DR
CMorrison@churchofscotland.org.uk   01382 561523
Marc A. Prowe   2000   2021
2 Boniface Place, Invergowrie, Dundee DD2 5DR
MProwe@churchofscotland.org.uk   01382 561523

7 Aberuthven and Dunning See Aberdalgie and Forteviot

8 Alloa: Ludgate (F W)
Dawn A. Laing BEd PGCertPD BD — 2020
28 Alloa Park Drive, Alloa FK10 1QY
DLaing@churchofscotland.org.uk
01259 213134

9 Alloa: St Mungo's (F H T W)
Sang Y. Cha BD MTh — 2011
contact@alloastmungos.org
37A Claremont, Alloa FK10 2DG
SCha@churchofscotland.org.uk
01259 723004
01259 213872

10 Almondbank Tibbermore (F W) linked with Methven and Logiealmond (F W)
Robert J. Malloch BD — 1987 2019
The Manse, Dalcrue Road, Pitcairngreen, Perth PH1 3EA
RMalloch@churchofscotland.org.uk
01738 583727

11 Alva (F W)
James N.R. McNeil BSc BD — 1990 1997
alvaparishchurch@gmail.com
34 Ochil Road, Alva FK12 5JT
JMcNeil@churchofscotland.org.uk
01259 760262
Anne F. Shearer BA DipEd CertCS — 2010 2018
(Auxiliary Minister)
10 Colsnaur, Menstrie FK11 7HG
AShearer@churchofscotland.org.uk
01259 769176

12 Alyth (F H W)
Michael J. Erskine MA BD — 1985 2012
The Manse, Cambridge Street, Alyth, Blairgowrie PH11 8AW
erskinemike@gmail.com
01828 632238

13 Arbirlot linked with Carmyllie
Vacant
Interim Moderator: Annette Gordon
The Manse, Arbirlot, Arbroath DD11 2NX
AGordon@churchofscotland.org.uk
01241 874613
01241 854478

14 Arbroath: Old and Abbey (F H W)
Vacant
Interim Moderator: Michael J. Goss
church.office@old-and-abbey-church.org.uk
MGoss@churchofscotland.org.uk
01241 877068
01241 410194

15 Arbroath: St Andrew's (F H W)
Vacant
Interim Moderator: Geoffrey Redmayne
office@arbroathstandrews.org.uk
GRedmayne@churchofscotland.org.uk
01241 431135
01674 675634

16 Arbroath: St Vigeans (F H W)
Guardianship of the Presbytery
Interim Moderator: Peter A. Phillips
office.stvigeans@gmail.com
PPhillips@churchofscotland.org.uk
01241 879567
01241 830464

17 Arbroath: West Kirk (F H W)
Christine Hay LLB CA BD   2020

arbroathwestkirk2019@gmail.com   **01241 434721**
1 Charles Avenue, Arbroath DD11 2EY   01241 554189
Christine.Hay@churchofscotland.org.uk

18 Ardler, Kettins and Meigle (F W)
Vacant   01828 640074
Interim Moderator: Michael J. Erskine   01828 632238

The Manse, Dundee Road, Meigle, Blairgowrie PH12 8SB
erskinemike@gmail.com

19 Ardoch (H W) linked with Blackford (F H W)
Mairi Perkins BA BTh   2012   2016

info@ardochparishchurch.org   01786 880948
Manse of Ardoch, Feddal Road, Braco, Dunblane   FK15 5RE
MPerkins@churchofscotland.org.uk

20 Auchterarder (F H T W)
Lynn M. McChlery BA BD MLitt PhD   2005   2019

admin@auchterarderparish.org   **01764 660152**
22 Kirkfield Place, Auchterarder PH3 1FP   01764 662399
LMcChlery@churchofscotland.org.uk

21 Auchtergaven and Moneydie (F W) linked with Redgorton and Stanley (W)   auchtergavenchurch@hotmail.co.uk
Vacant   **01738 788017**
Interim Moderator: Susan Thorburn
SThorburn@churchofscotland.org.uk   01821 642681

22 Auchterhouse (H)
Vacant   01382 580210
Interim Moderator: Donna M. Hays
DHays@churchofscotland.org.uk

23 Balfron (F W) linked with Fintry (F H W)
Vacant   01360 440285
Lesley A. Stanley MA PhD FBTS   2021   01506 671532
(Ordained Local Minister)   07415 683871
Interim Moderator: Alison E.P. Britchfield

admin@balfronchurch.org.uk
7 Station Road, Balfron, Glasgow G63 0SX
Lilac Cottage, Main Street, Gartmore, Stirling FK8 3RN
LStanley@churchofscotland.org.uk
ABritchfield@churchofscotland.org.uk

24 Balquhidder linked with Killin and Ardeonaig (H W)
Vacant   01567 820247
Interim Moderator: Jeffrey A. McCormick   07880 612858

The Manse, Killin FK21 8TN
JMcCormick@churchofscotland.org.uk

25 Bannockburn: Allan (F H T W) linked with Cowie and Plean (H T)   hiya@allanchurch.org
Vacant   01786 814692
Interim Moderator: Gary J. McIntyre   01786 474421
The Manse, Bogend Road, Bannockburn, Stirling FK7 8NP
GMcIntyre@churchofscotland.org.uk

26 **Bannockburn: Ladywell (F H W)**
Elizabeth M.D. Robertson (Miss) 1997
BD CertMin
57 The Firs, Bannockburn FK7 0EG
ERobertson@churchofscotland.org.uk
01786 812467

27 **Barry (W) linked with Carnoustie (F W)**
Michael S. Goss BD DPS 1991 2003
44 Terrace Road, Carnoustie DD7 7AR
MGoss@churchofscotland.org.uk
01241 410194
07787 141567

28 **Bendochy (W) linked with Coupar Angus: Abbey (W)**
Andrew F. Graham BTh DPS 2001 2016
Caddam Road, Coupar Angus, Blairgowrie PH13 9EF
Andrew.Graham@churchofscotland.org.uk
01828 627864

29 **Blackford** See Ardoch

30 **Blair Atholl and Struan linked with Braes of Rannoch linked with Foss and Rannoch (H)**
Vacant
Interim Moderator: Grace M. F. Steele
The Manse, Blair Atholl, Pitlochry PH18 5SX
GSteele@churchofscotland.org.uk
01796 481213
01887 820025

31 **Blairgowrie (F W)**
Benjamin J. A. Abeledo BTh DipTh PTh 1991 2019
blairgowrieparishchurch@gmail.com
The Manse, Upper David Street, Blairgowrie PH10 6HB
BAbeledo@churchofscotland.org.uk
01250 870986

32 **Braes of Rannoch** See Blair Atholl and Struan

33 **Brechin and Farnell (F H T W)**
Vacant
Interim Moderator: Malcolm I. G. Rooney
New charge formed by the union of Brechin: Gardner Memorial and Farnell
office@gardnermemorial.plus.com
15 Caldhame Gardens, Brechin DD9 7JJ
malc.rooney@gmail.com
01356 629191
01356 622034
01575 575334

34 **Bridge of Allan (F H W)**
Daniel (Dan) J. Harper BSc BD 2016
office@bridgeofallanparishchurch.org.uk
29 Keir Street, Bridge of Allan, Stirling FK9 4QJ
DHarper@churchofscotland.org.uk
01786 834155
01786 832753

35 **Buchanan linked with Drymen (F W)**
Vacant
Interim Moderator: Ian McVean
Buchanan Manse, Drymen, Glasgow G63 0AQ
ianmcvean@yahoo.co.uk
01360 660370
01360 870212
01360 440016

36 Buchlyvie (H W) linked with Gartmore (H W)
Vacant
buchlyviechurch@gmail.com   gartmorechurch@gmail.com

37 Callander (F H W)
Jeffrey A. McCormick BD DipMin   1984
The Manse, Killin FK21 8TN
JMcCormick@churchofscotland.org.uk
Tel/Fax: **01877 331409**
01567 820247
07880 612858

38 Cambusbarron: The Bruce Memorial (F H W)
Graham P. Nash MA BD   2006
14 Woodside Court, Cambusbarron, Stirling FK7 9PH
GPNash@churchofscotland.org.uk
01786 442068

39 Caputh and Clunie (H) linked with Kinclaven (H)
Vacant
Interim Moderator: Harry Mowbray
mowbrayh@outlook.com
01250 873479

40 Cargill Burrelton (F) linked with Collace (F)
Vacant
Interim Moderator: Gillian Munro
The Manse, Manse Road, Woodside, Blairgowrie PH13 9NQ
munrooth@gmail.com
01828 670384
01738 850066

41 Carmyllie See Arbirlot
42 Carnoustie See Barry

43 Carnoustie: Panbride (F H W)
Annette M. Gordon BD   2017
8 Arbroath Road, Carnoustie DD7 6BL
AGordon@churchofscotland.org.uk
01241 854478

44 Clackmannan (F H W) linked with Sauchie and Coalsnaughton (F)   office@clackmannankirk.org.uk
Vacant
Interim Moderator: Michael J. Goodison
The Manse, Port Street, Clackmannan FK10 4JH
MGoodison@churchofscotland.org.uk
01259 214238
01259 611109

45 Cleish (H W) linked with Fossoway: St Serf's and Devonside (F W)
Elisabeth M. Stenhouse BD   2006   2014
Station House, Station Road, Crook of Devon, Kinross KY13 0PG
EStenhouse@churchofscotland.org.uk
01577 842128

46 Collace See Cargill Burrelton

47 Colliston linked with Friockheim Kinnell linked with Inverkeilor and Lunan (H)
Peter A. Phillips BA   1995   2004   The Manse, Inverkeilor, Arbroath DD11 5SA   01241 830464
PPhillips@churchofscotland.org.uk

48 Comrie (F H W) linked with Dundurn (F H)
Craig Dobney BA BD   2020   **strathearnkirks@btinternet.com**   **01764 679555**
The Manse, Strowan Road, Comrie, Crieff PH6 2ES   01764 679196
CDobney@churchofscotland.org.uk

49 Coupar Angus: Abbey See Bendochy
50 Cowie and Plean See Bannockburn: Allan

51 Crieff (F H W)
Andrew J. Philip BSc BD   1996   2013   8 Strathearn Terrace, Crieff PH7 3AQ   01764 218976
APhilip@churchofscotland.org.uk

52 Dollar (F H W) linked with Glendevon linked with Muckhart (W) info@dollarparishchurch.org.uk   muckhartchurch@gmail.com
Vacant   2 Princes Crescent East, Dollar FK14 7BU   01259 740286
Interim Moderator: Ellen M. Larson Davidson   ELarsonDavidson@churchofscotland.org.uk   01786 871249

53 Drymen See Buchanan
54 Dull and Weem See Aberfeldy

55 Dunbarney (H) and Forgandenny (F W)
Allan J. Wilson BSc MEd BD   2007   **dfpoffice@btconnect.com**   **01738 812463**
Dunbarney Manse, Manse Road, Bridge of Earn, Perth PH2 9DY   01738 812211
AWilson@churchofscotland.org.uk

56 Dunblane: Cathedral (F H T W)
Colin C. Renwick BMus BD   1989   2014   **office@dunblanecathedral.org.uk**   **01786 825388**
Cathedral Manse, The Cross, Dunblane FK15 0AQ   01786 822205
CRenwick@churchofscotland.org.uk
Ruth Kennedy BA MA PGDipPsych   2022   6 Craigmore View, Aberfoyle FK8 3SJ   01877 389427
(Pioneer Minister with under 40s)   RKennedy@churchofscotland.org.uk
Alastair Munro RN BSc   2022   AMunro@churchofscotland.org.uk
(Ordained Local Minister)

57 Dunblane: St Blane's (F H W) linked with Lecropt (F H W)
Vacant   46 Kellie Wynd, Dunblane FK15 0NR   01786 825324
Ruth Kennedy BA MA PGDipPsych   2022   6 Craigmore View, Aberfoyle FK8 3SJ   01877 389427
(Pioneer Minister with under 40s)   RKennedy@churchofscotland.org.uk
Interim Moderator: Colin C. Renwick   CRenwick@churchofscotland.org.uk   01786 822205

58   Dundee: Balgay (F H W)
Nardia J. Sandison BAppSc BD MLitt   2019
150 City Road, Dundee DD2 2PW
NSandison@churchofscotland.org.uk
01382 903446

59   Dundee: Barnhill St Margaret's (F H W)
Andrew Gardner BSc BD PhD   1997   2021
(Interim Minister)
church.office@btconnect.com
2 St Margaret's Lane, Barnhill, Dundee DD5 2PQ
AGardner@churchofscotland.org.uk
01382 737294
01382 503012
07411 989344

60   Dundee: Broughty Ferry New Kirk (F H T W)
Vacant
office@broughtyferrynewkirk.org.uk
New Kirk Manse, 25 Ballinard Gardens, Broughty Ferry, Dundee DD5 1BZ
RGrahame@churchofscotland.org.uk
01382 738264
01382 778874

Interim Moderator: Roderick J. Grahame
01382 561873

61   Dundee: Broughty Ferry St James' (F H)
Guardianship of the Presbytery
Session Clerks: Lyn Edwards (Mrs)   kathelyneedwards@gmail.com
        David J.B. Murie   d.j.b.murie@gmail.com
01382 730552
01382 320493

62   Dundee: Broughty Ferry St Luke's and Queen Street (F W)
Vacant
22 Albert Road, Broughty Ferry, Dundee DD5 1AZ
Interim Moderator: Anita D.C. Kerr
Anita.Kerr@churchofscotland.org.uk
01382 732094
01382 779212
01382 456659

63   Dundee: Broughty Ferry St Stephen's and West (H W) linked with Dundee: Dundee (St Mary's) (H W)
office@dundeestmarys.co.uk
Keith F. Hall MA BD   1981   1994
33 Strathern Road, West Ferry, Dundee DD5 1PP
KHall@churchofscotland.org.uk
01382 226271
01382 778808

64   Dundee: Camperdown (H)
Guardianship of the Presbytery
Interim Moderator: Roderick J. Grahame
Camperdown Manse, Myrekirk Road, Dundee DD2 4SF
RGrahame@churchofscotland.org.uk
01382 561872

65   Dundee: Chalmers-Ardler (F H W)
Vacant
Interim Moderator: Gordon A. Campbell
40 St Martin Crescent, Dundee DD3 0SU
g.a.campbell@dundee.ac.uk
01382 561383

66   Dundee: Coldside (F W)
Vacant
Interim Moderator: Kenneth Andrew
kga@scot-int.com
01382 776765

67 Dundee: Craigiebank (H W) linked with Dundee: Douglas and Mid Craigie (F W)   **01382 731173**
Vacant
Brenda M.M. Elwell-Sutton   2022   BElwell-Sutton@churchofscotland.org.uk   07811 753391
(Ordained Local Minister)
Interim Moderator: Grant R. MacLaughlan   GMacLaughlan@churchofscotland.org.uk   07790 518041

68 Dundee: Douglas and Mid Craigie   See Dundee: Craigiebank

69 Dundee: Downfield Mains (F H W)   office@downfieldmainschurch.org   **07979 939092**
Nathan S. McConnell BS MA ThM PhD   2002   2016   9 Elgin Street, Dundee DD3 8NL   07979 939092
NMcConnell@churchofscotland.org.uk

70 Dundee: Dundee (St Mary's)   See Dundee: Broughty Ferry St Stephen's and West

71 Dundee: Fintry (F W)
Vacant   01382 458629
Catherine J. Brodie MA BA MPhil PGCE   2017   4 Clive Street, Dundee DD4 7AW   07432 513375
48h Cleghorn Street, Dundee DD2 2NJ
CBrodie@churchofscotland.org.uk
(Ordained Local Minister)
Interim Moderator: Alison E. P. Britchfield   ABritchfield@churchofscotland.org.uk   07415 683871

72 Dundee: Kingsgait (F H T W)   standrewsdundee@outlook.com   **01382 224860**
Anita D.C. Kerr MA   2007   2020   27 Mayfield Grove, Dundee DD4 7GZ   01382 456659
Anita.Kerr@churchofscotland.org.uk
New charge formed by the union of Dundee: Meadowside St Paul's and Dundee: St Andrew's

73 Dundee: Lochee (F H)
Roderick J. Grahame BD CPS   1991   2018   32 Clayhills Drive, Dundee DD2 1SX   01382 561872
DMin DipPSRP   RGrahame@churchofscotland.org.uk

74 Dundee: Logie and St John's Cross (F H W)   administrator@logies.org   **01382 668514**
Grant R. MacLaughlan BA BD   1998   2021   7 Hyndford Street, Dundee DD2 1HQ   07790 518041
GMacLaughlan@churchofscotland.org.uk

75 Dundee: Menzieshill (F W)
Robert Mallinson BD   2010   The Manse, Charleston Drive, Dundee DD2 4BD   01382 667446
RMallinson@churchofscotland.org.uk   07595 249089

76 Dundee: St David's High Kirk (H W)
Emma McDonald BD   2013   2018   EMcDonald@churchofscotland.org.uk   01382 322746

No.	Charge / Minister		Contact	Phone
77	**Dundee: Steeple (F H T W)** Vacant Interim Moderator: James Connolly		office@thesteeplechurch.org.uk JConnolly@churchofscotland.org.uk	**01382 200031** 07711 177655
78	**Dundee: Stobswell Trinity (F H W)** Jean A. Kirkwood BSc PhD BD	2015 2021	secretary@trinitychurchdundee.org 65 Clepington Road, Dundee DD4 7BQ JKirkwood@churchofscotland.org.uk	**01382 526071** 01382 526071

New charge formed by the union of Dundee: Stobswell and Dundee: Trinity

No.	Charge / Minister		Contact	Phone
79	**Dundee: Strathmartine (F H W)** Vacant Interim Moderator: Willie D. Strachan		19 Americanmuir Road, Dundee DD3 9AA WStrachan@churchofscotland.org.uk	**01382 825817** 01382 812423 07432 513375
80	**Dundee: West (F H L W)** James Connolly DipTh CertMin DipMin MA(Theol) DMin	1982 2020	enquiries@dundeewestchurch.org 22 Hyndford Street, Dundee DD2 1HX JConnolly@churchofscotland.org.uk	**07341 255354** 07711 177655
81	**Dundee: Whitfield (H)** Vacant Brenda M.M. Elwell-Sutton (Ordained Local Minister) Interim Moderator: Grant R. MacLaughlan	2022	53 Old Craigie Road, Dundee DD4 7JD BElwell-Sutton@churchofscotland.org.uk GMacLaughlan@churchofscotland.org.uk	**01382 503012** 07811 753391 07790 518041
82	**Dundurn** See Comrie			
83	**Dunkeld (H W)** R. Fraser Penny BA BD	1984 2001	The Manse, Cathedral Street, Dunkeld PH8 0AW RPenny@churchofscotland.org.uk	01350 727249
84	**Dunnichen, Letham and Kirkden (W)** Guardianship of the Presbytery Session Clerk: Irene McGugan		irene.mcgugan@btinternet.com	01307 818436
85	**Eassie, Nevay and Newtyle** Carleen J. Robertson (Miss) BD CertEd	1992	2 Kirkton Road, Newtyle, Blairgowrie PH12 8TS CRobertson@churchofscotland.org.uk	01828 650461

86	**Edzell (F H W)** A.S. Wayne Pearce MA PhD	2002	2017	**elgparish@btconnect.com** 19 Lethnot Road, Edzell, Brechin DD9 7TG ASWaynePearce@churchofscotland.org.uk	**01356 647815** 01356 648117

New charge formed by the union of Edzell Lethnot Glenesk and Fern Careston Menmuir

87	**Errol (F H W)** Vacant Interim Moderator: Graham W. Crawford			GCrawford@churchofscotland.org.uk	01738 626046
88	**Fallin (F W)** Alison J. Grainger BD CertEd	1995	2021	**info@fallinchurch.com** 5 Fincastle Place, Cowie, Stirling FK7 7DS AGrainger@churchofscotland.org.uk	01786 760512
89	**Fintry** See Balfron				
90	**Forfar: East and Old (F H W)** Barbara Ann Sweetin BD	2011		**eando_office@yahoo.co.uk** The Manse, Lour Road, Forfar DD8 2BB BSweetin@churchofscotland.org.uk	01307 248228
91	**Forfar: Lowson Memorial (F H W)** Karen M. Fenwick BSc BD MPhil PhD	2006		1 Jamieson Street, Forfar DD8 2HY KFenwick@churchofscotland.org.uk	**01307 460576** 01307 468585
92	**Forfar: St Margaret's (F H W)** Margaret J. Hunt (Mrs) MA BD	2014		**stmargaretsforfar@gmail.com** St Margaret's Manse, 15 Potters Park Crescent, Forfar DD8 1HH MHunt@churchofscotland.org.uk	**01307 464224** 01307 462044
93	**Fortingall, Glenlyon, Kenmore (H) and Lawers (W)** Vacant Interim Moderator: Robert D. Nicol			The Manse, Balnaskeag, Kenmore, Aberfeldy PH15 2HB RNicol@churchofscotland.org.uk	01887 830218 01887 820242
94	**Foss and Rannoch** See Blair Atholl and Struan				
95	**Fossoway: St Serf's and Devonside** See Cleish				
96	**Fowlis and Liff (F T W) linked with Lundie and Muirhead (F H T W)** enquiries@churches-flandlm.co.uk Donna M. Hays (Mrs) MTheol DipEd DipTMHA	2004		149 Coupar Angus Road, Muirhead of Liff, Dundee DD2 5QN DHays@churchofscotland.org.uk	01382 580210

97 Friockheim Kinnell See Colliston

98 Gargunnock (W) linked with Kilmadock (W) linked with Kincardine-in-Menteith (W)
Vacant
Interim Moderator: Val Rose   val.rose@btinternet.com   01259 722221

99 Gartmore See Buchlyvie

100 Glamis (H), Inverarity and Kinnettles (F W)
Guardianship of the Presbytery
Session Clerk: Mary Reid (Mrs)   mmreid@btinternet.com   01307 840999

101 Glendevon See Dollar
102 Grantully, Logierait and Strathtay See Aberfeldy
103 Guthrie and Rescobie See Aberlemno
104 Inchture and Kinnaird See Abernyte

105 Invergowrie (H W)   hello@invergowrieparishchurch.org
Catriona M. Morrison MA BD   1995   2020   2 Boniface Place, Invergowrie, Dundee   DD2 5DR
CMorrison@churchofscotland.org.uk
Marc A. Prowe   2000   2020   2 Boniface Place, Invergowrie, Dundee   DD2 5DR
MProwe@churchofscotland.org.uk

106 Inverkeilor and Lunan See Colliston

107 Isla Parishes (F W)
Stephen A. Blakey BSc BD CStJ   1977   2018   Balduff House, Kilry, Blairgowrie   PH11 8HS   01575 560226
SBlakey@churchofscotland.org.uk

108 Killearn (F H W)
Stuart W. Sharp MTheol DipPA   2001   2018   Killearn Kirk, Balfron Road, Killearn   G63 9NL   01360 550101
SSharp@churchofscotland.org.uk

109 Killin and Ardeonaig See Balquhidder
110 Kilmadock See Gargunnock
111 Kincardine-in-Menteith See Gargunnock
112 Kinclaven See Caputh and Clunie

113 Kinross (F H W) 1989 2009
Alan D. Reid MA BD
office@kinrossparishchurch.org
15 Green Wood, Kinross KY13 8FG
AReid@churchofscotland.org.uk
01577 862570
01577 862952

114 Kippen (F W) linked with Norrieston (F W) 2007 2015
Ellen M. Larson Davidson BA MDiv
The Manse, Main Street, Kippen, Stirling FK8 3DN
ELarsonDavidson@churchofscotland.org.uk
01786 871249

115 Kirkmichael, Straloch and Glenshee (W) linked with Rattray (H W) 1996 2012
Linda Stewart (Mrs) BD
The Manse, Alyth Road, Rattray, Blairgowrie PH10 7HF
Linda.Stewart@churchofscotland.org.uk
01250 872462

116 Lecropt See Dunblane: St Blane's

117 Logie (F H W) 1988 2022
Jan J. Steyn BA BD DipTheol
21 Craiglea, Causewayhead, Stirling FK9 5EE
JSteyn@churchofscotland.org.uk
01786 271809

118 Longforgan See Abernyte
119 Lundie and Muirhead See Fowlis and Liff

120 Menstrie (F H T W) 2013 2022
Michael J. Goodison BSc BD
7 Long Row, Menstrie FK11 7BA
MGoodison@churchofscotland.org.uk
01259 611109

121 Methven and Logiealmond See Almondbank Tibbermore

122 Mid Strathearn (H W)
Vacant
Interim Moderator: Marjorie Clark (Miss)
Beechview, Abercairney, Crieff PH7 3NF
marjorie.clark@btinternet.com
01764 652116
01738 637017

123 Monifieth South Angus (F H W)
Vacant
office@monifiethparishchurch.co.uk
8 Church Street, Monifieth, Dundee DD5 4JP
01382 699183
New charge formed by the union of Monifieth, and Monifieth and Newbigging and Murroes and Tealing

124 Montrose: Trinity (F W)
Vacant

Geoffrey Redmayne BSc BD MPhil	2000	2016	2 Rosehill Road, Montrose DD10 8ST	01674 672447
(Team Minister)			Inchbrayock Manse, Usan, Montrose DD10 9SD	01674 675634
			GRedmayne@churchofscotland.org.uk	
Ian Gray	2013	2017	The Mallards, 15 Rossie Island Road, Montrose DD10 9NH	01674 677126
(Ordained Local Minister)			IGray@churchofscotland.org.uk	

New charge formed by the union of Dun and Hillside, Montrose: Old and St Andrew's and Montrose: South and Ferryden

125 Muckhart See Dollar

126 Muthill (F H W) linked with Trinity Gask and Kinkell (F W)
Vacant

Interim Moderator: Mairi Perkins	The Manse, Station Road, Muthill, Crieff PH5 2AR	01764 681205
	mperkins@churchofscotland.org.uk	01786 880948

127 Norrieston See Kippen

128 Oathlaw Tannadice (F W) linked with The Glens and Kirriemuir United (F W)

John K. Orr BD MTh	2012	26 Quarry Park, Kirriemuir DD8 4DR	**01575 572819**
		JOrr@churchofscotland.org.uk	01575 572610

129 Orwell and Portmoak (F H W)
Vacant

Interim Moderator: Alan D. Reid	**orwellandportmoakchurch@gmail.com**	**01577 862100**
	areid@churchofscotland.org.uk	01577 862952

130 Perth: Craigie and Moncreiffe (F W)
Vacant

Robert F. Wilkie CertCS	2011	2012	The Manse, 46 Abbot Street, Perth PH2 0EE	01738 623748
(Auxiliary Minister)			24 Huntingtower Road, Perth PH1 2JS	01738 628301
Interim Moderator: Kenneth D. Stott			RWilkie@churchofscotland.org.uk	01738 625728
			KStott@churchofscotland.org.uk	

131 Perth: Kinnoull (F H W)

Graham W. Crawford BSc BD STM	1991	2016	1 Mount Tabor Avenue, Perth PH2 7BT	01738 626046
			GCrawford@churchofscotland.org.uk	07817 504042

132 Perth: Letham St Mark's (F H W)

James C. Stewart BD DipMin	1997	**office@lethamstmarks.org.uk**	**01738 446377**
		35 Rose Crescent, Perth PH1 1NT	01738 624167
		JStewart@churchofscotland.org.uk	

133 Perth: North (F W)
Kenneth D. Stott MA BD   1989   2017
info@perthnorthchurch.org.uk
2 Cragganmore Place, Perth PH1 3GJ
KStott@churchofscotland.org.uk
01738 **622298**
01738 625728

134 Perth: Riverside (F W)
David R. Rankin MA BD   2009   2014
perthriverside.bookings@gmail.com
44 Hay Street, Perth PH1 5HS
DRankin@churchofscotland.org.uk
01738 **622341**
07810 008754

135 Perth: St John's Kirk of Perth (F H W) linked with Perth: St Leonard's-in-the-Fields (H W)
Vacant
Interim Moderator: Craig Dobney
CDobney@churchofscotland.org.uk
St John's: 01738 **633192**
St Leonard's: 01738 **632238**
01764 679196

136 Perth: St Leonard's-in-the-Fields See Perth: St John's Kirk of Perth

137 Perth: St Matthew's (F T W)
Fiona C. Bullock (Mrs) MA LLB BD   2014
Office: 01738 **636757**; Vestry: 01738 **630725**
office@stmatts.org.uk
12 Craigieknowes Avenue, Perth PH2 0DL
FBullock@churchofscotland.org.uk
01738 570241

138 Pitlochry (H W)
Vacant
Interim Moderator: R. Fraser Penny
thetryst@btconnect.com
Manse Road, Moulin, Pitlochry PH16 5EP
RPenny@churchofscotland.org.uk
01796 **474010**
01796 472774
01350 727249

139 Port of Menteith See Aberfoyle
140 Rattray See Kirkmichael, Straloch and Glenshee
141 Redgorton and Stanley See Auchtergaven and Moneydie

142 St Madoes and Kinfauns (F W)
Marc F. Bircham BD MTh   2000
The Manse, St Madoes, Glencarse, Perth PH2 7NF
MBircham@churchofscotland.org.uk
01738 860837

143 Sauchie and Coalsnaughton See Clackmannan

144 Scone and St Martins (F W)
Maudeen I. MacDougall BA BD MTh   1978   2019
sconeandstmartinschurch@talktalk.net
The Manse, Burnside, Scone PH2 6LP
rev.maudeen@gmail.com
01738 **553900**
01738 551942

145 Stirling: Church of the Holy Rude (F H W) linked with Stirling: Viewfield Erskine (H)   holyrude@holyrude.org
Alan F. Miller BA MA BD   2000   2010   7 Windsor Place, Stirling FK8 2HY
AMiller@churchofscotland.org.uk   01786 465166

146 Stirling: North (F H W)   info@stirlingnorth.org   **01786 463376**
Scott McInnes MEng BD   2016   13 Calton Crescent, Stirling FK7 0BB   01786 463376
SMcInnes@churchofscotland.org.uk

147 Stirling: Park (F H T W)   parkchurchstirling@gmail.com   **01786 462400**
Attie van Wyk BTh LMus MDiv MTh   2005   2022   24 Laurelhill Gardens, Stirling FK8 2PT   01786 478269
AvanWyk@churchofscotland.org.uk

148 Stirling: St Mark's (T W)   stmarksstirling1@gmail.com   **01786 470733**
Barry J. Hughes MA BA   2011   2018   St Mark's Parish Church, Drip Road, Stirling FK8 1RE   07597 386762
BHughes@churchofscotland.org.uk

149 Stirling: St Ninians Old (F H W)   01786 474421
Gary J. McIntyre BD DipMin   1993   1998   7 Randolph Road, Stirling FK8 2AJ
GMcIntyre@churchofscotland.org.uk

150 Stirling: Viewfield Erskine See Stirling: Church of the Holy Rude

151 Strathblane (F H T W)   strathblanekirk@gmail.com   **01360 770418**
Vacant   2 Campsie Road, Strathblane, Glasgow G63 9AB   01360 770226

152 Tenandry
Guardianship of the Presbytery   01887 820819
Interim Moderator: Neil M. Glover   NGlover@churchofscotland.org.uk   07779 280074

153 The Glens and Kirriemuir United See Oathlaw Tannadice

154 Tillicoultry (F H W)   **01259 750340**
Alison E.P. Britchfield (Mrs) MA BD   1987   2013   2 Old Harbour Square, Stirling FK8 1RB   07415 683871
ABritchfield@churchofscotland.org.uk

155 Trinity Gask and Kinkell See Muthill

156 Tullibody: St Serf's (H W)

Drew Barrie BSc BD	1984	2016		22, The Cedars, Tullibody, Alloa FK10 2PX DBarrie@churchofscotland.org.uk	01259 213326

B. In other appointments: members of Presbytery

Allen, Valerie L. BMus MDiv DMin	1990	2015	Presbytery Chaplain	16 Pine Court, Doune FK16 6JE VL2allen@btinternet.com	01786 842577 07801 291538
Begg, Richard J. MA BD	2008	2016	Army Chaplain	12 Whiteyetts Drive, Sauchie FK10 3GE rbegg711@aol.com	07525 612914
Caldwell, Gary J. BSc BD	2007	2023	Chaplain, HM Prison Greenock	63 Skye Road, Cumbernauld, Glasgow G67 1PB gary.caldwell@prisons.gov.scot	07983 987465
Campbell, Gordon A. MA BD CDipAF DipHSM CMgr MCMI MIHM AssocCIPD AFRIN ARSGS FRGS FSAScot	2001	2004	Auxiliary Minister: an Honorary Chaplain: University of Dundee	2 Falkland Place, Kingoodie, Invergowrie, Dundee DD2 5DY g.a.campbell@dundee.ac.uk	01382 561383
Douglas, Fiona C. MBE MA BD PhD	1989	1997	Chaplain: University of Dundee	10 Springfield, Dundee DD1 4JE f.c.douglas@dundee.ac.uk	01382 384157
Fair, W. Martin BA BD DMin	1992	2023	Pathways to Ministry Manager, Faith Action Programme	121 George Street, Edinburgh EH2 4YN MFair@churchofscotland.org.uk	0131 225 5722
Ferguson, John F. BD DipMin DMin	1988	2022	Presbytery Clerk: Perth	Suite F3, Riverview House, Friarton Road, Perth PH2 8DF JFerguson@churchofscotland.org.uk	07596 868064
Gourlay, Heather	2021		Ordained Local Minister: supporting rural ministry in Angus	The Schoolhouse, Pitkennedy, Forfar DD8 2UJ HGourlay@churchofscotland.org.uk	01307 830372
Jack, Alison M. (Prof.) MA BD PhD SFHEA	1998	2022	Principal, New College; Professor, Bible and Literature, University of Edinburgh	5 Murdoch Terrace, Dunblane FK15 9JE alisonjack809@btinternet.com	01786 826953
McDonald, Ian J.M. MA BD	1984	2020	Chaplain, Palliative Care, Roxburghe House, NHS Tayside	11 James Grove, Kirkcaldy KY1 1TN IanJMMcdonald@churchofscotland.org.uk	07421 775644
Michie, Margaret	2013		Ordained Local Minister: Loch Leven Parish Grouping	3 Loch Leven Court, Wester Balgedie, Kinross KY13 9NE margaretmichie@btinternet.com	01592 840602
Nicol, Robert D. MA	2013	2019	Ordained Local Minister: Presbytery-wide	Rappla Lodge, Camserney, Aberfeldy PH15 2JF RNicol@churchofscotland.org.uk	01887 820242
Pandian, Ali R. BA BD PGCertHC DipPS	2017	2022	Chaplain, Rachel House Children's Hospice	Rachel House Children's Hospice, Avenue Road, Kinross KY13 8FX alipandian@chas.org.uk	01577 865777 07425 630904
Redpath, Anne	2022		Presbytery Chaplain, Discipleship and Mission	9 Beveridge Place, Kinross KY13 8QY ARedpath@churchofscotland.org.uk	
Shuttleworth, Margaret MA BD	2013	2020	Chaplain, HM Prison and YOI Stirling; HM YOI Polmont; Lilias Community Custody Unit, Glasgow	62 Toll Road, Kincardine, Alloa FK10 4QZ margaret.shuttleworth@prisons.gov.scot	01259 731002
Spencer, Daniel H. PhD	2023		Assistant Minister, Dundee Menzieshill Parish Grouping	DSpencer@churchofscotland.org.uk	07554 392895

Steele, Grace M.F. MA BTh	2014		Ordained Local Minister: Presbytery-wide	12a Farragon Drive, Aberfeldy PH15 2BQ GSteele@churchofscotland.org.uk	01887 820025
Stevenson, Beverley	2020		Ordained Local Minister	2 Robert Dick Court, Tullibody FK10 2BP BStevenson@churchofscotland.org.uk	07584 902508
Stewart, Anne E. BD CertMin	1998	2007	Chaplain: HM Prison Castle Huntly; Bella Community Custody Unit, Dundee	35 Rose Crescent, Perth PH1 1NT anne.stewart2@prisons.gov.scot	01738 624167
Stott, Anne M.	2019		Ordained Local Minister: Presbytery Pioneer Worker, Bertha Park	2 Cragganmore Place, Perth PH1 3GJ AStott@churchofscotland.org.uk	01738 625728
Strachan, Willie D. DipYCW MBA CertCS	2013	2020	Ordained Local Minister: Presbytery-wide	Ladywell House, Lucky Slap, Monikie, Dundee DD5 3QG WStrachan@churchofscotland.org.uk	07432 513375
Thorburn, Susan MTh	2014		Ordained Local Minister: Mission Development Worker, Presbytery of Fife	3 Daleally Farm Cottages, St Madoes Road, Errol, Perth PH1 7TJ SThorburn@churchofscotland.org.uk	01821 642681
Wallace, Catherine PGDipC DCS	1987	2021	Clinical Manager, Harbour Counselling Service, Perth	21 Durley Dene Crescent, Bridge of Earn PH2 9RD secretary@churchofscotland.org.uk	01738 621709
Wylie, Jonathan BSc BD MTh	2000	2016	Chaplain: Strathallan School	Strathallan School, Forgandenny, Perth PH2 9EG chaplain@strathallan.co.uk	01738 815098

C. Retaining: members of Presbytery

Allan, Jean (Mrs) DCS	1989	2011	(Deacon, Dundee: Craigiebank with Dundee: Douglas and Mid Craigie)	12C Hindmarsh Avenue, Dundee DD3 7LW jeannieallan45@googlemail.com	01382 827299 07709 959474
Ballentine, Ann M. MA BD DipRE	1981	2007	(Kirknewton and East Calder)	17 Nellfield Road, Crieff PH7 3DU annmballentine@gmail.com	01764 652567
Barr, T. Leslie LTh	1969	1997	(Kinross)	8 Fairfield Road, Kelty KY4 0BY leslie_barr@yahoo.co.uk	07727 718076
Barrett, Leslie M. BD FRICS	1991	2014	(Chaplain: University of Abertay, Dundee)	Dunelm Cottage, Logie, Cupar KY15 4SJ lesliembarrett@btinternet.com	01334 870396
Brennan, Anne J. BSc BD MTh	1999	2019	(Fortingall, Glenlyon, Kenmore and Lawers)	Dunmore House, Findo Gask, Auchterarder PH3 1HS annebrennan@yahoo.co.uk	01738 730350
Brough, Colin M. BSc BD	1998	2022	(Dundee: Fintry)	Westcroft, Station Road, Longforgan DD2 5EX colinbrough73@gmail.com	
Brown, Elizabeth JP RGN	1996	2007	(Auxiliary Minister, Perth: St John the Baptist)	8 Viewlands Place, Perth PH1 1BS liz.brown@blueyonder.co.uk	01738 552391
Brown, Marina D. MA BD MTh	2000	2012	(Hawick: St Mary's and Old)	Moneydie School Cottage, Luncarty, Perth PH1 3HZ revmd1711@btinternet.com	01738 582163
Brown, Scott J. CBE BD	1993	2023	(Buchlyvie with Gartmore)	SJBrown@churchofscotland.org.uk	07824 805888
Buchan, Alexander MA BD PGCE	1975	1992	(North Ronaldsay with Sanday)	59 Clifburn Road, Arbroath DD11 5BA revicbuchan@bluebucket.org	01241 878862
Buchan, Isabel C. (Mrs) BSc BD RE(PgCE)	1975	2019	(Buckie: North with Rathven)	59 Clifburn Road, Arbroath DD11 5BA revicbuchan@bluebucket.org	01241 878862
Buwert, Klaus O.F. LLB BD DMin	1984	2022	(Muthill with Trinity Gask and Kinkell)	55 Duncan Road, Letham, Forfar DD8 2PN	

Name	Years	Role	Address / Email	Tel.
Cairns, Evelyn BD	1987 2012	(Chaplain: Rachel House Children's Hospice, Kinross)	15 Talla Park, Kinross KY13 8AB / revelyn@btinternet.com	01577 863990
Calvert, Robert A. BSc BD DMin PhD	1983 2021	(Dundee: The Steeple)	5 Cowiefaulds Cottages, Gateside, Cupar KY14 7ST / robertacalvert@gmail.com	07532 029343
Campbell, Richard S. LTh	1993 2010	(Gargunnock with Kilmadock with Kincardine-in-Menteith)	3 David Farquharson Road, Blairgowrie PH10 6FD / revrichards@yahoo.co.uk	01250 876386
Campbell, Murdo M. BD DipMin	1997 2023	(Strathblane)	MCampbell@churchofscotland.org.uk	
Caskie, J. Colin BA BD	1977 2012	(Rhu and Shandon)	13 Anderson Drive, Perth PH1 1JZ / jcolincaskie@gmail.com	01738 445543
Clark, Marion A. (Rae) MA BD	2014 2022	(Clackmannan)	RClark@churchofscotland.org.uk	
Cloggie, June (Mrs)	1997 2006	(Auxiliary Minister, Callander)	11A Tulipan Crescent, Callander FK17 8AR / david.cloggie@hotmail.co.uk	01877 331021
Cochrane, James P.N. LTh	1994 2012	(Tillicoultry)	12 Sandpiper Meadow, Alloa Park, Alloa FK10 1QU / jamescochrane@pobroadband.co.uk	01259 218883
Coleman, Sidney H. BA BD MTh	1961 2001	(Glasgow: Merrylea)	15 Richmond Terrace, Dundee DD2 1BQ / sidney.h.coleman@gmail.com	01382 645824
Cook, Helen K.M. (Mrs) MA BD DipSW MComC	1974 2012	(Kingussie)	60 Pelstream Avenue, Stirling FK7 0BG / revhcook@btinternet.com	01786 464128
Corbett, Richard T. BSc MSc PhD BD	1992 2019	(Kilmallie)	Flat 309, Knights Court, 1 North William Street, Perth PH1 5NB / richard.t.corbett@btinternet.com	01738 626315
Craig, Joan H. MTheol DipCE CPS	1986 2005	(East Mainland)	7 Jedburgh Place, Perth PH1 1SJ / joanhcraig@btinternet.com	01738 580180
Dempster, Colin J. BD CertMin	1990 2016	(Mearns Coastal)	35 Margaret Lindsay Place, Monifieth DD6 4RD / Coldcoast@btinternet.com	01382 532368
Dingwall, Brian BTh CQSW	1999 2020	(Arbirlot with Carmyllie)	10 New Road, Rattray, Blairgowrie PH10 7RA / brian.d12@btinternet.com	07906 656847
Duncan, John C. MBE BD MPhil	1987 2021	(Leuchars: St Athernase)	21 Ravenscraig Gardens, Broughty Ferry, Dundee DD5 1LT / JDuncan@churchofscotland.org.uk	01382 480772
Dunnett, Linda (Mrs) BA DCS	1976 2016	(Deacon, Cowie and Plean with Fallin)	9 Tulipan Crescent, Callander FK17 8AR / lindadunnett@sky.com	01877 339640
Edwards, Dougal BTh	2013 2017	(Ordained Local Minister, Barry with Carnoustie)	25 Mackenzie Street, Carnoustie DD7 6HD	07838 041683 / 01241 852666
Ewart, William BSc BD	1972 2010	(Caputh and Clunie with Kinclaven)	22 Muirend Avenue, Perth PH1 1JL / ewe1@btinternet.com	
Ewart-Roberts, Peggy BA BD	2003 2022	(Caputh and Clunie with Kinclaven)	22 Muirend Avenue, Perth PH1 1JL / PEwart-Roberts@churchofscotland.org.uk	07775 712686
Fraser, Donald W. MA	1958 2010	(Monifieth)	1 Blake Avenue, Broughty Ferry, Dundee DD5 3LH / fraserdonald37@yahoo.co.uk	01382 477491
Gaston, A. Ray C. MA BD	1969 2002	(Leuchars: St Athernase)	'Hamewith', 13 Manse Road, Dollar FK14 7AL / gaston.arthur@yahoo.co.uk	07531 863316 / 01259 743202
Gilchrist, Ewen J. BD DipMin DipComm	1982 2017	(Cults)	9 David Douglas Avenue, Scone PH2 6QQ / ewengilchrist@btconnect.com	07747 746418
Gill, Peter G. BA MA	2008 2023	(Bannockburn: Allan with Cowie and Plean)	The Manse, Bogend Road, Bannockburn, Stirling FK7 8NP / PGill@churchofscotland.org.uk	01786 814692

Goring, Iain M. BSc BD	1976	2015	(Interim Minister, Edinburgh: St John's Colinton Mains)	4 Argyle Grove, Dunblane FK15 9DU imgoring@gmail.com	01786 821688
Gough, Ian G. MA BD MTh DMin	1974	2009	(Arbroath: Knox's with Arbroath: St Vigeans)	23 Keptie Road, Arbroath DD11 3ED iangough@btinternet.com	07891 838379
Graham, Alasdair G. BD DipMin	1981	2019	(Arbroath: West Kirk)	5 Robb Place, Perth PH2 0GB alasdairgraham704@btinternet.com	01738 626952
Graham, Sydney S. DipYL MPhil BD	1987	2009	(Iona with Kilfinichen and Kilvickeon and the Ross of Mull)	'Aspen', Milton Road, Luncarty, Perth PH1 3ES syd@sydgraham.plus.com	01738 829350
Gunn, Alexander M. MA BD	1967	2006	(Aberfeldy with Amulree and Strathbraan with Dull and Weem)	'Navarone', 12 Cornhill Road, Perth PH1 1LR sandygunn@btinternet.com	01738 443216
Haddow, Mary M. (Mrs) BD	2001	2022	(Pitlochry)	16 Hobens Drive, North Berwick EH39 5GZ mary_haddow@btconnect.com	
Halliday, Archibald R. BD MTh	1964	1999	(Duffus, Spynie and Hopeman)	8 Turretbank Drive, Crieff PH7 4LW roberthalliday343@btinternet.com	01764 656464
Humphrey, Jonathan W. BSc BD PhD	2015	2021	(Dundee: Chalmers Ardler)	Burnside, Kilcaldrum, Forfar DD8 1TW JHumphrey@churchofscotland.org.uk	07587 186424
Izett, William A.F.	1968	2000	(Law)	1 Duke Street, Clackmannan FK10 4EF william.izett@talktalk.net	01259 724203
Kay, Elizabeth (Miss) DipYCS	1993	2007	(Auxiliary Minister, Abernyte with Inchture and Kinnaird with Longforgan)	1 Kintail Walk, Inchture, Perth PH14 9RY ekay007@btinternet.com	01828 686029
Kelly, T. Clifford	1973	1993	(Ferintosh)	20 Whinfield Drive, Kinross KY13 8UB stankennon@outlook.com	01577 864946
Kennon, Stanley BA BD CertEd	1992	2022	(Abernethy and Dron and Arngask)	9 The Orchard, Woodside, Burrelton, Blairgowrie PH13 9NQ	
Knox, John W. MTheol	1992	1997	(Lochgelly: Macainsh)	2 Darroch Gate, Blairgowrie PH10 6GT ian.knox5@btinternet.com	01250 872733
Laidlaw, John J. MA	1964	1996	(Adviser in Religious Education)	14 Dalhousie Road, Barnhill, Dundee DD5 2SQ jacklaidlaw@blueyonder.co.uk	01382 477458
Laing, David J.H. BD DPS	1976	2014	(Dundee: Trinity)	18 Kerrington Crescent, Barnhill, Dundee DD5 2TN david.laing@live.co.uk	01382 739586
Lawson, James B. MA BD	1961	2002	(South Uist)	4 Cowden Way, Comrie, Crieff PH6 2NW james.lawson7@btopenworld.com	01764 679180
Lillie, Fiona L. (Mrs) BA BD MLitt	1995	2017	(Glasgow: St John's Renfield)	4 McVicars Lane, Dundee DD1 4LH fionalillie@btinternet.com	01382 229082
MacDonald, James W. BD	1976	2012	(Crieff)	'Mingulay', 29 Hebridean Gardens, Crieff PH7 3BP rev_up@btinternet.com	01764 654500
Macgregor, John BD	2001	2020	(Errol with Kilspindie and Rait)	1 Le Petit Vierzon, 16490 Hiesse, France john_macg@hotmail.com	
Mack, Lynne (Mrs)	2013	2019	(Ordained Local Minister, Gargunnock with Kilmadock with Kincardine-in-Menteith)	36 Middleton, Menstrie FK11 7HD LMack@churchofscotland.org.uk	01259 761465
MacMillan, Riada M. BD	1991	1998	(Perth: Craigend Moncreiffe with Rhynd)	73 Muirend Gardens, Perth PH1 1JR	01738 447259
MacRae, Malcolm H. MA PhD	1971	2010	(Kirkmichael, Straloch and Glenshee with Rattray)	10B Victoria Place, Stirling FK8 2QU malcolm.macrae1@btopenworld.com	01786 465547

Main, Douglas M. BD	1986	2014	(Errol with Kilspindie and Rait)	14 Madoch Road, St Madoes, Perth PH2 7TT revdmain@sky.com	01738 860867
Mair, Michael V.A. MA BD	1968	2007	(Dundee: Craigiebank with Douglas and Mid Craigie)	48 Panmure Street, Monifieth DD5 4EH mvamair@gmail.com	01382 530538
Majcher, Philip L. BD	1982	2020	(London: Crown Court)	5 Strathallan Bank, Ardargie, Forgandenny, Perth PH2 9FE pmajcher@me.com	
Malcolm, Alistair BD DPS	1976	2012	(Inverness: Inshes)	11 Kinclaven Gardens, Murthly, Perth PH1 4EX amalcolm067@btinternet.com	01738 710979
Malloch, Philip R.M. LLB BD	1970	2009	(Killearn)	8 Michael McParland Drive, Torrance, Glasgow G64 4EE pmalloch@mac.com	01360 620089
Mathew, J. Gordon MA BD	1973	2011	(Buckie: North)	45 Westhaugh Road, Stirling FK9 5GF jg.mathew@btinternet.com	01786 445951
McCarthy, David J. BSc BD	1985	2020	(Fresh Expressions Development Worker, Faith Nurture Forum)	Orchard House, Croft Avenue, Dunning PH2 0SG djmcclv@gmail.com	
McCormick, Alistair F.	1962	1998	(Creich with Rosehall)	14 Balmanno Park, Bridge of Earn, Perth PH2 9RJ	01738 813588
McCrum, Robert BSc BD CertMin	1982	2014	(Ayr: St James')	28 Rose Crescent, Perth PH1 1NT robert.mccrum@virgin.net	01738 447906
McFadzean, Iain MA BD CMgr FCMI MHGI	1989	2019	(Chief Executive: Work Place Chaplaincy Scotland)	2 Lowfield Crescent, Luncarty, Perth PH1 3FG iain.mcfadzean@wpcscotland.co.uk	01738 827338 07969 227696
McIntosh, Colin G. MA BD	1976	2013	(Dunblane: Cathedral)	Drumhead Cottage, Drum, Kinross KY13 0PR colinmcintosh4@btinternet.com	01577 840012
McKenzie, Alan BSc BD	1988	2013	(Bellshill: Macdonald Memorial with Bellshill: Orbiston)	89 Drip Road, Stirling FK8 1RN rev.a.mckenzie@btopenworld.com	01786 430450
McLean, Ian A. BSc BD DMin	1981	2023	(Montrose: Trinity)	9 Lunan Avenue, Montrose DD10 9DG IMcLean@churchofscotland.org.uk	01674 434672
McMillan, Edith F. (Mrs) MA BD	1981	2018	(Dundee: Craigiebank with Douglas and Mid Craigie)	39 Castlefield Court, Stepps, Glasgow G33 6NN wee_rev_edimac@btinternet.com	
McMillan, Stewart BD	1983	2022	(Dundee: Strathmartine)	39 Castlefield Court, Stepps, Glasgow G33 6NN SMcMillan@churchofscotland.org.uk	
McNaughton, David J.H. BA CA	1976	1995	(Killin and Ardeonaig)	14 Rankine Court, Wormit, Newport-on-Tay DD6 8TA	
McNicol, Bruce BL BD	1967	2006	(Jedburgh: Old and Edgerston)	22 Beechwood Gardens, Stirling FK8 2AX mcnicol942@gmail.com	01786 358308
Millar, Alexander M. MA BD MBA	1980	2018	(Stirling: St Columba's)	17 Mapledene Road, Scone, Perth PH2 6NX alexmillar0406@gmail.com	01738 550270
Millar, Jennifer M. (Mrs) BD DipMin	1986	2021	(Teacher: Religious and Moral Education)	17 Mapledene Road, Scone, Perth PH2 6NX ajrmillar@blueyonder.co.uk	01738 550270
Milne, Robert B. BTh	1999	2017	(Broughton, Glenholm and Kilbucho with Skirling with Stobo and Drumelzier with Tweedsmuir)	3 Mid Square, Comrie PH6 2EG rbmilne@aol.com	07803 609387
Mitchell, Alexander B. BD	1981	2014	(Dunblane: St Blane's)	24 Hebridean Gardens, Crieff PH7 3BP alex.mitchell6@btopenworld.com	
Moffat, Russel BD CPS MTh PhD	1986	2022	(Balquidder with Killin and Ardeonaig)	21 McKerrow Drive, Heathhall, Dumfries DG1 3SP russel.moffat@churchofscotland.org.uk	01764 652241

Name	(Appointment)			Address / Email	Tel
Mowbray, Harry BD CA	(Blairgowrie)	2003	2018	12 Isla Road, Blairgowrie PH10 6RR mowbrayh@gmail.com	01250 873479
Munro, Gillian BSc BD	(Head of Spiritual Care, NHS Tayside)	1989	2018	The Old Town House, 53 Main Street, Abernethy, Perth PH2 9JH munrooth@aol.com	01738 850066
Munro, Patricia M. BSc DCS	(Deacon, Perth: St John's Kirk of Perth with Perth: St Leonard's-in-the-Fields)	1986	2016	4 Hewat Place, Perth PH1 2UD patmunrodcs@gmail.com	01738 443088 07814 836314
Nelson, Robert C. BA BD	(Kilninian and Kilmore with Salen and Ulva with Tobermory with Torosay and Kinlochspelvie)	1980	2010	St Colme's, Perth Road, Birnam, Dunkeld PH8 0BH rcnelson49@btinternet.com	01350 727455
Nicoll, A. Norman BD	(Corby: St Andrew's)	2003	2020	14 Victoria Street, Forfar DD8 3BA	
Norrie, Graham MA BD	(Forfar: East and Old)	1967	2007	'Novar', 14A Wyllie Street, Forfar DD8 3DN grahamnorrie@hotmail.com	01307 468152
Notman, Alison BD	(Ardler, Kettins and Meigle)	2014	2020	6 Hall Street, Kettlebridge, Cupar KY15 7QF	
Ogilvie, Catriona (Mrs) MA BD	(Cumbernauld: Old)	1999	2015	Seberham Flat, 1A Bridge Street, Dollar FK14 7DF catriona.ogilvie1@btinternet.com	01259 742155
Ormiston, Hugh C. BSc BD MPhil PhD	(Kirkmichael, Straloch and Glenshee with Rattray)	1969	2004	Cedar Lea, Main Road, Woodside, Blairgowrie PH13 9NP	01828 670539
Ovens, Samuel B. BD	(Slamannan)	1982	1992	21 Bevan Drive, Alva FK12 5PD	01259 763456
Oxburgh, Brian H. BSc BD	(Tayport)	1980	2019	50 Ravensbay Park Gardens, Carnoustie DD7 7NY	
Paton, Iain F. BD FCIS	(Elie with Kilconquhar and Colinsburgh)	1980	2006	Muldoanich, Stirling Street, Blackford, Auchterarder PH4 1QG iain.f.paton@btinternet.com	01764 682234
Philip, Elizabeth A. C. MA BA PGCSE DCS	(Deacon, Crieff)	2007	2018	8 Strathearn Terrace, Crieff PH7 3AQ ephilipstitch@gmail.com	01764 218976 07970 767851
Porter, Jean T. (Mrs) BD DCS	(Deacon, Stirling: St Mark's)	2006	2022	3 Cochrie Place, Tullibody FK10 2RR JPorter@churchofscotland.org.uk	07729 316321
Quigley, Barbara D. (Mrs) MTheol ThM DPS	(Glasgow: St Andrew's East)	1979	2019	33 Castle Drive, Auchterarder PH3 1FU bdquigley@aol.com	07926 064235
Ramsay, Brian BD DPS MLitt	(Aberlemno with Guthrie and Rescobie)	1980	2022	The Manse, Guthrie, Forfar DD8 2TP	01241 828243 07713 919442
Redpath, James G. BD DipPTh	(Auchtermuchty with Edenshead and Strathmiglo)	1988	2016	9 Beveridge Place, Kinross KY13 8QY JRedpath@churchofscotland.org.uk	
Reid, R. Gordon BSc BD MIEE	(Carriden)	1993	2010	6 Bayview Place, Monifieth, Dundee DD5 4TN GordonReid@aol.com	01382 520519 07952 349884
Reynolds, Fiona J. LLB BD FdSc	(Monifieth)	2018	2023	7 Ruthven Place, Edinburgh EH16 5TU FReynolds@churchofscotland.org.uk	
Robertson, George R. LTh	(Udny and Pitmedden)	1985	2004	3 Slateford Gardens, Edzell, Brechin DD9 7SX geomag.robertson@btinternet.com	01356 647322
Robertson, James H. BSc BD	(Culloden: The Barn)	1975	2014	'Far End', 35 Mains Terrace, Dundee DD4 7BZ jimrob838@gmail.com	01382 522773 07595 465838
Robertson, Matthew LTh	(Cawdor with Croy and Dalcross)	1968	2002	Inver, Strathtay, Pitlochry PH9 0PG	01887 840780
Robson, George K. LTh DPS BA	(Dundee: Balgay)	1983	2011	11 Ceres Crescent, Broughty Ferry, Dundee DD5 3JN gkrobson@virginmedia.com	01382 901212
Rodger, Matthew A. BD	(Ellon)	1978	1999	1 Bank House, Airlie Street, Alyth PH11 8AH	01828 634265

Name			Charge	Address	Telephone
Rooney, Malcolm I.G. DipPE BEd BD	1993	2017	(The Glens and Kirriemuir: Old)	23 Mart Lane, Northmuir, Kirriemuir DD8 4TL / malc.rooney@gmail.com	01575 575334 / 07909 993233
Rose, Dennis S. DipTh LTh	1996	2016	(Arbuthnott, Bervie and Kinneff)	69 Blackthorn Grove, Menstrie FK11 7DX / dennis2327@aol.com	01259 692451
Rose, Lewis (Mr) DCS	1993	2010	(Deacon, Organiser, Industrial Chaplaincy)	6 Gauldie Crescent, Dundee DD3 0RR / lewis_rose48@yahoo.co.uk	01382 816580 / 07899 790466
Russell, John MA	1959	2000	(Tillicoultry)	Kilblaan, Gladstone Terrace, Birnam, Dunkeld PH8 0DP	01350 728896
Russell, Kenneth G. BD CertCE CertCounsS PGCertHC DipPRSP	1986	2020	(Chaplain: HM Prison Perth)	158 Bannockburn Road, Stirling FK7 0EW / kenrussell1000@hotmail.com	01786 812680
Saunders, Grace I.M. BSc BTh	2007	2022	(Cumbernauld: Condorrat)	65 Slade Gardens, Kirriemuir DD8 5AG / rev.grace.saunders@btinternet.com	
Scott, James MA BD	1973	2010	(Drumoak-Durris)	3 Blake Place, Broughty Ferry, Dundee DD5 3LQ / jimscott73@yahoo.co.uk	01382 739595
Searle, David C. MA DipTh FSAScot	1965	2002	(Warden: Rutherford House, Edinburgh)	Stonefall Lodge, 30 Abbey Lane, Grange, Errol PH2 7GB / dcs@davidsearle.plus.com	01821 641004
Sewell, Paul M.N. MA BD	1970	2010	(Berwick-upon-Tweed: St Andrew's Wallace Green and Lowick)	7 Bohun Court, Stirling FK7 7UT / paulmsewell@btinternet.com	01786 489969
Shewan, Michael R.R. MA BD CPS	1985	2022	(Aberdeen: North)	13 Hatton Road, Luncarty, Perth PH1 3UZ	
Simpson, James A. BSc BD STM DD	1960	1999	(Interim Minister, Brechin Cathedral)	'Dornoch', Perth Road, Bankfoot, Perth PH1 4ED / ja@simpsondornoch.co.uk	01738 787710
Sloan, Robert P. MA BD	1968	2007	(Interim Minister, Armadale)	1 Broomhill Avenue, Perth PH1 1EN / sloan12@virginmedia.com	01738 443904
Stenhouse, W. Duncan MA BD	1989	2006	(Dunbarney and Forgandenny)	32 Sandport Gait, Kinross KY13 8FB	01577 866992
Stewart, Alexander T. MA BD FSAScot	1975	2022	(Associate, Perth: St John's Kirk of Perth with St Leonard's-in-the-Fields)	36 Viewlands Terrace, Perth PH1 1BZ / alex.t.stewart@blueyonder.co.uk	01738 566675
Stewart, Robin J. MA BD STM	1959	1995	(Orwell with Portmoak)	'Oakbrae', Perth Road, Murthly, Perth PH1 4HF	01738 710220
Taylor, Caroline (Mrs)	1995	2014	(Leuchars: St Athernase)	7 Sunart Street, Broughty Ferry, Dundee DD5 3HW / caro234@btinternet.com	01382 770198
Taylor, C. Graham D. BSc BD FIAB	2001	2020	(Dundee: Broughty Ferry St Luke's and Queen Street)	The Smithy, Grange, Errol, Perth PH2 7TB / cgdtaylor@btinternet.com	07804 527103
Thomas, Martyn R.H. CEng MIStructE	1987	2002	(Fowlis and Liff with Lundie and Muirhead of Liff)	14 Kirkgait, Letham, Forfar DD8 2XQ / martyn317thomas@btinternet.com	01307 818084
Thomson, Raymond BD DipMin	1992	2013	(Slamannan)	8 Rhodders Grove, Alva FK12 5ER	01259 769083
Thomson, Steven BSc BD	2001	2022	(Cargill Burrelton with Collace)	Flat 02, 3 Rosebery Terrace, Glasgow G5 0AS	
Wallace, James K. MA BD STM	1988	2015	(Perth: St John's Kirk of Perth with St Leonard's-in-the-Fields)	21 Durley Dene Crescent, Bridge of Earn PH2 9RD / jkwministry@hotmail.com	01738 621709
Wallace, Sheila D. (Mrs) BA BD DCS	2009	2020	(Deacon, Grandtully, Logierait and Strathtay)	Little Orchard, Blair Atholl, Pitlochry PH18 5SH	01796 481647 / 07733 243046
Watt, Alan G.N. MTh CQSW DipCommEd	1996	2009	(Edzell Lethnot Glenesk with Fern Careston Menmuir)	6 Pine Way, Friockheim, Arbroath DD11 4WF / watt455@btinternet.com	01241 826018
Webster, Allan F. MA BD	1978	2013	(Workplace Chaplain, Tayside and North Fife)	42 McCulloch Drive, Forfar DD8 2EB / allanfwebster@aol.com	01307 464252 / 07546 276725
Whyte, William B. DipArch ARIBA BD	1973	2004	(Nairn: St Ninian's)	The Old Inn, Park Hill Road, Rattray, Blairgowrie PH10 7DS	01250 874401

Name	Ord.	Ind.	Charge / Appointment	Address / Email	Tel
Wilson, Hazel MA BD DipEd DipMS	1991	2015	(Dundee: Lochee)	2 Boe Court, Springfield Terrace, Dunblane FK15 9LU / hmwilson704@gmail.com	01786 825850
Wilson, James L. BD CPS	1986	2022	(Dundee: Whitfield)	Burnside Cottage, 97 Peebles Drive, Dundee DD4 0TF / r3vjw@aol.com	07885 618659
Wilson, John M. MA BD	1967	2004	(Altnaharra and Farr)	Berbice, The Terrace, Blair Atholl, Pitlochry PH18 5SZ	01796 481619

D. In other appointments: not members of Presbytery

Name	Ord.	Ind.	Appointment	Address / Email	Tel
Patterson, Philip W. BMus BD	1999	2022	Programme Co-ordinator, Veterans Chaplaincy Scotland	philip.patterson@vcscotland.org	07713 625792

E. Retaining: not members of Presbytery

Name	Ord.	Ind.	Charge	Address / Email	Tel
Dawson, Michael S. BTech BD	1979	2005	(Associate: Edinburgh: Holy Trinity)	9 The Broich, Alva FK12 5NR / mikpen.dawson@btinternet.com	01259 769309
Gillies, Janet E. BD	1998	2014	(Tranent)	33 Castle Road, Stirling FK9 5JD / jan.gillies@yahoo.com	01786 446222
Gordon, Elinor J. (Miss) BD	1988	2015	(Cumbernauld: Kildrum)	6 Balgibbon Drive, Callander FK17 8EU / elinorgordon@btinternet.com	01877 331049
Mackay, Kenneth D. DCS	1996	2020	(Deacon, Perth: Letham St Mark's)	15 Bank Street, Blairgowrie PH10 6DE	01250 369029 / 07891 203403
Morrice, Alastair M. MA BD	1968	2008	(International Church of Bishkek, Kyrgyzstan)	5 Brechin Road, Kirriemuir DD8 4BX / ambishkek@swissmail.org	01575 574102
Roderick, Maggie R. BA BD FRSA FTSI	2010	2018	(Menstrie)	34 Craiglea, Stirling FK9 5EE / MRoderick@churchofscotland.org.uk	01786 478113
Stevens, Linda (Mrs) BSc BD PGDipCouns	2006	2022	(West Angus Area Team Minister)	17 North Latch Road, Brechin DD9 6LE	

F. Inactive: not members of Presbytery

Name	Ord.	Ind.	Charge	Address / Email	Tel
Donald, Robert M. BA LTh	1969	2005	(Kilmodan and Colintraive)	20 Avon Crescent, Broughty Ferry, Dundee DD5 3TX / robandmoiradonald@yahoo.co.uk	
Dunsmore, Barry W. MA BD	1982	2018	(Aberdeen: St Machar's Cathedral)	33 Young Road, Victoria Park, Dunblane FK15 0FT / barrydunsmore@gmail.com	01786 643287
Gilmour, William M. MA BD	1969	2008	(Lecropt)	14 Pine Court, Doune FK16 6JE	01786 842928
Hamilton, David S.M. MA BD STM	1958	1996	(Lecturer, Practical Theology, University of Glasgow)	Linfield, Milton of Lawton, Arbroath DD11 4RU / dandmhamilton@gmail.com	01241 238369
Hastie, George I. MA BD	1971	2009	(Mearns Coastal)	23 Borrowfield Crescent, Montrose DD10 9BR	01674 672290
Liddiard, F.G. Bernard MA	1957	1971	(Brechin: Gardner Memorial and East)	34 Trinity Fields Crescent, Brechin DD9 6YF / bernardliddiard@btinternet.com	01356 622966

Name	Dates	(Charge)	Address	Email	Phone
McIntosh, Hamish N.M. MA	1949 1987	(Fintry)	Room 20, Pearson House, Erskine Home, Nursery Avenue, Bishopton PA7 5PU		01786 831081
Murray, Douglas R. MA BD	1965 2004	(Lausanne: The Scots Kirk)	32 Forth Park, Bridge of Allan, Stirling FK9 5NT	d-smurray@supanet.com	
Ramsay, Robert J. LLB NP BD	1986 2018	(Invergowrie)	50 Nethergray Road, Dundee DD2 5GT	s3rjr@tiscali.co.uk	01382 562481
Reid, Albert B. BSc BD	1966 2001	(Ardler, Kettins and Meigle)	1 Mary Countess Way, Glamis, Forfar DD8 1RF	abreid019@gmail.com	01307 840999
Shannon, W.G. MA BD	1955 1998	(Pitlochry)	19 Knockard Road, Pitlochry PH16 5HJ		01796 473533
Sloan, Robert BD	1997 2014	(Fauldhouse: St Andrew's)	3 Gean Grove, Blairgowrie PH10 6TL		01250 875286

G. Readers (active)

Archibald, Michael	Wychwood, Culdeesland Road, Methven, Perth PH1 3QE	michael.archibald@gmail.com	01783 840995
Beedie, Alexander W. (William)	68 Bloomfield Road, Arbroath DD11 3LQ	a.wbeedie38@gmail.com	01241 875001
Benneworth, Michael	7 Hamilton Place, Perth PH1 1BB	mbenneworth@hotmail.com	01738 628093
Davidson, Andrew	95 Needless Road, Perth PH2 0LD	a.r.davidson.91@cantab.net	01738 620839
Gray, Linda (Mrs)	8 Inchgarth Street, Forfar DD8 3LY	lindamgray@sky.com	01307 464039
Grier, Hunter	17 Station Road, Bannockburn, Stirling FK7 8LG	anneandhunter@gmail.com	01786 815192
Howat, David P.	Lilybank Cottage, Newton Street, Blairgowrie PH10 6HZ	david@thehowats.net	01250 874715
McPherson, Alistair M.	Springpark, Doune Road, Dunblane FK15 9AR		01786 826850
Montgomery, Nicola	8 Beechwood Terrace, Dundee DD2 1NW		
Patterson, Rosemary (Mrs)	Rowantree, Golf Course Road, Blairgowrie PH10 6LJ	pattersonrose.c@gmail.com	01250 876607
Stewart, Anne	Ballcraine, Murthly Road, Stanley, Perth PH1 4PN	anne.stewart13@btinternet.com	01738 828637
Walker, Eric	12 Orchard Brae, Kirriemuir DD8 4JY	eric.line15@btinternet.com	01575 572082
Walker, Pat (Mrs)	12 Orchard Brae, Kirriemuir DD8 4JY	pat.line15@btinternet.com	01575 572082
Weidner, Karl J. BD CertTh	4 Drumkelbo Road, Meigle PH12 8AD	kweidner@btinternet.com	07523 091786
Xenophontos-Hellen, Tim	23 Ancrum Drive, Dundee DD2 2JG	tim.xsf@btinternet.com	01382 630355
Yellowlees, Deirdre (Mrs)	Ringmill House, Gannochy Farm, Perth PH2 7JH	d.yellowlees@btinternet.com	(Work) 01382 567756 / 01738 633773 / 07920 805399

H. Ministries Development Staff

Name	Role	Email
Allen, Valerie L. (Rev) BMus MDiv DMin	Presbytery – Chaplain	VL2allen@btinternet.com
Barakat, Shona	Montrose Area – Youth and Children's Worker	SBarakat@churchofscotland.org.uk
Berry, Gavin R.	Dundee: Camperdown/Dundee: Lochee – Parish Assistant	GBerry@churchofscotland.org.uk
Clark, Ross	Dundee: Fintry – Discipleship, Mission and Development Worker	Ross.Clark@churchofscotland.org.uk
Ingram, Carla BA MLitt	Arbroath: St Andrew's – Children and Families Worker	CIngram@churchofscotland.org.uk
McKenzie, Matthew	Dundee: Lochee / Dundee: Camperdown – Youth and Families Worker	MMcKenzie@churchofscotland.org.uk
Slowman, Neil BA	Perth: Letham St Mark's – Community Development Worker	NSlowman@churchofscotland.org.uk
Smith, Jane	Perth: Riverside – Community Development Worker	JSmith@churchofscotland.org.uk
Stirling, Diane BSc DipCPC BTh	Dundee: Craigiebank linked with Douglas and Mid Craigie – Parish Assistant	DStirling@churchofscotland.org.uk
Stott, Anne M. (Rev)	Presbytery Pioneer Worker – Bertha Park	AStott@churchofscotland.org.uk

CITY AND TOWN ADDRESSES

Arbroath

Old and Abbey	West Abbey Street
St Andrew's	Hamilton Green
St Vigeans	St Vigeans Brae
West Kirk	Keptie Street

Dundee

Balgay	200 Lochee Road
Barnhill St Margaret's	10 Invermark Terrace
Broughty Ferry New Kirk	370 Queen Street
St James'	5 Fort Street
St Luke's and Queen Street	5 West Queen Street
St Stephen's and West	96 Dundee Road
Camperdown	22 Brownhill Road
Chalmers-Ardler	Turnberry Avenue
Coldside	Isla Street x Main Street
Craigiebank	Craigie Avenue at Greendykes Road
Douglas and Mid Craigie	Balbeggie Place
Downfield Mains	Haldane Street off Strathmartine Road
Dundee (St Mary's)	Nethergate
Fintry	Fintry Road x Fintry Drive
Kingsgait	2 King Street
Lochee	191 High Street, Lochee
Logie and St John's Cross	Shaftesbury Rd x Blackness Ave
Menzieshill	Charleston Drive, Menzieshill
St David's High Kirk	119A Kinghorne Road
Steeple	Nethergate
Stobswell Trinity	73 Crescent Street
Strathmartine	507 Strathmartine Road
West	130 Perth Road
Whitfield	Haddington Crescent

Forfar

East and Old	East High Street
Lowson Memorial	Jamieson Street
St Margaret's	West High Street

Perth

Craigie	Abbot Street
Kinnoull	Dundee Rd near Queen's Bridge
Letham St Mark's	Rannoch Road
Moncreiffe	Glenbruar Crescent
North	Mill Street near Kinnoull Street
Riverside	Bute Drive
St John's	St John's Street
St Leonard's-in-the-Fields	Marshall Place
St Matthew's	Tay Street

Stirling

Holy Rude	St John Street
North	Springfield Road
Park	Park Terrace
St Mark's	Drip Road
St Ninians Old	Kirk Wynd, St Ninians
Viewfield Erskine	Barnton Street

(9) NORTH EAST AND NORTHERN ISLES (F W)

Meets at Aberdeen Fountainhall at the Cross on Tuesdays 7 November and 5 December 2023. In 2024 meets on dates to be determined.

Clerk: REV. ELSPETH M. McKAY LLB LLM PGCert BD
Presbytery Office: Suite 2, Ocean Spirit House West, 33 Waterloo Quay, Aberdeen AB11 5BS   tel awaited
NorthEastandNorthernIsles@churchofscotland.org.uk

1 Aberdeen: Bridge of Don Oldmachar (F H W)
Darren M. Jalland BA   2022
secretary@oldmacharchurch.org   **01224 709299**
60 Newburgh Circle, Aberdeen AB22 8QZ   07546 738797
DJalland@churchofscotland.org.uk

2 Aberdeen: Craigiebuckler (F H W)
Kenneth L. Petrie MA BD   1984 1999
office@craigiebuckler.org.uk   **01224 315649**
185 Springfield Road, Aberdeen AB15 8AA   01224 315125
KPetrie@churchofscotland.org.uk

3 Aberdeen: Devana (F H W)   Fonthill Road: **01224 213093**
Holburn Street: **01224 961430**
admin@devanaparishchurch.org
J. Peter N. Johnston BSc BD   2001 2013
(Moderator)
54 Polmuir Road, Aberdeen AB11 7RT   01224 414747
PJohnston@churchofscotland.org.uk
David J. Stewart BD MTh DipMin   2000 2018
(Team Minister)
54 Woodstock Road, Aberdeen AB15 5JF   01224 317975
DStewart@churchofscotland.org.uk
New charge formed by the union of Aberdeen: Ferryhill, Aberdeen: St Mark's and Aberdeen: South Holburn

4 Aberdeen: Fountainhall (F H W)
office@fountainhallchurch.org.uk   **01224 002891**
Duncan C. Eddie MA BD   1992 1999
(Moderator)
31 Cranford Road, Aberdeen AB10 7NJ   01224 325873
DEddie@churchofscotland.org.uk
Robert L. Smith BS MTh PhD   2000 2013
(Team Minister)
13 Oakhill Road, Aberdeen AB15 5ER   01224 314773
RSmith@churchofscotland.org.uk
Tanya J. Webster BCom DipAcc BD   2011 2019
(Team Minister)
182 Midstocket Road, Aberdeen AB15 5HS   01224 561358
TWebster@churchofscotland.org.uk
New charge formed by the union of Aberdeen: Holburn West, Aberdeen: Midstocket, Aberdeen: Queen's Cross and Aberdeen: Rubislaw

5 Aberdeen: Hillside (F H W)
Vacant
info@aberdeenhillsideparish.church   **01224 494717**
New charge formed by the union of Aberdeen: High Hilton and Aberdeen: Woodside

6 **Aberdeen: Mannofield (F H T W)**
   Keith T. Blackwood BD DipMin   1997   2007
   office@mannofieldchurch.org.uk
   21 Forest Avenue, Aberdeen AB15 4TU
   KBlackwood@churchofscotland.org.uk
   01224 310087
   01224 315748

7 **Aberdeen: North (F H W)**
   Fiona Lister   2023
   office@aberdeennorthchurch.co.uk
   8 Corse Wynd, Kingswells, Aberdeen AB15 8TP
   FLIster@churchofscotland.org.uk
   01224 694121
   07905 770259

8 **Aberdeen: Ruthrieston West (F W)**
   Benjamin D. W. Byun   1992   2008
   BA MDiv MTh PhD
   53 Springfield Avenue, Aberdeen AB15 8JJ
   BByun@churchofscotland.org.uk
   01224 312706

9 **Aberdeen: St Columba's Bridge of Don (F H W)**
   Louis Kinsey BD DipMin TD   1991
   administrator@stcolumbaschurch.org.uk
   151 Jesmond Avenue, Aberdeen AB22 8UG
   LKinsey@churchofscotland.org.uk
   01224 825653
   01224 705337

10 **Aberdeen: St John's Church for Deaf People**
   P. Mary Whittaker BSc BD   2011
   11 Templand Road, Lhanbryde, Elgin IV30 8BR
   MWhittaker@churchofscotland.org.uk
   Text only 07501 454766

11 **Aberdeen: St Machar's Cathedral (F H T W)**
   Sarah A. Brown (Ms)   2012
   MA BD ThM DipYW/Theol PDCCE DipPS
   office@stmachar.com
   39 Woodstock Road, Aberdeen AB15 5EX
   Sarah.Brown@churchofscotland.org.uk
   01224 485988
   01224 539630

12 **Aberdeen: St Mary's (F H W)**
   Vacant
   stmaryschurch924@btinternet.com
   456 King Street, Aberdeen AB24 3DE
   01224 487227
   01224 633778

13 **Aberdeen: St Nicholas Kincorth, South of (W)**
   Edward C. McKenna BD DPS   1989
   The Manse, Kincorth Circle, Aberdeen AB12 5NX
   EMcKenna@churchofscotland.org.uk
   01224 872820

   Joseph K. Somevi BSc MSc PhD BTh   2015   2021
   MRICS MRTPI MIEMA CertCRS
   (Ordained Local Minister)
   97 Ashwood Road, Aberdeen AB22 8QX
   JSomevi@churchofscotland.org.uk
   01224 826362
   07886 533259

14 **Aberdeen: St Stephen's (F H W)**
   Maggie Whyte BD   2010
   6 Belvidere Street, Aberdeen AB25 2QS
   Maggie.Whyte@churchofscotland.org.uk
   01224 624443
   01224 635694

15   Aberdeen: Stockethill (F W)
Ian M. Aitken MA BD — 1999
52 Ashgrove Road West, Aberdeen   AB16 5EE
IAitken@churchofscotland.org.uk
01224 686929

16   Aberdeen: Torry St Fittick's (F H W)
Edmond Gatima BEng BD MSc MPhil PhD — 2013
st.fitticks@btconnect.com — 01224 899183
11 Devanha Gardens East, Aberdeen   AB11 7UH — 01224 588245
EGatima@churchofscotland.org.uk
Joseph K. Somevi BSc MSc PhD BTh MRICS MRTPI MIEMA CertCRS (Ordained Local Minister) — 2015 2021
97 Ashwood Road, Aberdeen   AB22 8QX — 01224 826362 / 07886 533259
JSomevi@churchofscotland.org.uk

17   Aberdour linked (W) with Pitsligo (F W)
Vacant
Interim Moderator: Ruth Mackenzie (Miss)
31 Blairmore Park, Rosehearty, Fraserburgh   AB43 7NZ
ursular@tiscali.co.uk
01346 571823 / 01779 480680

18   Aberlour (F H W)
Andrew I. M. Kimmitt MA(Div) — 2020
The Manse, Mary Avenue, Aberlour   AB38 9QU
AKimmitt@churchofscotland.org.uk
01340 871909 / 07752 306462

19   Aberluthnott (F W) linked with Laurencekirk (F H W)
Rosalind (Linda) E. Pollock (Miss) BD ThM ThM — 2001 2021
contact@parishchurchofaberluthnottandlaurencekirk.co.uk
The Manse, Aberdeen Road, Laurencekirk   AB30 1AJ
RPollock@churchofscotland.org.uk
01561 377013

20   Aboyne-Dinnet (F H W) linked with Cromar (F W)
Frank Ribbons MA BD DipEd — 1985 2011
49 Charlton Crescent, Aboyne   AB34 5GN
FRibbons@churchofscotland.org.uk
01339 887267

21   Arbuthnott, Bervie and Kinneff (F T W)
Andrew R. Morrison MA BA — 2019
5 West Park Place, Inverbervie, Montrose   DD10 0XA
Andrew.Morrison@churchofscotland.org.uk
01561 443325 / 07720 275028

22   Auchterless and Auchaber (W)
Stephen J. Potts BA — 2012
The Manse, Auchterless, Turriff   AB53 8BA
SPotts@churchofscotland.org.uk
01888 511058
New charge formed by the union of Auchaber United and Auchterless

23   Banchory-Ternan: East (F H W)
Vacant
info@banchoryeastchurch.com — 01330 820380
East Manse, Station Road, Banchory   AB31 5YP — 01330 822481

24 Banchory-Ternan: West (F H T W)
Antony A. Stephen MA BD   2001   2011

office@banchorywestchurch.com   **01330 822006**
The Manse, 2 Wilson Road, Banchory AB31 5UY   01330 822006
TStephen@churchofscotland.org.uk   07866 704738

25 Banff (F W) linked with King Edward (F W)
Vacant
Interim Moderator: Colin A. Strong

info@banffparishchurchofscotland.org.uk   **01262 818211**
7 Colleonard Road, Banff AB45 1DZ   01261 812107
CStrong@churchofscotland.org.uk   01771 637365

26 Barthol Chapel (F) linked with Tarves (F W)
Alison I. Swindells (Mrs) LLB BD DMin   1998   2017

8 Murray Avenue, Tarves, Ellon AB41 7LZ   01651 851295
ASwindells@churchofscotland.org.uk

27 Belhelvie (F H W)
Paul McKeown BSc PhD BD   2000   2005

belhelviecofs@btconnect.com
Belhelvie Manse, Balmedie, Aberdeen AB23 8YR   01358 742227
PMcKeown@churchofscotland.org.uk

28 Bellie and Speymouth (F W)
Seòras I. Orr MSc MTh   2018

11 The Square, Fochabers IV32 7DG   01343 820256
SOrr@churchofscotland.org.uk

29 Bennachie (F H W)
Neil W. Meyer BD MTh   2000   2014
(Moderator)
G. Euan D. Glen BSc BD   1992
(Team Minister)
Sheila M. Mitchell BD MTh   1995   2018
(Team Minister)
New charge formed by the union of Blairdaff and Chapel of Garioch, Cluny, Echt and Midmar, Kemnay, Kintore, and Monymusk

office@kemnayparish.church   **Kennay 01467 643883**
28 Oakhill Road, Kintore, Inverurie AB51 0FH   01467 632219
NMeyer@churchofscotland.org.uk
The Manse, 26 St Ninians, Monymusk, Inverurie AB51 7HF   01467 651470
GGlen@churchofscotland.org.uk
The Manse, Echt, Westhill AB32 7AB   01330 860004
SMitchell@churchofscotland.org.uk

30 Birnie and Pluscarden (W) linked with Elgin: High (W)
Vacant
Session Clerk, Birnie and Pluscarden: Alistair Farquhar
Session Clerk, Elgin: High: Hazel Dickson

The Manse, 7 Kirkton Place, Elgin IV30 6JR
alistair.farquhar@btinternet.com   01343 541328
hazelandjohn@mypostoffice.co.uk   01343 540949

31 Birsay, Harray and Sandwick (F W)
Moira Taylor-Wintersgill BD — 2022
The Manse, North Biggings Road, Dounby, Orkney KW17 2HZ — 01856 771599
MTaylor-Wintersgill@churchofscotland.org.uk

D. Kerr Wintersgill BA — 2022
The Manse, North Biggings Road, Dounby, Orkney KW17 2HZ — 01856 771599
KWintersgill@churchofscotland.org.uk

32 Birse and Feughside (W)
Amy C. Pierce BA BD — 2017 2019
The Manse, Finzean, Banchory AB31 6PB — 01330 850736 / 07814 194997
ACPierce@churchofscotland.org.uk

33 Braemar and Crathie (F W)
Kenneth I. Mackenzie DL BD CPS — 1990 2005
The Manse, Crathie, Ballater AB35 5UL — 01339 742208
KMacKenzie@churchofscotland.org.uk

34 Brimmond (F H W)
Jonathan A. Clipston BSc MDiv — 2020
office@brimmondchurch.org.uk — **01224 716161**
Brimmond Manse, Bucksburn, Aberdeen AB21 9SS — 01224 712594
JClipston@churchofscotland.org.uk

35 Buckie: North (F H W) linked with Rathven (F)
Jacobus Boonzaaier BA BCom(OR) BD MDiv PhD — 1996 2021
info@buckienorth-rathvenchurches.org — 01542 649644
20 Netherton Terrace, Findochty, Buckie AB56 4QD
JBoonzaaier@churchofscotland.org.uk

36 Buckie: South and West (F H) linked with Enzie (F)
Vacant
Session Clerk, Buckie: South and West: Wilma Smith — 01542 833895
Craigendarroch, 14 Cliff Terrace, Buckie AB56 1LX
parkgrove10@gmail.com
Session Clerk, Enzie: Gladys Murray (Mrs) — 01542 832383

37 Crimond (F W) linked with Lonmay (W)
Vacant
Session Clerk, Crimond: Irene Fowlie (Mrs) — 01346 532431 / 01771 637263
The Manse, Crimond, Fraserburgh AB43 8QJ
fowlie_@hotmail.com
strathelliefarm@btinternet.com
Session Clerk, Lonmay: Roy Kinghorn — 01346 532436

38 Cromar See Aboyne-Dinnet

39 Cruden (F H W)
Sean Swindells BD DipMin MTh — 1996 2019
8 Murray Avenue, Tarves, Ellon AB41 7LZ — 01651 851295 / 07791 755976
SSwindells@churchofscotland.org.uk

40 Cullen and Deskford (F T W)
Douglas F. Stevenson BD DipMin
  DipHE MScR MCOSCA MBACP   1991   2010
14 Seafield Road, Cullen, Buckie AB56 4AF
DStevenson@churchofscotland.org.uk   01542 841963

41 Culsalmond and Rayne (F W) linked with Daviot (F H W)
Mary M. Cranfield MA BD DMin   1989
The Manse, Daviot, Inverurie AB51 0HY
MCranfield@churchofscotland.org.uk   01467 671241

42 Cults (F H T W)
Shuna M. Dicks BSc BD   2010   2018
cultsparishchurch@btinternet.com
1 Cairnlee Terrace, Bieldside, Aberdeen AB15 9AE
SDicks@churchofscotland.org.uk   **01224 869028** / 01224 861692

43 Daviot   See Culsalmond and Rayne

44 Deer (F H)
Sheila M. Kirk BA LLB BD   2007   2010
The Manse, Abbey Street, Old Deer, Peterhead AB42 5JB
SKirk@churchofscotland.org.uk   01771 623582

45 Drumoak-Durris (F H W)
Vacant
drumoakdurrischurch2020@gmail.com
26 Sunnyside Drive, Drumoak, Banchory AB31 3EW   01330 811031

46 Duffus, Spynie and Hopeman (F H W)
Jenny M. Adams BEng BD MTh   2013
The Manse, Duffus, Elgin IV30 5QP
JAdams@churchofscotland.org.uk   01343 830276

47 Dyce (F H T W) linked with New Machar (F W)
Manson C. Merchant BD CPS   1992   2008
dyceparishchurch@outlook.com
admin-newmacharchurch@btconnect.com
100 Burnside Road, Dyce, Aberdeen AB21 7HA
MMerchant@churchofscotland.org.uk   **01224 771295** / 01224 722380

Joan I. Thorne BA TQFE CertCS   2019
  (Ordained Local Minister)
85 Mosside Drive, Portlethen, Aberdeen AB12 4QY
JThorne@churchofscotland.org.uk   07368 390832

48 East Mainland (W)
Christopher Wallace BD DipMin   1988   2022
eastmainlandchurch@gmail.com
The Manse, Holm, Orkney KW17 2SB
Christopher.Wallace@churchofscotland.org.uk   01856 781797

49 Eday
Vacant
Session Clerk: Johan Robertson   essonquoy@btinternet.com   01857 622251

50 Elgin: High See Birnie and Pluscarden

51 Elgin: St Giles' (H) and St Columba's South (F W)
Deon F. Oelofse BA MDiv LTh MTh   2002 2017   **stgileselgin@gmail.com**   **01343 551501**
18 Reidhaven Street, Elgin IV30 1QH   01343 208786
DOelofse@churchofscotland.org.uk

Sonia Palmer RGN   2017   94 Ashgrove Park, Elgin IV30 1UT   07748 700929
(Ordained Local Minister)   Sonia.Palmer@churchofscotland.org.uk

52 Ellon (F T W)
Alastair J. Bruce BD MTh PGCE   2015   **info@ellonparishchurch.co.uk**   **01358 725690**
The Manse, 12 Union Street, Ellon   AB41 9BA   01358 723787
ABruce@churchofscotland.org.uk

53 Enzie See Buckie: South and West

54 Evie and Rendall (F) linked with Firth (F H)   **Firth: 01856 761117**
Vacant
Session Clerk, Evie and Rendall: Eileen Fraser   eileenocot@hotmail.co.uk   01856 761409
Session Clerk, Firth: Janis Dickey   rbdickey@hotmail.com   01856 761396
Interim Moderator: Iain D. MacDonald   IMacDonald@churchofscotland.org.uk   01857 677357

55 Findochty (F T W) linked with Portknockie (F T W)
Vacant   20 Netherton Terrace, Findochty, Buckie   AB56 4QD   01542 649644
Interim Moderator: Louis C. Bezuidenhout   macbez@gmail.com   01542 839493

56 Fintray Kinellar Keithhall (F W)   **01224 790439**
Vacant
Interim Moderator: Sheila A. Craggs   sacraggs@outlook.com   01358 723055

57 Firth See Evie and Rendall

58 Flotta (W) linked with Orphir and Stenness (H W)
Vacant
Martin W.M. Prentice BVMS MRCVS   2013 2015   Cot of Howe, Cairston, Stromness, Orkney KW16 3JU   01856 851139
DipCS (Ordained Local Minister)   MPrentice@churchofscotland.org.uk   07795 817213
Session Clerk, Flotta: Isobel Smith   01856 701219

59 Foveran (W)
Vacant
Interim Moderator: Ibidun B. Daramola
The Manse, Foveran, Ellon AB41 6AP
01358 789288
07395 006113

60 Fraserburgh: Old (W)
Vacant
Interim Moderator: James Givan
fraserburghopc@btconnect.com
4 Robbie's Road, Fraserburgh AB43 7AF
jim.givan@btinternet.com
01346 510139
01346 515332
01261 833318

61 Fraserburgh: South (H) linked with Inverallochy and Rathen: East   info@southkirk.com
Vacant

62 Fraserburgh: West (F H T W) linked with Rathen: West (T W)
Vacant
Session Clerk, Fraserburgh: West: Jill Smith (Mrs)   4 Kirkton Gardens, Fraserburgh AB43 8TU   jill@fraserburgh-harbour.co.uk
Session Clerk, Rathen: West: Ian J. Campbell   cicfarmers@hotmail.co.uk
01346 513303
01346 517972
01346 532062

63 Fyvie linked with Rothienorman (F) 1990 2019
Alison Jaffrey (Mrs) MA BD FSAScot
The Manse, Peterwell Road, Fyvie, Turriff AB53 8RD
AJaffrey@churchofscotland.org.uk
01651 891961

64 Glenmuick (Ballater) (H W) 2014
David L.C. Barr
The Manse, Craigendarroch Walk, Ballater AB35 5ZB
DBarr@churchofscotland.org.uk
01339 756111

65 Hoy and Walls (F)
Vacant
Session Clerk: Anderson Sutherland
Interim Moderator: Marjory A. MacLean
MMacLean@churchofscotland.org.uk
01856 701363
01856 831648

66 Huntly Cairnie Glass (F) 1994
Thomas R. Calder LLB BD WS
The Manse, Queen Street, Huntly AB54 8EB
TCalder@churchofscotland.org.uk
01466 792630

67 Insch-Leslie-Premnay-Oyne (F H W) 1999 2015
Kay F. Gauld BD STM PhD
66 Denwell Road, Insch AB52 6LH
KGauld@churchofscotland.org.uk
01464 820404

68 Inverallochy and Rathen: East   See Fraserburgh: South

69 Inverurie: St Andrew's (F W)
Carl J. Irvine   BSc MEd BA   2017   2020
standrews@btinternet.com
1 Ury Dale, Inverurie   AB51 3XW
CIrvine@churchofscotland.org.uk
   01467 628740
   01467 629163

70 Inverurie: West (F T W)
Rhona P. Cathcart   BA BSc BD   2017
admin@inveruriewestchurch.org
West Manse, 1 Westburn Place, Inverurie   AB51 5QS
RCathcart@churchofscotland.org.uk
   01467 620285
   01467 620285

71 Keith: North, Newmill, Boharm and Rothiemay (F H W)
Amy C. Bender   BA PhD DDiv   2022
knnbrchurch@btconnect.com
North Manse, Church Road, Keith   AB55 5BR
ABender@churchofscotland.org.uk
   01542 886390
   01542 780486

72 Keith: St Rufus, Botriphnie and Grange (F H W)
J.P.L. (Wiekus) van Straaten   BA BTh   1997   2020
St Rufus Manse, Church Road, Keith   AB55 5BR
WvanStraaten@churchofscotland.org.uk
   01542 882799

73 King Edward   See Banff

74 Kingshill (F H W)
Stella Campbell   MA (Oxon) BD   2012
secretary.kingshillparish@gmail.com
The Manse, Manse Road, Kirkton of Skene, Westhill   AB32 6LX
SCampbell@churchofscotland.org.uk
   01224 742512
   01224 745955

New charge formed by the union of **Kingswells and Skene**

75 Kirkwall: East (F H W) linked with Shapinsay (F W)
Julia M. Meason   MTh MA MTh   2013
East Church Manse, Thoms Street, Kirkwall, Orkney   KW15 1PF
JMeason@churchofscotland.org.uk
   01856 874789

76 Kirkwall: St Magnus Cathedral (F H T W) linked with Rousay
G. Fraser H. Macnaughton
   MA BD DipCPC   1982   2002
Cathedral Manse, Berstane Road, Kirkwall, Orkney   KW15 1NA
FMacnaughton@churchofscotland.org.uk
   01856 873312

June Freeth   BA MA   2015
(Ordained Local Minister)
Cumlaquoy, Orkney   KW17 2ND
JFreeth@churchofscotland.org.uk
   01856 721449

77 Knockando, Elchies and Archiestown (H W) linked with Rothes (W) info@moraykirk.co.uk
Vacant
The Manse, Rothes, Aberlour AB38 7AF
01340 **831497**
01340 831381
Session Clerk, Knockando, Elchies and Archiestown:
Patricia North
patnorth82@gmail.com
01340 810687
Session Clerk, Rothes: Dennis Malcolm
dennis.malcolm46@icloud.com
01340 831319
07399 420695

78 Laurencekirk See Aberluthnott

79 Longside (W)
Robert A. Fowlie BD   2007
The Manse, Abbey Street, Old Deer, Peterhead AB42 5JB
RFowlie@churchofscotland.org.uk
01771 622228

80 Lonmay See Crimond

81 Lossiemouth: St Gerardine's High (H W) linked with Lossiemouth: St James (F T W)
Geoffrey D. McKee BA BA DipPS   1997   2014
The Manse, St Gerardine's Road, Lossiemouth IV31 6RA
GMcKee@churchofscotland.org.uk
01343 208852

82 Lossiemouth: St James' See Lossiemouth: St Gerardine's High

83 Macduff (F T W) contactus@macduffparishchurch.org
Vacant
10 Ross Street, Macduff AB44 1NS
Interim Moderator: Stephen J. Potts
SPotts@churchofscotland.org.uk
01261 832316
01888 511058

84 Marnoch (F W)
Vacant
Marnoch Manse, 53 South Street, Aberchirder, Huntly AB54 7TS
01466 781143

85 Maryculter Trinity (W) marycultertrinitychurch@btinternet.com
Vacant
The Manse, Kirkton of Maryculter, Aberdeen AB12 5FS
David Galbraith   2021
Myreside Steading, Auchenblae, Laurencekirk AB30 1TX
(Ordained Local Minister)
David.Galbraith@churchofscotland.org.uk
Interim Moderator: Antony A. Stephen
TStephen@churchofscotland.org.uk
01224 **735983**
01224 730150
01561 320779
01330 822811

86 Maud and Savoch (F W) linked with New Deer: St Kane's (F W)
Aileen M. McFie (Mrs) BD   2003   2018
The Manse, Fordyce Terrace, New Deer, Turriff AB53 6TD
ARobson@churchofscotland.org.uk
01771 **644097**
01771 644631

87 Meldrum and Bourtie (F W)
Alisa L. McDonald BA MDiv   2008   2020   **info@meldrumandbourtiechurch.com**
17 Benview Gardens, Oldmeldrum, Inverurie AB51 0FY
Alisa.McDonald@churchofscotland.org.uk
07968 000610
01651 872059

88 Methlick (F W)
Vacant
Interim Moderator: Paul McKeown
The Manse, Manse Road, Methlick, Ellon AB41 7DG
PMcKeown@churchofscotland.org.uk
01651 806264
01358 742227

89 Mid Deeside (F W)
Holly Smith BSIS MDiv MEd   2009   2019
Lochnagar, Beltie Road, Torphins, Banchory AB31 4JU
Holly.Smith@churchofscotland.org.uk
01339 889160
01339 882915

90 Monquhitter and New Byth linked with Turriff: St Andrew's (F)   **info@standrewsturriff.co.uk**
James M. Cook BSc MBA MDiv   1999   2002
St Andrew's Manse, Balmellie Road, Turriff AB53 4DP
JCook@churchofscotland.org.uk
01888 560304

91 Mortlach and Cabrach (F H)
Eduard Enslin BTh MDiv MTh LLB   2010   2020
Mortlach Manse, Ardean, Church Street, Dufftown, Keith, AB55 4AR
EEnslin@churchofscotland.org.uk
01340 820380

92 New Deer: St Kane's See Maud and Savoch
93 New Machar See Dyce

94 New Pitsligo linked with Strichen and Tyrie (F W)
Colin A. Strong BSc BD   1989   2020
Kingsville, Strichen, Fraserburgh AB43 6SQ
CStrong@churchofscotland.org.uk
01771 637365

95 Newtonhill (F W)
Vacant
39 St Ternans Road, Newtonhill, Stonehaven AB39 3PF
01569 730143

96 North Ronaldsay
Guardianship of the Presbytery
Interim Moderator: Kenneth Meason
kennymeason@yahoo.co.uk
01856 874789

97 Ordiquhill and Cornhill (H) linked with Whitehills
Vacant
Session Clerk, Ordiquhill and Cornhill: Frances Webster (Mrs)
Session Clerk, Whitehills: Jenny Abel (Mrs)
6 Craigneen Place, Whitehills, Banff AB45 2NE
william.webster@btconnect.com
jennyabel14@hotmail.co.uk
01261 861317
01466 751230
01261 861386

98 Orphir and Stenness See Flotta

99 Papa Westray (W) linked with Westray (W) 1993
Iain D. MacDonald BD DipChEd
The Manse, Hilldavale, Westray, Orkney KW17 2DW
IMacDonald@churchofscotland.org.uk
Tel/Fax 01857 677357
07710 443780

100 Peterculter (F H W)
Vacant
secretary@culterkirk.co.uk
7 Howie Lane, Peterculter AB14 0LJ
01224 735845
01224 735041

101 Peterhead: New (F) 1999 2021
Julia Pizzuto-Pomaco BA MA MDiv PhD
contact@peterheadnew.org
15 Inchmore Gardens, Boddam, Peterhead AB42 3BG
JPizzuto-Pomaco@churchofscotland.org.uk
01779 471714

102 Peterhead: St Andrew's (H W)
Guardianship of the Presbytery
Session Clerk: John Leslie
eil.ian@btinternet.com
01779 470571

103 Pitsligo See Aberdour
104 Portknockie See Findochty

105 Portlethen (F H W)
Vacant
portlethenpc@btconnect.com
18 Rowanbank Road, Portlethen, Aberdeen AB12 4NX
01224 782883
01224 780211

106 Portsoy (W) 2021
John Gow BA
portsoychurch@gmail.com
The Manse, 4 Seafield Terrace, Portsoy, Banff AB45 2QB
JGow@churchofscotland.org.uk
01261 843125
01261 838506

107 Rathen: West See Fraserburgh: West
108 Rathven See Buckie: North
109 Rothes See Knockando, Elchies and Archiestown
110 Rothienorman See Fyvie
111 Rousay See Kirkwall: St Magnus Cathedral

112 St Andrew's-Lhanbryd and Urquhart (F H W) 1979 2020
C. Breda Ludik BA BTh DipTheol MTh PhD
39 St Andrews Road, Lhanbryde, Elgin IV30 8PU
BLudik@churchofscotland.org.uk
01343 842017

113 St Cyrus (F W)
Guardianship of the Presbytery
Norman D. Lennox-Trewren CertCS   2018
(Ordained Local Minister)
32 Haulkerton Crescent, Laurencekirk AB30 1FB
NLennoxTrewren@churchofscotland.org.uk
01561 377359
Mearns Coastal has been renamed St Cyrus

114 St Fergus (F)
Jeffrey Tippner BA MDiv MCS PhD   1991   2012
26 Newton Road, St Fergus, Peterhead AB42 3DD
JTippner@churchofscotland.org.uk
01779 838287

115 Sanday
Vacant
Interim Moderator: June Freeth
JFreeth@churchofscotland.org.uk
01856 721449

116 Sandhaven
Guardianship of the Presbytery
Interim Moderator: Colin A. Strong
CStrong@churchofscotland.org.uk
01771 637365

117 Shapinsay See Kirkwall: East

118 Shetland (F)
ShetlandParish@churchofscotland.org.uk
Frances M. Henderson BA BD PhD   2006   2018
(Transition Minister/ Minister)
The Manse, 25 Hogalee, East Voe, Scalloway, Shetland ZE1 0UU
FHenderson@churchofscotland.org.uk
01595 881184
Irene A. Charlton (Mrs) BTh CPS   1994   1997
(Team Minister)
The Manse, Marrister, Symbister, Whalsay, Shetland ZE2 9AE
ICharlton@churchofscotland.org.uk
01806 566767
Vacant
(Team Minister)
The North Isles Manse, Gutcher, Yell, Shetland ZE2 9DF
07815 922889
Michelle McAdoo RMN BD   2023
(Pioneer Minister)
MMcAdoo@churchofscotland.org.uk

119 South Ronaldsay and Burray (F)
Marjory A. MacLean LLB BD PhD   1991   2020
St Margaret's Manse, Church Road, St Margaret's Hope,
Orkney KW17 2SR
MMacLean@churchofscotland.org.uk
01856 831648

120 Stonehaven: Carronside (H W)
secretary.dunnottarchurch@outlook.com
Sarah Smith BA MDiv MA   2017   2021
Dunnottar Manse, Stonehaven AB39 3XL
Sarah.Smith@churchofscotland.org.uk
01569 760930
01569 762166

121 Stonehaven: Fetteresso (H W)
Mark Lowey BD DipTh   2012   2021
office@fetteresso.org.uk   01569 **767689**
11 South Lodge Drive, Stonehaven   AB39 2PN   01569 549960
MLowey@churchofscotland.org.uk

122 Strathbogie Drumblade (F W)
Vacant
Interim Moderator: Carol H.M. Ford
strathbogiedrumblade@outlook.com   01466 792702
49 Deveron Park, Huntly   AB54 8UZ   01464 820332
CFord@churchofscotland.org.uk

123 Strichen and Tyrie See New Pitsligo

124 Stromness (F H)
Vacant
Interim Moderator: June Freeth
JFreeth@churchofscotland.org.uk   01856 721449

125 Stronsay: Moncur Memorial (W)
David I.W. Locke MA MSc BD   2000   2021
The Manse, Wardhill, Stronsay, Orkney KW17 2AG   01857 616284
DLocke@churchofscotland.org.uk

126 Tarves See Barthol Chapel
127 Turriff: St Andrew's See Monquhitter and New Byth

128 Turriff: St Ninian's and Forglen (H L W)
Kevin R. Gruer BSc BA   2011
info@stniniansandforglen.org.uk   01888 **560282**
4 Deveronside Drive, Turriff AB53 4SP   01888 563850
KGruer@churchofscotland

129 Udny and Pitmedden (F W)
Vacant
Interim Moderator: Sheila M. Mitchell
The Manse, Manse Road, Udny Green, Ellon AB41 7RS 01651 843794
SMitchell@churchofscotland.org.uk   01330 860004

130 West Gordon (Alford, Strathdon, Rhynie) (F H W)
John A. Cook MA BD DMin   1986   2000
enquiries@howetrinity.org.uk   01975 **562829**
The Manse, 110 Main Street, Alford AB33 8AD   01975 562282
John.Cook@churchofscotland.org.uk

Simon A. Crouch MCIPD CertCS   2019
(Ordained Local Minister)
Delhandy, Corgarff, Strathdon AB36 8YB   01975 651779
SCrouch@churchofscotland.org.uk   07713 101358
    New charge formed by the union of Cushnie and Tough, Howe Trinity, Noth, and Upper Donside

131 West Mearns (F W)
Brian D. Smith BD   1990 2016   The Manse, Fettercairn, Laurencekirk AB30 1UE   01561 340203
BSmith@churchofscotland.org.uk

132 Westray See Papa Westray
133 Whitehills See Ordiquhill and Cornhill

B. In other appointments: members of Presbytery

Craig, Gordon T. KHC BD DipMin   1988 2012   Chaplain to UK Oil and Gas Industry   Shell Exploration and Production, Tullos Complex, 1 Altens Farm Road, Aberdeen AB12 3FY   gordon.craig@ukoilandgaschaplaincy.com   01224 882600

Jeffrey, Kenneth S. BA BD PhD DMin   2002 2014   Senior Lecturer, School of Divinity, University of Aberdeen   The North Steading, Dalgairn, Cupar KY15 4PH   ksjeffrey@btopenworld.com   01334 653196

Lancaster, Craig MA BD   2004 2011   RAF Senior Chaplain   Chaplaincy Centre, RAF Cosford, Wolverhampton WV7 3EX   craig.lancaster102@mod.gov.uk   07789 993535

McKay, Elspeth M. LLB LLM PGCert BD   2014 2022   Clerk, Presbytery of the North East and the Northern Isles   Suite 2, Ocean Spirit House West, 33 Waterloo Quay, Aberdeen AB11 5BS   EMcKay@churchofscotland.org.uk

McWhirter, Christine BA   2022   Assistant Minister, Lossiemouth area and Presbytery duties   CMcWhirter@churchofscotland.org.uk

Murray, B. Ian BD   2002 2021   Buildings Officer, Presbytery of the North East and the Northern Isles   Kilmorie House, 6 Institution Road, Elgin IV30 1RP   IMurray@churchofscotland.org.uk   0131 376 3647

Stewart, William   2015 2016   Ordained Local Minister, Presbytery-wide   Denend, Strichen, Fraserburgh AB43 6RN   billandjunes@live.co.uk   01771 637256

Swinton, John (Prof.) BD PhD RMN RNMD FRSE FBA   1999 2012   Master of Christ's College, University of Aberdeen   51 Newburgh Circle, Bridge of Don, Aberdeen AB22 8XA   j.swinton@abdn.ac.uk   01224 825637

van Sittert, Paul BA BD   1997 2011   Chaplain: Army   1 LANCS, Salamanca Barracks, Episkopi, BFPO 53   padre.pvs@gmail.com

Wood, Donald   2023   Assistant Minister, Presbytery-wide   DWood@churchofscotland.org.uk

Young, David T. BA BD MTh   2007 2022   Chaplain: RAF   St Aidan's Church, RAF Lossiemouth, Moray IV31 6DS   david.young137@mod.gov.uk   01434 817193

C. Retaining: members of Presbytery

Anderson, Robert J.M. BD FInstLM   1993 2022   (Knockando, Elchies and Archiestown with Rothes)   20 Park Street, Burghead, Elgin IV30 5UG   bobjmanderson@gmail.com   01343 835401

Bain, Brian LTh   1980 2007   (Gask with Methven and Logiealmond)   Bayview, 13 Stewart Street, Portgordon, Buckie AB56 5QT   bricoreen@gmail.com   01542 831215

Bezuidenhout, Louis C. BA MA BD DD   1978 2020   (Interim Minister, Arrochar with Luss)   76 East Church Street, Buckie AB56 1LQ   macbez@gmail.com   01542 839493

Blair, Fyfe BA BD DMin   1989 2019   (Stonehaven: Fetteresso)   19 Crichie Place, Fettercairn, Laurencekirk AB30 1EZ   Fyfe.Blair@churchofscotland.org.uk   01561 340579

Boyd, Barry J. LTh DPS	1993	2020	(Forres: St Laurence)	11 Hazeldene Road, Aberdeen AB15 8LB	07778 731018
Boyd, Jean A. MSc BSc BA	2016	2023	(Drumoak-Durris)	Snaefell, Lochside Road, St Cyrus, Montrose DD10 0DB	07856 573606
Broadley, Linda J. (Mrs) LTh DipEd	1996	2013	(Dun and Hillside)	lindabroadley@btinternet.com	01674 850141
Butterfield, John A. BA BD MPhil DipTCP DipCC	1990	2022	(Stromness)	Bring Deeps, Buxa Road, Orphir, Orkney KW17 2RE	01856 811707
Cheyne, Regine U. (Mrs) MA BSc BD	1988	2022	(Noth)	38 Morven Place, Aboyne AB34 5EZ RCheyne@churchofscotland.org.uk	
Christie, Andrew C. LTh	1975	2000	(Banchory-Devenick and Maryculter/Cookney)	17 Broadstraik Close, Elrick, Aberdeen AB32 6JP	01224 746888
Coutts, Fred MA BD	1973	2012	(Head of Spiritual Care, NHS Grampian)	Ladebank, 1 Manse Place, Hatton, Peterhead AB42 0UQ fred.coutts@btinternet.com	01779 841320
Craggs, Sheila A. (Mrs)	2001	2016	(Auxiliary Minister, Ellon)	7 Morar Court, Ellon AB41 9GG sacraggs@outlook.com	01358 723055
Craig, Anthony J.D. BD	1987	2009	(Glasgow: Maryhill)	4 Hightown, Collieston, Ellon AB41 8RS aacraig@btinternet.com	01358 751247
Daramola, I.B. BA MA PhD	2020	2023	(Associate, Skene)	16 Glenhome Gardens, Dyce, Aberdeen AB21 7FG ian@idryden.freeserve.co.uk	07395 006113
Dryden, Ian MA DipEd	1988	2001	(New Machar)		01224 722820
Duff, Stuart M. BA	1997	2019	(Birnie and Pluscarden with Elgin: High)	7 Kirkton Place, Elgin IV30 6JR stuart.duff@gmail.com	01343 200233
Falconer, James B. MBE BD CertMin	1982	2018	(Chaplain, Aberdeen Royal Hospitals)	3 Brimmond Walk, Westhill AB32 6XH	01224 744621
Ford, Carolyn (Carol) H.M. DSD RSAMD BD	2003	2018	(Edinburgh: St Margaret's)	4 Mitchell Avenue, Huntly AB54 8DW CFord@churchofscotland.org.uk	01464 820332
Fortune, Elsie J. (Mrs) BSc BD	2003	2023	(Aberdeen: St Mary's)	EFortune@churchofscotland.org.uk	01857 616487
Graham, Jennifer D. (Mrs) BA MDiv PhD	2000	2011	(Eday with Stronsay: Moncur Memorial)	Lodge, Stronsay, Orkney KW17 2AN jdgraham67@gmail.com	01464 820332
Greig, Alan BSc BD	1977	2017	(Interim Minister, Avonbridge with Torphichen)	1 Dunnydeer Place, Insch AB52 6HP greig@kincarr.free-online.co.uk	01771 624684
Griffiths, Melvyn J. BTh DipTheol DMin	1978	2021	(Maryculter Trinity)	2 Chalmers Place, Fetterangus AB42 4ED thehayvn@btinternet.com	01358 723981
Hawthorn, Daniel MA BD DMin	1965	2004	(Belhelvie)	7 Crimond Drive, Ellon AB41 8BT donhawthorn@btinternet.com	01856 741318
Johnston, Wilma A. MTheol MTh	2006	2020	(East Mainland)	Notland, Denwick Road, Deerness KW17 2QL rev.wilmajohnston@gmail.com	07706 091968
King, Margaret MA DCS	2002	2012	(Deacon, Bellie with Speymouth)	56 Murrayfield, Fochabers IV32 7EZ margaretking889@gmail.com	01343 820937
Lamb, A. Douglas MA	1964	2002	(Dalry: St Margaret's)	9 Luther Drive, Laurencekirk AB30 1FE lamb.edzell@talk21.com	01561 376816
Legge, Rosemary (Mrs) BSc BD MTh	1992	2017	(Cushnie and Tough)	57 High Street, Archiestown, Aberlour AB38 7QZ revrl192@aol.com	01340 810304

Name	Ord	Ret	(Charge)	Address	Tel
Lundie, Ann V. (Miss) DCS	1972	2007	(Deacon, Aberdeen: St George's Tillydrone)	20 Langdykes Drive, Cove, Aberdeen AB12 3HW / ann.lundie@btopenworld.com	01224 898416
Macalister, Eleanor E. DipCEd BD	1994	2006	(Ellon)	Quarryview, Ythan Bank, Ellon AB41 7TH / macal1ster@aol.com	01358 761402
Macgregor, Alan BA BD PhD	1992	2022	(Marnoch)	Culag, 139 Main Street, Aberchirder, Huntly AB54 7TB / a.macgregor1947@gmail.com	
Macnee, Iain LTh BD MA PhD	1975	2011	(New Pitsligo with Strichen and Tyrie)	Wardend Cottage, Alvah, Banff AB45 3TR / macneeiain4@googlemail.com	01261 815647
McLeish, Robert S. LTh	1970	2000	(Insch-Leslie-Premnay-Oyne)	19 Western Road, Insch AB52 6JR	01464 820749
Mikelson, Joshua M. BA MDiv	2008	2023	(Kennay)	JMikelson@churchofscotland.org.uk	
Mitchell, Valerie A. MA FSA	2019	2022	(Ordained Local Minster: Presbytery-wide)	Brownhill of Ardo, Methlick AB41 7HS / VMitchell@churchofscotland.org.uk	01651 806005
Montgomerie, Jean B. (Miss) MA BD	1973	2006	(Forfar: St Margaret's)	12 St Ronan's Place, Peterculter, Aberdeen AB14 0QX / revjeanb@tiscali.co.uk	01224 732350
Morton, Alasdair J. MA BD DipEd FEIS	1960	2000	(Bowden with Newtown)	16 St Leonard's Road, Forres IV36 1DW / alasgilmor@hotmail.co.uk	01309 671719
Murray, Alan J.S. BSc BD PhD	2003	2023	(Banchory-Ternan: East)	Lade Cottage, Bleachers Way, Hunting Towerfield, Perth PH1 3NY / AJSMurray@churchofscotland.org.uk	
Murray, Alistair BD	1984	2018	(Inverness: Trinity)	7 Clunie Street, Banff AB45 1HY / a.murray111@btinternet.com	01261 390154
Noble, Alexander B. MA BD ThM	1982	2020	(Saltcoats: North)	93 Snipe Street, Ellon AB41 9FW	01358 268705
Notman, John R. BSc BD	1990	2023	(Dumfries: Troqueer)	2 Burnett Road, Stonehaven AB39 2EZ / notman@sky.com	
O'Brien, Hugh CSS MTheol	2001	2023	(Macduff)	HOBrien@churchofscotland.org.uk	
Purves, John P. S. MBE BSc BD	1978	2013	(Colombo, Sri Lanka: St Andrew's Scots Kirk)	Lonville Cottage, 20 Viewfield Road, Ballater AB35 5RD / john@thepurves.com	01339 754081
Reid, Richard M.C. BSc BD MTh	1991	2021	(Foveran)	13 Morningside Crescent, Inverurie AB51 4FA / reidricky322@gmail.com	07474 010915
Rodgers, D. Mark BA BD MTh	1987	2021	(Head of Spiritual Care, NHS Grampian)	63 Cordiner Place, Hilton, Aberdeen AB24 4SB / dmrodgers16@gmail.com	01224 379135
Rollo, George B. BD	1974	2010	(Elgin: St Giles' and St Columba's South)	'Struan', 13 Meadow View, Hopeman, Elgin IV30 5PL / rollos@gmail.com	01343 835226
Ross, David S. BSc MSc PhD BD	1978	2013	(Chaplain: HM Prison Aberdeen and HM Prison Peterhead)	3–5 Abbey Street, Old Deer, Peterhead AB42 5LN / padsross@btinternet.com	01771 623994
Ross, William B. LTh CPS	1988	2016	(Aberdour with Pitsligo)	5 Strathlene Court, Rathven AB55 3DD / williamross278@btinternet.com	01542 834418
Sanders, Martyn S. BA CertEd	2013	2020	(Blairdaff and Chapel of Garioch)	140 The Homend, Ledbury, Herefordshire HR8 1BZ	07814 164373
Sheret, Brian S. MA BD DPhil	1982	2009	(Glasgow: Drumchapel Drumry St Mary's)	59 Airyhall Crescent, Aberdeen AB15 7QS	01224 323032
Smith, Morris BD CertCE	1988	2013	(Cromdale and Advie with Dulnain Bridge with Grantown-on-Spey)	1 Urquhart Grove, New Elgin IV30 8TB / mosmith.themanse@btinternet.com	01343 545019
Steel, G. Hutton B. MA BD	1982	2022	(Aberdeen: High Hilton)	1 Fairview Road, Bridge of Don, Aberdeen AB22 8ZG	
Sutherland, Susan J. (Mrs) BD	2009	2022	(Aberdeen: North)	53 Westhill Grange, Westhill AB32 6QJ / SSutherland@churchofscotland.org.uk	07917 012024

Name	Dates	Charge / Appointment	Address	Telephone
Tait, Alexander	1967 1995	(Glasgow: St Enoch's Hogganfield)	Ingermas, Evie, Orkney KW17 2PH	01856 751477
Telfer, Iain J.M. BD DPS	1978 2018	(Chaplain: Royal Infirmary of Edinburgh)	66 High Street, Inverurie AB51 3XS iain_telfer@yahoo.co.uk	07749 993070
Thomson, Iain U. MA BD	1970 2011	(Skene)	4 Keirhill Gardens, Westhill AB32 6AZ iainuthomson@googlemail.com	01224 746743
Thorburn, Robert J. BD DipPS	1978 2017	(Fyvie with Rothienorman)	12 Slackadale Gardens, Turriff AB53 4UA rjthorburn@aol.com	01888 562278
Verster, W. Myburgh BA BTh LTh MTh	1981 2019	(Ordiquhill and Cornhill with Whitehills)	32 Newtown Drive, Macduff AB44 1SR myburghverster@gmail.com	
Wallace, William F. BDS BD	1968 2008	(Wick: Pulteneytown and Thrumster)	Lachlan Cottage, 29 Station Road, Banchory AB31 5XX williamfwallace39@gmail.com	01330 822259
Watson, John M. LTh	1989 2009	(Aberdeen: St Mark's)	20 Greystone Place, Newtonhill, Stonehaven AB39 3UL johnmutchwatson2065@btinternet.com	01569 730604 07733 334380
Weir, James J.C.M. BD CertMin	1991 2018	(Aberdeen: St George's Tillydrone)	114 Hilton Heights, Woodside, Aberdeen AB24 4QF	01224 901430
Whyte, David W. LTh	1993 2011	(Boat of Garten, Duthil and Kincardine)	1 Lemanfield Crescent, Garmouth, Fochabers IV32 7LS whytedj@btinternet.com	01343 870667
Wishart, James BD	1986 2009	(Deer)	Upper Westshore, Burray, Orkney KW17 2TE jwishart06@btinternet.com	01856 731672
Youngson, Elizabeth J.B. BD	1996 2015	(Aberdeen: Mastrick)	47 Corse Drive, The Links, Dubford, Aberdeen AB23 8LN elizabeth.youngson@btinternet.com	07788 294745

D. In other appointments: not members of Presbytery

Name	Dates	Appointment	Address	Telephone
Smith, Hilary W. BD DipMin MTh PhD	1999 2016	Tutor in Theology, Vanuatu Spiritual Care Development Minister	Vaughan Park Anglican Retreat Centre, New Zealand oxfordsmith28@yahoo.co.nz	0064 21 0283 5435
Strachan, David G. BD DPS FRSA	1978 1988	Producer, Religious Television	24 Kennay Place, Aberdeen AB15 8SG dgstrachan@btinternet.com	01224 324032

E. Retaining; not members of Presbytery

Name	Dates	Charge	Address	Telephone
Anderson, David MA BD	1975 1999	(Fordyce)	Rowan Cottage, Aberlour Gardens, Aberlour AB38 9LD maurvid@hotmail.com	01340 871906
Brown, Robert F. MA BD ThM	1971 2008	(Aberdeen: Queen's Cross)	55 Hilton Drive, Aberdeen AB24 4NJ Bjacob546@aol.com	01224 491451
Gardner, Bruce K. MA BD PhD	1988 2011	(Aberdeen: Bridge of Don Oldmachar)	21 Hopetoun Crescent, Bucksburn, Aberdeen AB21 9QY drbruckgardner@aol.com	07891 186724
Grieg, Charles H.M. MA BD	1976 2016	(Dunrossness and St Ninian's incl. Fair Isle with Sandwick, Cunningsburgh and Quarff)	6 Hayhoull Place, Bigton, Shetland ZE2 9GA chm.greig@btinternet.com	01950 422468
Groves, Ian B. BD CPS	1989 2016	(Inverurie: West)	28 Parkhill Circle, Dyce, Aberdeen AB21 7FN ian@thegroves.me.uk	01224 774380

Hamilton, Helen D. (Miss) BD	1991	2002	(Glasgow: St James' (Pollok))	The Cottage, West Tilbouries, Maryculter, Aberdeen AB12 5GD / helenhamilton125@gmail.com	01224 739632
Hobson, Diane L. (Mrs) BA BD	2002	2017	(Aberdeen: St Mark's)	173B Blatchcombe Road, Paignton, Devon TQ3 2JP / diane.hobson@me.com	07850 962007
Hutchison, Alison M. (Mrs) BD DipMin	1988	2013	(Chaplain, Aberdeen General Hospitals)	Ashfield, Drumoak, Banchory AB31 5AG / ahutch@hotmail.co.uk	01330 811309
MacLean, Elspeth J. (Mrs) BVMS BD	2011	2021	(Forth: St Paul's)	17 Mameulah Crescent, Newmachar AB21 0WG / revmum55@gmail.com	
McDonald, Alan D. LLB BD MTh DLitt DD	1979	2016	(Cameron with St Andrews: St Leonard's)	13 Ashley Hall Gardens, Linlithgow EH49 7DN	07762 966393
Munro, Flora J. BD DMin	1993	2015	(Portlethen)	87 Gairn Terrace, Aberdeen AB10 6AY / floramunro@aol.com	
Nicholson, Thomas S. BD DPS	1982	2020	(Gordon: St Michael's with Greenlaw with Legerwood with Westruther)	Sandy Hill, St Margaret's Hope, Orkney KW17 2RN / TNicholson@churchofscotland.org.uk	
Robertson, Blair MA BD ThM	1990	2016	(Head of Chaplaincy and Spiritual Care, NHS Greater Glasgow and Clyde)	West End Guest House, 282 High Street, Elgin IV30 1AG / blair.robertson@tiscali.co.uk	07952 558766
Smith, William A. LTh	1972	1978	(Blairdaff with Monymusk)	82 Ashgrove Road West, Aberdeen AB16 5EE / bill2us@aol.com	01224 681866
Strachan, Ian M. MA BD	1959	1994	(Ashkirk with Selkirk)	'Cardenwell', Glen Drive, Dyce, Aberdeen AB21 7EN	01224 772028
Williamson, Magnus J.C.	1982	1999	(Fetlar with Yell)	Creekhaven, Houl Road, Scalloway, Shetland ZE1 0XA	01595 880023
Wilson, Andrew G.N. MA BD DMin	1977	2012	(Aberdeen: Rubislaw)	Auchintarph, Coull, Tarland, Aboyne AB34 4TT / agn.wilson@gmail.com	01339 880918

F. Inactive: not members of Presbytery

Ferguson, Ronald MA BD ThM DLitt	1972	2001	(Kirkwall: St Magnus Cathedral)	Vinbreck, Orphir, Orkney KW17 2RE / ronbluebrazil@aol.com	01856 811353
Forbes, John W.A. BD	1973	1999	(Edzell Lethnot with Fern, Careston and Menmuir with Glenesk)	Little Ennochie Steading, Finzean, Banchory AB31 4LX / jr6666@icloud.com	01330 850785
Grainger, Harvey L. LTh	1975	2004	(Kingswells)	13 St Ronan's Crescent, Peterculter, Aberdeen AB14 0RL / harveygrainger@btinternet.com	01224 739824
Haddow, Angus H. BSc	1963	1999	(Methlick)	25 Lerwick Road, Aberdeen AB16 6RF / marjory.haddow@gmail.com	01224 969521
Main, Alan (Prof.) TD MA BD STM PhD DD	1963	2001	(Practical Theology, University of Aberdeen)	Kirkfield, Barthol Chapel, Inverurie AB51 8TD / a.main993@btinternet.com	01651 806773
Richardson, Thomas C. LTh ThB	1971	2004	(Cults: West)	19 Kinkell Road, Aberdeen AB15 8HR / tomandpatrich@gmail.com	07956 308687
Stewart, James C. MA BD STM FSAScot	1960	2000	(Aberdeen: Kirk of St Nicholas)	Ashley House Residential Home, 4 King's Gate, Aberdeen AB15 4EJ	01224 648878
Wilson, Thomas F. BD	1984	1996	(Aberdeen: North of St Andrew)	55 Allison Close, Cove, Aberdeen AB12 3WG	01224 873501
Wood, James L.K.	1967	1995	(Aberdeen: Ruthrieston West)	1 Glen Drive, Dyce, Aberdeen AB21 7EN / james@jamesinez.plus.com	01224 722543

G. Readers (active)

Barker, Tim	South Silverford Croft, Longmanhill, Banff AB45 3SB	tbarker05@aol.com	01261 851839
Bell, Robert BSc FIStructE MICE	27 Mearns Drive, Stonehaven AB39 2DZ	r.bell282@btinternet.com	01569 767173 / 07733 014826
Bichard, Susanna (Mrs)	Beechlee, Haddo Lane, Tarves, Ellon AB41 7JZ	smbichard@aol.com	01651 851345
Broere, Teresa (Mrs)	3 Balnastraid Cottages, Dinnet, Aboyne AB34 5NE	broere@btinternet.com	01339 880058
Brown, Lillian (Mrs)	45 Main Street, Aberchirder, Huntly AB54 7ST	mabroon64@gmail.com	01466 780330
Coles, Stephen	43 Mearns Walk, Laurencekirk AB30 1FA	steve@sbcco.com	01561 378400
Cooper, Gordon	1 Kirkbrae View, Cults, Aberdeen AB15 9RU	ga_cooper@hotmail.co.uk	01224 964165
Cumming, Grant	Dunedin, 2 Reidhaven Street, Elgin IV30 1QG	cumminggrant@gmail.com	01343 540023
Dicken, Marion (Mrs)	12 MacDonald Park, St Margaret's Hope, Orkney KW17 2AL	mj44@hotmail.co.uk	01856 831687
Doak, Alan B.	17 Chievres Place, Ellon AB41 9WH	alanbdoak@aol.com	01358 721819
Findlay, Patricia (Mrs)	Douglas View, Tullynessle, Alford AB33 8QR	p.a.findlay@btopenworld.com	01975 562379
Forbes, Jean (Mrs)	Greenmoss, Drybridge, Buckie AB56 5JB	dancingfeet@tinyworld.co.uk	01542 831646 / 07974 760337
Forsyth, Alicia (Mrs)	Rothie Inn Farm, Forgue Road, Rothienorman, Inverurie AB51 8YH	aliciaforsyth56@gmail.com	01651 821359
Gillespie, Jean (Mrs)	16 St Colm's Quadrant, Eday, Orkney KW16 3PH	jrw2810@btinternet.com	01856 701406
Givan, James	Zimra, Longmanhill, Banff AB45 3RP	jim.givan@btinternet.com	01261 833318 / 07753 458864
Grant, Margaret (Mrs)	22 Elphin Street, New Aberlour, Fraserburgh AB43 6LH	mgrant3120@gmail.com	01346 561341
Gray, Peter (Prof.)	165 Countesswells Road, Aberdeen AB15 7RA	pmdgray@bcs.org.uk	01224 318172
Greig, Martin	85 Macaulay Drive, Aberdeen AB15 8FL	mgreig@aberdeencity.gov.uk	07920 806332
Harrison, Christine BA	16 Allt-Na-Coire, Tomnavoulin, Ballindalloch AB37 9JE	chrsthnrrsn42@googlemail.com	01897 590630 / 07930 048565
Hine, Kath (Ms)	2 Burnside Cottage, Rothiemay, Huntly AB54 7JX	kath.hine@gmail.com	01542 870680
Howard, Chris	Pegal, Glaitness Road, Kirkwall KW17 1BA	2201csb@gmail.com	01856 873271 / 07510 320607
Jones, Josephine (Mrs) BA CertEd LRAM	Moorside, Firth, Orkney KW17 2JZ	yetminstermusic@googlemail.com	01856 761899
MacLeod, Ali (Ms)	11 Pitfour Crescent, Fetterangus, Peterhead AB42 4EL	aliowl@hotmail.com	01771 622992 / 07821 670705
Macnee, Anthea (Mrs)	Wardend Cottage, Alvah, Banff AB45 3TR	macneeian4@googlemail.com	01261 815647
Mair, Dorothy L.T. (Miss)	Flat F, 15 The Quay, Newburgh, Ellon AB41 6DA	dorothymair2@aol.com	01358 788832 / 07505 051305
McCafferty, W. John	Lynwood, Cammachmore, Stonehaven AB39 3NR	wjmccafferty@yahoo.co.uk	01569 730281 / 07768 925122
McDonald, Rhoda (Miss)	16 St Andrew's Drive, Fraserburgh AB43 2PX	techmc@callnetuk.com	01346 514052
McFie, David	The Manse, Fordyce Terrace, New Deer, Turriff AB53 6TD	waverley710@gmx.co.uk	01771 644631
Middleton, Robin B. (Capt.)	7 St Ternan's Road, Newtonhill, Stonehaven AB39 3PF	robbiemiddleton7@hotmail.com	01569 730852
Pirie, Maggie (Mrs)	Uppermill Cottage, Auchterless, Turriff AB53 8AU	maggie.pirie@btinternet.com	01888 511059
Pomfret, Valerie (Mrs)	3 Clumly Avenue, Kirkwall, Orkney KW15 1YU	vpomfret@btinternet.com	
Robertson, Johan (Mrs)	Essonquoy, Eday, Orkney KW17 2AB	essonquoy@btinternet.com	01857 622251

Name	Address	Email	Phone
Simpson, Andrew C.	10 Wood Street, Banff AB45 1JX	andy.louise1@btinternet.com	
Simpson, Elizabeth (Mrs)	Connemara, 33 Golf Road, Ballater AB35 5RS	connemara33@yahoo.com	01261 812538
Sneddon, Richard	100 West Road, Peterhead AB42 2AQ	richard.sneddon@btinternet.com	01339 755597

H. Ministries Development Staff

Name	Role	Email
Adam, Pamela BD	Ellon – Parish Assistant	PAdam@churchofscotland.org.uk
Amalanand, John C.	Aberdeen: Devana – Mission Development Worker, Families and Students	JAmalanand@churchofscotland.org.uk
Angus, Natalie	Dyce – Youth and Family Worker	NAngus@churchofscotland.org.uk
Baker, Paula (Mrs)	Birnie and Pluscarden linked with Elgin: High – Parish Assistant	PBaker@churchofscotland.org.uk
Bruce, Nicola P.S. BA MTh	Ellon – Parish Assistant, Mission Development	NBruce@churchofscotland.org.uk
Cross, Peter	Ellon – Parish Assistant	PCross@churchofscotland.org.uk
Dick, Janet	Presbytery – Mission and Discipleship Development Worker	Janet.Dick@churchofscotland.org.uk
Griffiths Weir, K. Ellen	Shetland – Youth and Children's Worker	EWeir@churchofscotland.org.uk
Mikelson, Heather (Rev)	Presbytery – Mission Development Worker	HMikelson@churchofscotland.org.uk
Mitchell, William	Aberdeen: Hillside – Parish Assistant	WMitchell@churchofscotland.org.uk
Richardson, Frances	Shetland – Administrator and Treasurer	FRichardson@churchofscotland.org.uk
Simms, Michele MA	Shetland – Parish Development Worker	MSimms@churchofscotland.org.uk
Stigant, Victoria J.	Presbytery - Youth Work Facilitator	VStigant@churchofscotland.org.uk
Taylor, Valerie Assoc-CIPD PGDip	Aberdeen: Torry St Fittick's – Ministry Assistant	VTaylor@churchofscotland.org.uk

ABERDEEN ADDRESSES

Church	Address
Bridge of Don Oldmachar	Ashwood Park, Springfield Road
Craigiebuckler	
Devana	Fonthill Road x Polmuir Road; and Holburn Street
Fountainhall	Albyn Place; and Mid Stocket Road
Hillside	Hilton Drive
Mannofield	Great Western Road x Craigton Road
North	
Ruthrieston West	Greenfern Road, Mastrick
St Columba's Bridge of Don	Broomhill Road
St John's for the Deaf	(contact Minister)
St Machar's Cathedral	The Chanonry
St Mary's	King Street
St Nicholas Kincorth, South of	Kincorth Circle
St Stephen's	Powis Place
Stockethill	Cairncry Community Centre
Torry St Fittick's	Walker Road
	Braehead Way, Bridge of Don

Worship in the Parish of Shetland held at:

Aith	11 Wirliegert, Aith, Bixter ZE2 9NW
Baltasound St John's	Baltasound, Unst ZE2 9DX
Brae	Grindwell, Brae, Delting ZE2 9QW
Bridgend, Burra Isle	Freefield Road, Bridge End, Burra Isle ZE2 9LD
Cullivoe	Cullivoe, Yell ZE2 9DD
Lerwick St Columba's	Greenfield Place, Lerwick ZE1 0EQ
Luma St Margaret's	Methodist Chapel, Vidlin, Lunnasting ZE2 9QE
Ollaberry	Ollaberry, Northmavine ZE2 9QW
Sandwick	Sandwick ZE2 9HW
Scalloway	Main Street, Scalloway ZE1 0TR
Walls St Paul's	Pier Road, Walls ZE2 9PF
Whalsay	Church Hall, Symbister, Whalsay ZE2 9AD

(10) CLÈIR EILEAN Ì: HIGHLANDS AND HEBRIDES

A new presbytery to be formed on 1 January 2024 by the union of the presbyteries of Argyll, Abernethy, Inverness, Lochaber, Ross, Sutherland, Caithness, Lochcarron-Skye and Uist. The first meeting to be on a day and at a time to be determined by the Clèir Eilean Ì: Highlands and Hebrides Transition Team.

Clerk: to be appointed

As the union has yet to take place, the presbyteries continuing until the end of 2023 are listed separately, below.

(10.1) ARGYLL (F W)

Meets in the Village Hall, Tarbert, Loch Fyne, Argyll on the first Tuesday of December. For details, contact the Presbytery Clerk.

Clerk:	MR W. STEWART SHAW DL BSc	59 Barone Road, Rothesay, Isle of Bute PA20 0DZ argyll@churchofscotland.org.uk	07775 926541
Treasurer:	REV. DAVID CARRUTHERS BD	The Manse, Park Road, Ardrishaig, Lochgilphead PA30 8HE DCarruthers@churchofscotland.org.uk	01546 603269

1 Appin (F) linked with Lismore
Dugald J. Cameron BD DipMin MTh   1990   2021   An Mansa, 11 Tyneribbie Place, Appin, Argyll PA38 4DS   Appin 01631 730280
Dugald.Cameron@churchofscotland.org.uk

2 Ardchattan (F H W) linked with Coll (F W) linked with Connel (F W)
Willem J. Bezuidenhout   1977   2019   St Oran's Manse, Connel, Oban PA37 1PJ   01631 710214
BA BD MHEd MEd   WBezuidenhout@churchofscotland.org.uk   07484 333923
                                                                                      Coll 01879 230366

3 Barra (GD) linked with South Uist (GD W)
Lindsay Schluter ThE CertMin PhD   1995   2016   The Manse, Cuithir, Grean, Isle of Barra HS9 5XU   01871 810230
L.Schluter@churchofscotland.org.uk   07835 913963

4 Bute, United Church of (F W)
Vacant
Session Clerk: James McMillan   jamessmcmillan@btinternet.com   01700 502755
                                                                        07889 988219

5 **Campbeltown: (F H W) linked with Saddell and Carradale (H W) linked with Southend (F H W) (South Kintyre)**
Steven Sass BTh MDiv LTh 2001 2023 The Manse, Southend, Campbeltown PA28 6RQ 07838 434416
Campbeltown was formed by the union of Campbeltown: Highland and Campbeltown: Lorne and Lowland

6 **Coll** See Ardchattan

7 **Colonsay and Oronsay (W)**
Guardianship of the Presbytery
Session Clerk: William Leigh Knight (Dr) copsessionclerk@gmail.com 07808 586370

8 **Connel** See Ardchattan

9 **Cowal Kirk (F H W)** **admin@cowalkirk.org**
Everisto Musedza BTh 2015 2023 The Manse, 13 Dhailling Park, Hunter Street, 01369 702256
Kirn, Dunoon, PA23 8FB 07748 347487
EMusedza@churchofscotland.org.uk
Alexander J. (Sandy) MacPherson MA BSc 2021 8 Queens View, Marine Parade, Kirn, Dunoon PA23 8LF 01369 707969
FRSA (Ordained Local Minister) SMacPherson@churchofscotland.org.uk

10 **Dalriada Mid Argyll (F W)**
David Carruthers BD 1998 The Manse, Kiluskland Road, Ardrishaig, Lochgilphead PA30 8HE 01546 603269
DCarruthers@churchofscotland.org.uk
New charge formed by the union of Ardrishaig, Glassary, Kilmartin and Ford, Lochgilphead, North Knapdale, and South Knapdale

11 **Glenorchy and Strathfillan (W)**
Vacant
Session Clerk, Strathfillan: Janet Buchanan (Mrs) janetbuchanan567@btinternet.com 01866 833308
New charge formed by the union of Glenorchy and Innishael, and Strathfillan

12 **Iona (W) linked with Kilfinichen and Kilvickeon and the Ross of Mull (W)**
Vacant
Session Clerk, K&K&RoM: Linda Dawson (Mrs) Maolbhuide, Fionnphort, Isle of Mull PA66 6BP 01681 700718

13 **Jura (GD) linked with North and West Islay (GD) linked with South Islay (GD H W) (Islay and Jura)**
William F. Hunter MA BD 1986 2023 The Manse, Bowmore, Isle of Islay PA43 7LH 01496 810271
WHunter@churchofscotland.org.uk

14 **Kilchrenan and Dalavich (W) linked with Muckairn (W)**
Thomas W. Telfer BA MDiv 1986 2018 Muckairn Manse, Taynuilt PA35 1HW 01866 822204
TTelfer@churchofscotland.org.uk

15 Kilfinichen and Kilvickeon and the Ross of Mull See Iona

16 Kilmore and Oban (F GD W)
Vacant
Session Clerks: Sine MacVicar (Miss)
John MacLean

obancofs@btinternet.com
Kilmore and Oban Manse, Ganavan Road, Oban PA34 5TU
s.macvicar52@btinternet.com
john.maclean56@btinternet.com

01631 **562405**
01631 566253
01631 710090
01631 565519

17 Kilmun, Strone and Ardentinny: The Shore Kirk (H W)
Janet K. MacKellar BSc ProfCertMgmt   2019
FCMI (Ordained Local Minister)

Laurel Bank, 23 George Street, Dunoon PA23 8TE
JMackellar@churchofscotland.org.uk

01369 705549

18 Lismore See Appin

19 Lochgoilhead (H) and Kilmorich linked with Strachur and Strathlachlan (Upper Cowal)
Robert K. Mackenzie MA BD PhD   1976   1998

The Manse, Strachur, Cairndow PA27 8DG
RKMackenzie@churchofscotland.org.uk

01369 860246

20 Mid Kintyre and Gigha (H W) linked with Tarbert, Loch Fyne and Kilberry (F H W) (North Kintyre)
Lyn M. Peden (Mrs) BD   2010   2020

The Manse, Campbeltown Road, Tarbert, Argyll PA29 6SX
LPeden@churchofscotland.org.uk

01880 820158

Mid Kintyre and Gigha was formed by the union of Gigha & Cara, Kilcalmonell, Killean & Kilchenzie and Skipness

21 Muckairn See Kilchrenan and Dalavich

22 Netherlorn (F W)
Vacant
Session Clerk: Fiona Cruikshanks

The Manse, Kilmelford, Oban PA34 4XA
netherlornsessionclerk@gmail.com

01852 200565
01852 314375

Netherlorn was formed by the union of Craignish, Kilbrandon & Kilchattan, and Kilninver & Kilmelford

23 North and West Islay See Jura

24 North Mull (F GD H W)
Elizabeth A. Gibson (Mrs) MA MLitt BD   2003   2021

The New Manse, Gruline Road, Salen, Aros, Isle of Mull PA72 6JF
egibson@churchofscotland.org.uk

01680 300655

25 Rothesay: Trinity (H W)
Sibyl A. Tchaikovsky BA BD MLitt 2018 12 Crichton Road, Rothesay, Isle of Bute PA20 9JR 01700 504047
STchaikovsky@churchofscotland.org.uk

26 Saddell and Carradale See Campbeltown
27 Southend See Campbeltown
28 South Islay See Jura
29 South Uist See Barra
30 Strachur and Strathlachlan See Lochgoilhead and Kilmorich
31 Tarbert, Loch Fyne and Kilberry See Mid Kintyre and Gigha

32 Tiree (F GD W)
Vacant
Interim Moderator: Aileen Binner The Manse, Scarinish, Isle of Tiree PA77 6TN 01879 220377
ABinner@churchofscotland.org.uk 01631 710264

33 West Cowal (H)
David Mitchell BD DipPTheol MSc 1988 2006 West Cowal Manse, Kames, Tighnabruaich PA21 2AD 01700 811045
DMitchell@churchofscotland.org.uk

New charge formed by the union of Kilfinan and Kilmodan & Colintraive and Kyles

34 West Lochfyneside: Cumlodden, Inveraray and Lochgair (F W)
Dorothy M. Wallace BA 2021 The Manse, Inveraray PA32 8XT 01499 302459
Dorothy.Wallace@churchofscotland.org.uk

B. In other appointments: members of Presbytery

Anderson, David P. BSc BD 2002 2007 Senior Army Chaplain 4 Infantry Brigade and HQ North East, Bourlon Barracks, Pl"ymer Road, Catterick Garrison DL9 3AD
David.Anderson646@mod.gov.uk

Ross, Kenneth R. OBE BA BD PhD 1982 2019 Theological Educator, Africa Zomba Theological College, PO Box 130, Zomba, Malawi
kross@thinkingmission.org

C. Retaining: members of Presbytery

Barge, Nigel L. BSc BD 1991 2021 (Torrance) 2 Lephinmore Cottage, Strathlachlan, Cairndow PA27 8BU
NBarge@churchofscotland.org.uk

Campbell, Roderick D.M. TD MStJ BD 1975 2019 (Cumlodden, Lochfyneside and Lochgair Windy Ridge, Glen Loanan, Taynuilt PA35 1EY 01866 822623
DMin FSAScot with Glenaray and Inveraray) Roderick.Campbell@churchofscotland.org.uk

Cringles, George G. BD CertMin 1981 2017 (Coll with Connel) The Moorings, Ganavan Road, Oban PA34 5TU 01631 564215
george.cringles@gmail.com

Earl, Jenny MA BD	2007	2023	(Iona with Kilfinichen and Kilvickeon and the Ross of Mull)	Kenilworth Cottage, Victoria Park, Minard, Inveraray PA 32 8YN	
Fulcher, Christine P. BEd CertCS	2012	2022	(Ordained Local Minister, Team Minister, South Argyll)	Jura, The Steading, Kilmelford PA34 4XA CFulcher@churchofscotland.org.uk	01852 200538
Fulcher, Stephen BA MA	1993	2022	(Campbeltown: Highland with Saddell and Carradale with Southend)	Jura, The Steading, Kilmelford PA34 4XA steve.f2000@btinternet.com	01852 200538
Griffiths, Ruth I. (Mrs)	2004	2020	(Auxiliary Minister, Dunoon: The High Kirk with Innellan with Toward)	Kirkwood, Mathieson Lane, Innellan, Dunoon PA23 7TA	01369 830145
Henderson, Grahame McL. BD CPS	1974	2008	(Kirn)	6 Gerhallow, Bullwood Road, Dunoon PA23 7QB ghende5884@aol.com	01369 702433
Hood, H. Stanley C. MA BD	1966	2000	(London: Crown Court)	10 Dalriada Place, Kilmichael Glassary, Lochgilphead PA31 8QA	01546 606168
Jones, John Owain MA BD FSAScot	1981	2023	(United Church of Bute)	28 Ardgowan Square, Greenock PA16 8NJ johnowainjones1@gmail.com	07806 623677
Lind, Michael J. LLB BD	1984	2012	(Campbeltown: Highland)	Maybank, Station Road, Conon Bridge, Dingwall IV7 8BJ mijylind@gmail.com	01349 865932
Macfarlane, James MTh PhD	1991	2011	(Lochgoilhead and Kilmorich)	'Lindores', 11 Bullwood Road, Dunoon PA23 7QJ mac.farlane@btinternet.com	01369 710626
Marshall, Freda (Mrs) BD FCII	1993	2005	(Colonsay and Oronsay with Kilbrandon and Kilchattan)	Allt Mhaluidh, Glenview, Dalmally PA33 1BE mail@freda.org.uk	01838 200693
McIvor, Anne (Miss) SRD BD	1996	2013	(Gigha and Cara)	20 Albyn Avenue, Campbeltown PA28 6LY annemcivor@btinternet.com	07901 964825
McLaren, Glenda M. (Ms) DCS	1990	2020	(Deacon, Dunoon: St John's with Kirn and Sandbank)	Kiona, 1 Trinity Lane, Innellan PA23 7TS gmmclaren1330@gmail.com	07743 763054
Mill, David GCSI MA BD	1978	2018	(Kilmun, Strone and Ardentinny: The Shore Kirk)	The Hebrides, 107 Bullwood Road, Dunoon PA23 7QN revandevmill@aol.com	01369 707544
Millar, Margaret R.M. (Miss) DipChE BTh	1977	2008	(Kilchrenan and Dalavich with Muckairn)	Fearnoch Cottage, Fearnoch, Taynuilt PA35 1JB macoje@btinternet.com	01866 822416
Park, Peter B. BD MCIBS	1997	2014	(Fraserburgh: Old)	Hillview, 24 McKelvie Road, Oban PA34 4GB peterpark9@btinternet.com	01631 565849
Ritchie, Walter M.	1973	1999	(Uphall: South)	Hazel Cottage, Barr Mor View, Kilmartin, Lochgilphead PA31 8UN	01546 510343
Scott, Randolph MA BD	1991	2013	(Jersey: St Columba's)	18 Lochan Avenue, Kirn, Dunoon PA23 8HT rev.rs@hotmail.com	01369 703175
Smith, Hilda C. (Miss) MA BD MSc	1992	2021	(Lochgilphead)	Ardmore, Kilmory Road, Lochgilphead PA31 8SZ hilda.smith2@btinternet.com	01546 603191
Stewart, Joseph LTh	1979	2011	(Dunoon: St John's with Sandbank)	7 Glenmorag Avenue, Dunoon PA23 7LG	01369 703438
Wilkinson, W. Brian MA BD	1968	2007	(Glenaray and Inveraray)	3 Achlonan, Taynuilt PA35 1JJ williambrian35@btinternet.com	01866 822036

D. In other appointments: not members of Presbytery
Nil

E. Retaining: not members of Presbytery

Webster, Peter BD DipPS	1977	2014	(Edinburgh: Portobello St James')	6 Newton Park, Dunoon PA23 7ST peterwebster101@hotmail.com	07572 813695

F. Inactive: not members of Presbytery

Beautyman, Paul H. MA BD PGCCE	1993	2019	(Youth Adviser, Presbytery of Argyll)	59 Alexander Street, Dunoon PA23 7BB paulbeautyman67@gmail.com	01546 600316
Dunlop, Alistair J. MA	1965	2004	(Saddell and Carradale)	8 Pipers Road, Cairnbaan, Lochgilphead PA31 8UF dunrevn@btinternet.com	01631 567471
Gray, William LTh	1971	2006	(Kilberry with Tarbert)	Lochnagar, Longsdale Road, Oban PA34 5DZ gray98@hotmail.com	01499 500629
MacLeod, Roderick MBE MA BD PhD(Edin) PhD(open)	1966	2011	(Cumlodden, Lochfyneside and Lochgair)	Creag-nam-Barnach, Furnace, Inveraray PA32 8XU mail@revroddy.co.uk	01870 610320
Muir, Eleanor D. MTheol DipPTheol	1986	2015	(Fowlis Wester, Madderty and Monzie with Gask)	Heatherdale, 6 Lochcarnan, South Uist HS8 5NU eleanordmuir@gmail.com	

G. Readers (active)

Allan, Douglas	1 Camplen Court, Rothesay, Isle of Bute PA20 0NL	douglas.allan423@gmail.com	01700 502331
Binner, Aileen (Mrs)	Ailand, North Connel, Oban PA37 1QX	binners@ailand.plus.com	01631 710264
Logue, David	3 Braeface, Tayvallich, Lochgilphead PA31 89N	david@loguenet.co.uk	01546 870647
Malcolm, James	Courtyard Cottage, Barmor View, Kilmartin PA31 8UN	jgrmalcolm@btinternet.com	01546 510540
McHugh, Douglas	Tigh Na Criche, Cairndow, Argyll PA27 8BY	dmchugh6@gmail.com	01369 860147
McLellan, James A.	West Drimvore, Lochgilphead PA31 8SU	james.mclellan8@btinternet.com	01546 606403
Mills, Peter A.	Northton, Ganavan, Oban PA34 5TU	peter@peteramills.com	
Morrison, John L.	Tigh na Barnashaig, Tayvallich, Lochgilphead PA31 8PN	jolomo@thejolomostudio.com	01546 870637
Ramsay, Matthew M.	Portnastorm, Carradale, Campbeltown PA28 6SB	kintyre@fishermensmission.org.uk	01583 431381
Scouller, Alastair	15 Allanwater Apartments, Bridge of Allan, Stirling FK9 4DZ	scouller@globalnet.co.uk	01786 832496
Sinclair, Margaret (Ms)	2 Quarry Place, Furnace, Inveraray PA32 8XW	margaret_sinclair@btinternet.com	01499 500633
Stather, Angela (Ms)	1 Dunlossit Cottages, Port Askaig, Isle of Islay PA46 7RB	angstat@btinternet.com	01496 840726
Thornhill, Christopher R.	4 Ardfern Cottages, Ardfern, Lochgilphead PA31 8QN	c.thornhill@btinternet.com	01852 300011
Zielinski, Jeneffer C. (Mrs)	7 Wallace Court, Ferguslie Street, Sandbank, Dunoon PA23 8QA	jenefferzielinski@gmail.com	01369 706136

H. Ministries Development Staff

Binner, Aileen	Presbytery – Ministries Co-ordinator, South Argyll	ABinner@churchofscotland.org.uk
D'Silva, Emily	Kilmore and Oban – Parish Assistant	EDSilva@churchofscotland.org.uk
Hay, Alison	Presbytery – Ministries Co-ordinator, North and East Argyll	AHay@churchofscotland.org.uk
Whyte, Susan	Presbytery – Youth Worker – Team Leader	SWhyte@churchofscotland.org.uk
Wilson, John K. (Kenny)	Presbytery – Youth and Children's Worker	KWilson@churchofscotland.org.uk

(10.2) ABERNETHY (W)

Meets at Boat of Garten on the first Tuesday of October, November and December.

| Clerk: | REV JAMES A.I. MacEWAN MA BD | Rapness, Station Road, Nethy Bridge PH25 3DN abernethy@churchofscotland.org.uk | 01479 821116 |

1 Abernethy (F H W) linked with Boat of Garten (H), Carrbridge (H) and Kincardine (F W)

| Graham T. Atkinson MA BD MTh | 2006 | 2019 | The Manse, Deshar Road, Boat of Garten PH24 3BN GAtkinson@churchofscotland.org.uk | 01479 831637 |

2 Alvie and Insh (H W) linked with Rothiemurchus and Aviemore (H W)

| Charles J. Finnie LTh DPS | 1991 | 2019 | The Manse, 8 Dalfaber Park, Aviemore PH22 1QF CFinnie@churchofscotland.org.uk | 01479 810280 |

3 Boat of Garten, Carrbridge and Kincardine See Abernethy

4 Cromdale (H) and Advie (F W) linked with Grantown-on-Spey and Dulnain Bridge (F H W)

Vacant   The Manse, Golf Course Road, Grantown-on-Spey PH26 3HY   01479 872084
Session Clerk, Cromdale and Advie: Diane Brazier (Mrs)   dbrazier39@gmail.com   01479 872547
Session Clerk, Grantown-on-Spey and Dulnain Bridge: wmsteele33@aol.com   01479 870154
William Steele (Dr)

Grantown-on-Spey and Dulnain Bridge formed by the union of Grantown-on-Spey and Dulnain Bridge

5 Grantown-on-Spey and Dulnain Bridge See Cromdale and Advie

6 Kingussie (F H W) linked with Laggan (H) and Newtonmore (H W)

Vacant   The Manse, Fort William Road, Newtonmore PH20 1DG   01540 673238
Session Clerk, Kingussie: Sandy Peebles (Mr)   sandy@ats.me.uk   01540 661965
Session Clerk, Laggan and Newtonmore: Alison Armstrong (Mrs)   alisonmabel@hotmail.com   07841 502991

7 Laggan and Newtonmore See Kingussie

8 Rothiemurchus and Aviemore See Alvie and Insh

9 Tomintoul (H), Glenlivet and Inveraven
Guardianship of the Presbytery
Session Clerk: Margo Stuart (Mrs)   margoandedward@hotmail.co.uk   01807 580239

B. In other appointments: members of Presbytery

Thomson, Mary Ellen (Mrs)	2014	Ordained Local Minister: Presbytery Chaplain to Care Homes	Elm Cottage, Main Street, Newtonmore PH20 1DR Mary.Thomson@churchofscotland.org.uk	01479 667226

C. Retaining: members of Presbytery

Duncanson, Mary B. (Ms) BTh	2013	2023	(Ordained Local Minister, Cromdale and Advie with Grantown-on-Spey and Dulnain Bridge)	
MacEwan, James A.I. MA BD	1973	2012	(Abernethy with Cromdale and Advie)	Rapness, Station Road, Nethy Bridge PH25 3DN wurrus@hotmail.co.uk	01479 821116
Ritchie, Christine A.Y. (Mrs) BD DipMin	2002	2012	(Braes of Rannoch with Foss and Rannoch)	25 Beachen Court, Grantown-on-Spey PH26 3JD gandcritchie.70@gmail.com	01479 873419
Walker, Donald K. BD	1979	2018	(Abernethy with Boat of Garten, Carrbridge and Kincardine)	Jabulani, Seafield Avenue, Grantown-on-Spey PH26 3JQ dwalkerjabulani@gmail.com	01479 870104

D. In other appointments: not members of Presbytery
Nil

E. Retaining: not members of Presbytery

Bardgett, Frank D. MA BD PhD	1987	2001	(Department of National Mission)	Tigh an Iasgair, Street of Kincardine, Boat of Garten PH24 3BY iasgair1@icloud.com	01479 831751
Whyte, Ron C. BD CPS	1990	2013	(Alvie and Insh with Rothiemurchus and Aviemore)	13 Hillside Avenue, Kingussie PH21 1PA ron4xst@btinternet.com	01540 661101 07979 026973

F. Inactive: not members of Presbytery
Nil

G. Readers (active)

Bardgett, Alison (Mrs)	Tigh an Iasgair, Street of Kincardine, Boat of Garten PH24 3BY	iasgair10@icloud.com	01479 831751
Black, Barbara J. (Mrs)	Carn Eilrig, Nethy Bridge PH25 3EE	bjcarneilrig54@gmail.com	01479 821641

H. Ministries Development Staff

Black, Barbara J. (Mrs)	Tomintoul, Glenlivet and Inveraven – Parish Assistant	BBlack@churchofscotland.org.uk
Bowker, Thomas	Presbytery – Fresh Expressions Worker (South)	TBowker@churchofscotland.org.uk

(10.3) INVERNESS (W)

Meets at Inverness, in Inverness: Inshes East on the third Tuesday of November 2023.

Clerk: REV. TREVOR G. HUNT BA BD   7 Woodville Court, Culduthel Avenue, Inverness IV2 6BX   07753 423333
inverness@churchofscotland.org.uk

1 Alves and Burghead (F W) linked with Kinloss and Findhorn (W)
Dewald Louw BTh MDiv   2007   2021   The Manse, 4 Manse Road, Kinloss, Forres IV36 3GH   01309 690474
DLouw@churchofscotland.org.uk   07464 847803

2 Ardersier (H) linked with Petty (F)
Vacant
Fiona S. Morrison BA   2019   2023   The Manse, Ardersier, Inverness IV2 7SX   01667 462224
(Ordained Local Minister; Assistant   8 Essich Gardens, Inverness IV2 6BW   07710 331746
Minister)   FMorrison@churchofscotland.org.uk

3 Cawdor (F H) linked with Croy and Dalcross (F H)
Robert E. Brookes BD   2009   2016   Hillswick, Regoul, Geddes, Nairn IV12 5SB   01667 404686
RBrookes@churchofscotland.org.uk

4 Croy and Dalcross See Cawdor

5 Culloden: The Barn (F H W)
Vacant   **admin@barnchurch.org.uk**   **01463 798946**
Interim Moderator: David Whillis   45 Oakdene Court, Culloden IV2 7XL   01463 795430
DWhillis@churchofscotland.org.uk   01463 232304

6 Dallas linked with Forres: St Leonard's (F H W) linked with Rafford (F)   **stleonardsforres@gmail.com**
Vacant   St Leonard's Manse, Nelson Road, Forres IV36 1DR   01309 672380
John A. Morrison BSc BA PGCE   2013   35 Kirkton Place, Elgin IV30 6JR   01343 550199
(Ordained Local Minister)   JMorrison@churchofscotland.org.uk
Interim Moderator: Dewald Louw   DLouw@churchofscotland.org.uk   01309 690474
07464 847803

7 Daviot and Dunlichity (W) linked with Moy, Dalarossie and Tomatin (W)
Vacant
Interim Moderator: Robert E. Brookes
RBrookes@churchofscotland.org.uk
01667 404686

8 Dores and Boleskine
Vacant
Interim Moderator: Scott A. McRoberts
SMcRoberts@churchofscotland.org.uk
01463 230308
07535 290092

9 Dyke and Edinkillie (F W) 1994 2019
Richard G. Moffat BD
Dyke and Edinkillie Manse, Westview, Mundole, Forres IV36 2TA
RMoffat@churchofscotland.org.uk
01309 271321

10 Forres: St Laurence (F H W)
Vacant
Interim Moderator: Linda A.W. Walker
office@stlaurencechurchforres.org.uk
12 Mackenzie Drive, Forres IV36 2JP
LWalker@churchofscotland.org.uk
01309 672260
01667 456082
07842 311057

11 Forres: St Leonard's See Dallas

12 Inverness: Crown (F H W) 1991 2020
Douglas R. Robertson BSc BD
office@crown-church.co.uk
39 Southside Road, Inverness IV2 4XA
DRRobertson@churchofscotland.org.uk
01463 231140
01463 230537

13 Inverness: Dalneigh and Bona (GD H W)
Vacant
Interim Moderator: Len Cazaly
9 St Mungo Road, Inverness IV3 5AS
len_cazaly@btinternet.com
01463 232339
01463 794469

14 Inverness: Hilton (F W) 1994
Duncan MacPherson LLB DipLP BD
office@hiltonchurch.org.uk
66 Culduthel Mains Crescent, Inverness IV2 6RG
DMacPherson@churchofscotland.org.uk
01463 233310
01463 231417

15 Inverness: Inshes East (H W) 1987 2013
David S. Scott MA BD
48 Redwood Crescent, Milton of Leys, Inverness IV2 6HB
David.Scott@churchofscotland.org.uk
01463 226727
01463 772402
New charge formed by the union of Inverness: East and Inverness: Inshes

16 Inverness: Kinmylies (F H W) 2009 2018
Scott Polworth LLB BD
2 Balnafettack Place, Inverness IV3 8TQ
SPolworth@churchofscotland.org.uk
01463 714035
01463 559137

No.	Congregation / Minister		Contact
17	**Inverness: Ness Bank (F H T W)** Vacant Interim Moderator: Ian A. Manson		**nessbankchurch@gmail.com** 15 Ballifeary Road, Inverness IV3 5PJ IManson@churchofscotland.org.uk	**01463 221812** 01463 234653 01463 783824
18	**Inverness: Old High St Stephen's (T W)** Vacant Interim Moderator: Duncan MacPherson		**invernesschurch@gmail.com** 24 Damfield Road, Inverness IV2 3HU DMacPherson@churchofscotland.org.uk	**07934 285924** 01463 250802 01463 231417
19	**Inverness: St Columba's (F H T W)** Scott A. McRoberts BD MTh	2012	**info@stcolumbainverness.org** 25 Moriston Road, Inverness IV2 6HN SMcRoberts@churchofscotland.org.uk	01463 832601
20	**Inverness: Trinity (F H W)** Vacant Interim Moderator: Fraser K. Turner		**invernesstrinitychurch@yahoo.co.uk** 60 Kenneth Street, Inverness IV3 5PZ fraseratq@yahoo.co.uk	**01463 221490** 01463 234756 01463 794004
21	**Kilmorack and Erchless (F W)** Ian A. Manson BA BD	1989 2016	'Roselynn', Croyard Road, Beauly IV4 7DJ IManson@churchofscotland.org.uk	01463 783824
22	**Kiltarlity and Kirkhill (F W)** Andrew (Drew) P. Kuzma DipTheol BA	2007 2021	Wardlaw Manse, Wardlaw Road, Kirkhill IV5 7NZ AKuzma@churchofscotland.org.uk	01463 831132
23	**Kinloss and Findhorn** See Alves and Burghead			
24	**Moy, Dalarossie and Tomatin** See Daviot and Dunlichity			
25	**Nairn: Old (H W)** Alison C. Mehigan BD DPS	2003 2015	**secretary.nairnold@btconnect.com** 15 Chattan Gardens, Nairn IV12 4QP AMehigan@churchofscotland.org.uk	**01667 452382** 01667 453777
26	**Nairn: St Ninian's (H) and Auldearn and Dalmore (F W)** Thomas M. Bryson BD	1997 2015	The Manse, Auldearn, Nairn IV12 5SX TBryson@churchofscotland.org.uk	01667 451675
27	**Petty** See Ardersier			
28	**Rafford** See Dallas			

29 Urquhart and Glenmoriston (F H W)
Vacant

Blairbeg, Drumnadrochit, Inverness IV3 6UG

01456 450231

B. In other appointments

Name			Appointment	Address	Contact
Archer, Morven (Mrs)	2013	2020	Ordained Local Minister: Presbytery Assistant Minister	42 Firthview Drive, Inverness IV3 8QE MArcher@churchofscotland.org.uk	01463 237840
Finlayson, Stuart A. BA	2022		Community Pioneer Minister, Forres and West Moray	SFinlayson@churchofscotland.org.uk	07557 472745
Fraser, Jonathan MA(Div) MTh ThM PhD	2012	2019	Lecturer: Highland Theological College	9 Broom Drive, Inverness IV2 4EG Jonathan.Fraser@uhi.ac.uk	07749 539981
Morrison, Hector BSc BD MTh CertITL	1981	2009	Principal: Highland Theological College	24 Oak Avenue, Inverness IV2 4NX	01463 238561
Robertson, Michael A. BA	2014	2022	Chaplain, Raigmore Hospital, Inverness	Raigmore Hospital, Old Perth Road, Inverness IV2 3UJ Michael.Robertson@churchofscotland.org.uk	07740 984395
Whillis, David (Dr) DipHE	2020		Ordained Local Minister: Presbytery-wide minister to over 60s community	Helen's Lodge, Inshes, Inverness IV2 5BG DWhillis@churchofscotland.org.uk	01463 232304

C. Retaining

Name				Address	Contact
Andrews, J. Edward MA BD DipCG FSAScot	1985	2005	(Armadale)	Dunnichen, 1B Cameron Road, Nairn IV12 5NS edward.andrews@btinternet.com	01667 459466 07808 720708
Archer, Nicholas D.C. BA BD	1971	1992	(Dores and Boleskine)	3 Ferntower Place, Culloden, Inverness IV2 7TL na.overcome7@gmail.com	01463 793538
Attenburrow, A. Anne BSc MB ChB	2006	2018	(Auxiliary Minister, Dallas with Forres: St Leonard's with Rafford)	71 Osprey Crescent, Nairn IV12 5LG AAttenburrow@churchofscotland.org.uk	01667 457582 07860 934727
Buell, F. Bart BA MDiv	1980	1995	(Urquhart and Glenmoriston)	6 Towerhill Place, Cradlehall, Inverness IV2 5FN bartbuell@talktalk.net	01463 794634
Cleland, Robert	1997	2022	(Ardersier with Petty)	35 High Street, Ardersier, Inverness IV2 7QE	
Forbes, Farquhar A.M. MA BA	2016	2022	(Associate, Inverness: Inshes)	The Heights, Inverarnie, Inverness IV2 6XA FForbes@churchofscotland.org.uk	01808 521450
Getliffe, Dot L.J. (Mrs) BA BD DipEd DCS	2006	2021	(Deacon, Inverness Old High St Stephen's)	136 Ardness Place, Lochardil, Inverness IV2 4QY DGetliffe@churchofscotland.org.uk	01463 716051
Hunt, Trevor G. BA BD	1986	2011	(Evie with Firth with Rendall)	7 Woodville Court, Culduthel Avenue, Inverness IV2 6BX trevorghunt@gmail.com	07753 423333
MacGregor, Neil I.M. BD	1995	2019	(Strathbogie Drumblade)	1 Abban Place, Inverness IV3 8GZ NMacGregor@churchofscotland.org.uk	07989 902722
MacLean, Gillean P. (Ms) BA BD PGDipCouns CertPS	1994	2023	(Lausanne: The Scots Kirk)	GMacLean@churchofscotland.org.uk	
MacPherson, Alexander J. BD	1986	2021	(Buchanan with Drymen)	8 Little Cullernie Park, Balloch, Inverness IV2 7FQ revalexj1@gmail.com	
McRoberts, T. Douglas BD CPS FRSA	1975	2014	(Malta: St Andrew's Scots Church)	24 Redwood Avenue, Inverness IV2 6HA doug.mcroberts@btinternet.com	01463 772594

Mitchell, Joyce (Mrs) DCS	1994	2010	(Deacon, Edinburgh: Holy Trinity)	Sunnybank, Farr, Inverness IV2 6XG stanleymitchell121@btinternet.com	01808 521285
Morton, Gillian M. (Mrs) MA BD	1983	1996	(Chaplain, Borders General Hospital)	16 St Leonard's Road, Forres IV36 1DW gillianmorton@hotmail.co.uk	01309 671719
Prentice, Donald K. BSc BD DipPsych MSc MLitt	1989	2023	(Dallas with Forres: St Leonard's with Rafford)	DPrentice@churchofscotland.org.uk	
Ritchie, Bruce BSc BD PhD	1977	2013	(Dingwall: Castle Street)	16 Brinckman Terrace, Westhill, Inverness IV2 5BL brucezomba@hotmail.com	01463 791389
Robertson, Peter BSc BD	1988	1998	(Dallas with Forres: St Leonard's with Rafford)	17 Ferryhill Road, Forres IV36 2GY peterrobertsonforres@talktalk.net	01309 676769
Turner, Fraser K. LTh	1994	2007	(Kiltarlity with Kirkhill)	20 Caulfield Avenue, Inverness IV2 5GA fraseratq@yahoo.co.uk	01463 794004
Walker, Linda A.W. BA CertCS	2008	2022	(Auxiliary Minister, Presbytery of Glasgow)	39 Elmgrove, Achareidh, Nairn IV12 4SL LWalker@churchofscotland.org.uk	01667 456082 07842 311057
Watt, Hugh F. BD DPS DMin	1986	2023	(Urquhart and Glenmoriston)	7 The Cairns, Muir of Ord IV6 7AT HWatt@churchofscotland.org.uk	
Younger, Alastair S. BScEcon ASCC	1969	2008	(Inverness: St Columba High)	33 Duke's View, Slackbuie, Inverness IV2 6BB younger873@btinternet.com	01463 242873

D. In other appointments: not members of Presbytery
Nil

E. Retaining: not members of Presbytery

Stewart, Fraser M.C. BSc BD	1980	2017	(Kilmuir and Logie Easter)	44 Great Glen Place, Inverness IV3 8FA fraserstewart1955@hotmail.com	01463 832589

F. Inactive: not members of Presbytery

Chisholm, Archibald F. MA	1957	1997	(Braes of Rannoch with Foss and Rannoch)	32 Seabank Road, Nairn IV12 4EU arch32@btinternet.com	01667 452001
Minto, Joan E. (Mrs) MA BD	1993	1997	(Wemyss)	1 Lochaber Cottages, Forres IV36 2RL joanminto.123@gmail.com	07800 669074
Munro, Sheila BD DipPsych	1995	2021	(RAF Chaplain)		07468 339330
Stirling, G. Alan S. MA	1960	1999	(Leochel Cushnie and Lynturk with Tough)	97 Lochlann Road, Culloden, Inverness IV2 7HJ	01463 798313
Waugh, John L. LTh	1973	2002	(Ardclach with Auldearn and Dalmore)	58 Wyvis Drive, Nairn IV12 4TP jswaugh31@gmail.com	01667 456397

G. Readers (active)

Appleby, Jonathan	91 Cradlehall Park, Inverness IV2 5DB	jon.wyvis@gmail.com	01463 791470
Cazaly, Leonard	9 Moray Park Gardens, Culloden, Inverness IV2 7FY	len_cazaly@btinternet.com	01463 794469
Cook, Arnett D.	66 Millerton Avenue, Inverness IV3 8RY	arnett.cook@btinternet.com	01463 224795
Dennis, Barry	5 Loch Ness View, Dores, Inverness IV2 6TW	barrydennis@live.co.uk	01463 751393
King, Fiona	23 Torr Gardens, Dores, Inverness IV2 6TS	kingdores@btinternet.com	01463 751293
MacInnes, Ailsa (Mrs)	Kilmartin, 17 Southside Road, Inverness IV2 3BG	ailsa.macinnes@btopenworld.com	01463 230321 / 07704 485055
Robertson, Hendry	Park House, 51 Glenurquhart Road, Inverness IV3 5PB	hendryrobertson046@btinternet.com	01463 231858 / 07929 766102
Roberston, Stewart J.H.	6 Raasay Road, Inverness IV2 3LR	sjhro@tiscali.co.uk	01463 417937
Roden, Vivian (Mrs)	15 Old Mill Road, Tomatin, Inverness IV13 7YW	vroden@btinternet.com	01808 511355 / 07887 704915

H. Ministries Development Staff
Nil

INVERNESS ADDRESSES

Inverness

Church	Address
Crown	Kingsmills Road x Midmills Road
Dalneigh and Bona	St Mary's Avenue
Hilton	Druid Road x Tomatin Road
Inshes East	Inshes Retail Park
Kinmylies	Kinmylies Way
Ness Bank	Ness Bank x Castle Road
Old High	Old Edinburgh Road x Southside Road
St Stephen's	
St Columba	Drummond School, Drummond Road
Trinity	Huntly Place x Upper Kessock Street

Nairn

Church	Address
Old	Academy Street x Seabank Road
St Ninian's	High Street x Queen Street

(10.4) LOCHABER (F W)

Meets at Fort William MacIntosh Hall on the last Tuesday of October and the first Tuesday of December.

Clerk:	REV STEWART GOUDIE BSc BD	Church of Scotland Manse, Annie's Brae, Mallaig PH41 4RG lochaber@churchofscotland.org.uk	01687 462514 07957 237757
Treasurer:	MRS CONNIE ANDERSON	faoconnie@gmail.com	

1 **Acharacle (H) and Ardnamurchan (F W) linked with Ardgour, Morvern and Strontian (F H T W)**

Donald G.B. McCorkindale BD DipMin	1992	2011	The Manse, 2 The Meadows, Strontian, Acharacle PH36 4HZ DMcCorkindale@churchofscotland.org.uk	01967 402234 07554 176580

New charge formed by the union of Acharacle and Ardnamurchan, and of Ardgour and Kingairloch, Morvern, and Strontian

2 **Ardgour, Morvern and Strontian** See Acharacle and Ardnamurchan

3 Fort Augustus (W) linked with Glengarry (W)

Anthony M. Jones   1994   2018   The Manse, Fort Augustus PH32 4BH   01320 366210
BD DPS DipTheol CertMin FRSA   AJones@churchofscotland.org.uk

4 Fort William Kilmallie (F H W) linked with Kilmonivaig (F W)

Vacant   The Manse, The Parade, Fort William PH33 6BA   01397 702297
Rory N. MacLeod BA BD   1986   2021   Kilmallie Manse, Corpach, Fort William PH33 7JS   01397 772736
(Team Minister)   RNMacLeod@churchofscotland.org.uk
Session Clerk, FWK: Mabel Wallace (Mrs)   thewallace@talk21.com   01397 703635
Session Clerk, Kilmonivaig: Gordon Smith   gordonsmith934@btinternet.com   01397 712375

5 Glengarry See Fort Augustus

6 Kilmonivaig See Fort William Kilmallie

7 Kinlochleven (H W) linked with South Lochaber (H W)

Malcolm A. Kinnear MA BD PhD   2010   The Manse, Lochaber Road, Kinlochleven PH50 4QW   01855 831227
MKinnear@churchofscotland.org.uk
Marion Kinnear (Mrs) BD   2009   2021   The Manse, Lochaber Road, Kinlochleven PH50 4QW   01855 831227 / 07519 635976
(Auxiliary Minister)   Marion.Kinnear@churchofscotland.org.uk

South Lochaber was formed by the union of Duror, Glencoe: St Munda's, and Nether Lochaber

8 North West Lochaber (F H W)

Stewart Goudie BSc BD   2010   2018   Church of Scotland Manse, Annie's Brae, Mallaig PH41 4RG   01687 462514 / 07957 237757
SGoudie@churchofscotland.org.uk

9 South Lochaber See Kinlochleven

B. In other appointments: members of Presbytery
Nil

C. Retaining; members of Presbytery

Anderson, David M. MSc FCOptom   1984 2017   (Ordained Local Minister, Cawdor with Croy and Dalcross)   'Mirlos', 1 Dumfries Place, Fort William PH33 6UQ   01397 702091
David.Anderson@churchofscotland.org.uk
Muirhead, Morag Y. (Mrs)   2013 2022   (Ordained Local Minister, Fort William Kilmallie with Kilmonivaig)   6 Dumbarton Road, Fort William PH33 6UU   01397 703643
MMuirhead@churchofscotland.org.uk
Stoddart, Alexander C. BD   2001 2022   (Duror with Glencoe: St Munda's)   33 Sandilands Grove, Newburgh Road, Abernethy   PH2 9LH   07593 598741
sandystoddart1@outlook.com

Varwell, Adrian P.J. BA BD PhD	1983 2011	(Fort Augustus with Glengarry)	19 Enrick Crescent, Kilmore, Drumnadrochit, Inverness IV63 6TP adrian.varwell@btinternet.com	01456 459352
Winning, A. Ann MA DipEd BD	1984 2006	(Morvern)	'Westering', 13C Carnoch, Glencoe, Ballachulish PH49 4HQ awinning009@btinternet.com	01855 811929

D. In other appointments: not members of Presbytery
Nil

E. Retaining: not members of Presbytery
Nil

F. Inactive: not members of Presbytery

Millar, John L. MA BD	1981 1990	(Fort William: Duncansburgh with Kilmonivaig)	Flat 0/1, 12 Chesterfield Gardens, Glasgow G12 0BF johnmillar123@btinternet.com	0141 339 4090
Ramsay, Alan MA	1967 2007	(Fort William: MacIntosh Memorial)	12 Riverside Grove, Lochyside, Fort William PH33 7RD	01397 702054

G. Readers (active)

Gill, Ella (Mrs)	5 Camus Inas, Acharacle PH36 4JQ	ellagill768@gmail.com	01967 431834
Skene, William	Tiree, Gairlochy, Spean Bridge PH34 4EQ	bill.skene@lochaber.presbytery.org.uk	01397 712594

H. Ministries Development Staff
MacLeod, Rory N. (Rev) BA BD — Fort William Kilmallie linked with Kilmonivaig – Team Minister — RNMacLeod@churchofscotland.org.uk

(10.5) ROSS (W)

Meets in Dingwall: Castle Street Church on the first Tuesday of October, November and December.

Clerk:	MRS CATH CHAMBERS	184 Kirkside, Alness IV17 0RH ross@churchofscotland.org.uk	01349 882026

1 Alness
Vacant — 27 Darroch Brae, Alness IV17 0SD — 01349 882238

Michael J. Macdonald (Auxiliary Minister)	2004	2014	73 Firhill, Alness IV17 0RT Michael.Macdonald@churchofscotland.org.uk	01349 884268
2 Avoch (W) linked with Fortrose and Rosemarkie (W) Warren R. Beattie BSc BD MSc PhD	1990	2019	5 Ness Way, Fortrose IV10 8SS WBeattie@churchofscotland.org.uk	01381 620111
3 Contin (H W) linked with Foddery and Strathpeffer (H W) Ronald Gall BSc BD	1985	2021	The Manse, Contin, Strathpeffer IV14 9ES RGall@churchofscotland.org.uk	01997 421028
4 Cromarty (W) linked with Resolis and Urquhart (W) Terrance T. Burns BA MA	2004	2017	The Manse, Culbokie, Dingwall IV7 8JN TBurns@churchofscotland.org.uk	01349 877452
Carol Rattenbury BA (Ordained Local Minister)	2017	2022	Balloan Farm House, Alcaig, Conon Bridge, Dingwall IV7 8HU CRattenbury@churchofscotland.org.uk	01349 877323
5 Dingwall: Castle Street (F H W) Drausio P. Goncalves	1993	2019	16 Achany Road, Dingwall IV15 9JB DGoncalves@churchofscotland.org.uk	01349 866792
6 Dingwall: St Clement's (H W) Bruce Dempsey BD	1997	2014	8 Castlehill Road, Dingwall IV15 9PB BDempsey@churchofscotland.org.uk	01349 292055
7 Fearn Abbey and Nigg (W) linked with Tarbat (W) Vacant Session Clerk, Fearn Abbey and Nigg: James Maxwell Session Clerk, Tarbat: Douglas Gordon			jimmymaxwell62@gmail.com d.gordon123@btinternet.com	01862 871883
8 Ferintosh (F W) Stephen Macdonald BD MTh	2008	2018	Ferintosh Manse, Leanaig Road, Conon Bridge, Dingwall IV7 8BE SMacdonald@churchofscotland.org.uk	01349 861275 07570 804193
9 Foddery and Strathpeffer See Contin **10 Fortrose and Rosemarkie** See Avoch				

11	**Invergordon (W)**			**invergordonparishchurch@live.co.uk**	
	Brian Macleod BA MDiv	2021	2022	The Manse, Cromlet Drive, Invergordon IV18 0BA	01463 731930
				BMacleod@churchofscotland.org.uk	
12	**Killearnan (F H W) linked with Knockbain (F H W)**				
	Susan Cord		2016	14 First Field Avenue, North Kessock, Inverness IV1 3JB	
				SCord@churchofscotland.org.uk	
13	**Kilmuir and Logie Easter (F)**				
	Alistair J. Drummond BSc BD ThM	1986	2020	The Manse, Delny, Invergordon IV18 0NW	01862 842280
				ADrummond@churchofscotland.org.uk	
14	**Kiltearn (H)**				
	Donald A. MacSween BD	1991	1998	The Manse, Swordale Road, Evanton, Dingwall IV16 9UZ	01349 830472
				DMacSween@churchofscotland.org.uk	
15	**Knockbain** See Killearnan				
16	**Lochbroom and Ullapool (F GD W)**			**info@ullapoolkirk.co.uk**	**01854 612360**
	Heidi J. Hercus BA		2018	The Manse, 11 Royal Park, Mill Street, Ullapool IV26 2XT	01854 613146
				HHercus@churchofscotland.org.uk	
17	**Resolis and Urquhart** See Cromarty				
18	**Rosskeen (F W)**				
	Philip Gunn BSc BA		2020	Rosskeen Manse, 15 Perrins Road, Alness IV17 0SX	01349 884252
				PGunn@churchofscotland.org.uk	
19	**Tain (F W)**				
	Andrew P. Fothergill BA	2012	2017	14 Kingsway Avenue, Tain IV19 1NJ	01862 892296
				AFothergill@churchofscotland.org.uk	
20	**Tarbat** See Fearn Abbey and Nigg				
21	**Urray and Kilchrist (F W)**			**urraychurch@gmail.com**	
	Monika R.W. Redman BA BD	2003	2021	Woodville, Ord Road, Muir of Ord IV6 7XL	01463 871625
				MRedman@churchofscotland.org.uk	

B. In other appointments: members of Presbytery

Name			Appointment	Address / Email	Tel
Bissett, James	2016	2021	Ordained Local Minister, on loan to Inverness: Old High Stephen's	JBissett@churchofscotland.org.uk	
McGowan, Andrew T. B. (Prof) BD STM PhD	1979	2019	Director, Rutherford Centre for Reformed Theology	18 Davis Drive, Alness IV17 0ZD, AMcGowan@churchofscotland.org.uk	01340 880762
Munro, Irene BA		2019	Ordained Local Minister: Presbytery Chaplain to vulnerable groups in residential care	1 Wyvis Crescent, Conan Bridge, Dingwall IV7 8BZ, IMunro@churchofscotland.org.uk	01349 865752

C. Retaining; members of Presbytery

Bell, Graeme K. BA BD CertMS	1983	2017	(Glasgow: Carnwadric)	4 Munro Terrace, Rosemarkie, Fortrose IV10 8UR, graemekbell@googlemail.com	07591 180101
Horne, Douglas A. BD	1977	2009	(Tain)	151 Holm Farm Road, Culduthel, Inverness IV2 6BF, douglas.horne@talktalk.net	01463 712677
Lincoln, John BA BD MPhil	1986	2014	(Balquhidder with Killin and Ardeonaig)	59 Obsdale Park, Alness IV17 0TR, johnlincoln@minister.com	01349 882791
MacLeod, Kenneth Donald BD CPS	1989	2019	(Invergordon)	10 Scott Crescent, Greenfaulds, Cumbernauld, Glasgow G67 4LG, kd-macleod@tiscali.co.uk	07808 416767
McLeod, John MA	1958	1993	(Resolis and Urquhart)	'Benview', 19 Balvaird, Muir of Ord IV6 7RQ, sheilaandjohn@yahoo.co.uk	01463 871286
Munro, James A. BD DMS	1979	2013	(Port Glasgow: Hamilton Bardrainney)	1 Wyvis Crescent, Conon Bridge, Dingwall IV7 8BZ, james781munro@btinternet.com	01349 865752
Scott, David V. BTh	1994	2014	(Fearn Abbey and Nigg with Tarbat)	29 Sunnyside, Culloden Moor, Inverness IV2 5ES, russanntwo@btinternet.com	01463 795802
Smith, Russel BD	1994	2013	(Dingwall: St Clement's)	1 School Road, Conon Bridge, Dingwall IV7 8AE	01349 861011
Warwick, Ivan C. TD BD DipPS DipEcum	1980	2014	(Paisley: St James')	Ardcruidh Croft, Heights of Dochcarty, Dingwall IV15 9UF, L70rev@btinternet.com	01349 861464, 07787 535083

D. In other appointments: not members of Presbytery
Nil

E. Retaining: not members of Presbytery

Bell, Sandra L.N. (Mrs) DCS	2001	2013	(Deacon: Chaplain, Glasgow Royal Infirmary)	4 Munro Terrace, Rosemarkie, Fortrose IV10 8UR	
McKean, Alan T. BD CertMin	1982	2018	(Avoch with Fortrose and Rosemarkie)	15 Park Road, Kirn, Dunoon PA23 8JL	01369 700016
McLean, Gordon LTh CertMS	1972	1992	(Edinburgh: Currie)	Beinn Dhorain, Kinnettas Square, Strathpeffer IV14 9BD, gmaclean@hotmail.co.uk	01997 421380

McWilliam, Thomas M. MA BD	1964 2003	(Contin)	Flat 3, 13 Culduthel Road, Inverness IV2 4AG	01463 718981
			tommcw@tommcwl.plus.com	
Porter, Carol Anne B. (Mrs) BEd BD	2009 2017	(Alloa: Ludgate)	The Cottages, Dornoch Firth Caravan Park, Meikle Ferry South, Tain IV19 1JX	01862 892292
			ca.porter@icloud.com	
Tallach, John M. MA MLitt DipPhil	1970 2010	(Cromarty)	29 Firthview Drive, Inverness IV3 8NS	01463 418721
			johntallach@talktalk.net	

F. Inactive: not members of Presbytery
Nil

G. Readers (active)

Finlayson, Michael R.	Amberlea, Glenskiach, Evanton, Dingwall IV16 9UU	finlayson935@btinternet.com	01349 830598
Greer, Kathleen (Mrs) MEd	17 Duthac Wynd, Tain IV19 1LP	greer2@talktalk.net	01862 892065
Jackson, Simon	Broomton Farm, Balintore IV20 1XN	simonjackson@procam.co.uk	01862 832831
Jamieson, Patricia A. (Mrs)	9 Craig Avenue, Tain IV19 1JP	happjam179@yahoo.co.uk	01862 893154
McAlpine, James	5 Cromlet Park, Invergordon IV18 0RN	jmca2@tiscali.co.uk	01349 852801

H. Ministries Development Staff
Nil

(10.6) SUTHERLAND (F)

Meets at Lairg on the first Tuesday of November and December.

Clerk: REV. IAN W. McCREE BD   **Tigh Ardachu, Mosshill, Brora KW9 6NG   01408 621185**
sutherland@churchofscotland.org.uk

1   Altnaharra and Farr (F W) linked with Melness and Tongue (F H)
Vacant
Interim Moderator: Mary J. Stobo   The Manse, Bettyhill, Thurso KW14 7SS   01641 521208
MStobo@churchofscotland.org.uk   01863 766868

2   Assynt and Stoer (F W)
Iain A. MacLeod BA   2012   2020   info@assyntcofs.org   01571 844342
The Manse, Canisp Road, Lochinver, Lairg IV27 4LH   07795 014889
IMacleod@churchofscotland.org.uk

3 Clyne (H W) linked with Kildonan and Loth Helmsdale (F H W)   info@brorachurchofscotland.org
Lorna H. Tunstall MA MDiv   2020
40 Golf Road, Brora KW9 6QS
LTunstall@churchofscotland.org.uk
01408 536005

4 Creich (W) linked with Kincardine Croick and Edderton (W) linked with Rosehall (W)   info@kyleofsutherlandchurches.org
Vacant
Interim Moderator: John B. Sterrett
The Manse, Ardgay IV24 3BG
JSterrett@churchofscotland.org.uk
01863 766285
Tel/Fax 01408 633295

5 Dornoch Cathedral (F H W)
Vacant
Interim Moderator: Iain A. MacLeod
1 Allan Gardens, Dornoch IV25 3PD
IMacLeod@churchofscotland.org.uk
01862 810296
01571 844342

6 Durness and Kinlochbervie (F W)
Andrea M. Boyes (Mrs) RMN BA(Theol)   2013   2017
Manse Road, Kinlochbervie, Lairg IV27 4RG
ABoyes@churchofscotland.org.uk
01971 521287

7 Eddrachillis
Vacant
Interim Moderator: John B. Sterrett
Church of Scotland Manse, Scourie, Lairg IV27 4TQ
JSterrett@churchofscotland.org.uk
01971 502431
01408 633295

8 Golspie (W)
John B. Sterrett BA BD PhD   2007
pray@standrewgolspie.org
The Manse, Fountain Road, Golspie KW10 6TH
JSterrett@churchofscotland.org.uk
Tel/Fax 01408 633295

9 Kildonan and Loth Helmsdale See Clyne
10 Kincardine Croick and Edderton See Creich

11 Lairg (F H W) linked with Rogart (H W)
Vacant
Hilary M. Gardner (Miss)   2010   2018
(Auxiliary Minister)
Interim Moderator: Sydney L. Barnett
Cayman Lodge, Kincardine Hill, Ardgay IV24 3DJ
HGardner@churchofscotland.org.uk
sydneylb43@gmail.com
01863 766107
01408 621569

12 Melness and Tongue See Altnaharra and Farr
13 Rogart See Lairg
14 Rosehall See Creich

B. In other appointments: members of Presbytery

| Stobo, Mary J. (Mrs) BA | 2013 | Ordained Local Minister; Community Healthcare Chaplain | Druim-an-Sgairnich, Ardgay IV24 3BG
MStobo@churchofscotland.org.uk | 01863 766868 |

C. Retaining: members of Presbytery

Chambers, S. John OBE BSc	1972 2009	(Inverness: Ness Bank)	Bannlagan Lodge, 4 Earls Cross Gardens, Dornoch IV25 3NR chambersdornoch@btinternet.com	01862 811520
Cushman, Beverly W. BA MDiv MA PhD	1977 2023	(Altnaharra and Farr with Melness and Tongue)	Royston, Stemster, Halkirk KW12 6UX BCushman@churchofscotland.org.uk	01955 661265
MacPherson, John BSc BD	1993 2021	(Eddrachillis)	23 Drumfield Road, Inverness IV2 4XH	01463 230038
McCree, Ian W. BD	1971 2011	(Clyne with Kildonan and Loth Helmsdale)	Tigh Ardachu, Mosshill, Brora KW9 6NG ianmccree@live.co.uk	01408 621185
McKay, Margaret M. (Mrs) MA BD MTh	1991 2003	(Auchaber United with Auchterless)	2 Mackenzie Gardens, Dornoch IV25 3RU megsie38@gmail.com	01862 811859

D. In other appointments: not members of Presbytery
Nil

E. Retaining; not members of Presbytery

| Muckart, Graeme W.M. MTh MSc FSAScot | 1983 2009 | (Kincardine, Croick and Edderton) | Torr Gorm, Davochfin, Dornoch IV25 3RW
gw2m.kildale@gmail.com | 01862 810428
07737 424565 |
| Thomson, Alexander BSc BD MPhil PhD | 1973 2012 | (Rutherglen: Old) | 4 Munro Street, Dornoch IV25 3RA
alexander.thomson6@btinternet.com | 01862 811650 |

F. Inactive: not members of Presbytery
Nil

G. Readers (active)

| Baxter, A. Rosie (Dr) | Daylesford, Invershin, Lairg IV27 4ET | drrosiereid@yahoo.co.uk | 01549 421326
07748 761694 |
| Roberts, Irene (Miss) | Flat 4, Harbour Buildings, Main Street, Portmahomack, Tain IV20 1YG | ireneroberts43@hotmail.com | 01862 871166
07854 436854 |

H. Ministries Development Staff
Nil

(10.7) CAITHNESS (W)

Meets alternately at Wick and Thurso on the first Tuesday of November and December.

Clerk: REV. HEATHER STEWART — Burnthill, Thrumster, Wick KW1 5TR
caithness@churchofscotland.org.uk
01955 651717

1 Halkirk Westerdale linked with Watten
Vacant
Interim Moderator: Sheila Cormack (Mrs)
Wester Cottage, Dunnet, by Thurso KW14 8XP
01847 851274

2 Latheron (W)
Vacant
Heather Stewart (Mrs)   2013   2017
(Ordained Local Minister)
parish-of-latheron@btconnect.com
Central Manse, Main Street, Lybster KW3 6BN   01593 721706
Burnthill, Thrumster, Wick KW1 5TR   01955 651717
Heather.Stewart@churchofscotland.org.uk

3 North Coast (F W)
Vacant
Session Clerk: Graham Cameron
cameroncroik@gmail.com
01641 571246

4 Pentland
Janet A. Easton-Berry BA BA   2016   2021
The Manse, Canisbay, Wick KW1 4YH
JEaston-Berry@churchofscotland.org.uk
01955 611551

5 Thurso: St Peter's and St Andrew's (F H W)
David S.M. Malcolm BD   2011   2014
11 Castle Gardens, Barrock Street, Thurso KW14 7GZ
David.Malcolm@churchofscotland.org.uk
01847 895186

6 Thurso: West (H W)
Vacant
Interim Moderator: Lyall Rennie
LRennie@churchofscotland.org.uk
01955 611756

7 Watten See Halkirk Westerdale

8 Wick: Pulteneytown (H) and Thrumster (F W)
Andrew A. Barrie BD   2013   2017
The Manse, Coronation Street, Wick KW1 5LS
Andrew.Barrie@churchofscotland.org.uk
01955 606192
07791 663439

9   Wick: St Fergus (F W)
Vacant
Interim Moderator: Heather Stewart

contact@wickstferguschurch.org.uk
Mansefield, Miller Avenue, Wick KW1 4DF   01955 602167
caithness@churchofscotland.org.uk   01955 651717

B. In other appointments: members of Presbytery
Nil

C. Retaining: members of Presbytery

Duncan, Esme (Miss)	2013	2017	(Ordained Local Minister, Caithness)	Avalon, Upper Warse, Canisbay, Wick KW1 4YD	01955 611455
				EDuncan@churchofscotland.org.uk	
Macartney, David J.B. BA	2017	2023	(North Coast)	DMacartney@churchofscotland.org.uk	
Nugent, John BD	1999	2020	(Wick: St Fergus)	39 Argyle Square, Wick KW1 5AJ	07493 857689
Rennie, Lyall	2014	2019	(Ordained Local Minister, Pentland)	Ruachmarra, Lower Warse, Canisbay, Wick KW1 4YB	01955 611756
				LRennie@churchofscotland.org.uk	

D. In other appointments: not members of Presbytery
Nil

E. Retaining: not members of Presbytery
Nil

F. Inactive: not members of Presbytery
Nil

G. Readers (active)

MacDonald, Morag (Dr)	Orkney View, Portskerra, Melvich KW14 7YL	liliasmacdonald@btinternet.com	01641 531281
O'Neill, Leslie	Holytree Cottage, Parkside, Lybster KW3 6AS	leslie_oneill@hotmail.co.uk	01593 721738
O'Neill, Maureen (Mrs)	Holytree Cottage, Parkside, Lybster KW3 6AS	oneill.maureen@yahoo.com	01593 721738

H. Ministries Development Staff

Petersen, Robert	Wick: Pulteneytown and Thrumster – Mission Development Worker	RPetersen@churchofscotland.org.uk
Rennie, Lyall (Rev)	Pentland – Parish Assistant	LRennie@churchofscotland.org.uk

CAITHNESS Communion Sundays

Halkirk Westerdale	Apr, Jul, Oct	
Latheron	Apr, Jul, Sep, Nov	
North Coast	Mar, Easter, Jun, Sep, Dec	
Pentland: Canisbay	1st Jun, Nov	
Dunnet	last May, Nov	
Keiss	1st May, 3rd Nov	
Olrig	last May, Nov	
Thurso: St Peter's and St Andrew's	Mar, Jun, Sep, Dec	
West	4th Mar, Jun, Nov	
Watten	1st Jul, Dec	
Wick: Pulteneytown and Thrunster	1st Mar, Jun, Sep, Dec	
St Fergus	Apr, Oct	

(10.8) LOCHCARRON – SKYE (F W)

Meets in conference annually and in Kyle as required and, where possible, online.

Clerk: REV. RODERICK A.R. MacLEOD MA MBA BD DMin
The Manse, 6 Upper Breakish, Isle of Skye IV42 8PY
lochcarronskye@churchofscotland.org.uk
01471 822416

1 Applecross, Lochcarron and Torridon (F GD)
Guardianship of the Presbytery
Interim Moderator: Stuart J. Smith
The Manse, Colonel's Road, Lochcarron, Strathcarron IV54 8YG
Stuart.Smith@churchofscotland.org.uk
01520 722783
01445 712645

2 Bracadale and Duirinish (GD)
Guardianship of the Presbytery
Interim Moderator: Roderick A.R. MacLeod
RMacLeod@churchofscotland.org.uk
01471 822416

3 Gairloch and Dundonnell (F W)
Stuart J. Smith BEng BD MTh   1994   2016
Church of Scotland Manse, The Glebe, Gairloch IV21 2BT
Stuart.Smith@churchofscotland.org.uk
01445 712645

4 Glenelg, Kintail and Lochalsh (F W)
Frederick W. Vincent BA BD MPhil   1990   2021
The Manse, Glebe Road, Inverinate, Kyle of Lochalsh IV40 8HE
FVincent@churchofscotland.org.uk
07971 507952

5 Kilmuir and Stenscholl (F GD)
Vacant
Interim Moderator: John H. Lamont
1 Totescore, Kilmuir, Isle of Skye IV51 9YN
jhlamont@btinternet.com
01470 542297
01445 731888
07714 720753

6   Portree (GD W)
Sandor Fazakas BD MTh   1977   2007   Viewfield Road, Portree, Isle of Skye IV51 9ES   01478 611868
SFazakas@churchofscotland.org.uk

7   Snizort (GD H)
Vacant
Interim Moderator: Donald E.MacRae   The Manse, Kensaleyre, Snizort, Portree, Isle of Skye IV51 9XE   01470 532453
dmgair@aol.com   01445 712235

8   Strath and Sleat (F GD W)
Roderick A.R. MacLeod   1994   2015   The Manse, 6 Upper Breakish, Isle of Skye IV42 8PY   01471 822416
   MA MBA BD DMin
RMacLeod@churchofscotland.org.uk

B. In other appointments: members of Presbytery
Nil

C. Retaining: members of Presbytery
MacLeod-Mair, Alisdair T.   2001   2022   (Snizort)   Flat 2/2, 44 Leven Street, Glasgow G41 2JE
   MEd DipTheol   revalisdair@hotmail.com
Martin, George M. MA BD   1987   2005   (Applecross, Lochcarron and Torridon)   2 Cliffton Place, Poolewe, Achnasheen IV22 2JU   0131 343 3937
Morrison, Derek   1995   2013   (Gairloch and Dundonnell)   8(1) Buckingham Terrace, Edinburgh EH4 3AA   01445 781333
   dereknmorrison1@aol.com
Stutter, Anita Drs (MA)   2008   2020   (Applecross, Lochcarron and Torridon)   Aros, Slumbay, Lochcarron IV54 8YQ   01520 722139
   AStutter@churchofscotland.org.uk

D. In other appointments: not members of Presbytery
Drummond, Norman W. (Prof.)   1976   1997   President, Columba 1400   c/o Columba 1400 Ltd., Staffin, Isle of Skye IV51 9JY   01478 611400
   CBE MA BD DUniv FRSE

E. Retaining: not members of Presbytery
Nil

F. Inactive: not members of Presbytery
Nil

G. Readers (active)
Lamont, John H. BD   6 Tigh na Fiiine, Aultbea, Achnasheen IV22 2JE   jhlamont@btinternet.com   07714 720753
MacRae, Donald E.   Nethania, 52 Strath, Gairloch IV21 2DB   dmgair@aol.com   01445 712235

H. Ministries Development Staff
Sikorski, Anne   Presbytery – Mission and Ministry Development Worker   ASikorski@churchofscotland.org.uk

(10.9) UIST

Meets on the first Tuesday of November in Lochmaddy.

Clerk: REV. GAVIN J. ELLIOTT MA BD   5a Aird, Isle of Benbecula HS7 5LT   01870 602726
uist@churchofscotland.org.uk

1 **Benbecula (F GD H) linked with Carinish (F GD H W)**   info@carinish-church.org.uk
Vacant
Ishabel Macdonald   2011   'Cleat Afe Ora', 18 Carinish, Isle of North Uist HS6 5HN   01876 580367
(Ordained Local Minister)   Ishie.Macdonald@churchofscotland.org.uk

2 **Berneray and Lochmaddy (GD H) linked with Kilmuir and Paible (GD)**
Alen J.R. McCulloch MA BD   1990   2017   Church of Scotland Manse, Paible, Isle of North Uist HS6 5HD   01876 510310
AMcCulloch@churchofscotland.org.uk

3 **Carinish** See Benbecula
4 **Kilmuir and Paible** See Berneray and Lochmaddy

5 **Manish-Scarista (GD H)**   Church of Scotland Manse, Scarista, Isle of Harris HS3 3HX   01859 550200
Vacant   01859 520494
Session Clerk: Paul Alldred   paul.alldred@outlook.com

6 Tarbert (F GD H T W)
Ian Murdo M. MacDonald DPA BD   2001   2015   The Manse, Manse Road, Tarbert, Isle of Harris HS3 3DF   01859 502231
Ian.MacDonald@churchofscotland.org.uk

B. In other appointments: members of Presbytery
Nil

C. Retaining: members of Presbytery

Elliott, Gavin J. MA BD	1976	2015	(Ministries Council)	5a Aird, Isle of Benbecula HS7 5LT	01870 602726
				gavkondwani@gmail.com	
MacIver, Norman BD	1976	2011	(Tarbert)	57 Boswell Road, Wester Inshes, Inverness IV2 3EW	01463 236586
				norman@n-cmaciver.freeserve.co.uk	
Morrison, Donald John	2001	2019	(Auxiliary Minister, Tarbert)	22 Kyles, Tarbert, Isle of Harris HS3 3BS	01859 502341
				DMorrison@churchofscotland.org.uk	
Petrie, Jackie G.	1989	2011	(South Uist)	7B Malaclete, Isle of North Uist HS6 5BX	01876 560804
				jackiegpetrie@yahoo.com	
Smith, Murdo MA BD	1988	2011	(Manish-Scarista)	Aisgeir, 15A Upper Shader, Isle of Lewis HS3 3MX	

D. In other appointments: not members of Presbytery
Nil

E. Retaining: not members of Presbytery
Nil

F. Inactive: not members of Presbytery
Nil

G. Readers (active)

MacNab, Ann (Mrs)	Druim Skilivat, Scolpaig, Lochmaddy, Isle of North Uist HS6 5DH	annabhan@hotmail.com	01876 510701

H. Ministries Development Staff
Nil

UIST Communion Sundays

Benbecula	2nd Mar, Sep	
Berneray and Lochmaddy	4th Jun, last Oct	Manish-Scarista	3rd Apr, 1st Oct
Carinish	4th Mar, Aug	Tarbert	2nd Mar, 3rd Sep
Kilmuir and Paible	1st Jun, 3rd Nov	

(11) LEWIS

Meets at Stornoway, in St Columba's Church Hall, on the second Tuesday of March, June, September and November and at other times as required.

Clerk: REV. BEN JOHNSTONE MA BD DMin   Loch Alain, 5 Breaclete, Bernera, Isle of Lewis HS2 9LT   **01851 612445**
lewis@churchofscotland.org.uk   **07444 125719**

1 Barvas (F GD H W)
Dougie Wolf BA(Theol)   2017   Church of Scotland Manse, Lower Barvas, Isle of Lewis HS2 0QY   01851 840218
DWolf@churchofscotland.org.uk

2 Carloway (F GD H)
Duncan M. Macaskill   1992   2019   Church of Scotland Manse, Knock, Carloway, Isle of Lewis HS2 9AU   **01851 643211**
BA BD MPhil DMin   DMacaskill@churchofscotland.org.uk   01851 643761

3 Cross Ness (F GD H T W)
John M. Nicolson BD DipMin   1997   2019   **crossnesschurch@gmail.com**
Church of Scotland Manse, Cross Skigersta Road, Ness,   07899 235355
Isle of Lewis HS2 0TB
JNicolson@churchofscotland.org.uk

4 Kinloch (F GD H)
Iain M. Campbell BD   2004   2008   Laxay, Lochs, Isle of Lewis HS2 9LA   01851 830218
Iain.Campbell@churchofscotland.org.uk

5 Knock (GD H)
Guardianship of the Presbytery
Interim Moderator: Iain M. Campbell   Iain.Campbell@churchofscotland.org.uk   01851 830218

6 Lochs-Crossbost (GD H)
Guardianship of the Presbytery
Interim Moderator: Donald Macleod   donaldmacleod25@btinternet.com   01851 704516

7 Lochs-in-Bernera (F GD H) linked with Uig (F GD H)
Hugh Maurice Stewart DPA BD   2008   Church of Scotland Manse, Uigen, Miavaig, Isle of Lewis HS2 9HX   01851 672388
HStewart@churchofscotland.org.uk

8 Stornoway: High (F GD H W)
Gordon M. Macleod BA   2017   2019

Woodside, Laxdale Lane, Stornoway, Isle of Lewis HS1 0DR   07717 065739
GMacleod@churchofscotland.org.uk

9 Stornoway: Martin's Memorial (F H W)
Thomas MacNeil MA BD   2002   2006

enquiries@martinsmemorial.org.uk   **01851 700820**
Martin's Memorial Manse, Matheson Road, Stornoway,   01851 704238
Isle of Lewis HS1 2LR
TMacNeil@churchofscotland.org.uk

10 Stornoway: St Columba (F GD H)
William J. Heenan BA MTh   2012

St Columba's Manse, Lewis Street, Stornoway, Isle of Lewis HS1 2JF   **01851 701546**
WHeenan@churchofscotland.org.uk   01851 705933
                                                                      07837 770589

11 Uig See Lochs-in-Bernera

B. In other appointments: members of Presbytery

Shadakshari, T.K. BTh BD MTh	1998	2006	Head of Spiritual Care, Western Isles Health Board	23D Benside, Newmarket, Stornoway, Isle of Lewis HS2 0DZ Home 01851 701727 Office 01851 704704 07403 697138
				tk.shadakshari@nhs.scot

C. Retaining: members of Presbytery

Amed, Paul LTh DPS	1992	2015	(Barvas)	6 Scotland Street, Stornoway, Isle of Lewis HS1 2JQ 01851 706450
				paul.amed@outlook.com
Jamieson, Esther M.M. (Mrs) BD	1984	2002	(Glasgow: Penilee St Andrew)	1 Redburn, Bayview, Stornoway, Isle of Lewis HS1 2UU 01851 704789
				iandejamieson@btinternet.com
Johnstone, Ben MA BD DMin	1973	2013	(Strath and Sleat)	Loch Alain, 5 Breaclete, Bernera, Isle of Lewis HS2 9LT 01851 612445 07444 125719
				benonbernera@gmail.com
Maclean, Donald A. DCS	1988	1990	(Deacon, Tarbert)	8 Upper Barvas, Isle of Lewis HS2 0QX 01851 840454
Macleod, William	1957	2006	(Uig)	54 Lower Barvas, Isle of Lewis HS2 0QY 01851 840217

D. In other appointments: not members of Presbytery
Nil

E. Retaining: not members of Presbytery
Nil

F. Inactive: not members of Presbytery
Nil

G. Readers (active)

Macleod, Donald	14 Balmerino Drive, Stornoway, Isle of Lewis	HS1 2TD	donaldmacleod25@btinternet.com	01851 704516
Macmillan, Iain	34 Scotland Street, Stornoway, Isle of Lewis	HS1 2JR	iainmacmillan.alba34@gmail.com	01851 704826
				07943 420817

H. Ministries Development Staff
Nil

LEWIS Communion Sundays

Barvas	3rd Mar, Sep	Knock	3rd Apr, 1st Nov
Carloway	1st Mar, last Sep	Lochs-Crossbost	4th Mar, Sep
Cross Ness	2nd Mar, Oct	Lochs-in-Bernera	1st Apr, 2nd Sep
Kinloch	3rd Mar, 2nd Jun, 2nd Sep	Stornoway: High	3rd Feb, last Aug

Stornoway: Martin's Memorial	3rd Feb, last Aug, 1st Dec, Easter
Stornoway: St Columba	3rd Feb, last Aug
Uig	3rd Jun, 4th Oct

(12) ENGLAND AND CHANNEL ISLANDS (F)

Meets at London, in Crown Court Church, on the second Tuesday of February and the second Saturday of October, and at St Columba's, Pont Street, on the second Tuesday of June.

Clerk: REV. ALISTAIR CUMMING MSc CCS FInstLM FLPI   50 Burgh Heath Road, Epsom KT17 4LX   england@churchofscotland.org.uk   07534 943986

1 Corby (F H W)
Vacant
Interim Moderator: Scott M. Rennie
New charge formed by the union of Corby: St Andrew's and Corby: St Ninian's
The Manse, 46 Glyndebourne Gardens, Corby, Northants NN18 0PZ
SRennie@churchofscotland.org.uk
01536 265245
01536 669478
020 7278 5022

2 Guernsey: St Andrew's in the Grange (F H W)
Justin W. Taylor BTh MTh MTh   2018   2022
The Manse, Le Villocq, Castel, Guernsey GY5 7SB
JTaylor@churchofscotland.org.uk
01481 257345

3 Jersey: St Columba's (F H T W)
Vacant
Interim Moderator: Alistair Cumming
18 Claremont Avenue, St Saviour, Jersey JE2 7SF
ACumming@churchofscotland.org.uk
01534 730659
07534 943986

4 London: Crown Court (F H T W)
Scott M. Rennie MA BD STM FRSA   1999   2022
53 Sidmouth Street, London WC1H 8JX
SRennie@churchofscotland.org.uk
020 7836 5643
020 7278 5022

5 London: St Columba's (F H T W) linked with Newcastle: St Andrew's (H T W)   office@stcolumbas.org.uk   **St Columba's: 020 7584 2321**
C. Angus MacLeod MA BD   1996   2012
29 Hollywood Road, Chelsea, London SW10 9HT   Office 020 7584 2321
Angus.MacLeod@churchofscotland.org.uk
William McLaren MA BD   1990   2021
St Columba's, Pont Street, London SW1X 0BD   Office 020 7584 2321
(Associate Minister)
WMcLaren@churchofscotland.org.uk

6 Newcastle: St Andrew's   See London: St Columba's

B. In other appointments: members of Presbytery

Binks, Mike   2007   2015   Auxiliary Minister – Churches Together in Corby   Hollybank, 10 Kingsbrook, Corby NN18 9HY   07590 507917
MBinks@churchofscotland.org.uk

Cumming, Alistair MSc CCS FInstLM FLPI   2010   2013   Presbytery Clerk: Auxiliary Minister   50 Burgh Heath Road, Epsom KT17 4LX   07534 943986
ACumming@churchofscotland.org.uk

Name			Position	Address / Contact	Telephone
Francis, James MBE BD PhD	2002	2009	Army Chaplain	37 Milburn Road, Coleraine BT52 1QT JFrancis@churchofscotland.org.uk	02870 353869
Langlands, Cameron H. BD MTh ThM PhD MInstLM	1995	2012	Head of Spiritual and Pastoral Care, South London and Maudsley NHS Foundation Trust	Maudsley Hospital, Denmark Road, London SE5 8AZ Cameron.Langlands@slam.nhs.uk	020 3228 2815 07971 169791
Lovett, Mairi F. BSc BA DipPS MTh	2005	2013	Hospital Chaplain	Royal Brompton Hospital, Sydney Street, London SW3 6NP m.lovett@rbht.nhs.uk	020 7351 8060
MacKay, Stewart A. BA	2009	2020	Army Chaplain	ATR (P) 3ATR, Alexander Barracks, Pirbright, Woking GU24 0QQ Stewart.Mackay762@mod.gov.uk	
MacKenzie, Hector M.	2008		Army Chaplain	ITC (C) 2ITB, Helles Barracks, Catterick Garrison DL9 4HH Hector.MacKenzie657@mod.gov.uk	
Mather, James BA DipArch MA MBA	2010	2019	Auxiliary Minister: Woodley Airfield Church	24 Ellison Road, Barnes, London SW13 0AD JMather@churchofscotland.org.uk	020 8876 6540 07836 715655
McLay, Neil BA BD MTh	2006	2012	Army Chaplain	HQ SE, Taurus House, Cavans Road, Aldershot GU11 2LQ Neil.McLay100@mod.gov.uk	
McMahon, John K.S. MA BD	1998	2012	Head of Spiritual and Pastoral Care, West London NHS Trust	Broadmoor Hospital, Crowthorne, Berkshire RG45 7EG john.mcmahonrev@westlondon.nhs.uk	01344 754098
Middleton, Paul (Prof) BMus BD ThM PhD FRSA FHEA	2000	2018	New Testament and Early Christianity, University of Chester	10 Raymond Street, Chester CH1 4EL p.middleton@chester.ac.uk	01244 378766
Thom, David J. BD DipMin	1999	2015	Army Chaplain	HQ SHAPE, EJSU, SHAPE, BFPO 26 revdjt@gmail.com	
Walker, R. Forbes BSc BD ThM	1987	2013	School Chaplain, Emmanuel School, London	15 Selhurst New Court, Selhurst New Road, London SE25 5PT revrfw@gmail.com	
Ward, Michael J. BSc BD PhD MA PGCE	1983	2009	Training and Development Officer: Presbyterian Church of Wales	Apt 6, Bryn Hedd, Conwy Road, Penmaen-mawr, Gwynedd LL34 6BS revmw@btopenworld.com	07765 598816
Wright, Allan BVMS MRCVS	2021		Ordained Local Minister: Pioneer Minister to Veterinary Community in NE England	27 Prospect Terrace, Burnopfield, Newcastle NE16 6EL AWright@churchofscotland.org.uk	07984 541587

C. Retaining; members of Presbytery

Name			Position	Address / Contact	Telephone
Anderson, Andrew F. MA BD	1981	2011	(Edinburgh: Greenside)	58 Reliance Way, Oxford OX4 2FG andrew.relianceway@gmail.com	01865 778397
Cairns, W. Alexander BD	1978	2006	(Corby: St Andrew's)	Kirkton House, Kirkton of Craig, Montrose DD10 9TB sandy.cairns@btinternet.com	07808 588045
Cameron, R. Neil	1976	2005	(Chaplain: Army)	neilandminacameron@yahoo.co.uk	
Clark, Christine M. BA BD MTh DMin	2006	2019	(Chaplain, Royal Hospital for Sick Children, Edinburgh)	CClark@churchofscotland.org.uk	07444 819237
Lunn, Dorothy I.M.	2002	2016	(Auxiliary Minister, Newcastle: St Andrew's)	14 Bellerby Drive, Ouston, Co.Durham DH2 1TW dorothylunn@hotmail.com	0191 492 0647
Macfarlane, Peter T. BA LTh	1970	1994	(Chaplain: Army)	4 rue de Rives, 37160 Abilly, France	
Mills, Peter W. CB BD DD CPD	1984	2018	(East Neuk Trinity with St Monans)	16 Pearce Drive, Lawley, Telford TF3 5IQ	

Ogg, M. Fiona (Mrs) BA BD	2012 2021	(Acharacle with Ardnamurchan)	6a Stamford Road, Essendine, Stamford PE9 4LQ Fiona.Ogg@churchofscotland.org.uk	
Pitkeathly, David G. LLB DipLP BD	1996 2021	(Border Kirk)	11 Butlers Road, Horsham, Sussex RH13 6AJ david.pitkeathly@btinternet.com	07546 064607
Stone, Lance B. BD MTh PhD	1978 2021	(Amsterdam: English Reformed Church)	Flat C Branksome Court, 2 Sudbourne Road, London SW2 5AQ LStone@churchofscotland.org.uk	07443 321184

D. In other appointments: not members of Presbytery
Nil

E. Retaining: not members of Presbytery

| Hutchison, David S. BSc BD ThM | 1991 2022 | (Chaplain: University of Aberdeen) | 40 The Lane, Alwoodley, Leeds LS17 7BS | |

F. Inactive: not members of Presbytery
Nil

G. Readers (active)

| Menzies, Rena (Mrs) | 40 Elizabeth Avenue, St Brelade's, Jersey JE3 8GR | menzfamily@jerseymail.co.uk | 01534 741095 |
| Milligan, Elaine (Mrs) | 16 Surrey Close, Corby, Northants NN17 2TG | elainemilligan@ntlworld.com | 01536 205259 |

H. Ministries Development Staff
McLaren, William (Rev) MA BD   London: St Columba's with Newcastle: St Andrew's – Associate Minister   WMcLaren@churchofscotland.org.uk

ADDRESSES

Corby	Beanfield Avenue
Guernsey	The Grange, St Peter Port
Jersey	Midvale Road, St Helier
London: Crown Court	Crown Court WC2
London: St Columba's	Pont Street SW1
Newcastle	Sandyford Road

(13) INTERNATIONAL CHARGES (F W)

Meets over the weekend of the second Sunday of March and October, hosted by congregations in mainland Europe.

Clerk: REV. DEREK G. LAWSON LLB BD

16 Rue de la Madeleine, 22210 La Chèze, France
international@churchofscotland.org.uk
clerk@internationalpresbytery.net
www.internationalpresbytery.net
0033 6 09 57 66 71

1 Amsterdam: English Reformed Church (F T W)
Vacant

info@erc.amsterdam
Jan Willem Brouwersstraat 9, NL-1071 LH Amsterdam, The Netherlands
Church address: Begijnhof 48, 1012WV Amsterdam
0031 20 672 2288

Interim Moderator: James M. Brown
JBrown@churchofscotland.org.uk
0049 234 133363

2 Bermuda: Christ Church, Warwick (F H W)
Alistair G. Bennett BSc BD   1978   2016

christchurch@logic.bm
1 Steele's Drive, Paget PG03, Bermuda
ABennett@churchofscotland.org.uk
Church address: Christ Church, Middle Road, Warwick, Bermuda
Mailing address: PO Box WK 130, Warwick WK BX, Bermuda
001 441 236 1882
001 441 236 0400

3 Bochum: English-Speaking Christian Congregation (Associated congregation) (W)
Anja Nicole Stuckenberger
(*Joint Pastors, not ministers of the CofS*)
Emmanuel Mote-Ndasah

Ev. Stadtakademie Bochum, Westring 26a, 44787 Bochum
astuckenberger@ekvw.de
Church address: Pauluskirche, Grabenstrasse 9, 44787 Bochum
0049 234 962904 ext 661
0049 175 2518757

4 Brussels: St Andrew's (F H W)
Eric W. Foggitt MA BSc BD   1991   2020

secretary@churchofscotland.be
23 Square des Nations, B-1000 Brussels, Belgium
EFoggitt@churchofscotland.org.uk
Church address: Chaussée de Vieurgat 181, 1050 Brussels
0032 2 649 02 19
0032 2 672 40 56

5 Budapest: St Columba's (F W)
Aaron C. Stevens BA MDiv MACE   2004   2006

Locsei ut 14, 4e, 21a, 1147, Budapest, Hungary
AStevens@churchofscotland.org.uk
0036 30 567 6356
0036 70 615 5394

Szabina Sztojka (*Associate Minister, Reformed Church of Hungary*)   2021
sztojka.szabina@reformatus.hu
Church address: Vörösmarty utca 51, 1064 Budapest

6 Colombo, Sri Lanka: St Andrew's Scots Kirk (F W)
Guardianship of the Presbytery

Interim Moderator: Norman M. Hutcheson

churchofficer@scotskirk.lk   **0094 112 323 765**
73 Galle Road, Colpetty, Colombo 3, Sri Lanka   0094 112 386 774
minister@standrewsscotskirk.org
Church address: 73 Galle Road, Colpetty, Colombo   01556 610102
norman.hutcheson@gmail.com

7 Geneva (F W)   1977   2017
Laurence H. Twaddle MA BD MTh

6 chemin Taverney, 1218 Geneva, Switzerland   **0041 22 788 08 31**
LTwaddle@churchofscotland.org.uk   0041 22 788 08 31
Church address: Auditoire de Calvin, 1 Place de la Taconnerie, Geneva

8 Lausanne: The Scots Kirk (F H W)
Vacant
Interim Moderator: Graham Austin

26 Avenue de Rumine, CH-1005 Lausanne, Switzerland   0041 21 323 98 28
Church address: 26 Avenue de Rumine, Lausanne
GAustin@churchofscotland.org.uk   0031 10 412 5709

9 Lisbon: St Andrew's (F W)
Guardianship of the Presbytery

Session Clerk: Nina O'Donnell

lisbonstandrewschurch@gmail.com   00351 213 951 165
Rua Coelho da Rocha, N°75 - 1°
Campa de Ourique, 1350-073 Lisbon, Portugal
cofslx@netcabo.pt
Church address: Rua da Arriaga, Lisbon   00351 21 483 8750
sessionclerklisbon@gmail.com

10 Malta: St Andrew's Scots Church (H W)   2020
Beata (Betsi) Thane MA BD

2 Casa Cappella, Triq L-Infanterija, KKP 1270 Hal-Kirkop, Malta   00356 993 53246
minister@saintandrewsmalta.com
Church address: 210 Old Bakery Street, Valletta, Malta

11 Paris: The Scots Kirk (F W)
Vacant
Interim Moderator: Lawrence H. Twaddle

10 Rue Thimmonier, F-75009 Paris, France   0033 1 48 78 47 94
LTwaddle@churchofscotland.org.uk   0041 22 788 08 31
Church address: 17 Rue Bayard, 75009 Paris

12 Rome: St Andrew's (F W)
Vacant
Interim Moderator: Aaron C. Stevens

scotskirkrome@gmail.com   Tel 0039 06 482 7627
Via XX Settembre 7, 00187 Rome, Italy   Fax 0039 06 487 4370
Church address: Via XX Settembre 7, 00187 Rome   0036 70 615 5394
AStevens@churchofscotland.org.uk

13 Rotterdam: Scots International Church (F W) 1997 2020
Graham Austin BD
info@scotsintchurch.com
Schiedamse Vest 121, 3012BH Rotterdam, The Netherlands
GAustin@churchofscotland.org.uk
Church address: Schiedamsesingel 2, Rotterdam, The Netherlands
0031 10 412 4779
0031 10 412 5709

14 Trinidad: Greyfriars St Ann's, Port of Spain (W) linked with Arouca and Sangre Grande
Vacant
50 Frederick Street, Port of Spain, Trinidad
001 868 623 6684
Interim Moderator: Alistair G. Bennett
ABennett@churchofscotland.org.uk
001 441 236 0400

B. In other appointments: members of Presbytery

Bom, Irene M.E. BA DipCS   2008   (Ordained Local Minister-Worship and Prayer Promoter)
Bergpolderstraat 53A, NL-3038 KB Rotterdam, The Netherlands   0031 10 265 1703
ibsalem@xs4all.nl

Evans-Boiten, Joanne H.G. BD   2004 2018   (Retreat Centre Director)
Colomba le Roc. 510 Chemin du Faurat, Belmontet, 46800 Montcuq en Quercy, France   0033 5 65 22 13 11
Joanne.evansboiten@gmail.com

McGeoch, Graham G. MA BD MTh PhD   2009 2017   (Theology Lecturer)
Faculdade Unida de Vitoria. R.Eng. Fabio Ruschi, 161 Bento Ferreira, Vitoria ES 29050-670, Brazil
graham@fuv.edu.br

C. Retaining; members of Presbytery

Brown, James M. MA BD   1982 2022   (Bochum: English-Speaking Christian Congregation)
Verkehrsstrasse 37, 44809 Bochum, Germany   0049 234 133363
JBrown@churchofscotland.org.uk

Homewood, I. Maxwell MSc BD   1997 2003   (Edinburgh: Drylaw)
Ander Fließwiese 26, D-14052 Berlin, Germany   0049 151 2758 6921
maxhomewood@me.com

Lawson, Derek G. LLB BD   1998 2020   (Rotterdam: Scots International Church)
16 Rue de la Madeleine, 22210 La Chèze, France   0036 09 57 66 71
DLawson@churchofscotland.org.uk

MacLean, Ewen D. BA BD DipBI   1995 2022   (Gibraltar: St Andrew's)
Flat 201 Sunrise, Royal Ocean Plaza, Ocean Village, Gibraltar GX11 1AA 2009   00350 200 77040
Ewen.Maclean@churchofscotland.org.uk

Pitkeathly, Thomas C. MA CA BD   1984 2004   (Brussels: St Andrew's)
77 St Thomas Road. Lytham St. Anne's FY8 1JP   01253 789634
tpitkeathly@yahoo.co.uk

Pot, Joost BSc   1992 2004   (Auxiliary Minister, Rotterdam: Scots International Church)
joostpot@gmail.com

Reamonn, Paraic BA BD   1982 2018   (Jerusalem: St Andrew's)
395B Route de Mandement, 1281 Ruissin, Switzerland   0041 22 776 4834
PReamonn@churchofscotland.org.uk

D. In other appointments: not members of Presbytery
Nil

E. Retaining: not members of Presbytery
Nil

F. Inactive: not members of Presbytery
Nil

G. Readers (active)
Campbell, Cindy (Mrs)   9 Cavello Heights, Sandys MA 05, Bermuda   cindyfcampbell@gmail.com   001 441 234 3797
Goodman, Alice (Mrs)   Route de Sallaz 23, Rivaz 1071, Switzerland   alice.goodman@epfl.ch   0041 21 946 1727

H. Ministries Development Staff
Nil

(14) JERUSALEM

Clerk: JOANNA OAKLEY-LEVSTEIN BA   **St Andrew's, Galilee, PO Box 104, Tiberias 14100, Israel   00972 50 5842517**
j.oak.lev@gmail.com

Jerusalem and Tiberias: St Andrew's (F W)
D. Stewart Gillan BSc MDiv PhD   1985   2022   **jerusalem@churchofscotland.org.uk**   00972 2 673 2401
St Andrew's Scots Memorial Church, 1 David Remez Street,
PO Box 8619, Jerusalem 91086, Israel
SGillan@churchofscotland.org.uk
tiberias@churchofscotland.org.uk

Muriel B. Pearson (Ms) MA BD PGCE   2004   2021   St Andrew's, Galilee, 1 Gdud Barak Street,   +447951 888860
(Associate Minister)   PO Box 104, Tiberias 14100, Israel
MPearson@churchofscotland.org.uk

G. Reader (active)
Oakley-Levstein, Joanna (Mrs) BA   Mevo Hamma, 12934, Israel   j.oak.lev@gmail.com   00972 50 584 2517

SECTION 6

Additional Lists of Personnel

Ministers not members of Presbytery are now listed in Section 5 under each Presbytery: Employed part D, Retaining part E, Inactive part F.

Readers and Ministries Development Staff are now listed in Section 5 under each Presbytery: parts G and H respectively

LIST A – ORDAINED LOCAL MINISTERS AND AUXILIARY MINISTERS

Those in active service only*. Where only one date is given it is the year of ordination and appointment. Contact details are under the relevant Presbytery in Section 5.
(* Those registered Retaining and Inactive are listed under the relevant presbyteries.)

NAME	ORD	APP	APPOINTMENT	OLM / Aux
1. EDINBURGH AND WEST LOTHIAN				
Addis, Reuben	2023		Edinburgh: Gorgie Dalry Stenhouse	OLM
Haggarty, Kay O.N. BEd	2021		Edinburgh: Gracemount with Edinburgh: Liberton	OLM
Hardman Moore, Susan (Prof.) MA MAR PhD FRHistS	2013		New College, University of Edinburgh	OLM
Henderson, Derek R. MA DipTCP DipCS	2017		Abercorn linked with Pardovan, Kingscavil and Winchburgh	OLM
Kennedy, Fiona	2022		Edinburgh: Barclay Viewforth, Craiglockhart, Polwarth, St Michael's	OLM
Kirkland, Nikki J. BSc	2021		Edinburgh: St Nicholas' Sighthill	OLM
MacLeod Rivett, Mary A. BA MA PhD	2023		Edinburgh: Granton	OLM
McKenzie, Janet R. (Mrs) BA DipHS CertCS	2016		Edinburgh: Tron Kirk (Gilmerton and Moredun)	OLM
Munn, Derek B.	2022		Edinburgh: Dalmeny with Edinburgh: Queensferry	OLM
Quilter, Alison I. DipCS	2018		Polbeth Harwood linked with West Kirk of Calder	OLM
Riddell, Thomas S. BSc CEng FIChemE	1993	1994	Linlithgow: St Michael's	Aux
Tweedie, Fiona J. BSc PhD	2011	2014	Statistician, Church Offices	OLM
Welsh, Rita M. BA PhD	2017		Edinburgh: Holy Trinity	OLM
2. LOTHIAN AND BORDERS				
Don, Andrew MBA	2006	2013	Newton	OLM
Harrison, Frederick CertCT	2013	2021	Aberlady and Gullane	OLM
Watson, Michael D. CertCS	2013	2019	Traprain	OLM
3. SOUTH WEST				
Bellis, Pamela A. BA DipTheol	2014	2022	Balmaclellan, Kells and Dalry linked with Carsphairn	OLM
Hogg, James	2018	—		OLM
Hume, David MSc PhD CertHE	2020		Alloway	Aux
Mack, Elizabeth A. (Miss) DipPE	1994	2018	Lochend and New Abbey	OLM
McLeod, Tom	2014	2015	Craigie Symington linked with Prestwick: South	OLM
Wallace, Mhairi	2013	2017	Kirkmichael, Tinwald and Torthorwald	OLM
Watt, Kim CertThS	2015		Presbytery-wide	OLM
4. CLYDE				
Breingan, Mhairi M. BSc CertCS	2011	2019	Paisley: St George's	OLM
Millar, Ian J. BA	2020	2022	Dumbarton: Riverside linked with Dumbarton: St Andrew's linked with Dumbarton: West	OLM

Name			Charge	Type
Stevenson, Stuart CertCE	2011	——	Craigrownie linked with Garelochhead linked with Rosneath: St Modan's	OLM
		——	——	OLM
5. GLASGOW				
Forsythe, Ruth (Mrs) DipRS MCS	2017	2018	Glasgow: Knightswood Anniesland Trinity	OLM
Grieve, Leslie E.T. BSc BA	2014	——	Glasgow: Colston Wellpark	OLM
Hunt, Roland BSc PhD CertEd	2016	——	Glasgow: Carmyle linked with Glasgow: Mount Vernon	OLM
Sturrock, Roger D. (Prof.) BD MD FCRP	2014	——	Glasgow: Kelvinside Hillhead and Glasgow: Wellington	OLM
6. FORTH VALLEY AND CLYDESDALE				
Anderson, Fiona DipHE	2020	2023	Dalserf	OLM
Fyfe, Lorna K. BD	2020	——	——	OLM
Hacking, Philip R.	2021	——	——	OLM
MacDonald, Monica J. (Mrs)	2014	——	Slamannan	OLM
Murphy, Jim	2014	——	——	OLM
Sarle, Andrew BSc BD	2013	——	Falkirk: Bainsford	OLM
Wandrum, David C.	1993	——	Carriden	Aux
White, Anne W. BA CQSW DipHE	2018	2017	Falkirk: Grahamston United	OLM
7. FIFE				
Mateos, Margaret B.	2018	——	Dunfermline: St Leonard's	OLM
Whittle, Sarah BA MA PhD	2022	——	Kingsbarns	OLM
8. PERTH				
Brodie, Catherine J. MA BA MPhil PGCE	2017	——	Dundee: Fintry	OLM
Campbell, Gordon A. MA BD CDipAF DipHSM CMgr MCMI MIHM AssocCIPD AFRIN ARSGS FRGS FSAScot	2001	2004	An Honorary Chaplain, University of Dundee	Aux
Elwell-Sutton, Brenda M.M.	2022	——	Dundee: Craigiebank with Dundee: Douglas and Mid Craigie; Dundee: Whitfield	OLM
Gourlay, Heather	2021	——	Supporting rural ministry in Angus	OLM
Gray, Ian	2013	2017	Montrose: Old and St Andrew's	OLM
Michie, Margaret (Mrs)	2013	——	Loch Leven Parish Grouping	OLM
Munro, Alastair RN BSc	2022	——	Dunblane: Cathedral	OLM
Nicol, Robert D. MA	2013	——	Fortingall, Glenlyon, Kenmore and Lawers	OLM
Shearer, Anne F. BA DipEd CertCS	2010	——	Alva	Aux
Stanley, Lesley MA PhD FBTS	2021	——	Balfron with Fintry	OLM
Steele, Grace M.F. MA BTh	2014	——	Presbytery-wide	OLM
Stevenson, Beverley	2020	——	——	OLM
Stott, Anne M.	2019	——	Presbytery Pioneer Worker, Bertha Park	OLM
Strachan, Willie D. DipYCW MBA CertCS	2013	2020	Presbytery-wide	OLM
Thorburn, Susan (Mrs) MTh	2014	2019	Mission Development Worker, Presbytery of Fife	OLM

Name			Charge	
Wilkie, Robert F. CertCS	2011	2012	Perth: Craigie and Moncrieffe	Aux
9. NORTH EAST AND NORTHERN ISLES				
Crouch, Simon A. MCIPD CertCS	2019		West Gordon (Alford, Strathdon, Rhynie)	OLM
Freeth, June BA MA	2015		Kirkwall: St Magnus Cathedral linked with Rousay	OLM
Galbraith, David	2021		Maryculter Trinity	OLM
Lennox-Trewren, Norman D. CertCS	2018		Mearns Coastal	OLM
Palmer, Sonia RGN	2017		Elgin: St Giles' and St Columba's South	OLM
Prentice, Martin W.M. BVMS MRCVS DipCS	2013	2015	Flotta linked with Orphir and Stenness	OLM
Somevi, Joseph K. BSc MSc PhD MRICS MRTPI MIEMA CertCRS	2015	2021	Aberdeen: St Nicholas Kincorth, South of; and Aberdeen: Torry St Fittick's	OLM
Stewart, William	2015		Presbytery-wide	OLM
Thorne, Joan I. BA TQFE CertCS	2019	2016	Dyce linked with New Machar	OLM
10.1 ARGYLL				
MacKellar, Janet K. BSc ProfCertMgmt FCMI	2019		Kilmun, Strone and Ardentinny: The Shore Kirk	OLM
MacPherson, Alexander J. MA BSc FRSA	2021		Cowal Kirk	OLM
10.2 ABERNETHY				
Thomson, Mary Ellen (Mrs)	2014		Presbytery Chaplain to Care Homes	OLM
10.3 INVERNESS				
Archer, Morven (Mrs)	2013	2020	Presbytery Assistant Minister	OLM
Morrison, Fiona S. BA	2019	2023	Ardersier linked with Petty	OLM
Morrison, John A. BSc BA PGCE	2013		Dallas linked with Forres: St Leonard's linked with Rafford	OLM
Whillis, David (Dr) DipHE	2020		Presbytery-wide minister to over 60s community	OLM
10.4 LOCHABER				
Kinnear, Marion (Mrs) BD	2009	2021	Kinlochleven linked South Lochaber	Aux
10.5 ROSS				
Bissett, James	2016		Contin linked with Fodderty and Strathpeffer	OLM
Macdonald, Michael J.	2004	2014	Alness	Aux
Munro, Irene BA	2019		Presbytery Chaplain to vulnerable groups in residential care	OLM
Rattenbury, Carol BA	2017	2022	Cromarty linked with Resolis and Urquhart	OLM
10.6 SUTHERLAND				
Gardner, Hilary M. (Miss)	2010		Lairg linked with Rogart	Aux
Stobo, Mary J. (Mrs) BA	2013	2018	Community Healthcare Chaplain	OLM
10.7 CAITHNESS				
Stewart, Heather (Mrs)	2013	2017	Latheron	OLM

10.8 LOCHCARRON-SYKE

10.9 UIST

Macdonald, Ishabel	2011	Benbecula linked with Carinish	OLM

11. LEWIS

12. ENGLAND AND CHANNEL ISLANDS

Binks, Mike	2007	Churches Together in Corby	Aux
Cumming, Alistair MSc CCS FInstLM FLPI	2010	Presbytery Clerk, England and Channel Islands	Aux
Mather, James BA DipArch MA MBA	2010	Woodley Airfield Church	Aux
Wright, Allan BVMS MRCVS	2021	Pioneer Minister to Veterinary Community in NE England	OLM

13. INTERNATIONAL CHARGES

Bom, Irene M.E. BA DipCS	2008	Worship Resourcing	OLM

LIST B – DIACONATE

Those in active service. Contact details are under the relevant Presbytery in Section 5.

Prior to the General Assembly of 2002, Deacons were commissioned. In 2002 existing Deacons were ordained, as have been those subsequently.

NAME	ORD	APP	APPOINTMENT	PRESBYTERY
Beck, Isobel BD DCS	2014	2016	Kilwinning: Abbey	3 South West
Blair, Fiona (Miss) DCS	1994	2015	Beith	3 South West
Cathcart, John Paul (Mr) DCS	2000	2023	Presbytery Vacant Charge Enabler	5 Glasgow
Corrie, Margaret (Miss) DCS	1989	2013	Armadale	1 Edinburgh and West Lothian
Crocker, Liz (Mrs) DipComEd DCS	1985	2015	Edinburgh: Tron Kirk (Gilmerton and Moredun)	1 Edinburgh and West Lothian
Cuthbertson, Valerie (Miss) DipTMus DCS	2003		Cumbernauld: Old	5 Glasgow
Evans, Mark (Mr) BSc MSc DCS	1988	2006	Head of Spiritual Care and Bereavement Lead, NHS Fife (for 2023 seconded to Scottish Government as National Spiritual Care Strategic Advisor Operational Lead)	1 Edinburgh and West Lothian
Forsyth, Kirsty C. BD DCS	2022		Edinburgh: Richmond Craigmillar	1 Edinburgh and West Lothian
Gargrave, Mary S. (Mrs) DCS	1989	2002	Glasgow: Carnwadric	5 Glasgow
Hamilton, James (Mr) DCS	1997	2000	Glasgow: Maryhill Ruchill	5 Glasgow
Hamilton, Karen M. (Mrs) DCS	1995	2014	Glasgow: Cambuslang	5 Glasgow
Herbert, Claire BD DCS	2019		Chaplain, Lodging House Mission, Glasgow	5 Glasgow

	COM/ORD	RET		
Love, Joanna R. (Ms) BSc DCS	1992	2009	Iona Community: Wild Goose Resource Group	5 Glasgow
McPheat, Elspeth (Miss) DCS	1985	2001	CrossReach: Manager, St Margaret's House, Polmont	1 Edinburgh and West Lothian
Pennykid, Gordon J. BD DCS	2015	2018	Chaplain, HM Prison Edinburgh	1 Edinburgh and West Lothian
Robertson, Pauline (Mrs) BA CertTheol BD DCS	2003			1 Edinburgh and West Lothian
Scott, Pamela (Mrs) BD DCS	2017		Lochgelly and Benarty: St Serf's	7 Fife
Thomson, Jacqueline (Mrs) MTh DCS	2004	2008	Buckhaven and Wemyss	7 Fife
Wallace, Catherine (Mrs) PGDipC DCS	1987	2021	Clinical Manager, The Harbour Counselling Service, Perth	8 Perth
Wilson, Angela DCS	2015	2021	Community Outreach Worker, Southern Ministry Cluster	6 Forth Valley and Clydesdale

Registered as Retaining or Inactive

Those who are retired and registered under the Registration of Ministries Act (Act 2, 2017, as amended) as 'Retaining' or 'Inactive.' Only those 'Inactive' Deacons who have given consent under the GDPR to publication of their details are included. Contact details are under the relevant Presbytery in Section 5.

NAME	COM/ORD	RET	PRESBYTERY
Allan, Jean (Mrs) DCS	1989	2011	8C Perth
Beaton, Margaret S. (Miss) DCS	1989	2015	5C Glasgow
Bell, Sandra L.N. (Mrs) DCS	2001	2013	10.5E Ross
Buchanan, Marion (Mrs) MA DCS	1983	2019	2F Lothian and Borders
Crawford, Morag (Miss) MSc DCS	1977	2021	1C Edinburgh and West Lothian
Dunnett, Linda (Mrs) BA DCS	1976	2016	8C Perth
Getliffe, Dot L.J. (Mrs) BA BD DipEd DCS	2006	2021	10.3C Inverness
Gilroy, Lorraine (Mrs) DCS	1988	1994	6C Forth Valley and Clydesdale
Gordon, Margaret (Mrs) DCS	1998	2012	1C Edinburgh and West Lothian
Gray, Christine M. (Mrs) DCS	1969	2003	5F Glasgow
Gray, Greta (Miss) DCS	1992	2014	4C Clyde
Hughes, Helen (Miss) DCS	1977	2008	5C Glasgow
Johnston, Mary (Miss) DCS	1988	2003	4F Clyde
King, Margaret MA DCS	2002	2012	9C North East and Northern Isles
Lundie, Ann V. (Miss) DCS	1972	2007	9C North East and Northern Isles
Lyall, Ann (Miss) DCS	1980	2022	5C Glasgow
MacDonald, Anne (Miss) BA DCS	1980	2023	5C Glasgow
Mackay, Kenneth D. DCS	1996	2020	8E Perth
MacKinnon, Ronald M. (Mr) DCS	1996	2012	3F South West

Maclean, Donald A. (Mr) DCS	1988	11C Lewis
McCully, M. Isobel (Miss) DCS	1974	4F Clyde
McIntosh, Kay (Mrs) DCS	1990	1C Edinburgh and West Lothian
McLaren, Glenda M. (Ms) DCS	1990	10.1 Argyll
McLellan, Margaret DCS	1986	5C Glasgow
McNaughton, Janette (Miss) DCS	1982	5C Glasgow
Merrilees, Ann (Miss) DCS	1994	1E Edinburgh and West Lothian
Miller, Elsie M. (Miss) DCS	1974	5C Glasgow
Mitchell, Joyce (Mrs) DCS	1994	10,3C Inverness
Mulligan, Anne MA DCS	1974	1C Edinburgh and West Lothian
Munro, Patricia M. BSc DCS	1986	8C Perth
Nicholson, David (Mr) DCS	1994	5C Glasgow
Nicol, Joyce (Mrs) BA DCS	1974	4F Clyde
Ogilvie, Colin (Mr) BA DCS	1998	6C Forth Valley and Clydesdale
Philip, Elizabeth A. C. (Mrs) MA BA PGCSE DCS	2007	8C Perth
Porter, Jean T. (Mrs) BD DCS	2006	8C Perth
Rennie, Agnes M. (Miss) DCS	1974	1C Edinburgh and West Lothian
Rose, Lewis (Mr) DCS	1993	8C Perth
Steele, Marilynn J. (Mrs) BD DCS	1999	2C Lothian and Borders
Steven, Gordon R. BD DCS	2000	2F Lothian and Borders
Teague, Yvonne (Mrs) DCS	1965	1C Edinburgh and West Lothian
Urquhart, Barbara (Mrs) DCS	1986	3C South West
Wallace, Sheila D. (Mrs) BA BD DCS	2009	8C Perth
Wilson, Muriel (Miss) MA BD DCS	1997	3C South West
Wright, Lynda (Miss) BEd DCS	1979	7C Fife

LIST C – HEALTHCARE CHAPLAINS

SCOTTISH GOVERNMENT

National Spiritual Care Strategic Advisor Operational Lead
Mr Mark Evans DCS, Planning & Quality Division, Health & Social Care Directorates, Scottish Government, St Andrew's House, Edinburgh EH1 3DG; mark.evans2@gov.scot

LOTHIAN

Head of Spiritual Care and Bereavement
Vacant

Spiritual Care Office: The Royal Infirmary of Edinburgh, 51 Little France Crescent, Edinburgh EH16 4SA; 0131 242 1990
Full details of chaplains and contacts in all hospitals: www.nhslothian.scot > Our Services > Spiritual Care

Chaplaincy team includes from the Church of Scotland:
Rev. Joanne G. Foster, Western General Hospital, Edinburgh; joanne.foster2@nhslothian.scot.nhs.uk; 0131 537 1400
Rev. Dr Rosie Magee, Royal Infirmary of Edinburgh; rosie.magee@nhslothian.scot.nhs.uk; 0131 242 1997
Rev. Marjory McPherson, Royal Infirmary of Edinburgh; marjory.mcpherson@nhslothian.scot.nhs.uk; 0131 242 1992

Outwith NHS
Rev. Erica M. Wishart, St Columba's Hospice, 15 Boswall Road, Edinburgh EH5 3RW; EWishart@churchofscotland.org.uk; 0131 551 1381

BORDERS

Head of Spiritual Care
Rev. Michael D. Scouler; michael.scouler@borders.scot.nhs.uk; 01896 826565
Spiritual Care Department: Chaplaincy Centre, Borders General Hospital, Melrose TD6 9BS; 01896 826564
Further information: www.nhsborders.scot.nhs.uk > Patients and Visitors > Our services > Chaplaincy Centre

DUMFRIES AND GALLOWAY

Spiritual Care Lead
Rev. Nathan Mesnikoff, Dumfries and Galloway Royal Infirmary; 01387 246246 Ext 31544
DGRI Sanctuary Office, Cargenbridge, Dumfries DG2 8RX dg.spiritual-care@nhs.scot
Further information: https://dghscp.co.uk/spiritual-care-support

AYRSHIRE AND ARRAN

Head of Spiritual Care, Staff Care and Person-Centred Care
Andy Gillies, University Hospital Crosshouse, Kilmarnock Road KA2 0BE; 07866 984823
Point of contact for all chaplains: Susan Robertson, 01583 825988
University Hospital Crosshouse Healthcare Chaplain: Karen Crosbie
University Hospital Ayr Healthcare Chaplain: Elaine Hough
Ailsa Hospital Healthcare Chaplain: Suzanne Algeo
Irvine Central Healthcare Chaplain: Colin Scott
Further information: www.nhsaaa.net > Services A-Z > Chaplaincy service

GREATER GLASGOW AND CLYDE

Spiritual Care Service Manager: Dawn Allan;dawn.allan3@ggc.scot.nhs.uk
Chaplains Office, Inverclyde Royal Hospital, Larkfield Road, Greenock PA16 0XN; 07814 313249
Spiritual Care Administrator: chaplains@ggc.scot.nhs.uk
Further information: www.nhsggc.org.uk > Services Directory > Spiritual Care

Healthcare chaplains from Church of Scotland:
Rev. Paul G.R. Grant, Glasgow Royal Infirmary; 0141 201 6300
Rev. Jeanette L. Peel, Chaplains Office, Inverclyde Royal Hospital; 07903 681003; 01475 504759

FORTH VALLEY

Head of Spiritual Care: Pauline Donnelly, Person Centred Manager
Spiritual Care Centre: Forth Valley Royal Hospital, Larbert FK5 4WR; 01324 566071
Chaplain Team: Mary Anne Burgoyne, David Harper, Sharon McPhee
Further information: www.nhsforthvalley.com > Services A–Z > Spiritual Care Centre

LANARKSHIRE

Head of Spiritual Care and Wellbeing
Paul Graham, paul.graham@lanarkshire.scot.nhs.uk; 07717 815581
Spiritual Care and Wellbeing Office: Law House, Airdrie Road, Carluke ML8 5EP; spiritualcare@lanarkshire.scot.nhs.uk; 01698 754251
Further information: www.nhslanarkshire.org.uk > Our services A–Z > Spiritual care

FIFE

Interim Head of Spiritual Care and Bereavement Lead
Mr Ian Campbell, Department of Spiritual Care, Victoria Hospital, Hayfield Road, Kirkcaldy KY2 5AH;
ian.campbell3@nhs.scot; 01592 648158
Victoria Hospital, Kirkcaldy and NHS Fife Community Hospitals: Chaplain's Office: 01592 648158 or 01592 729675
Queen Margaret Hospital, Dunfermline: Chaplains Office: 01383 674136
Mental Health and Community Chaplain, Adamson and Stratheden Hospitals: 07976 918909
Further information: www.nhsfife.org > Spiritual Care

Chaplaincy team includes from the Church of Scotland:

Rev. Gordon I. Strang, Victoria Hospital, Kirkcaldy; 01592 648158

Rev. Eileen A. Miller, Queen Margaret Hospital, Dunfermline; 01383 674136

TAYSIDE

Head of Spiritual Care: Rev. Alan Gibbon

The Wellbeing Centre, Royal Victoria Hospital, Dundee DD2 1SP; lynne.downie@nhs.scot; 01382 423110

Further information: www.nhstayside.scot.nhs.uk > Our Services A-Z > Spiritual Care and Wellbeing

Chaplaincy team includes from the Church of Scotland:

Rev. Ian J.M. McDonald, Palliative Care Chaplain, Roxburghe House, Dundee; ian.mcdonald2@nhs.scot; 01382 423110

Outwith NHS

Rev. Ali R. Pandian, CHAS, Rachel House Children's Hospice, Avenue Road, Kinross KY13 8FX; APandian@churchofscotland.org.uk; 01577 865777

GRAMPIAN

Lead Chaplain

Gillian Douglas, Chaplains' Office, Aberdeen Royal Infirmary, Foresterhill, Aberdeen AB25 2ZN; gram.chaplaincy@nhs.scot; 01224 553166

Further information: www.nhsgrampian.co.uk > Home > Our services > A-Z > Spiritual Care

ORKNEY

Spiritual Care Team

ork.chaplaincy@nhs.scot; 01856 888184

Further information: www.ohb.scot.nhs.uk/service/chaplaincy-and-spiritual-care

SHETLAND

Spiritual Care Lead

Rev Canon Neil Brice, neil.brice@nhs.scot; 01595 743662; 07771 380989

Further information: www.shb.scot.nhs.uk/hospital/spiritualcare.asp

HIGHLAND

Lead Chaplain
Janet Davidson, Raigmore Hospital, Old Perth Road, Inverness IV2 3UJ; janet.davidson2@nhs.scot; 01463 704463
Further information: www.nhshighland.scot.nhs.uk

Chaplaincy team includes from the Church of Scotland:
Lead Chaplain Staff Support
Rev. Michael A. Robertson, Raigmore Hospital; mike.robertson@nhs.scot; 01463 704463

WESTERN ISLES HEALTH BOARD

Lead Chaplain
Rev. T. K. Shadakshari, 23D Benside, Newmarket, Stornoway, Isle of Lewis HS2 0DZ; tk.shadakshari@nhs.scot; (Office) 01851 704704; (Home) 01851 701727; (Mbl) 07403 697138

NHS SCOTLAND

Interim Head of Programme, Health & Social Care Chaplaincy & Spiritual Care, NHS Education for Scotland
Audrey Taylor, Principal Educator, NHS Education for Scotland, audrey.taylor@nhs.scot; 07984 772697

Spiritual Care Specialist Research Lead
Rev. Iain J.M.Telfer, iain.telfer@nhs.scot; 01224 805120; 07554 222232
NHS Education for Scotland, Forest Grove House, Foresterhill Road, Aberdeen AB25 2ZP

Church of Scotland Chaplains in NHS ENGLAND
Rev. Dr Cameron H. Langlands, Head of Spiritual and Pastoral Care, South London and Maudsley NHS Foundation Trust, Maudsley Hospital, Denmark Road, London SE3 8AZ; Cameron.Langlands@slam.nhs.uk; 020 3228 2815; 07971 169791
Rev. Mairi F. Lovett, Chaplain, Royal Brompton Hospital, Sydney Street, London SW3 6NP; m.lovett@rbht.nhs.uk; 020 7351 8060
Rev. John K.S. McMahon, Head of Spiritual and Pastoral Care, West London NHS Trust, Broadmoor Hospital, Crowthorne, Berkshire RG45 7EG; john.mcmahonrev@westlondon.nhs.uk; 01344 754098

LIST D – HM FORCES CHAPLAINS

The columns give years of ordination and commissioning.

NAME	ORD	COM	ADDRESS
ROYAL NAVY			
Ashley-Emery, Stephen BD DPS RN	2006	2019	CTL, The Chaplaincy, HMS Sultan, Military Road, Gosport PO12 3BY Stephen.Ashley-Emery100@mod.gov.uk
Dalton, Mark F. BD DipMin RN	2002	2002	The Chaplaincy, HMS Neptune, HM Naval Base Clyde, Faslane, Helensburgh G84 8HL Mark.Dalton242@mod.gov.uk
Davidson, Mark R. MA BD STM PhD PhD RN	2005	2011	Principal AFCC, Armed Forces Chaplaincy Centre, Beckett House, Defence Academy of the United Kingdom, Shrivenham SN6 8LA Mark.Davidson122@mod.gov.uk
Royal Naval Reserve Nil			
ARMY			
Anderson, David P. BSc BD	2002	2007	DACG 4 Infantry Brigade and HQ North East, Bourlon Barracks, Pluymer Road, Catterick Garrison DL9 3AD David.Anderson646@mod.gov.uk
Begg, Richard J. MA BD	2008	2016	3 RSME Regiment, Gibraltar Barracks, Blackwater, Camberley GU17 9LP Richard.Begg100@mod.gov.uk
Berry, Geoff T. BSc BD	2009	2012	3 SCOTS, Fort George, Ardersier, Inverness IV2 7TE Geoff.Berry102@mod.gov.uk
Cobain, Alan R. BD	2000	2017	HQ SW, Building 56, Jellabad Barracks, Tidworth SP9 7BQ Alan.Cobain100@mod.gov.uk
Frail, Nicola R. BLE MBA MDiv	2000	2012	Chaplains Office, DM(SW), Whittington Barracks, Lichfield WS14 9PY Nicola.Frail188@mod.gov.uk
Francis, James MBE BD PhD	2002	2009	HQ Regional Command, Montgomery House, Queen's Avenue, Aldershot GU11 2JN James.Francis369@mod.gov.uk
Kellock, Chris N. MA BD	1998	2012	Permanent Joint Headquarters, Sandy Lane, Northwood HA6 3HP Christopher.Kellock935@mod.gov.uk
MacKay, Stewart A. BA	2009	2009	ATR (P) 3ATR, Alexander Barracks, Pirbright, Woking GU24 0QQ Stewart.Mackay762@mod.gov.uk
MacKenzie, Hector M.	2008	2008	ITC (C) 2ITB, Helles Barracks, Catterick Garrison DL9 4HH Hector.MacKenzie657@mod.gov.uk
Macpherson, Duncan J. BSc BD	1993	2002	HQ 1 Deep Recce Strike Brigade Combat Team, Building 57, Delhi Barracks, Tidworth SP9 7DX Duncan.Macpherson183@mod.gov.uk

Name	Year	Address
McLay, Neil BD MTh	2006	HQ SE, Taurus House, Cavans Road, Aldershot GU11 2LQ Neil.McLay100@mod.gov.uk
Thom, David J. BD DipMin DipPS DipLM	1999	HQ SHAPE, EJSU, BFPO 26 David.Thom410@mod.gov.uk
van Sittert, Paul BA BD	1997	1 LANCS, Salamanca Barracks, Episkopi, BFPO 53 Paul.VanSittert218@mod.gov.uk

Army Reserve

Name	Year	Address
Goodison, Michael J. BSc BD	2013	105 Regiment Royal Artillery, Army Reserve Centre, Crawfordsburn Road, Newtonards Michael.Goodison100@mod.gov.uk
Jeffrey, Kenneth S. BA BD PhD DMin	2002	7 SCOTS, Queens Barracks, 131 Dunkeld Road, Perth PH1 5BT 8472jeffre@armymail.mod.uk
Mair, Michael J. MStJ BD MTh	2014	32 (Scottish) Signal Regiment, 21 Jardine Street, Glasgow G20 6JU 5558mai@armymail.mod.uk
Rowe, Christopher J. BA BD	2008	5 Military Intelligence Battalion, Edinburgh Castle, Edinburgh EH1 2NG 9607row@armymail.mod.uk

Officiating Chaplains to the Military

Name	Year	Address
Blakey, Stephen A. BSc BD	1977	Staff Chaplain, HQ Scotland, Forthside, Stirling FK7 7RR
Duncan, John C. MBE BD MPhil	1987	Waterloo Lines, Leuchars Station, St Andrews KY1 0JX
Gardner, Neil N. DL CStJ MA BD	1991	Edinburgh Universities Officers' Training Corps, 301 Colinton Road, Edinburgh EH13 0LA
Rankin, Lisa-Jane BD CPS	2003	2 Bn Royal Regiment of Scotland, Glencorse Barracks, Penicuik EH26 0QH
Selemani, Ecilo LTh MTh	1993	51 Infantry Brigade and HQ Scotland, Forthside, Stirling FK7 7RR

ROYAL AIR FORCE

Name	Year	Address
Lancaster, Craig MA BD	2004	Chaplaincy Centre, RAF Cosford, Wolverhampton WV7 3EX craig.lancaster102@mod.gov.uk
Young, David T. BA BD MTh	2007	St Aidan's Church, RAF Lossiemouth, Moray IV31 6DS david.young137@mod.gov.uk

Royal Air Force Reserve
Nil

Sea Cadets

Campbell, Gordon MA BD	Sea Cadets Dundee, East Camperdown Street, Dundee DD1 3LG
Fletcher, Suzanne G. BA MDiv MA DMin	Sea Cadets Dunbar, ACF Building, Castle Park Barracks, 33 North Road, Dunbar EH42 1EU
MacKay, Colin (Mr)	Sea Cadets Wick, The Scout Hall, Kirkhill, Wick KW1 4PN
May, John S. (Iain) BSc MBA BD	Sea Cadets Leith, Prince of Wales Dock, Leith, Edinburgh EH6 7DX
Robertson, Pauline DCS BA CertTheol	Sea Cadets Musselburgh, 9-11 South Street, Musselburgh EH21 6AT
Ross, Sarah L. BD MTh PGDipCS	Sea Cadets East Kilbride, Army Reserve Centre, Whitemoss, East Kilbride G74 2HP
Templeton, James L. BSc BD	Sea Cadets Methil, Harbour View, Methil KY8 3RF

Army Cadet Force

Blackwood, Keith T. BD DipMin — 2 Bn The Highlanders, ACF, Cadet Training Centre, Rocksley Drive, Boddam, Peterhead AB42 3BA — 01334 857136

Dicks, Shuna M. BSc BD — 2 Bn The Highlanders, ACF, Cadet Training Centre, Rocksley Drive, Boddam, Peterhead AB42 3BA — 07891 501859

Mackenzie, Cameron BD — Lothian and Borders Bn, ACF, Drumshoreland House, Broxburn EH52 5PF

McCulloch, Alen J.R. MA BD — 1 Highlanders Bn, ACF, Gordonville Road, Inverness IV2 4SU

Selemani, Ecilo LTh MTh — Glasgow and Lanarkshire Bn, ACF, Gilbertfield Road, Cambuslang, Glasgow G72 8YP

Swindells, Sean BD DipMin MTh — Angus and Dundee Bn, ACF, Barry Buddon Cadet Training Centre, by Carnoustie DD7 7RY

Wilson, Fiona A. BD — West Lowland Battalion, ACF, Fusilier House, Seaforth Road, Ayr KA8 9HX

Air Training Corps

Regional Chaplain, Scotland & N. Ireland — Alistair K. Ridland MStJ MA BD PGDip MRAeS MInstLM RAFAC — chaplain.sni@rafac.mod.gov.uk

North Scotland Wing

Wing Chaplain & 2405 Sqn — Russel Smith BD — russanntwo@yahoo.co.uk — 01349 861011

107 (Aberdeen) Sqn — James L.K. Wood — james@jamesinez.plus.com — 01224 722543

379 (County of Ross) Sqn — Michael J. Macdonald — Michael.Macdonald@churchofscotland.org.uk — 01349 884268

423DF (Speyside) Sqn — Robert J.M. Anderson BD FInstLM — bobjmanderson@gmail.com — 01343 835401

446 (Forres) Sqn — Donald K. Prentice BSc BD MSc MLitt — DPrentice@churchofscotland.org.uk

1298 (Huntly) Sqn — Kay F. Gauld BD STM PhD — KGauld@churchofscotland.org.uk — 01464 820404

1796 (Thurso) Sqn — David J.B. Macartney BA — DMacartney@churchofscotland.org.uk

2367 (Banchory) Sqn — Frank Ribbons MA BD DipEd — FRibbons@churchofscotland.org.uk — 01339 887267

Central Scotland Wing

Wing Chaplain & 2450 (Dudhope) Sqn — C. Graham D. Taylor BSc BD FIAB — AT Corps, MOD Leuchars KY16 0JX

775 (Burntisland) Sqn — Alan Sharp BSc BD — Unity Hall, Links Place, Burntisland KY3 9DY

859 (Dalgety) Sqn — Christine M. Sime BSc BD — CSime@churchofscotland.org.uk

1370 (Leven) Sqn — Jacqueline Thomson MTh DCS — Jacqueline.Thomson@churchofscotland.org.uk — 07806 776560

1743 (Crieff) Sqn — Robert D. Nicol MA — RNicol@churchofscotland.org.uk — 01887 820242

2288 (Montrose) Sqn — Ian A. McLean BSc BD DMin — IMcLean@churchofscotland.org.uk — 01674 434672

2435 (St Andrews) Sqn — Gavin R. Boswell BTheol — GBoswell@churchofscotland.org.uk — 01383 271548

South East Scotland Wing

Wing Chaplain — Regional Chaplain at present

132 (North Berwick) Sqn — Neil J. Dougall BD DipMin DMin — NDougall@churchofscotland.org.uk — 01620 892132

867 (Denny) Sqn — F. Derek Gunn BD — RevDerekGunn@hotmail.com — 01324 624938

870 (Dreghorn) Sqn, Edinburgh — Peter Nelson BSc BD — PNelson@churchofscotland.org.uk — 07500 057889

1716 (Roxburgh) Sqn — Sheila W. Moir MTheol — SMoir@churchofscotland.org.uk — 01835 822255

2535 (Livingston) Sqn — Nelu I. Balaj BD MA ThD — NBalaj@churchofscotland.org.uk — 01506 411888

West Scotland Wing

Wing Chaplain & 2166 (Hamilton) Sqn — I. Ross Blackman BSc MBA BD CertTh — RBlackman@churchofscotland.org.uk — 01698 640185

327 (Kilmarnock) Sqn — Kristina I. Hine BS MDiv — KHine@churchofscotland.org.uk — 01563 257172

498 (Wishaw) Sqn
1001 (Monklands) Sqn

Ian Douglas (Mr) (Reader)
Robert A. Hamilton BA BD

IDouglas@churchofscotland.org.uk   07742 022423
RHamilton@churchofscotland.org.uk   01236 763022

VETERANS CHAPLAINCY SCOTLAND

VCS provides pastoral care for military veterans and their families across Scotland. Working alongside local churches, and with a wide range of veteran charities, we provide individual veterans with a proactive listening ear, supporting them through the challenges of life. We seek to provide an approachable, confidential, experienced chaplaincy which mirrors the quality of ministry delivered by our serving chaplains. Our twenty chaplains, deployed across Scotland, are professionally qualified and recognised for their pastoral gifts. Our support is only a phone call or text away on 07521 638848, the first step to hope, healing and acceptance.

Programme Coordinator: Philip W. Patterson BMus BD   philip.patterson@vcscotland.org   07713 625792
Administrator: Stephen A. Blakey BSc BD   stephen.blakey@vcscotland.org

LIST E – MISSION PARTNERS SERVING INTERNATIONALLY

AFRICA

Malawi: Church of Central Africa Presbyterian, Synod of Livingstonia
Dr Linus Malu (2018)   Legal Officer, Church and Society Department, PO Box 112, Mzuzu, Malawi
mnabuikemalu@yahoo.com

www.ccapsolinia.org
office +265 265 1 311 133
mobile +265 994 652 345

Mr Gary Brough (2019)   Capacity Development Facilitator, CCAP General Assembly Office,
PO Box 30398, Lilongwe, Malawi
ccapgeneral@africa-online.net

office + 265 79 6064
mobile +265 883 626 500

Malawi: Church of Central Africa Presbyterian, Synods of Livingstonia, Nkhoma and Blantyre
Mozambique: Evangelical Church of Christ
South Sudan: Presbyterian Church of South Sudan
Rev Dr Kenneth R Ross (2019)   Theological Educator: Africa, based at:
Zomba Theological College, PO Box 130, Zomba
KRoss@churchofscotland.org.uk

+265 1 524 419

Zambia: United Church of Zambia
Mr Keith and Mrs Ida Waddell (2016)   Special Needs Support and Health Support, UCZ,
Mwandi Mission, Box 60693, Livingstone, Zambia
keithida2014@gmail.com

http://uczsynod.org
mobile (Keith) +260 977 143 692
mobile (Ida) +260 964 761 039

EUROPE

Budapest

Rev Aaron C. Stevens (2023)

Regional Liaison (Central Europe) & Minister, St Columba's, Budapest
Scottish Mission, Vörösmarty utca 51, 1064 Budapest
AStevens@churchofscotland.org.uk

www.scottishmission.org
+36 (70) 615 5394

Rome

Ms Fiona Kendall (2018)
(Ecumenical appointment: Methodist
Church UK; Global Ministries USA)

Mediterranean Hope, Federation of Protestant Churches in Italy,
Via Firenze 38, 00138 Roma, Italy
FKendall@churchofscotland.org.uk

www.mediterraneanhope.com
00 39 (0)6 4825 120

Vacant

Regional Ecumenical Liaison Officer & Minister, St Andrew's Rome
Reformed Ecumenical Office, Via Firenze 38, 00138 Roma, Italy
St Andrew's Church, Via Venti Settembre 7, 00187 Roma, Italy

www.presbyterianchurchrome.org
+39 06 474 5537
00 39 06 482 7627

MIDDLE EAST: ISRAEL & PALESTINE

Jerusalem

Rev Dr D. Stewart Gillan (2022)

St Andrew's Jerusalem, PO Box 8619, Jerusalem 91086, Israel
SGillan@churchofscotland.org.uk

www.standrewsjerusalem.org
+972 2 673 2401

Tiberias

Rev Muriel C. Pearson (2021)

St Andrew's Galilee, PO Box 104, Tiberias 14100, Israel
MPearson@churchofscotland.org.uk

https://standrewsgalilee.com
+447951 888860

The Church of Scotland also operates:

St Andrew's House Hotel, Jerusalem
Originally 'Hospice' and opened in 1930 beside St Andrew's Church in central Jerusalem.   23 bedrooms, meeting rooms, Fairtrade handcrafts sales.
General Manager: Mrs Lilian Lepejian, PO Box 8619, 1 David Remez Street, Jerusalem 910986, Israel.   www.scotsguesthouse.com   info@scotsguesthouse.com
+972 2 673 2401

The Scots Hotel, Tiberias
Hotel & Wellness Centre, opened in 2004 in the historic compound of the Scottish Hospital.   69 bedrooms, restaurant, wine bar, swimming pool, spa,
historical visitors centre. General Manager: Mr Shaul Hadas, 1 Gdud Barak Street, Tiberias, Israel.   www.scotshotels.com   info@scotshotels.co.il
+972 4 671 0710

Tabeetha School, Jaffa
An English speaking school founded in 1863, where girls and boys of different languages, faiths and cultures are educated together through an English curriculum leading
to IGCSE, GCSE and A level qualifications accepted by universities in Israel and elsewhere. Executive Director: Mrs Mona Ashkar PO Box 8170, 21 Jeffet Street, Jaffa
61081, Israel.   www.tabeethaschool.org   +972 3 682 1581

See also the Presbyteries of International Charges and Jerusalem (Section 5: 13 and 14)

LIST F – PRISON CHAPLAINS

SCOTTISH PRISON SERVICE CHAPLAINCY ADVISER (Church of Scotland)
Rev. Dr Sheena Orr
SPS HQ, One Lochside, 1 Lochside Avenue, Edinburgh EH12 9DJ
sheena.orr@prisons.gov.scot
0131 330 3575; 07922 649160

ADDIEWELL
Rev. Chris Galbraith
Rev. Kay Gilchrist
HM Prison Addiewell, Station Road, Addiewell, West Calder EH55 8QA
chris.galbraith@sodexogov.co.uk
KGilchrist@churchofscotland.org.uk
01506 874500

CASTLE HUNTLY
Rev. Anne E. Stewart
HM Prison Castle Huntly, Longforgan, Dundee DD2 5HL
anne.stewart2@prisons.gov.scot
01382 319388

DUMFRIES
Rev. Neil Campbell
HM Prison Dumfries, Terregles Street, Dumfries DG2 9AX
neil.campbell2@prisons.gov.scot
01387 294214

DUNDEE: BELLA
Rev. Anne E. Stewart
Bella Community Custody Unit, 81 Ann Street, Dundee DD3 7TF
anne.stewart2@prisons.gov.scot
01382 319388

EDINBURGH
Mr Gordon Pennykid DCS
Rev. Keith Graham
Rev. David Swan
Rev. Bob Akroyd (Free Church)
HM Prison Edinburgh, 33 Stenhouse Road, Edinburgh EH11 3LN
gordon.pennykid@prisons.gov.scot
KEGraham@churchofscotland.org.uk
david.swan@prisons.gov.scot
robert.akroyd@prisons.gov.scot
0131 444 3115

GLASGOW: BARLINNIE
Rev. Jill Clancy
Rev. Paul Innes (Assemblies of God)
Rev. Jonathan Keefe
Rev. John Murfin (Elim)
HM Prison Barlinnie, 81 Lee Avenue, Riddrie, Glasgow G33 2QX
jill.clancy@prisons.gov.scot; JClancy@churchofscotland.org.uk
paul.innes@prisons.gov.scot
jonathan.keefe@prisons.gov.scot
john.murfin@prisons.gov.scot
0141 770 2059

GLASGOW LILIAS
Rev. Margaret Shuttleworth
Lilias Community Custody Unit, 41 Shawpark Street, Wyndford, Glasgow G20 9BT
margaret.shuttleworth@prisons.gov.scot

GLENOCHIL
Rev. Graham Bell (Baptist)
Rev. Philip Hacking
HMPrison Glenochil, King o' Muir Road, Tullibody FK10 3AD
graham.bell@prisons.gov.scot
philip.hacking@prisons.gov.scot
01259 767211

GRAMPIAN
Rev. Paul Innes (Assemblies of God)
Mrs Julie Innes (Assemblies of God)
HM Prison and Young Offender Institution, South Road, Peterhead AB42 2YY
paul.innes@prisons.gov.scot
julie.innes@prisons.gov.scot
01779 485744

GREENOCK
Rev. Gary Caldwell
HM Prison Greenock, Old Inverkip Road, Greenock PA16 9AH
gary.caldwell@prisons.gov.scot
01475 787801

INVERNESS
Rev. Dr Hugh Watt
Rev. John Beadle (Methodist)
HM Prison Inverness, Duffy Drive, Inverness IV2 3HN
hugh.watt@prisons.gov.scot
john.beadle@methodist.org.uk
01463 229020

KILMARNOCK
Rev. John Murfin (Elim)
HM Prison Kilmarnock, Mauchline Road, Kilmarnock KA1 5AA
john.murfin@prisons.gov.scot
01563 548928

LOW MOSS
Rev. Martin Forrest
Ms Fiona Morrison
Rev. John Craib (Baptist)
HM Prison Low Moss, 190 Crosshill Road, Bishopbriggs, Glasgow G64 2QB
martin.forrest@prisons.gov.scot
fiona.morrison@prisons.gov.scot
john.craib@prisons.gov.scot
0141 762 9727

PERTH
Rev. Douglas Creighton
Chaplaincy Centre, HM Prison Perth, 3 Edinburgh Road, Perth PH2 7JH
douglas.creighton@prisons.gov.scot
01738 458216

POLMONT
Rev. Hillary Nyika (Baptist)
Rev. Margaret Shuttleworth
Chaplaincy Centre, HM Young Offender Institution Polmont, Brightons, Falkirk FK2 0AB
hillary.nyika@prisons.gov.scot
margaret.shuttleworth@prisons.gov.scot
01324 722241

SHOTTS
Rev. John Caldwell (Apostolic Church UK)
Rev. Murdo MacLean
HM Prison Shotts, Canthill Road, Shotts ML7 4LE
john.caldwell@prisons.gov.scot
murdo.maclean@prisons.gov.scot
01501 824071

STIRLING
Rev. Margaret Shuttleworth
Mrs Deirdre Yellowlees
HM Prison and Young Offender Institution, Cornton Road, Stirling FK9 5NU
margaret.shuttleworth@prisons.gov.scot
deirdre.yellowlees@prisons.gov.scot
01786 835300

LIST G – UNIVERSITY CHAPLAINS

ABERDEEN
Rev. Marylee Anderson MA BD
m.anderson@abdn.ac.uk
01224 272137

ABERTAY, DUNDEE
Vacant

CAMBRIDGE
Rev. Nigel Uden (U.R.C. and C. of S.)
nigel.uden@downingplaceurc.org
01223 314586

DUNDEE
Rev. Fiona C. Douglas MBE MA BD PhD
Rev. Gordon A. Campbell MA BD (Honorary)
f.c.douglas@dundee.ac.uk
g.a.campbell@dundee.ac.uk
01382 384156
01382 384045

EDINBURGH
Rev. Harriet A. Harris MBE BA DPhil — chaplain@ed.ac.uk — 0131 650 2595; 07896 244792
Rev. Geoffrey Baines (Associate Chaplain) — g.baines@ed.ac.uk — 0131 650 9502; 07940 348121
Rev. Dr Urzula Glienecke (Associate Chaplain) — urzula.glienecke@ed.ac.uk

EDINBURGH NAPIER (Honorary Chaplains)
— chaplaincy@napier.ac.uk
Rev. Karen K. Campbell BD MTh DMin — KKCampbell@churchofscotland.org.uk — 0131 447 4359
Rev. Michael J. Mair MStJ BD MTh — MMair@churchofscotland.org.uk — 0131 334 1730

GLASGOW
Rev. Carolyn Kelly PhD — chaplain@glasgow.ac.uk — 0141 330 4160
Rev. Roger D. Sturrock BD MD FCRP (Honorary) — RSturrock@churchofscotland.org.uk — 0141 339 0454
Rev. Richard Baxter MA BD (Honorary) — RBaxter@churchofscotland.org.uk — 07958 541418

GLASGOW CALEDONIAN
Rev. Alastair S. Duncan MA BD — ADuncan@churchofscotland.org.uk — 07968 852083

HERIOT-WATT, EDINBURGH
Rev. Jane M. Howitt MA BD — J.M.Howitt@hw.ac.uk — 0131 451 4508

OXFORD
Vacant

ROBERT GORDON, ABERDEEN
Rev. Canon Isaac. M. Poobalan BD MTh DMin — chaplaincy@rgu.ac.uk — 01224 640119

ST ANDREWS
Rev. Donald G. MacEwan MA BD PhD — dgm21@st-andrews.ac.uk — 01334 462865
Rev. Samantha J. Ferguson MTheol (Assistant) — sjf6@st-andrews.ac.uk — 01334 461766

STIRLING
Rev. Lesley Stanley MA PhD FBTS — lesley.stanley@stir.ac.uk — 01786 467164

STRATHCLYDE, GLASGOW
Meg Masson — meg.masson@strath.ac.uk — 0141 548 2212
Rev. Tara P. Granados BA MDiv — TGranados@churchofscotland.org.uk — 07380 830030

LIST H – REPRESENTATIVES ON COUNCIL EDUCATION COMMITTEES

Aberdeen City	Ms Hilda Smith	smith09@hotmail.com	01224 311309
Aberdeenshire	Rev. Carl J. Irvine	CIrvine@churchofscotland.org.uk	01467 629163
Angus	Vacant		
Argyll and Bute	Rev. Alexander J. MacPherson	SMacPherson@churchofscotland.org.uk	01369 707969
City of Edinburgh	Mrs Fiona E. Beveridge	fbeveridge1@gmail.com	0131 661 8831
Clackmannanshire	Rev. Sang Y. Cha	SCha@churchofscotland.org.uk	01259 213872
Comhairle nan Eilean Siar	Rev. Hugh M. Stewart	berneralwuig@btinternet.com	01851 672388
Dumfries and Galloway	Mr Robert McQuistan	mcquistan@mcquistan.plus.com	01671 820327
Dundee City	Ms Margaret McVean	margaret.mcvean@btinternet.com	01382 860894
East Ayrshire	Dr David F. Lewis	iadl@btinternet.com	01292 570663
East Dunbartonshire	Mrs Barbara Jarvie	jarviebj@gmail.com	01360 319729
East Lothian	Mr Ray Lesso	ray.lesso@gmail.com	07884 448224
East Renfrewshire	Mrs Fiona M. Gilchrist	fionagilchrist0@gmail.com	0141 391 9551
Falkirk	Mrs Agnes Mullen	mullenagnescc@gmail.com	07447 393343
Fife	Vacant		
Glasgow City	Mr James Hamilton DCS	James.Hamilton@churchofscotland.org.uk	0141 558 3195; 07584 137314
Highland	Mr William Skene	bill.skene@lochaber.presbytery.org.uk	01397 712594
Inverclyde	Rev. David W.G. Burt	dwgburt@btinternet.com	07971 431185
Midlothian	Mrs Elizabeth Morton	elizabethmorton180@gmail.com	0131 663 8916
Moray	Ms. Sheila A. Brumby	sheilabrumby50@btinternet.com	01340 831588
North Ayrshire	Mr Andrew J. Bruce	andrew_bruce2@sky.com	07484 150461
North Lanarkshire	Margaret S. Clarkson	clarkson492@btinternet.com	01698 261723
Orkney Islands	Rev. G. Fraser H. Macnaughton	FMacnaughton@churchofscotland.org.uk	01856 873312
Perth and Kinross	Mrs Margaret B. Conroy	margaretbconroy@hotmail.com	07817 627725
Renfrewshire	Miss Mary Jane Bird	mjbird55@gmail.com	
Scottish Borders	Rev. Dr Adam J.J. Hood	AHood@churchofscotland.org.uk	01289 332787
Shetland Islands	Ms K. Ellen Griffiths Weir	EWeir@churchofscotland.org.uk	
South Ayrshire	Rev. David R. Gemmell	DGemmell@churchofscotland.org.uk	01292 864140
South Lanarkshire	Ms Gillian D. Coulter	gillcoulter55@yahoo.com	01899 810339
Stirling	Mr Colin O'Brien	cobrien20@btinternet.com	01360 660616
West Dunbartonshire	Vacant		
West Lothian	Mrs Lynne McEwen	lynnemcewen@hotmail.co.uk	07933 352935

LIST I – MINISTERS ORDAINED FOR SIXTY YEARS AND UPWARDS

Year	Date	Name	Charge
1948	6 October	George Davidson Wilkie OBE BL	(Kirkcaldy: Viewforth)
1949	14 February	Hamish Norman Mackenzie McIntosh MA	(Fintry)
1951	6 November	Alexander Gordon McGillivray MA BD STM	(Edinburgh: Presbytery Clerk)
1953	21 October	Donald Maciver Ross MA	(Industrial Mission Organiser)
	6 December	Mark Wilson	(Church of North India)
1954	17 January	Arthur William Alexander Main MA BD	(Kirkintilloch: St David's Memorial)
	6 June	Ian Murray Pollock Davidson MBE MA BD	(Stirling: Allan Park South with Stirling: Church of the Holy Rude)
1955	10 August	Michael Muir Dickie BSc	(Ayr: Castlehill)
	14 November	David Wishart Torrance MA BD	(Earlston)
	14 December	William Gault Shannon MA BD	(Pitlochry)
1957	11 January	William Macleod	(Uig)
	8 April	Thomas Stewart McGregor MBE MA BD	(Chaplain: Edinburgh Royal Infirmary)
	15 July	Alexander Brown Cairns MA	(Turin)
	3 November	George Gordon Cameron MA BD STM	(Edinburgh: Juniper Green)
	7 November	Robert Milne Tuton MA	(Glasgow: Shettleston Old)
	24 November	Archibald Freeland Chisholm MA	(Braes of Rannoch with Foss and Rannoch)
	24 November	Francis George Bernard Liddiard MA	(Brechin: Gardner Memorial and East)
		Peter Owen Price CBE KHC BA FPhS	(Blantyre: Old)
1958	11 June	William Moncur McKenzie DA	(Dumfries: Troqueer)
	13 July	Donald William Fraser MA	(Monifieth)
	23 October	David Sage Millen Hamilton MA BD STM	(Lecturer, Practical Theology, University of Glasgow)
	14 December	Francis Campbell Tollick BSc DipEd	(Port Glasgow: St Martin's)
	23 December	John McLeod MA	(Resolis and Urquhart)
1959	16 March	Robert James Stewart MA BD STM	(Orwell with Portmoak)
	12 April	Ian Morrison Strachan MA BD	(Ashkirk with Selkirk)
	31 May	John Russell MA	(Tillicoultry)
	5 July	James Lindsay Wilkie MA BD	(Executive Secretary, Board of World Mission)
	28 October	Andrew Stark Taylor BTh FPhS	(Greenock: The Union)
1960	6 January	Alasdair James Morton MA BD DipEd FEIS	(Bowden with Newtown)
	13 January	Ralph Colley Philip Smith MA STM	(Director, Audio-Visual Productions)
	5 July	Derek Haley BD DPS	(Chaplain: Gartnavel Royal Hospital, Glasgow)
	15 July	Iain McDougall Roy MA BD	(Stevenston: Livingstone)
	13 September	James Charles Stewart MA BD STM	(Aberdeen: Kirk of St Nicholas)
	14 September	George Alan Simpson Stirling MA	(Leochel Cushnie and Lynturk with Tough)
	21 September	James Alexander Simpson BSc BD STM DD	(Interim Minister, Brechin Cathedral)
	17 November	Alistair Andrew Benvie Davidson MA BD	(Grange with Rothiemay)
1961	8 April	Douglas Niven Alexander MA BD	(Bishopton)
	26 April	Archibald Iain Campbell MA DipEd	(Busby)
	26 April	John Pattison Cubie MA BD	(Caldwell)
	21 May	James Harkness KVCO CB OBE KHC MA DD	(Chaplain General, Army)
	June	Sidney Hall Coleman BA BD MTh	(Glasgow: Merrylea)
	24 October	James Barbour Lawson MA BD	(South Uist)

		Name	Charge
	17 November	Alexander Cunningham MA BD	(Glasgow: Presbytery Clerk)
1962	11 January	Robin Graeme Brown BA BD	(Birsay with Rousay)
	4 March	John Mackenzie Kellet MA	(Edinburgh: Leith South)
	6 April	Ian Andrew Moir MA BD	(Adviser for Urban Priority Areas)
	12 June	Alastair Fleming McCormick	(Creich with Rosehall)
	26 August	David Ferguson Huie MA BD	(Rome: St Andrew's)
	25 September	Ronald Stanton Blakey MA BD MTh	(Assembly Council)
		John Diamond Rennie MA	(Broughton, Glenholm and Kilbucho with Skirling with Stobo and Drumelzier with Tweedsmuir)
	10 October	John Spencer MA BD	(Dumfries: Lincluden with Holywood)
	11 November	Donald Murray Stephen TD MA BD ThM	(Edinburgh: Marchmont St Giles')
	14 December	George Angus Chalmers MA BD MLitt	(Catrine with Sorn)
	December	Hugh Rutherford Wylie MA DD FCIBS	(Hamilton: Old)
1963	11 January	William Johnstone MA BD DLitt	(Professor of Hebrew and Semitic Languages, University of Aberdeen)
	17 April	Kenneth Charles Lawson MA BD	(Director, Ecumenical Spirituality Programme, Scottish Churches Open College)
	13 September	Stephen Anton Pacitti MA	(Black Mount with Culter with Libberton and Quothquan)
	19 September	Angus Halley Haddow BSc	(Methlick)
	25 October	John Stevenson MA BD PhD HonFEIS	(General Secretary, Department of Education)
	27 October	Alan Main TD MA BD STM PhD DD	(Professor of Practical Theology, University of Aberdeen)
	4 December	James Ainslie McIntyre MA BD	(Lecturer, New Testament, University of Glasgow)
		Gordon Calderwood MacPherson MA BD MTh	(Associate, Kilmarnock: Henderson)

LIST J – DECEASED MINISTERS AND DEACONS

The following ministers and deacons have died since the list in the previous volume of the Year Book was compiled.

NAME	ORD	RET	CHARGE
2018 *(notified late 2022)*			
Wallace, Donald Stewart QHC	1950	1990	(Chaplain, Royal Caledonian Schools)
2022			
Ballentine, Thomas Crawford MPhil BD	1981	1983	(Cummertrees with Mouswald with Ruthwell)
Birss, Alan David DL OStJ MA BD	1979	2020	(Paisley: Abbey)
Fawkes, George Miller Allan BSc BA JP	1979	2000	(Lonmay with Rathen: West)
Gaddes, Donald Rutherford	1961	1994	(Kelso: North and Ednam)
Logan, Robert James Victor MA BD	1962	2001	(Abdie and Dunbog with Newburgh)
Martin, James Davidson MA BD MA PhD	1962	n/a	(Senior Lecturer, Hebrew and Old Testament, University of St Andrews)
McLachlan, Ian Kenneth MA BD	1999	2019	(Barr with Dailly with Girvan: South)

Name			Location
Morrison, Angus Wilson MA BD	1959	1999	(Kildalton and Oa)
Osbeck, John Robert BD	1979	2011	(Aberdeen: St John's Church for Deaf People)
Paterson, John Hay BD	1977	2000	(Kirkintilloch: St David's Memorial Park)
Poole, Ann McColl DipEd ACE LTh	1983	2003	(Dyke with Edinkillie)
Ramsay, William Grant	1967	1999	(Glasgow: Springburn)
Riggans, Walter BD MA PhD	1971	1980	(Church of Scotland Centre, Tiberias, Israel)
Rogerson, Stuart Douglas BSc BD	1980	2001	(Strathaven: West)
Scott, George Grant	1965	1973	(Dundee: Camperdown)
Scott, Thomas Tait	1968	1989	(Kilmarnock: St Marnock's)
Smith, John Murdo BEM	1956	1992	(Lochmaddy and Trumisgarry)
Stewart, Diane Elizabeth BD CertMin	1988	2006	(Milton of Campsie)
Taylor, Ian BSc BEd MA LTh	1983	1997	(Abdie and Dunbog with Newburgh)
Westmarland, Colin Andrew MBE BD	1971	2002	(Malta: St Andrew's Scots Church)
Williams, Andrew Denis MA	1965	1977	(Dundee: St James')
Wilson, James Hay LTh	1970	1996	(Cleland)

2023

Name			Location
Alexander, Eric John MA BD	1958	1997	(Glasgow: St George's Tron)
Almond, David M. BD	1996	2016	(Kirkmahoe)
Bain, Hugh MA	1965	1978	(Dunning)
Beveridge, Sydney Edwin Peebles BA	1959	2004	(Brydekirk with Hoddom)
Birse, George Stewart CA BD BSc	1980	2013	(Ayr: Newton Wallacetown)
Burns, Marjory DCS	1997	2012	(Deacon, Bellshill: Macdonald Memorial with Bellshill: Orbiston)
Campbell, Donald BD	1998	2016	(Houston and Killellan)
Combe, Neil Robert BSc MSc BD	1984	2015	(Hawick: St Mary's and Old with Hawick: Teviot and Roberton)
Currie, Ian Samuel MBE BD	1975	2010	(United Church of Bute)
Drysdale, James Potter Reid	1967	1999	(Brechin: Gardner Memorial)
Durno, Richard C. DipSW CQSW PGCertCouns NVQ BSL (Level 4)	1989	1998	(Glasgow: John Ross Memorial Church for Deaf People and Ayrshire Mission to the Deaf)
Geddes, Alexander John MA BD	1960	1998	(Stewarton: St Columba's)
Goskirk, John Leslie LTh	1968	2010	(Lairg with Rogart)
Gregory, James Charles LTh	1968	1992	(Blantyre: St Andrew's)
MacLennan, Alasdair John BD DipCE	1979	2001	(Resolis and Urquhart)
McLean, John MA BD	1967	2003	(Bathgate: Boghall)
Niven, William Wallace LTh	1982	1995	(Alness)
Noble, George Strachan	1972	2000	(Carfin with Newarthill)
Owen, Catherine Weir MTh	1984	1987	(Wishaw: Chalmers)
Phenix, Douglas William BSc BD STM	1967	1980	(Cumbernauld: Abronhill)
Raeburn, Graham Bruce MTh	2004		(Newmains: Bonkle with Newmains: Coltness Memorial
Reid, David MSc LTh FSAScot	1962	1992	(Largoward with St Monans)
Scott, James Finlay	1957	1997	(Dyce)
Smith, Catherine DCS	1964	2003	(Deacon, Presbytery Assistant, Presbytery of Shetland)
Smith, Hamish Gault	1965	1993	(Auchterless with Rothienorman)
Thomson, William BD	2001	2023	(Stenhouse and Carron)
Watts, Anthony Edward BD	1999	2013	(Glenmuick (Ballater))

SECTION 7

Legal Names and Scottish Charity Numbers: Presbyteries and Congregations

Those presbyteries, all congregations in Scotland, and those congregations furth of Scotland which are registered with OSCR, the Office of the Scottish Charity Regulator

For a complete list of legal names see:

www.churchofscotland.org.uk > Resources > Yearbook > Section 7

Further information

All documents, as defined in the Charities References in Documents (Scotland) Regulations 2007, must specify the Charity Number, Legal Name of the congregation, any other name by which the congregation is commonly known and the fact that it is a Charity. For more information, please refer to the Law Department circular on the Regulations on the Church of Scotland website.

www.churchofscotland.org.uk > Resources > Law Department Circulars > Charity Law

SECTION 8

Church Buildings: Ordnance Survey National Grid References

Please go to: www.churchofscotland.org.uk > Resources > Yearbook > Section 8

SECTION 9

Parish and Congregational Changes

The parish structure of the Church of Scotland is constantly being reshaped as the result of unions, linkages and the dissolutions.

Section 9A, 'Parishes and Congregations: names no longer in use', records one of the inevitable consequences of these changes, the disappearance of the names of many former parishes and congregations. There are, however, occasions when for legal and other reasons it is important to be able to identify the present-day successors of those parishes and congregations whose names are no longer in use and which can therefore no longer be easily traced. A list of all such parishes and congregations, with full explanatory notes, may be found at:

www.churchofscotland.org.uk/Resources/Yearbook > Section 9A

Section 9B, 'Recent Readjustment and other Congregational Changes', below, lists all instances of union, linkage and dissolution, since the compilation of the 2022–23 Year Book.

1. Edinburgh and West Lothian

   Blackridge linked with **Harthill: St Andrew's**: linkage severed

   Edinburgh: Bristo Memorial Craigmillar and **Edinburgh: Richmond Craigmillar** united as **Edinburgh: Richmond Craigmillar**

   Edinburgh: Cramond and **Edinburgh: Old Kirk and Muirhouse** united as **Edinburgh: Northwest Kirk: Cramond and Old Kirk and Muirhouse**

   Edinburgh: Dalmeny linked with **Edinburgh: Queensferry** united as **Edinburgh: Dalmeny and Queensferry**

   Edinburgh: Meadowbank and **Edinburgh: Willowbrae** united as **Edinburgh: Meadowbank and Willowbrae**

2. Lothian and Borders

   Aberlady and **Gullane** united as **Aberlady and Gullane**

Bilston linked with **Roslin**: linkage severed

Bilston and **Loanhead** united as **Loanhead and Bilston**

Broughton, Glenholm and Kilbucho linked with **Carlops** linked with **Kirkurd and Newlands** linked with **Skirling** linked with **Tweedsmuir** linked with **West Linton: St Andrew's**: linkage severed

Broughton, Glenholm and Kilbucho, **Skirling** and **Tweedsmuir** united as **Upper Tweeddale**

Carlops linked with **Kirkurd and Newlands** linked with **Upper Tweeddale** linked with **West Linton: St Andrew's**

Dalkeith: St John's and King's Park and **Newton** united as **Dalkeith: St John's and Newton**

5. Glasgow

Cumbernauld: Kildrum and **Cumbernauld: St Mungo's** united as **Cumbernauld: Kildrum and St Mungo's**

Glasgow: Balshagray Victoria Park and **Glasgow: Partick South** united as **Glasgow: Partick Victoria Park**

Glasgow: Blawarthill linked with **Glasgow: St Columba**

Glasgow: Carntyne and **Glasgow: Cranhill** united as **Glasgow: Carntyne and Cranhill**

Glasgow: John Ross Memorial Church for Deaf People and **Glasgow: Queen's Park Govanhill** united as **Glasgow: Queen's Park Govanhill** *(incorporating John Ross Memorial Deaf Local Mission Church)*

Glasgow: Maryhill and **Glasgow: Ruchill Kelvinside** united as **Glasgow: Maryhill Ruchill**

7. Fife

East Neuk Trinity linked with **St Monans**: linkage severed

Leuchars: St Athernase and **Tayport** united as **Leuchars: St Athernase and Tayport**

8. Perth

Auchterhouse linked with **Monikie and Newbigging and Murroes and Tealing**: linkage severed

Brechin: Gardner Memorial linked with **Farnell** united as **Brechin and Farnell**

Clackmannan linked with **Sauchie and Coalsnaughton**

Dun and Hillside, **Montrose: Old and St Andrew's** and **Montrose: South and Ferryden** united as **Montrose: Trinity**

Dundee: Meadowside St Paul's and **Dundee: St Andrew's** united as **Dundee: Kingsgait**

Dundee: Stobswell and **Dundee: Trinity** united as **Dundee: Stobswell Trinity**

Edzell Lethnot Glenesk linked with **Fern Careston Menmuir** united as **Edzell**

Kilspindie and Rait dissolved

Monifieth and **Monikie and Newbigging and Murroes and Tealing** united as **Monifieth South Angus**

9. North East and Northern Isles

Aberdeen: Ferryhill, Aberdeen: St Mark's and **Aberdeen: South Holburn** united as **Aberdeen: Devana**

Aberdeen: High Hilton and **Aberdeen: Woodside** united as **Aberdeen: Hillside**

Aberdeen: Holburn West, Aberdeen: Midstocket, Aberdeen: Queen's Cross and **Aberdeen: Rubislaw** united as **Aberdeen: Fountainhall**

Auchaber United and **Auchterless** united as **Auchterless and Auchaber**

Cluny linked with **Monymusk**: linkage severed

Blairdaff and Chapel of Garioch, Cluny, Echt and Midmar, Kemnay, Kintore, and **Monymusk** united as **Bennachie**

Cushnie and Tough, Howe Trinity, Noth, and **Upper Donside** united as **West Gordon (Alford, Strathdon, Rhynie)**

Dyce linked with **New Machar**

Evie and Rendell linked with **Firth** linked with **Rousay**: linkage with **Rousay** severed

Kirkwall: St Magnus Cathedral linked with **Rousay**

Kingswells and **Skene** united as **Kingshill**

Mearns Coastal renamed **St Cyrus**

10.1 Argyll

Ardrishaig linked with South Knapdale: linkage severed

Glassary, Kilmartin and Ford linked with North Knapdale: linkage severed

Ardrishaig, Glassary, Kilmartin and Ford, Lochgilphead, North Knapdale and **South Knapdale** united as **Dalriada Mid Argyll**

Campbeltown: Highland linked with **Saddell and Carradale** linked with **Southend**: linkage severed

Campbeltown: Highland and **Campbeltown: Lowland** united as **Campbeltown**

Campbeltown linked with **Saddell and Carradale** linked with **Southend**

Gigha and Cara linked with **Kilcalmonell** linked with **Killean and Kilchenzie**: linkage severed

Skipness linked with **Tarbert, Loch Fyne and Kilberry**: linkage severed

Gigha and Cara, Kilcalmonell, Killean and Kilchenzie and **Skipness** united as **Mid Kintyre and Gigha**

Mid Kintyre and Gigha linked with **Tarbert, Loch Fyne and Kilberry**

Glenorchy and Innishael and **Strathfillan** united as **Glenorchy and Strathfillan**

Kilbrandon and Kilchattan linked with **Kilninver and Kilmelford**: linkage severed

Craignish, **Kilbrandon and Kilchattan** and **Kilninver and Kilmelford** united as **Netherlorn**

Kilfinan, Kilmodan and Colintraive, and **Kyles** united as **West Cowal**

10.2 Abernethy

Cromdale and Advie linked with **Dulnain Bridge** linked with **Grantown-on-Spey**: linkage severed

Dulnain Bridge and **Grantown-on-Spey** united as **Grantown-on-Spey and Dulnain Bridge**

Cromdale and Advie linked with **Grantown-on-Spey and Dulnain Bridge**

10.3 Inverness

Inverness: East and **Inverness: Inshes** united as **Inverness : Inshes East**

10.4 Lochaber

Acharacle and **Ardnamurchan** united as **Acharacle and Ardnamurchan**

Ardgour and Kingairloch, **Morvern** and **Strontian** united as **Ardgour, Morvern and Strontian**

Acharacle and Ardnamurchan linked with **Ardgour, Morvern and Strontian**

Kinlochleven linked with **Nether Lochaber**: linkage severed

Duror, Glencoe: St Munda's, and **Nether Lochaber** united as **South Lochaber**

Kinlochleven linked with **South Lochaber**

12.   England – renamed England and the Channel Islands

Corby: St Andrew's and **Corby: St Ninian's** united as **Corby**

13.   International Charges

Gibraltar: St Andrew's dissolved

Presbytery of Lothian, Presbytery of Melrose and Peebles, Presbytery of Duns and **Presbytery of Jedburgh** united as **Presbytery of Lothian and Borders** *(see Note A. below)*

Presbytery of Stirling, Presbytery of Dunkeld and Meigle, Presbytery of Perth, Presbytery of Dundee and **Presbytery of Angus** united as **Presbytery of Perth** *(see Note B. below)*

Presbytery of Aberdeen and Shetland, Presbytery of Kincardine and Deeside, Presbytery of Gordon, Presbytery of Buchan, Presbytery of Moray and **Presbytery of Orkney** united as **Presbytery of the North East and the Northern Isles** *(see Note C. below)*

Historical Note

A. Presbytery of Lothian and Borders

The presbyteries created in 1581 (or shortly thereafter) included the Presbyteries of Peebles, Dalkeith, Haddington, Dunbar, Duns, Chirnside, Jedburgh, and Selkirk (renamed Melrose 1613–1640).

> In 1609 the Presbytery of Kelso was disjoined from Duns and Jedburgh.
> In 1613 the Presbytery of Earlston was disjoined from Selkirk (and renamed Lauder between 1768–1876).

Following the 1929 union:

> Haddington and Dunbar were united as the Presbytery of Haddington & Dunbar;
> Duns and Chirnside were united as the **Presbytery of Duns**;
> Jedburgh was divided, part uniting with Kelso to form the Presbytery of Jedburgh & Kelso and part uniting with Langholm to form the Presbytery of Hawick; and
> Earlston and Selkirk were united as the Presbytery of Melrose.

In 1972 Jedburgh & Kelso and Hawick were united as the **Presbytery of Jedburgh**.
In 1976:

> Dalkeith and Haddington & Dunbar were united as the **Presbytery of Lothian**; and
> Peebles and Melrose were united as the **Presbytery of Melrose and Peebles**.

B. (new) Presbytery of Perth

The 1581 presbyteries included the Presbyteries of Dunkeld, Perth, Auchterarder, Stirling, Dunblane, Meigle, **Dundee**, Brechin, Arbroath, and Fordoun.

> In 1611 the Presbytery of Forfar was disjoined from Meigle, Dundee, Brechin and Arbroath.
> In 1836 the Presbytery of Weem was disjoined from Dunkeld.

Following the 1929 union:

> Dunkeld and Weem were united as the Presbytery of Dunkeld;
> Stirling and Dunblane were united as the Presbytery of Stirling & Dunblane; and
> Brechin and Fordoun were united as the Presbytery of Brechin & Fordoun.

In 1961 Forfar, Arbroath, and Brechin & Fordoun were united as the Presbytery of Angus & Mearns.
In 1976:

> Dunkeld and Meigle were united as the **Presbytery of Dunkeld & Meigle**;
> Perth and Auchterarder were united as the **Presbytery of Perth**; and
> Angus & Mearns was renamed the **Presbytery of Angus**, with part disjoined to the Presbytery of Kincardine and Deeside.

In 1977 Stirling and Dunblane was renamed the **Presbytery of Stirling**.

C. Presbytery of the North East and the Northern Isles

The 1581 presbyteries included the Presbyteries of Aberdeen, Kincardine O'Neil, Alford, Garioch, Crimond, Banff (later Cullen), Strathbogie, Inveraven, Elgin, Forres, Orkney (later Kirkwall), and Shetland (subsequently Scalloway, and later Lerwick).

> In 1597 the Presbytery of Ellon was disjoined from Aberdeen.
> In 1621 Crimond was renamed the Presbytery of Deer.
> In 1632 the Presbytery of Aberlour was disjoined from Inveraven.
> By 1638 the Presbytery of Turriff was disjoined from Banff.
> In 1638 Cullen was renamed the Presbytery of Fordyce.

In 1707 the Presbytery of North Isles was disjoined from Kirkwall.

In 1725 the Presbytery of Cairston was disjoined from Kirkwall.

In 1830 the Presbytery of Burravoe was disjoined from Lerwick.

In 1848 the Presbytery of Olnafirth was disjoined from Lerwick and Burravoe.

Following the 1929 union:

Aberdeen and Ellon were united as the Presbytery of Aberdeen;

Aberlour, Elgin, and Forres were united as the Presbytery of Elgin;

Cairston, Kirkwall, and North Isles were united as the **Presbytery of Orkney**; and

Burravoe, Lerwick, and Olnafirth were united as the Presbytery of Shetland.

In 1961 Fordyce and Strathbogie were united as the Presbytery of Strathbogie & Fordyce.

In 1962 Alford and Deeside were united as the Presbytery of Deeside & Alford.

In 1976:

Deer and Turriff were united as the **Presbytery of Buchan**;

Elgin and Strathbogie & Fordyce were united as the **Presbytery of Moray**; and

Deeside & Alford was renamed the **Presbytery of Kincardine & Deeside**, with part added from Angus & Mearns.

Garioch was renamed the **Presbytery of Gordon**.

In 2020 Aberdeen and Shetland were united as the **Presbytery of Aberdeen & Shetland**.

In 2021 part of Moray was transferred to Inverness.

SECTION 10

Congregational
Statistics
2022

Comparative Statistics: 1982–2022

	2022	2012	2002	1992	1982
Communicants	270,300	415,705	571,698	752,719	918,991
Elders	22,500	34,138	42,992	46,238	47,697

NOTES ON CONGREGATIONAL STATISTICS

Com   Number of communicants at 31 December 2022.

Eld   Number of elders at 31 December 2022.

G   Membership of the Guild including Young Woman's Groups and others as recorded on the 2022 annual return submitted to the Guild Office.

In22   Ordinary General Income for 2022. Ordinary General Income consists of members' offerings, contributions from congregational organisations, regular fund-raising events, income from investments, deposits and so on. This figure does not include extraordinary or special income, or income from special collections and fund-raising for other charities.

M&M   Final amount allocated to congregations to contribute for Ministries and Mission after allowing for Presbytery-approved amendments up to 31 December 2022, but before deducting stipend endowments and normal allowances given for locum purposes in a vacancy or guardianship.

–18   This figure shows 'the number of children and young people aged 17 years and under who are involved in the life of the congregation'.

The statistics for the congregations now in the united Presbyteries of Lothian and Borders, Perth, and the North East and Northern Isles are shown under the new presbyteries.

Some congregations were united or dissolved after 31 December 2022. Their statistics are shown as the entities they were at that date, but their names are shown in italics – details of the readjustment are given in Section 9B.

Figures may also not be available for congregations which failed to submit the appropriate schedule. Where the figure for the number of elders is missing, then in nearly every case the number of communicants relates to the previous year.

Congregation	Com	Eld	G	In22	M&M	–18
1. Edinburgh and West Lothian						
Abercorn	63	7	-	15,371	9,253	-
Pardovan, Kingscavil and Winchburgh	203	17	-	54,060	35,366	-
Armadale	417	35	18	-	41,549	85
Avonbridge	40	-	-	5,996	5,324	-
Torphichen	104	14	-	35,956	17,090	1
Bathgate: Boghall	182	20	19	90,255	54,179	59
Bathgate: High	370	28	18	81,376	55,699	47
Bathgate: St John's	303	12	17	-	35,328	39
Blackburn and Seafield	204	19	-	96,812	38,808	46
Blackridge	56	10	-	21,522	12,805	-
Breich Valley	98	10	19	30,176	22,416	5
Broxburn	261	18	-	61,511	43,889	3
Edinburgh: Balerno	475	43	24	136,048	74,297	-
Edinburgh: Barclay Viewforth	268	29	-	172,938	105,468	33
Edinburgh: Blackhall St Columba's	573	48	-	201,560	101,355	6
Edinburgh: Broughton St Mary's	148	22	-	109,647	49,789	16
Edinburgh: Canongate	319	21	-	116,275	77,374	2
Edinburgh: Carrick Knowe	304	41	44	79,745	36,939	200
Edinburgh: Colinton	730	40	-	278,792	104,982	12
Edinburgh: Corstorphine Craigsbank	325	30	-	114,920	55,707	58
Edinburgh: Corstorphine Old	345	24	-	89,223	61,969	18
Edinburgh: Corstorphine St Anne's	339	44	57	121,569	62,722	48
Edinburgh: Corstorphine St Ninian's	510	66	29	177,759	89,402	-
Edinburgh: Craiglockhart	314	36	21	134,306	76,857	55
Edinburgh: Craigmillar Park	133	8	19	61,931	33,897	1
Edinburgh: Reid Memorial	167	9	-	106,109	58,754	-
Edinburgh: Cramond	822	59	-	275,444	164,342	12
Edinburgh: Currie	392	24	47	131,667	75,437	19
Edinburgh: Dalmeny	93	6	-	60,552	20,447	14
Edinburgh: Queensferry	450	42	42	129,630	65,726	58
Edinburgh: Davidson's Mains	380	52	-	236,565	110,548	37
Edinburgh: Drylaw	71	10	-	44,512	12,812	6
Edinburgh: Duddingston	361	36	-	-	66,727	129
Edinburgh: Fairmilehead	464	44	38	153,952	77,260	57
Edinburgh: Gorgie Dalry Stenhouse	148	15	-	90,810	59,737	59
Edinburgh: Gracemount	20	-	-	23,030	9,231	-
Edinburgh: Liberton	642	50	40	270,752	110,299	40
Edinburgh: Granton	146	23	-	61,224	25,644	3
Edinburgh: Greenbank	608	68	27	271,923	122,925	242
Edinburgh: Greenside	78	17	-	36,693	29,023	2
Edinburgh: Greyfriars Kirk	292	32	-	156,945	86,639	10
Edinburgh: High (St Giles')	427	33	-	-	157,571	-
Edinburgh: Holy Trinity	219	27	-	127,153	78,199	55
Edinburgh: Inverleith St Serf's	274	26	23	120,004	59,215	184
Edinburgh: Juniper Green	253	20	-	105,585	55,815	10
Edinburgh: Kirkliston	206	24	45	99,191	55,480	48
Edinburgh: Leith North	121	16	-	58,420	39,939	4
Edinburgh: Leith St Andrew's	127	18	-	77,889	43,037	-
Edinburgh: Leith South	229	39	-	137,271	68,576	119

Congregation	Com	Eld	G	In22	M&M	–18
Edinburgh: Liberton Northfield	113	7	-	42,283	25,040	240
Edinburgh: Marchmont St Giles'	194	20	-	140,696	74,101	74
Edinburgh: Mayfield Salisbury	412	50	-	273,369	124,933	33
Edinburgh: Meadowbank	22	3	-	21,674	26,799	-
Edinburgh: Morningside	359	54	-	205,822	102,843	24
Edinburgh: Morningside United	101	-	-	89,625	1,015	-
Edinburgh: Murrayfield	419	20	-	185,202	81,104	25
Edinburgh: Newhaven	135	14	-	107,130	43,237	110
Edinburgh: Old Kirk and Muirhouse	60	16	-	31,923	21,599	97
Edinburgh: Palmerston Place	323	28	-	188,853	95,011	60
Edinburgh: Pilrig St Paul's	176	12	13	64,956	32,423	-
Edinburgh: Polwarth	126	18	-	60,560	51,406	3
Edinburgh: Portobello and Joppa	727	67	51	202,412	129,213	159
Edinburgh: Priestfield	98	13	-	92,437	47,784	43
Edinburgh: Ratho	169	10	-	39,387	32,229	11
Edinburgh: Richmond Craigmillar	78	7	-	-	32,340	16
Edinburgh: St Andrew's and St George's West	254	39	-	228,993	142,201	9
Edinburgh: St Andrew's Clermiston	130	7	-	-	31,881	5
Edinburgh: St Catherine's Argyle	81	6	-	75,383	32,851	20
Edinburgh: St Cuthbert's	229	25	-	-	70,586	-
Edinburgh: St David's Broomhouse	111	15	-	29,519	18,145	14
Edinburgh: St John's Colinton Mains	169	19	-	62,778	34,098	88
Edinburgh: St Margaret's	171	25	22	-	36,187	-
Edinburgh: St Martin's	75	12	-	-	12,361	10
Edinburgh: St Michael's	283	24	30	78,791	42,135	8
Edinburgh: St Nicholas' Sighthill	289	16	-	-	21,622	12
Edinburgh: St Stephen's Comely Bank	107	10	-	105,849	56,067	16
Edinburgh: Slateford Longstone	150	8	22	50,955	20,549	27
Edinburgh: Stockbridge	175	10	-	130,849	52,964	18
Edinburgh: Tron Kirk (Gilmerton and Moredun)	75	10	-	45,598	15,522	14
Edinburgh: Wardie	423	36	48	126,398	76,536	115
Edinburgh: Willowbrae	81	12	-	44,338	31,580	1
Fauldhouse: St Andrew's	159	7	-	40,929	25,880	-
Harthill: St Andrew's	145	9	21	53,124	30,903	6
Kirknewton and East Calder	273	33	26	-	55,825	62
Kirk of Calder	407	29	21	85,764	48,596	-
Linlithgow: St Michael's	1,190	85	45	-	158,738	80
Linlithgow: St Ninian's Craigmailen	320	30	47	-	39,461	21
Livingston: Old	263	31	14	90,123	54,953	81
Livingston: United	229	30	-	68,554	47,277	184
Polbeth Harwood	137	12	-	45,668	14,402	-
West Kirk of Calder	200	15	-	70,195	43,775	30
Strathbrock	231	18	18	71,019	56,322	-
Uphall: South	136	22	-	40,461	32,876	6
Whitburn: Brucefield	148	12	24	76,591	53,204	-
Whitburn: South	294	26	-	69,187	41,965	72

2. Lothian and Borders

Aberlady and Gullane	437	23	-	71,016	66,046	38
Ale and Teviot United	351	21	-	22,084	29,759	10

Congregation	Com	Eld	G	In22	M&M	–18
Ashkirk	26	3	-	-	6,195	-
Ettrick and Yarrow	132	10	-	17,184	28,810	-
Selkirk	271	22	-	59,093	31,510	12
Ayton and District Churches	259	-	12	21,713	27,299	-
Belhaven	468	27	50	79,254	53,904	60
Spott	82	6	-	14,404	10,709	-
Berwick-upon-Tweed: St Andrew's Wallace Green and Lowick	259	15	-	60,229	32,725	3
Bilston	65	3	12	11,588	6,311	-
Bonnyrigg	492	45	40	100,288	63,777	23
Bowden and Melrose	589	31	22	-	71,939	17
Caddonfoot	135	11	-	17,164	10,286	1
Stow: St Mary of Wedale and Heriot	120	9	-	20,656	19,023	-
Broughton, Glenholm and Kilbucho	112	7	22	13,771	8,855	-
Carlops	46	10	-	24,767	13,596	5
Kirkurd and Newlands	66	11	8	12,948	12,692	2
Skirling	56	4	-	10,756	4,907	1
Tweedsmuir	34	3	-	-	2,981	-
West Linton: St Andrew's	151	15	-	-	20,552	12
Cavers and Kirkton	82	6	-	-	11,327	-
Hawick: Trinity	426	31	24	-	26,777	-
Channelkirk and Lauder	338	13	9	-	37,091	3
Cheviot Churches	256	17	16	-	41,884	2
Chirnside	69	-	-	13,092	10,131	-
Hutton and Fishwick and Paxton	56	-	-	7,908	9,111	-
Cockenzie and Port Seton: Chalmers Memorial	142	26	19	83,476	51,022	-
Cockenzie and Port Seton: Old	182	19	20	48,593	26,869	10
Cockpen and Carrington	130	19	32	-	23,990	-
Lasswade and Rosewell	200	15	-	29,996	21,929	20
Coldingham and St Abbs	48	-	-	39,471	24,588	-
Eyemouth	86	-	16	43,541	21,468	-
Coldstream and District Parishes	343	25	-	43,937	37,926	-
Eccles and Leitholm	124	-	-	22,230	16,059	-
Dalkeith: St John's and King's Park	464	24	31	-	65,248	86
Dalkeith: St Nicholas Buccleuch	296	14	-	51,713	29,324	-
Dirleton	158	-	-	-	40,423	-
North Berwick: Abbey	224	25	27	96,578	52,093	312
Dryburgh District Churches	289	24	11	39,791	37,136	4
Dunbar	268	13	14	83,865	70,796	8
Dunglass	246	8	-	17,834	19,036	15
Duns and District Parishes	509	30	30	80,703	61,263	50
Earlston	304	16	10	34,917	29,346	21
Eddleston	90	7	-	-	7,914	-
Peebles: Old	337	22	-	-	62,542	-
Stobo and Drumelzier	74	7	-	21,933	14,627	1
Fogo	86	13	-	-	5,564	51
Galashiels	598	39	27	136,021	89,782	40
Garvald and Morham	31	-	-	-	6,844	-
Haddington: West	186	17	-	59,699	31,894	10
Gladsmuir	141	-	-	-	16,530	-

Congregation	Com	Eld	G	In22	M&M	–18
Longniddry	251	38	25	79,955	44,864	5
Gordon: St Michael's	52	6	-	7,392	5,991	4
Gorebridge	136	-	-	128,387	70,559	-
Greenlaw	65	3	11	-	9,914	1
Haddington: St Mary's	422	38	-	121,989	65,671	19
Hawick: Burnfoot	59	9	-	12,541	11,633	27
Hawick: St Mary's and Old	291	15	17	-	28,821	40
Hawick: Teviot and Roberton	175	12	12	54,740	32,428	40
Hawick: Wilton	222	17	-	-	30,043	48
Teviothead	48	3	-	3,481	3,475	-
Hobkirk and Southdean	121	-	10	8,534	16,073	-
Ruberslaw	205	-	11	25,893	22,956	-
Humbie	63	7	-	28,415	16,595	12
Yester, Bolton and Saltoun	242	23	-	48,169	32,125	20
Innerleithen, Traquair and Walkerburn	274	24	24	-	37,249	14
Jedburgh: Old and Trinity	515	-	23	-	37,886	-
Kelso Country Churches	164	13	-	15,252	26,580	-
Kelso: North and Ednam	798	57	-	117,616	72,800	8
Kelso: Old and Sprouston	365	20	-	-	32,219	2
Legerwood	51	-	-	-	4,898	-
Loanhead	258	23	22	-	36,816	35
Lyne and Manor	89	9	-	31,691	18,658	-
Peebles: St Andrew's Leckie	426	24	-	152,232	70,192	132
Musselburgh: Northesk	265	-	28	58,726	34,212	-
Musselburgh: St Andrew's High	228	-	15	-	39,209	-
Musselburgh: St Clement's and St Ninian's	50	5	-	19,118	14,149	-
Musselburgh: St Michael's Inveresk	320	31	-	85,274	52,258	7
Newbattle	255	23	-	60,445	36,163	90
Newton	75	3	-	26,586	11,037	-
North Berwick: St Andrew Blackadder	544	27	22	-	102,321	50
Ormiston	118	8	29	32,615	25,834	4
Pencaitland	124	2	-	-	21,694	-
Oxnam	116	11	-	-	6,082	3
Penicuik: North	327	26	-	64,697	43,626	21
Penicuik: Trinity	199	20	28	-	72,300	-
Prestonpans: Prestongrange	206	11	14	61,047	36,560	15
Roslin	184	6	-	21,216	15,099	-
Tranent	190	17	35	67,582	37,445	8
Traprain	631	30	30	89,224	69,469	34
Tyne Valley	244	25	-	61,673	54,897	16

3. South West

Alloway	839	85	-	-	123,658	120
Annan: Old	306	32	41	46,367	33,687	-
Dornock	90	5	-	-	4,905	1
Annan: St Andrew's	376	39	-	61,189	34,207	35
Brydekirk	43	-	-	-	5,187	-
Annbank	208	18	14	43,011	18,495	-
Tarbolton	242	22	18	53,762	33,220	38
Applegarth, Sibbaldbie and Johnstone	99	6	7	-	8,216	-

Congregation	Com	Eld	G	In22	M&M	–18
Lochmaben	169	15	24	66,392	37,608	-
Ardrossan: Park	330	26	28	64,723	46,262	15
Ardrossan and Saltcoats: Kirkgate	160	26	-	76,329	52,040	7
Arnsheen Barrhill and Colmonell: St Colmon	91	8	-	20,596	17,174	5
Ballantrae	205	12	7	28,257	30,579	-
Auchinleck	280	-	23	-	19,548	-
Catrine	80	6	-	14,818	13,098	-
Ayr: Auld Kirk of Ayr	358	30	-	66,039	46,355	-
Ayr: Castlehill	431	42	37	114,417	52,763	65
Ayr: Newton Wallacetown	166	31	34	-	65,154	60
Ayr: St Andrew's	183	18	-	-	33,165	80
Ayr: St Columba	842	86	55	246,175	150,530	9
Ayr: St James'	267	19	-	-	39,276	-
Ayr: St Leonard's	317	41	-	64,789	63,274	-
Dalrymple	110	8	-	-	15,769	-
Ayr: St Quivox	91	13	-	40,778	28,378	50
Balmaclellan, Kells and Dalry	104	16	12	27,130	23,608	-
Carsphairn	71	6	-	8,623	4,922	-
Barr	27	4	-	3,015	3,160	-
Dailly	94	8	-	10,734	7,820	-
Girvan: South	205	20	-	29,166	17,983	3
Beith	557	48	19	86,101	62,503	32
Bengairn Parishes	66	12	-	20,809	25,347	-
Castle Douglas	296	21	16	50,692	32,690	2
Border Kirk	248	32	-	52,186	34,973	10
Brodick	106	14	-	41,313	28,755	-
Corrie	23	4	-	16,274	10,846	-
Lochranza and Pirnmill	50	9	-	-	15,793	-
Shiskine	48	9	17	20,446	18,871	-
Caerlaverock	95	7	-	11,262	6,472	-
Dumfries: St Mary's-Greyfriars'	263	26	26	-	37,505	-
Caldwell	195	17	-	45,982	38,062	18
Dunlop	323	30	14	65,069	49,613	60
Canonbie United	71	8	-	26,679	20,693	7
Liddesdale	80	8	-	28,066	18,940	-
Closeburn	157	-	-	30,857	17,593	-
Kirkmahoe	138	11	-	-	19,212	-
Colvend, Southwick and Kirkbean	149	-	-	24,382	42,975	-
Corsock and Kirkpatrick Durham	44	8	-	18,172	13,146	1
Crossmichael, Parton and Balmaghie	59	8	-	-	18,424	-
Coylton	282	17	-	32,430	23,147	2
Drongan: The Schaw Kirk	138	15	-	26,508	21,708	5
Craigie and Symington	243	20	16	41,691	34,497	6
Prestwick: South	197	31	-	83,217	52,354	-
Crosshill	104	-	19	-	9,504	-
Maybole	182	22	9	49,653	36,543	1
Crosshouse	198	28	16	44,791	36,099	5
Cumbrae	173	14	24	40,214	39,686	51
Largs: St John's	555	28	-	-	70,343	15
Cummertrees, Mouswald and Ruthwell	155	12	-	-	22,060	-

Congregation	Com	Eld	G	In22	M&M	–18
Dalbeattie and Kirkgunzeon	301	19	-	-	31,898	-
Urr	147	8	-	-	11,122	-
Dalmellington	103	12	-	11,197	11,891	15
Patna: Waterside	113	6	-	-	12,176	-
Dalry: St Margaret's	432	47	-	-	82,555	30
Dalry: Trinity	130	13	-	86,404	52,254	58
Dalton and Hightae	161	6	-	9,960	11,387	-
St Mungo	42	-	-	6,809	7,487	-
Darvel	237	16	26	42,278	27,874	6
Dreghorn and Springside	261	27	23	76,379	55,928	35
Dumfries: Maxwelltown West	294	28	25	69,861	47,658	-
Dumfries: Northwest	208	5	-	-	18,003	-
Dumfries: St George's	418	44	24	107,608	58,392	19
Dumfries: St Michael's and South	557	34	21	52,447	53,967	5
Dumfries: Troqueer	222	14	19	122,332	48,844	35
Dundonald	410	30	34	-	35,045	23
Dunscore	159	15	-	32,883	18,232	13
Glencairn and Moniaive	125	5	-	27,972	20,174	-
Durisdeer	120	4	-	6,556	12,717	-
Penpont, Keir and Tynron	135	10	-	18,082	16,250	4
Thornhill	107	8	-	21,102	16,938	-
Ervie Kirkcolm	152	9	-	16,411	14,186	4
Leswalt	244	14	-	22,522	13,685	2
Fairlie	156	14	14	56,433	44,425	18
Largs: St Columba's	274	9	-	77,697	48,101	5
Fenwick	257	18	24	-	34,366	10
Fisherton	102	14	-	13,917	9,427	3
Kirkoswald	157	16	8	44,559	21,462	10
Galston	427	39	56	73,809	60,428	9
Gatehouse and Borgue	209	16	-	51,949	32,408	13
Tarff and Twynholm	117	11	23	18,393	18,089	1
Girvan: North	464	35	-	68,095	44,024	26
Glasserton and Isle of Whithorn	74	3	-	-	10,301	-
Whithorn: St Ninian's Priory	285	7	-	37,162	21,398	30
Gretna: Old, Gretna: St Andrew's, Half Morton and Kirkpatrick Fleming	265	-	-	32,652	26,076	-
Hoddom, Kirtle-Eaglesfield and Middlebie	166	17	-	21,715	19,841	-
Hurlford	225	16	20	45,531	35,731	1
Inch	161	13	5	15,288	12,255	3
Luce Valley	192	13	17	29,445	27,751	6
Irongray, Lochrutton and Terregles	144	20	-	30,860	18,643	-
Irvine: Fullarton	341	21	39	118,251	67,805	90
Irvine: Girdle Toll	126	10	17	26,781	19,734	40
Irvine: St Andrew's	223	-	-	-	21,109	-
Irvine: Mure Relief	308	30	20	58,034	50,169	90
Irvine: Old	270	-	-	54,621	40,675	-
Kilbirnie: Auld Kirk	252	-	-	29,252	32,027	-
Kilbirnie: St Columba's	427	27	-	50,069	37,314	-
Kilmarnock: Kay Park	395	38	18	114,844	75,650	10
Kilmarnock: New Laigh Kirk	688	64	37	223,414	134,338	90

Congregation	Com	Eld	G	In22	M&M	–18
Kilmarnock: St John's Onthank	133	13	-	19,588	20,121	2
Kilmarnock: St Kentigern's	181	22	-	40,796	31,016	45
Kilmarnock: St Marnock's	944	70	37	195,700	145,668	300
Kilmaurs: St Maur's Glencairn	243	11	21	62,160	35,633	50
Kilmory	24	3	-	-	8,003	-
Lamlash	59	7	-	-	22,934	3
Kilwinning: Abbey	426	47	22	100,945	69,571	14
Kilwinning: Mansefield Trinity	164	-	21	39,509	31,813	-
Kirkconnel	179	10	-	12,173	17,745	-
Sanquhar: St Bride's	306	14	11	30,303	21,563	-
Kirkcowan	88	10	-	26,999	18,587	-
Wigtown	134	10	9	35,295	19,135	50
Kirkcudbright	405	21	-	92,996	50,028	30
Kirkinner	96	5	6	404	10,393	-
Mochrum	198	8	15	-	11,872	3
Sorbie	80	7	-	16,932	11,194	-
Kirkmabreck	102	10	12	14,564	11,639	-
Monigaff	222	-	-	7,432	9,917	-
Kirkmaiden	137	7	-	12,187	14,772	6
Kirkmichael	182	14	17	25,502	14,058	1
Straiton: St Cuthbert's	142	11	14	-	12,135	5
Kirkmichael, Tinwald and Torthorwald	326	26	16	15,650	28,325	-
Kirkpatrick Juxta	86	3	-	10,620	6,550	-
Moffat: St Andrew's	273	29	20	-	38,850	12
Wamphray	51	4	-	5,914	5,279	4
Langholm, Eskdalemuir, Ewes and Westerkirk	374	18	-	-	35,634	10
Largs: Clark Memorial	519	63	-	123,706	75,436	2
Lochend and New Abbey	171	17	10	40,682	23,084	-
Lockerbie: Dryfesdale, Hutton and Corrie	376	21	27	49,893	36,266	1
Lugar	148	10	15	24,317	13,897	4
Old Cumnock: Old	286	18	21	65,424	37,093	-
Mauchline	310	22	28	-	42,179	-
Sorn	118	11	12	17,594	11,857	-
Monkton and Prestwick: North	205	24	32	77,609	54,972	1
Muirkirk	137	13	-	18,410	10,884	2
Old Cumnock: Trinity	256	17	14	38,009	26,633	13
New Cumnock	208	16	12	55,461	42,464	3
Newmilns: Loudoun	135	5	15	-	22,960	-
Ochiltree	201	19	-	26,426	19,309	-
Stair	195	16	12	45,958	30,416	26
Penninghame	350	18	17	91,273	60,498	27
Portpatrick	192	9	18	14,520	15,466	-
Stoneykirk	209	15	16	-	20,647	-
Prestwick: Kingcase	475	59	25	81,544	62,708	31
Prestwick: St Nicholas'	429	50	33	113,084	76,158	18
Saltcoats: North	199	17	7	-	25,484	6
Saltcoats: St Cuthbert's	194	23	11	61,269	51,291	10
Stevenston: Ardeer	84	16	-	9,516	20,623	-
Stevenston: Livingstone	165	16	9	32,721	27,209	17
Stevenston: High	180	15	23	70,017	51,643	24

Congregation	Com	Eld	G	In22	M&M	–18
Stewarton: John Knox	238	27	22	116,598	57,976	40
Stewarton: St Columba's	346	32	47	71,226	56,983	47
Stranraer	751	36	26	-	94,671	80
Troon: Old	667	42	-	115,299	71,545	10
Troon: Portland	381	42	-	-	68,134	11
Troon: St Meddan's	532	58	23	-	76,685	100
Tundergarth	28	4	-	-	4,285	-
West Kilbride	328	40	-	120,514	76,246	120
Whiting Bay and Kildonan	60	9	-	29,456	21,223	1

4. Clyde

Congregation	Com	Eld	G	In22	M&M	–18
Arrochar	47	14	-	-	13,041	2
Luss	77	13	6	-	26,603	3
Baldernock	153	13	-	24,375	20,177	1
Milngavie: St Paul's	602	81	90	188,444	113,417	32
Barrhead: Bourock	376	26	32	79,491	53,701	64
Barrhead: St Andrew's	290	33	22	-	82,367	221
Bearsden: Baljaffray	348	6	36	105,135	52,740	101
Bearsden: Cross	438	62	17	-	97,841	42
Bearsden: Killermont	496	53	31	-	93,091	120
Bearsden: New Kilpatrick	1,062	96	50	290,275	173,538	32
Bearsden: Westerton Fairlie Memorial	267	25	37	95,087	63,168	34
Bishopton	575	49	-	117,892	65,654	30
Bonhill	328	37	-	-	39,435	-
Renton: Trinity	128	12	-	-	18,168	8
Bridge of Weir: Freeland	347	34	-	138,672	81,808	72
Bridge of Weir: St Machar's Ranfurly	269	21	23	83,013	57,361	15
Cardross	321	36	21	86,064	53,031	44
Clydebank: Faifley	165	-	31	48,718	25,940	-
Clydebank: Kilbowie St Andrew's	196	19	12	46,488	26,091	97
Clydebank: Radnor Park	71	13	-	35,825	22,421	-
Clydebank: Waterfront	118	22	-	34,404	28,849	6
Dalmuir: Barclay	136	19	-	29,613	24,263	-
Craigrownie	128	14	-	30,989	16,266	-
Garelochhead	105	12	-	-	29,709	6
Rosneath: St Modan's	74	10	16	31,003	15,635	2
Dumbarton: Riverside	410	60	34	109,401	66,222	186
Dumbarton: St Andrew's	84	16	-	24,266	17,084	-
Dumbarton: West Kirk	125	25	-	-	31,597	12
Duntocher: Trinity	157	16	46	-	28,943	-
Elderslie Kirk	365	34	24	-	61,626	120
Erskine	269	24	53	-	61,305	105
Gourock: Old Gourock and Ashton	497	52	25	136,873	73,072	360
Greenock: St Ninian's	193	13	-	-	15,566	18
Gourock: St John's	336	42	-	101,631	75,529	141
Greenock: East End	45	5	-	-	4,956	10
Greenock: Mount Kirk	279	30	-	-	38,728	140
Greenock: Lyle Kirk	622	43	-	-	80,874	87
Greenock: St Margaret's	137	22	-	29,229	22,522	4
Greenock: Wellpark Mid Kirk	397	42	-	77,141	61,405	51

Congregation	Com	Eld	G	In22	M&M	–18
Greenock: Westburn	432	46	20	95,321	72,339	18
Helensburgh	707	50	15	255,174	112,451	25
Rhu and Shandon	140	15	7	-	41,358	5
Houston and Killellan	634	68	56	-	87,311	250
Howwood	96	14	19	43,201	29,428	5
Johnstone: St Paul's	286	52	-	72,144	48,415	61
Inchinnan	206	24	26	-	38,044	7
Inverkip	272	23	13	-	46,474	15
Skelmorlie and Wemyss Bay	183	27	-	53,818	47,240	-
Johnstone: High	166	27	18	88,616	56,142	62
Johnstone: St Andrew's Trinity	160	19	-	24,946	21,203	47
Kilbarchan	357	46	-	96,656	70,336	30
Kilmacolm: Old	304	36	-	-	73,350	15
Kilmacolm: St Columba	110	17	-	-	56,106	5
Kilmaronock Gartocharn	160	12	-	20,574	13,024	6
Lomond	302	32	20	109,161	65,136	11
Langbank	103	12	-	-	27,191	-
Linwood	128	14	-	-	27,764	1
Milngavie: Cairns	265	27	-	174,024	90,532	8
Milngavie: St Luke's	309	15	-	64,920	45,343	-
Neilston	345	22	13	103,957	70,149	132
Old Kilpatrick Bowling	176	9	-	35,971	40,723	10
Paisley: Abbey	387	33	-	-	93,393	45
Paisley: North	328	40	-	-	46,056	6
Paisley: Oakshaw Trinity	399	52	-	155,712	61,084	92
Paisley: St George's	339	48	24	112,387	79,619	10
Paisley: St Mark's Oldhall	344	33	45	129,852	66,255	50
Paisley: Sherwood Greenlaw	277	47	-	107,028	74,968	43
Paisley: South	297	50	-	-	77,187	115
Paisley: West	272	36	-	55,369	51,268	69
Port Glasgow: Hamilton Bardrainney	178	17	13	35,662	26,889	33
Port Glasgow: New	418	56	21	-	52,033	270
Renfrew: North	496	63	27	-	69,965	129
Renfrew: Trinity	239	18	-	95,260	61,610	12

5. Glasgow

Congregation	Com	Eld	G	In22	M&M	–18
Bishopbriggs: Kenmure	198	19	17	68,378	58,657	24
Bishopbriggs: Springfield Cambridge	527	26	60	146,185	82,395	16
Broom	386	39	-	154,188	77,847	107
Burnside Blairbeth	383	29	68	208,421	136,385	75
Busby	170	27	20	82,893	43,440	5
Cadder	381	56	43	-	91,338	69
Cambuslang	474	35	32	152,671	84,845	16
Cambuslang: Flemington Hallside	292	20	28	50,141	40,015	-
Campsie	126	21	17	55,666	34,888	-
Chryston	276	20	12	143,292	75,493	25
Cumbernauld: Abronhill	142	12	17	47,107	40,739	1
Cumbernauld: Condorrat	254	28	29	74,352	44,422	71
Cumbernauld: Kildrum	222	18	-	31,658	32,216	3
Cumbernauld: St Mungo's	139	26	-	47,822	25,360	3

Congregation	Com	Eld	G	In22	M&M	−18
Cumbernauld: Old	245	36	-	57,302	44,824	40
Eaglesham	429	46	34	138,736	83,434	268
Fernhill and Cathkin	201	17	-	-	25,380	58
Gartcosh	59	10	-	38,407	11,634	62
Glenboig	93	6	-	12,429	7,160	4
Giffnock: Orchardhill	268	38	-	188,288	93,038	187
Giffnock: South	509	46	31	189,265	102,147	25
Giffnock: The Park	214	14	-	60,403	39,356	-
Greenbank	646	59	49	191,376	126,515	250
Kilsyth: Anderson	209	21	38	-	42,927	77
Kilsyth: Burns and Old	330	27	30	74,505	49,136	15
Kirkintilloch: St Columba's Hillhead	232	32	30	-	73,362	9
Kirkintilloch: St David's Memorial Park	430	36	20	92,480	50,191	12
Kirkintilloch: St Mary's	612	37	-	131,657	72,032	10
Lenzie: Old	372	39	-	141,474	76,342	30
Lenzie: Union	500	45	45	215,262	107,453	210
Maxwell Mearns Castle	241	23	-	-	94,300	46
Mearns	489	39	-	-	115,770	34
Milton of Campsie	281	21	34	81,198	49,054	31
Moodiesburn	113	9	-	72,204	34,602	19
Netherlee and Stamperland	651	59	72	236,028	152,305	-
Newton Mearns	318	35	21	133,787	70,110	-
Rutherglen: Old	181	18	-	57,918	37,719	2
Rutherglen: Stonelaw	263	22	-	136,211	78,848	12
Rutherglen: West and Wardlawhill	410	42	-	-	45,351	51
Stepps	176	12	-	57,481	33,450	6
Thornliebank	104	11	23	44,682	27,526	7
Torrance	182	17	-	104,190	60,314	61
Williamwood	354	41	21	-	60,134	471
Glasgow: Baillieston Mure Memorial	281	26	44	-	50,301	90
Glasgow: Baillieston St Andrew's	237	19	13	56,470	40,696	14
Glasgow: Balshagray Victoria Park	95	23	-	67,718	55,790	2
Glasgow: Barlanark Greyfriars	49	10	12	21,717	12,515	159
Glasgow: Blawarthill	143	19	20	21,726	11,344	56
Glasgow: St Columba	120	13	-	-	14,493	8
Glasgow: Bridgeton St Francis in the East	55	12	11	33,258	20,432	16
Glasgow: Broomhill Hyndland	415	64	20	179,588	100,860	100
Glasgow: Calton Parkhead	70	11	-	16,333	5,777	4
Glasgow: Cardonald	221	33	-	94,980	63,467	56
Glasgow: Carmunnock	154	20	-	37,678	27,881	-
Glasgow: Carmyle	58	3	-	14,391	10,152	48
Glasgow: Kenmuir Mount Vernon	113	10	-	78,751	35,932	23
Glasgow: Carntyne and Cranhill	233	17	-	-	51,366	132
Glasgow: Carnwadric	67	10	-	40,752	19,912	-
Glasgow: Castlemilk	92	18	10	-	14,178	8
Glasgow: Cathcart Old	195	29	21	-	49,595	9
Glasgow: Cathcart Trinity	255	37	-	-	99,665	22
Glasgow: Cathedral (High or St Mungo's)	299	29	-	83,090	74,759	-
Glasgow: Causeway (Tollcross)	146	24	18	-	30,997	43
Glasgow: Clincarthill	172	23	32	95,769	51,166	15

Congregation	Com	Eld	G	In22	M&M	–18
Glasgow: Colston Milton	45	6	-	20,145	7,811	8
Glasgow: Colston Wellpark	72	8	-	23,055	19,131	12
Glasgow: Croftfoot	219	33	21	-	48,805	144
Glasgow: Dennistoun New	145	24	-	71,542	49,785	43
Glasgow: Drumchapel St Andrew's	138	25	-	-	25,486	45
Glasgow: Drumchapel St Mark's	74	-	-	19,931	3,481	-
Glasgow: Easterhouse	53	7	-	-	7,846	92
Glasgow: Eastwood	146	34	-	118,268	60,375	5
Glasgow: Gairbraid	119	-	-	17,858	11,871	-
Glasgow: Gallowgate	126	6	-	-	15,026	5
Glasgow: Garthamlock and Craigend	53	11	-	-	4,278	59
Glasgow: Gorbals	96	10	-	58,392	18,870	12
Glasgow: Govan and Linthouse	135	14	20	84,783	43,005	58
Glasgow: Hillington Park	245	30	25	86,448	37,262	100
Glasgow: Ibrox	103	24	-	-	28,183	16
Glasgow: John Ross Memorial (for Deaf People)	50	2	-	-	-	-
Glasgow: Jordanhill	290	45	37	195,670	94,968	19
Glasgow: Kelvinbridge	29	11	-	22,367	30,924	28
Glasgow: Kelvinside Hillhead	135	19	-	68,824	41,131	-
Glasgow: King's Park	402	49	-	120,102	77,134	19
Glasgow: Kinning Park	117	16	-	26,004	20,380	-
Glasgow: Knightswood Anniesland Trinity	298	29	-	-	83,572	131
Glasgow: Langside	175	39	-	89,797	56,802	6
Glasgow: Maryhill Ruchill	122	12	-	-	51,516	76
Glasgow: Merrylea	218	23	-	-	43,678	1
Glasgow: Newlands South	346	35	-	125,915	77,425	8
Glasgow: Partick South	81	9	-	56,864	32,591	15
Glasgow: Partick Trinity	119	-	-	-	50,561	-
Glasgow: Pollokshaws	77	17	-	47,778	23,372	6
Glasgow: Pollokshields	104	18	-	-	39,501	8
Glasgow: Possilpark	80	13	-	-	16,596	22
Glasgow: Queen's Park Govanhill	106	18	-	111,840	65,158	7
Glasgow: Robroyston	50	4	-	-	5,507	-
Glasgow: Ruchazie	30	5	-	-	2,063	30
Glasgow: St Andrew and St Nicholas	250	23	18	71,524	44,472	180
Glasgow: St Andrew's East	32	10	17	-	17,215	-
Glasgow: St Andrew's West	138	15	14	-	49,765	-
Glasgow: St Christopher's Priesthill and Nitshill	55	8	-	-	19,966	10
Glasgow: St David's Knightswood	135	16	-	70,383	48,423	13
Glasgow: St Enoch's Hogganfield	92	11	-	-	19,920	-
Glasgow: St George's Tron	69	7	-	-	2,762	3
Glasgow: St James' (Pollok)	94	18	-	37,408	25,365	65
Glasgow: St John's Renfield	273	39	-	143,504	87,366	122
Glasgow: St Paul's	27	7	-	29,286	3,973	285
Glasgow: St Rollox	70	7	-	45,295	27,539	22
Glasgow: Sandyford Henderson Memorial	179	15	-	121,481	86,998	10
Glasgow: Sandyhills	183	21	30	-	41,340	43
Glasgow: Scotstoun	60	5	-	47,987	33,651	-
Glasgow: Shawlands Trinity	186	21	-	86,329	55,772	100
Glasgow: Sherbrooke Mosspark	282	38	18	-	96,363	10

Congregation	Com	Eld	G	In22	M&M	–18
Glasgow: Shettleston New	187	27	15	-	46,628	120
Glasgow: Springburn	175	13	14	-	35,260	53
Glasgow: Toryglen	36	4	-	25,889	9,773	-
Glasgow: Trinity Possil and Henry Drummond	43	4	-	45,700	36,360	8
Glasgow: Tron St Mary's	69	12	-	-	24,794	22
Glasgow: Wallacewell	35	-	-	15,625	1,489	-
Glasgow: Wellington	92	24	-	-	65,346	5
Glasgow: Whiteinch	53	7	-	66,912	32,748	10
Glasgow: Yoker	87	7	-	-	9,730	6

6. Forth Valley and Clydesdale

Congregation	Com	Eld	G	In22	M&M	–18
Airdrie: Cairnlea	437	40	16	-	80,406	72
Calderbank	111	11	13	31,332	15,808	32
Airdrie: Clarkston	277	24	8	54,256	45,660	130
Airdrie: High	143	29	-	64,620	38,205	75
Caldercruix and Longriggend	130	9	-	42,007	33,324	5
Airdrie: Jackson	292	40	16	83,176	54,868	190
Airdrie: New Monkland	240	29	25	70,693	43,515	55
Greengairs	100	8	-	-	12,067	2
Airdrie: New Wellwynd	610	79	-	163,478	100,044	43
Airdrie: St Columba's	197	14	-	19,791	11,121	-
Airth	112	6	14	21,905	25,211	6
Bellshill: Central	133	30	26	46,257	34,205	5
Bellshill: West	353	26	-	71,324	39,815	16
Biggar	265	20	25	123,254	64,554	20
Black Mount	64	4	10	-	11,007	-
Blackbraes and Shieldhill	132	17	11	18,538	16,907	-
Muiravonside	136	13	-	-	25,978	-
Blantyre: Livingstone Memorial	161	20	-	56,857	28,170	9
Blantyre: St Andrew's	145	18	-	58,858	28,893	10
Blantyre: Old	206	14	-	57,161	45,145	11
Bo'ness: Old	259	22	9	56,170	36,639	3
Bo'ness: St Andrew's	309	11	-	-	28,811	90
Bonnybridge: St Helen's	153	14	-	-	32,860	-
Bothkennar and Carronshore	151	16	-	24,995	19,968	17
Bothwell	424	42	26	222,512	75,110	23
Brightons	510	24	32	-	85,447	190
Cairngryffe	128	12	8	19,437	19,669	7
Libberton and Quothquan	71	9	-	10,542	10,946	-
Symington	122	12	-	21,103	18,958	-
Carluke: Kirkton	506	40	32	115,914	79,494	450
Carluke: St Andrew's	149	10	17	37,119	30,308	3
Carluke: St John's	460	37	25	91,066	54,909	21
Carnwath	80	9	14	-	8,680	2
Carstairs	140	9	11	46,001	28,568	2
Carriden	278	35	18	49,278	37,970	-
Chapelhall	165	23	28	49,272	25,471	28
Kirk o' Shotts	124	9	-	-	17,020	14
Cleland	124	5	-	2,428	13,856	-
Wishaw: St Mark's	220	21	29	50,826	41,436	123

Congregation	Com	Eld	G	In22	M&M	–18
Coalburn and Lesmahagow	372	25	12	58,530	51,748	4
Coatbridge: Blairhill Dundyvan	203	20	17	43,277	39,230	19
Coatbridge: Middle	213	33	20	26,450	23,762	127
Coatbridge: Calder	227	13	-	29,846	30,084	-
Coatbridge: Old Monkland	81	12	-	37,558	29,515	-
Coatbridge: New St Andrew's	452	40	28	109,339	67,363	164
Coatbridge: Townhead	102	17	-	-	19,329	46
Crossford	123	4	-	29,324	18,969	-
Kirkfieldbank	72	6	-	-	10,965	2
Dalserf	158	20	19	44,902	44,242	3
Denny: Old	248	32	18	53,760	35,117	50
Haggs	196	23	-	35,283	22,683	20
Denny: Westpark	327	28	19	78,493	62,334	35
Douglas Valley	214	17	29	-	37,343	-
Dunipace	153	18	-	63,541	36,467	54
East Kilbride: Claremont	318	36	-	-	81,488	30
East Kilbride: Greenhills	106	9	11	-	17,945	5
East Kilbride: Moncrieff	490	31	50	113,244	69,570	110
East Kilbride: Mossneuk	238	7	-	50,127	18,287	41
East Kilbride: Old	536	51	22	-	75,519	32
East Kilbride: South	123	20	-	52,336	44,302	139
East Kilbride: Stewartfield	25	4	-	9,113	6,416	-
East Kilbride: West	228	19	-	56,627	31,076	-
East Kilbride: Westwood	249	22	-	-	41,744	5
Falkirk: Bainsford	96	10	-	-	17,429	98
Falkirk: Camelon	140	14	-	-	41,387	4
Falkirk: Grahamston United	360	42	19	-	9,554	41
Falkirk: Laurieston	139	19	17	38,541	21,584	-
Redding and Westquarter	84	11	-	26,934	14,853	-
Falkirk: St Andrew's West	345	21	-	59,540	48,402	13
Falkirk: Trinity	370	29	15	184,339	95,011	19
Forth: St Paul's	277	19	28	-	34,158	110
Grangemouth: Abbotsgrange	261	35	-	-	37,141	140
Grangemouth: Kirk of the Holy Rood	241	24	-	49,317	33,134	3
Grangemouth: Zetland	442	47	28	80,162	66,288	66
Hamilton: Cadzow	315	39	28	100,757	69,982	32
Hamilton: Gilmour and Whitehill	89	19	-	58,547	27,867	4
Hamilton: West	155	28	-	61,913	38,489	25
Hamilton: Hillhouse	316	25	-	-	52,062	80
Hamilton: Old	409	57	-	-	96,027	75
Hamilton: St John's	428	42	28	-	81,281	216
Hamilton: South	125	15	20	58,881	31,478	9
Quarter	86	10	-	27,543	14,372	-
Hamilton: Trinity	228	18	-	47,782	31,076	4
Holytown	127	21	19	40,088	28,184	43
New Stevenston: Wrangholm Kirk	61	7	-	-	19,762	2
Kirkmuirhill	124	6	37	80,569	54,223	10
Lanark: Greyfriars	426	39	-	-	53,453	35
Lanark: St Nicholas'	419	32	27	114,480	70,897	40
Larbert: East	512	49	34	122,315	83,209	33

Congregation	Com	Eld	G	In22	M&M	–18
Larbert: Old	217	15	-	87,081	46,581	37
Larbert: West	288	25	21	65,319	42,622	-
Larkhall: New	292	48	36	-	75,241	96
Larkhall: Trinity	131	14	21	35,876	23,041	77
Law	152	11	15	-	26,752	51
Motherwell: Crosshill	206	32	47	63,611	46,056	-
Motherwell: St Margaret's	338	15	-	27,505	20,856	4
Motherwell: Dalziel St Andrew's	383	51	43	140,386	82,487	110
Motherwell: North	119	21	25	49,172	39,077	80
Wishaw: Craigneuk and Belhaven	100	19	-	-	27,852	11
Motherwell: St Mary's	565	84	47	148,743	91,510	310
Motherwell: South	372	40	58	115,873	55,288	24
Newarthill and Carfin	162	15	-	48,735	40,854	57
Newmains: Bonkle	95	15	-	31,093	21,810	9
Newmains: Coltness Memorial	157	18	22	51,483	35,504	4
Overtown	242	30	30	64,522	32,999	98
Polmont: Old	264	21	-	90,297	59,000	10
Shotts: Calderhead Erskine	346	30	27	87,140	53,829	-
Slamannan	90	6	-	-	17,166	20
Stenhouse and Carron	277	19	-	-	36,565	10
Stonehouse: St Ninian's	336	44	40	-	4,832	150
Strathaven: Avendale Old and Drumclog	422	49	36	138,710	78,776	28
Strathaven: Trinity	779	105	30	166,159	98,985	236
Uddingston: Burnhead	244	22	8	-	32,372	15
Uddingston: Old	337	35	25	131,831	87,684	-
Uddingston: Viewpark	338	56	-	103,214	66,599	81
Upper Clyde	166	7	11	14,383	17,316	4
Wishaw: Cambusnethan North	360	36	-	63,059	46,834	32
Wishaw: Cambusnethan Old and Morningside	313	25	-	38,321	43,363	60
Wishaw: Old	160	20	-	37,658	22,089	30
Wishaw: South Wishaw	146	9	24	73,392	47,971	15

7. Fife

Congregation	Com	Eld	G	In22	M&M	–18
Aberdour: St Fillan's	309	12	-	65,791	47,813	-
Anstruther and Cellardyke: St Ayle	329	30	32	71,059	56,093	-
Crail	262	22	22	49,885	32,057	2
Auchterderran Kinglassie	262	19	19	47,988	36,539	3
Auchtertool	63	-	-	-	8,198	-
Kirkcaldy: Linktown	186	24	23	48,074	37,925	6
Balmerino	100	10	-	-	15,252	-
Wormit	135	12	27	-	23,050	-
Beath and Cowdenbeath: North	113	11	-	43,675	34,597	3
Boarhills and Dunino	118	-	-	18,955	21,171	-
St Andrews: Holy Trinity	204	21	30	145,379	60,413	-
Buckhaven and Wemyss	163	18	12	-	31,244	-
Burntisland	224	27	18	-	33,645	5
Cairneyhill	80	17	-	27,317	14,508	-
Limekilns	212	30	-	70,532	46,506	6
Cameron	83	10	-	22,184	13,906	-
St Andrews: St Leonard's	370	35	25	136,916	74,997	5

Congregation	Com	Eld	G	In22	M&M	–18
Carnbee	80	-	-	8,125	8,855	-
Pittenweem	204	-	-	13,808	11,078	-
Carnock and Oakley	122	13	16	38,081	29,040	-
Ceres, Kemback and Springfield	281	17	-	-	59,720	26
Cowdenbeath: Trinity	226	22	10	62,439	45,428	4
Creich, Flisk and Kilmany	70	10	-	20,288	15,901	1
Culross and Torryburn	45	8	-	25,644	30,924	-
Cupar: Old and St Michael of Tarvit	425	29	21	139,014	77,746	20
Monimail	68	-	-	-	14,523	-
Cupar: St John's and Dairsie United	530	35	19	-	60,953	12
Dalgety	430	32	23	127,485	72,984	30
Dunfermline: Abbey	450	38	-	130,775	73,175	30
Dunfermline: East	95	7	-	117,277	12,637	70
Dunfermline: Gillespie Memorial	100	14	14	-	18,837	-
Dunfermline: North	131	13	-	23,409	16,417	-
Dunfermline: St Andrew's Erskine	148	17	9	55,522	31,592	-
Dunfermline: St Leonard's	239	22	27	-	45,667	41
Dunfermline: St Margaret's	169	23	-	85,918	43,957	-
Dunfermline: St Ninian's	124	21	18	-	28,373	3
Dunfermline: Townhill and Kingseat	155	19	-	56,442	37,067	32
Dysart: St Clair	349	19	11	-	19,918	1
East Neuk Trinity	252	19	41	78,794	55,549	4
Edenshead	258	20	11	38,387	31,666	-
Falkland	95	9	-	22,614	24,047	-
Freuchie	109	-	18	32,174	17,475	-
Glenrothes: Christ's Kirk	150	13	15	42,507	22,803	1
Glenrothes: St Columba's	287	41	-	68,295	37,598	36
Glenrothes: St Margaret's	212	23	22	51,007	36,702	50
Glenrothes: St Ninian's	170	27	11	60,362	47,144	4
Howe of Fife	201	14	-	-	37,605	9
Inverkeithing	162	18	-	49,933	41,461	7
North Queensferry	42	-	-	18,161	10,206	-
Kelty	169	16	15	74,787	44,455	5
Kennoway, Windygates and Balgonie: St Kenneth's	345	31	29	87,193	63,813	2
Kilrenny	84	10	-	26,829	21,264	1
Kinghorn	204	21	-	72,885	28,756	10
Kingsbarns	62	6	-	15,252	10,268	11
Kirkcaldy: Abbotshall	300	27	-	72,683	46,150	6
Kirkcaldy: Bennochy	328	26	-	57,269	48,142	6
Kirkcaldy: Pathhead	268	23	24	74,360	44,999	60
Kirkcaldy: St Bryce Kirk	280	22	21	-	56,168	2
Kirkcaldy: Templehall and Torbain United	271	-	19	79,130	41,884	-
Largo	241	25	16	79,575	49,160	6
Largoward	44	-	-	-	5,443	-
Leslie: Trinity	106	8	-	11,741	10,990	3
Leuchars: St Athernase	233	-	14	-	27,003	-
Leven	320	21	32	-	58,563	-
Lindores	246	27	-	44,338	30,983	45
Lochgelly and Benarty: St Serf's	171	22	-	56,760	36,731	5
Markinch and Thornton	360	27	-	75,257	59,605	25

Congregation	Com	Eld	G	In22	M&M	–18
Methil: Wellesley	242	24	18	-	24,308	49
Methilhill and Denbeath	162	-	20	30,946	19,622	-
Newport-on-Tay	301	37	-	106,482	47,001	34
Rosyth	184	18	-	51,331	22,001	-
St Andrews: St Mark's	432	36	14	-	98,641	18
St Monans	183	7	25	33,395	34,645	15
Saline and Blairingone	117	11	-	38,395	28,463	2
Tulliallan and Kincardine	186	22	-	47,249	32,686	63
Tayport	196	-	-	-	26,704	-

8. Perth

Congregation	Com	Eld	G	In22	M&M	–18
Aberdalgie and Forteviot	165	-	-	19,941	16,099	-
Aberuthven and Dunning	177	-	-	37,507	33,036	-
Aberfeldy	140	13	-	68,330	28,914	150
Dull and Weem	113	13	11	-	21,845	1
Grantully, Logierait and Strathtay	125	9	7	30,207	27,861	2
Aberfoyle	57	5	8	14,589	10,389	-
Port of Menteith	49	9	-	15,453	9,784	-
Aberlemno	171	11	-	26,676	17,586	12
Guthrie and Rescobie	198	-	-	-	16,303	-
Abernethy and Dron and Arngask	241	17	-	32,254	34,728	9
Abernyte	79	10	-	15,803	13,845	3
Inchture and Kinnaird	120	22	-	38,899	25,627	16
Longforgan	140	10	11	-	33,457	-
Alloa: Ludgate	261	17	10	66,728	40,456	10
Alloa: St Mungo's	282	22	16	71,317	44,647	12
Almondbank Tibbermore	164	13	12	-	30,746	36
Methven and Logiealmond	63	15	-	-	15,855	-
Alva	378	50	-	86,805	51,680	73
Alyth	581	-	-	67,088	48,932	-
Arbirlot	116	8	-	36,453	15,751	-
Carmyllie	86	12	-	-	16,798	5
Arbroath: Old and Abbey	348	21	-	89,250	47,502	4
Arbroath: St Andrew's	448	37	32	138,863	86,123	47
Arbroath: St Vigeans	400	33	12	65,566	40,532	6
Arbroath: West Kirk	705	61	32	88,872	68,638	87
Ardler, Kettins and Meigle	334	15	17	41,033	28,229	-
Ardoch	140	12	24	42,719	26,094	-
Blackford	76	10	-	21,404	13,062	45
Auchterarder	495	29	35	169,454	77,598	-
Auchtergaven and Moneydie	433	21	17	-	28,827	-
Redgorton and Stanley	274	10	25	-	25,623	30
Auchterhouse	111	10	-	23,743	18,648	-
Balfron	106	11	-	-	23,797	4
Fintry	91	8	-	16,120	14,701	2
Balquhidder	62	8	-	29,211	11,255	4
Killin and Ardeonaig	68	9	4	35,170	15,447	5
Bannockburn: Allan	216	26	-	53,899	33,762	10
Cowie and Plean	142	8	-	14,449	7,902	2
Bannockburn: Ladywell	318	14	-	-	16,942	11

Congregation	Com	Eld	G	In22	M&M	–18
Barry	158	6	19	23,038	15,411	4
Carnoustie	241	18	15	72,035	39,774	3
Bendochy	65	5	-	13,820	16,785	-
Coupar Angus: Abbey	234	16	-	31,793	23,955	-
Blair Atholl and Struan	89	10	-	15,225	21,313	-
Braes of Rannoch	14	4	-	2,778	4,989	2
Foss and Rannoch	70	7	-	12,425	8,479	-
Blairgowrie	618	42	26	-	72,671	36
Brechin: Gardner Memorial	408	17	-	60,515	36,317	12
Farnell	114	12	-	-	9,839	10
Bridge of Allan	576	39	38	120,458	70,222	65
Buchanan	93	7	-	13,436	17,715	-
Drymen	192	19	-	55,144	44,786	8
Buchlyvie	125	10	-	23,628	16,344	6
Gartmore	54	8	-	-	14,432	2
Callander	297	18	24	70,057	60,873	39
Cambusbarron: The Bruce Memorial	245	21	-	87,418	44,876	7
Caputh and Clunie	112	12	-	15,699	19,922	-
Kinclaven	94	11	13	21,901	14,002	-
Cargill Burrelton	104	14	13	23,581	18,916	7
Collace	94	7	-	12,892	8,582	-
Carnoustie: Panbride	548	28	-	-	47,014	20
Clackmannan	289	20	20	67,773	52,315	6
Sauchie and Coalsnaughton	345	17	14	45,509	33,883	8
Cleish	105	9	-	33,403	24,467	-
Fossoway: St Serf's and Devonside	181	15	-	48,964	33,244	-
Colliston	153	5	-	14,553	10,164	-
Friockheim Kinnell	111	-	22	15,590	13,189	-
Inverkeilor and Lunan	99	6	-	18,485	14,442	1
Comrie	310	27	9	97,215	59,992	40
Dundurn	49	8	-	18,709	10,458	-
Crieff	454	18	15	60,402	53,491	-
Dollar	197	20	52	84,777	58,173	10
Glendevon	26	-	-	-	1,630	-
Muckhart	77	6	-	-	17,406	11
Dun and Hillside	298	25	8	-	33,557	1
Dunbarney and Forgandenny	474	22	21	86,087	55,579	24
Dunblane: Cathedral	708	61	21	213,612	121,579	218
Dunblane: St Blane's	257	23	34	80,764	61,095	-
Lecropt	124	12	-	51,976	23,377	2
Dundee: Balgay	195	14	-	-	35,814	-
Dundee: Barnhill St Margaret's	600	37	-	-	90,582	32
Dundee: Broughty Ferry New Kirk	509	35	40	97,540	61,302	-
Dundee: Broughty Ferry St James'	121	10	14	31,049	19,713	5
Dundee: Broughty Ferry St Luke's and Queen Street	228	12	55	-	33,442	5
Dundee: Broughty Ferry St Stephen's and West	260	16	-	55,212	31,120	-
Dundee: Dundee (St Mary's)	461	41	-	50,406	46,816	-
Dundee: Camperdown	52	8	-	14,734	16,996	-
Dundee: Chalmers Ardler	129	19	-	66,442	50,235	7
Dundee: Coldside	144	13	-	44,843	25,936	50

Congregation	Com	Eld	G	In22	M&M	–18
Dundee: Craigiebank	91	5	-	-	13,277	-
Dundee: Douglas and Mid Craigie	84	7	-	18,398	11,116	21
Dundee: Downfield Mains	217	11	-	93,816	55,223	20
Dundee: Fintry	77	4	-	40,441	28,069	7
Dundee: Kingsgait	575	53	41	-	89,321	6
Dundee: Lochee	302	15	31	59,391	35,854	181
Dundee: Logie and St John's Cross	205	15	28	90,113	42,417	6
Dundee: Menzieshill	222	-	-	-	19,919	-
Dundee: St David's High Kirk	92	8	-	-	27,175	-
Dundee: Steeple	130	16	-	125,170	75,721	-
Dundee: Stobswell	202	12	-	37,554	35,425	-
Dundee: Strathmartine	180	21	18	-	30,865	-
Dundee: Trinity	196	27	-	-	33,438	9
Dundee: West	223	21	18	86,639	47,118	-
Dundee: Whitfield	32	4	-	-	8,332	1
Dunkeld	288	22	-	77,289	68,110	20
Dunnichen, Letham and Kirkden	195	13	12	25,690	17,302	-
Eassie, Nevay and Newtyle	171	13	16	21,041	18,988	20
Edzell Lethnot Glenesk	319	18	14	37,338	27,676	25
Fern Careston Menmuir	91	5	-	10,943	11,972	6
Errol	219	14	-	34,894	33,335	37
Fallin	220	14	-	-	14,466	65
Forfar: East and Old	404	36	24	-	70,515	150
Forfar: Lowson Memorial	530	40	29	109,665	75,683	248
Forfar: St Margaret's	371	26	16	66,257	44,121	60
Fortingall, Glenlyon, Kenmore and Lawers	92	-	10	27,445	26,671	-
Fowlis and Liff	122	12	-	-	28,156	-
Lundie and Muirhead	235	19	-	36,127	26,869	-
Gargunnock	100	8	-	14,822	19,420	7
Kilmadock	70	7	-	17,652	18,437	-
Kincardine-in-Menteith	62	3	-	9,938	8,827	-
Glamis, Inverarity and Kinettles	316	25	-	45,230	42,706	11
Invergowrie	213	41	18	53,201	36,455	7
Isla Parishes	116	10	9	-	26,859	4
Killearn	291	15	42	74,613	56,536	4
Kinross	576	20	25	150,635	74,854	62
Kippen	142	13	11	38,661	24,298	6
Norrieston	76	8	5	22,720	17,685	5
Kirkmichael, Straloch and Glenshee	57	4	-	6,989	10,458	-
Rattray	229	13	-	27,971	20,788	-
Logie	427	27	-	66,069	51,591	3
Menstrie	282	19	16	54,148	41,008	1
Mid Strathearn	278	23	9	51,956	46,148	10
Monifieth	504	42	31	114,328	73,726	106
Monikie and Newbigging and Murroes and Tealing	388	17	13	33,109	34,379	-
Montrose: Old and St Andrew's	494	37	9	76,363	50,917	48
Montrose: South and Ferryden	249	-	-	61,918	36,107	-
Muthill	189	16	9	43,366	30,979	15
Trinity Gask and Kinkell	37	-	-	-	4,762	-
Oathlaw Tannadice	97	6	-	16,953	17,407	-

Congregation	Com	Eld	G	In22	M&M	–18
The Glens and Kirriemuir United	987	58	37	96,067	69,881	15
Orwell and Portmoak	345	28	-	60,411	49,818	20
Perth: Craigie and Moncrieffe	459	-	15	-	53,734	-
Perth: Kinnoull	341	37	15	-	43,875	75
Perth: Letham St Mark's	394	-	-	120,033	69,975	-
Perth: North	690	37	42	200,864	126,971	10
Perth: Riverside	62	-	-	-	28,101	-
Perth: St John's Kirk of Perth	324	24	-	78,676	54,917	-
Perth: St Leonard's-in-the-Fields	347	28	-	-	50,175	-
Perth: St Matthew's	346	31	20	146,504	66,814	170
Pitlochry	266	21	14	75,947	49,995	1
St Madoes and Kinfauns	257	35	-	71,307	42,112	147
Scone and St Martins	709	30	39	111,000	70,487	37
Stirling: Church of the Holy Rude	114	11	-	-	25,437	-
Stirling: Viewfield Erskine	199	17	9	34,187	21,087	-
Stirling: North	323	25	22	86,130	35,864	20
Stirling: Park	417	43	-	-	74,908	30
Stirling: St Mark's	143	10	-	34,204	17,608	19
Stirling: St Ninian's Old	540	44	-	117,547	61,433	48
Strathblane	137	16	33	75,950	44,077	8
Tenandry	32	8	-	15,143	13,738	-
Tillicoultry	350	51	22	82,627	55,137	64
Tullibody: St Serf's	270	21	25	-	34,992	35

9. North East and Northern Isles

Congregation	Com	Eld	G	In22	M&M	–18
Aberdeen: Bridge of Don Oldmachar	148	10	-	48,438	27,412	52
Aberdeen: Craigiebuckler	657	53	18	-	73,157	6
Aberdeen: Ferryhill	269	34	-	83,392	53,726	100
Aberdeen: High Hilton	340	-	-	36,988	34,244	-
Aberdeen: Holburn West	264	31	25	102,050	59,346	5
Aberdeen: Mannofield	714	57	19	177,589	90,788	10
Aberdeen: Midstocket	363	34	31	104,080	67,342	30
Aberdeen: North	337	-	21	-	62,534	-
Aberdeen: Queen's Cross	349	36	-	211,717	82,380	-
Aberdeen: Rubislaw	359	-	31	117,924	88,021	-
Aberdeen: Ruthrieston West	187	-	9	65,370	46,616	-
Aberdeen: St Columba's Bridge of Don	207	13	-	98,696	54,008	20
Aberdeen: St John's Church for Deaf People	82	-	-	-	-	-
Aberdeen: St Machar's Cathedral	413	31	-	-	94,716	12
Aberdeen: St Mark's	305	36	32	71,779	86,057	8
Aberdeen: St Mary's	210	32	-	58,262	43,962	58
Aberdeen: St Nicholas Kincorth, South of	261	25	-	53,016	41,402	60
Aberdeen: St Stephen's	112	16	13	-	43,269	10
Aberdeen: South Holburn	344	30	15	-	62,418	11
Aberdeen: Stockethill	83	-	-	30,233	12,379	-
Aberdeen: Torry St Fittick's	242	12	18	-	35,410	7
Aberdeen: Woodside	103	22	-	-	35,852	4
Aberdour	92	-	8	9,362	7,449	-
Pitsligo	74	-	-	19,964	9,844	-
Aberlour	183	16	28	41,345	22,188	-

Congregation	Com	Eld	G	In22	M&M	–18
Aberluthnott	57	-	-	13,537	9,655	-
Laurencekirk	197	6	-	24,113	14,020	1
Aboyne-Dinnet	230	8	11	42,746	27,955	9
Cromar	167	15	-	27,797	21,682	-
Arbuthnott, Bervie and Kinneff	227	17	-	65,375	43,518	50
Auchterless and Auchaber	242	15	-	22,454	26,569	1
Banchory-Ternan: East	436	23	9	64,143	51,953	5
Banchory-Ternan: West	548	15	12	83,463	67,264	30
Banff	324	18	-	-	52,708	-
King Edward	121	-	-	13,156	15,937	-
Barthol Chapel	63	6	-	6,881	7,502	1
Tarves	211	13	24	35,747	26,307	9
Belhelvie	282	28	12	81,249	56,283	49
Bellie and Speymouth	292	17	21	56,524	42,617	100
Birnie and Pluscarden	164	16	-	35,402	30,441	24
Elgin: High	204	28	-	62,788	38,359	3
Birsay, Harray and Sandwick	258	-	22	38,985	25,995	-
Birse and Feughside	191	11	-	33,347	27,718	23
Blairdaff and Chapel of Garioch	277	-	-	24,050	22,900	-
Braemar and Crathie	165	-	-	-	40,333	-
Brimmond	469	25	27	-	88,398	40
Buckie: North	251	23	27	50,226	30,472	16
Rathven	53	-	11	-	9,182	-
Buckie: South and West	164	16	-	29,159	27,991	-
Enzie	45	-	-	2,962	5,420	-
Cluny	148	5	-	-	18,256	13
Monymusk	84	4	-	-	12,123	37
Crimond	129	-	-	21,219	15,727	-
Lonmay	83	8	9	12,508	11,497	-
Cruden	282	18	16	33,690	25,889	8
Cullen and Deskford	233	12	11	49,234	40,436	-
Culsalmond and Rayne	144	4	-	-	10,401	4
Daviot	130	6	-	8,536	8,884	1
Cults	577	56	34	163,668	100,747	50
Cushnie and Tough	212	6	-	12,323	16,268	1
Deer	489	13	15	-	35,356	-
Drumoak-Durris	344	8	-	44,330	39,959	3
Duffus, Spynie and Hopeman	178	27	-	49,921	34,901	9
Dyce	757	42	44	125,864	65,632	120
New Machar	332	-	-	51,252	42,862	-
East Mainland	217	-	12	31,440	18,598	-
Echt and Midmar	235	8	-	29,035	21,688	10
Eday	2	-	-	-	1,354	-
Elgin: St Giles' and St Columba's South	454	-	37	107,480	69,925	-
Ellon	1,220	62	-	166,804	109,524	20
Evie and Rendall	59	5	-	-	16,705	32
Firth	61	4	-	24,023	10,964	8
Findochty	30	8	9	23,260	12,037	20
Portknockie	48	6	14	24,399	13,545	40
Fintray Kinellar Keithhall	124	9	-	-	26,065	-

Congregation	Com	Eld	G	In22	M&M	–18
Flotta	20	-	-	3,649	2,235	-
Orphir and Stenness	111	11	-	17,057	15,770	-
Foveran	176	5	-	27,319	27,750	1
Fraserburgh: Old	394	-	44	-	69,032	-
Fraserburgh: South	229	16	-	-	26,017	-
Inverallochy and Rathen: East	64	6	-	-	9,320	11
Fraserburgh: West	365	40	-	53,549	37,054	94
Rathen: West	64	7	-	7,703	5,952	-
Fyvie	153	12	14	35,228	26,094	5
Rothienorman	92	-	-	17,113	9,522	-
Glenmuick (Ballater)	214	-	-	28,673	26,133	-
Howe Trinity	392	17	32	78,978	47,249	20
Hoy and Walls	33	5	-	-	3,503	2
Huntly Cairnie Glass	551	-	9	-	36,790	-
Insch-Leslie-Premnay-Oyne	289	24	12	-	35,031	15
Inverurie: St Andrew's	785	19	-	-	63,926	4
Inverurie: West	486	35	20	96,152	51,453	3
Keith: North, Newmill, Boharm and Rothiemay	390	38	16	34,920	66,104	2
Keith: St Rufus, Botriphnie and Grange	766	51	24	62,380	45,561	6
Kemnay	403	-	-	72,478	52,788	-
Kingswells	257	18	9	41,181	27,143	-
Kintore	596	27	-	-	58,204	40
Kirkwall: East	275	-	-	-	38,145	-
Shapinsay	30	5	-	7,896	5,329	-
Kirkwall: St Magnus Cathedral	428	25	18	-	45,161	-
Rousay	10	-	-	5,170	2,416	-
Knockando, Elchies and Archiestown	182	17	-	35,955	25,503	19
Rothes	240	12	11	-	24,262	8
Longside	363	19	-	63,909	45,643	34
Lossiemouth: St Gerardine's High	146	10	-	32,351	32,249	-
Lossiemouth: St James'	176	12	33	44,667	27,809	7
Macduff	500	27	-	-	55,849	180
Marnoch	304	15	12	36,850	24,887	6
Maryculter Trinity	121	13	7	43,146	29,847	22
Maud and Savoch	158	12	-	24,611	19,219	10
New Deer: St Kane's	222	12	17	40,590	27,019	-
Meldrum and Bourtie	287	20	31	72,872	47,154	16
Methlick	293	-	14	-	44,212	-
Mid Deeside	441	32	15	70,212	43,045	20
Monquhitter and New Byth	235	16	-	16,317	19,175	-
Turriff: St Andrew's	393	23	14	-	24,195	54
Mortlach and Cabrach	271	-	10	28,456	23,738	-
New Pitsligo	229	-	-	20,427	13,159	-
Strichen and Tyrie	311	16	20	52,881	32,721	14
Newtonhill	197	9	14	24,442	21,459	28
North Ronaldsay	6	3	-	-	900	-
Noth	169	5	-	19,720	18,614	-
Ordiquhill and Cornhill	126	9	9	11,265	6,230	15
Whitehills	247	-	18	27,371	18,785	-
Papa Westray	7	4	-	7,298	3,388	-

Congregation	Com	Eld	G	In22	M&M	–18
Westray	74	17	21	-	19,800	45
Peterculter	447	40	-	100,395	64,962	58
Peterhead: New	429	23	24	-	38,445	20
Peterhead: St Andrew's	344	-	9	35,766	26,404	-
Portlethen	229	11	-	53,434	40,498	6
Portsoy	236	10	14	48,450	26,700	1
St Andrew's-Lhanbryd and Urquhart	274	35	26	68,670	43,585	4
St Cyrus	197	11	-	23,230	26,005	-
St Fergus	88	-	9	-	7,259	-
Sanday	42	-	5	-	6,478	-
Sandhaven	63	-	-	-	2,429	-
Shetland	733	85	82	-	109,424	70
Skene	995	52	39	156,431	86,111	109
South Ronaldsay and Burray	99	4	12	23,879	10,228	-
Stonehaven: Carronside	684	20	-	-	51,201	4
Stonehaven: Fetteresso	483	28	24	-	93,069	162
Strathbogie Drumblade	347	22	16	48,390	36,582	10
Stromness	247	29	12	40,450	27,220	1
Stronsay: Moncur Memorial	48	6	-	12,418	6,871	1
Turriff: St Ninian's and Forglen	465	16	13	-	42,681	13
Udny and Pitmedden	214	18	-	39,765	40,056	30
Upper Donside	289	10	-	-	26,615	25
West Mearns	395	-	14	-	42,250	-

10.1 Argyll

Appin	78	12	16	29,634	14,851	-
Lismore	34	-	-	-	8,861	-
Ardchattan	72	10	-	33,032	18,942	8
Coll	16	3	-	7,561	2,396	-
Connel	92	13	3	-	19,620	3
Ardrishaig	108	20	-	28,829	20,942	-
South Knapdale	26	4	-	-	8,183	2
Barra	31	2	-	-	8,812	-
South Uist	38	4	-	18,735	10,285	4
Bute, United Church of	352	32	21	66,681	45,022	2
Campbeltown: Highland	247	23	-	30,951	24,252	-
Saddell and Carradale	134	13	16	-	21,006	-
Southend	199	14	12	25,235	16,878	3
Campbeltown: Lorne and Lowland	610	27	-	74,772	53,273	14
Colonsay and Oronsay	8	2	-	13,790	7,424	4
Cowal Kirk	644	83	31	-	96,384	-
Craignish	37	2	-	-	5,239	-
Gigha and Cara	24	6	-	-	4,658	2
Kilcalmonell	28	9	-	5,335	5,117	10
Killean and Kilchenzie	82	8	7	-	13,492	3
Glassary, Kilmartin and Ford	77	8	-	15,827	12,829	-
North Knapdale	43	7	-	-	20,674	1
Glenorchy and Innishael	38	5	-	-	5,238	-
Strathfillan	18	5	-	-	4,046	-
Iona	10	4	-	-	10,951	-

Congregation	Com	Eld	G	In22	M&M	–18
Kilfinichen and Kilvickeon and the Ross of Mull	24	3	-	8,055	2,029	1
Jura	19	5	-		5,406	-
North and West Islay	91	23	-	28,080	30,199	-
South Islay	103	17	-	62,698	34,114	1
Kilbrandon and Kilchattan	98	13	-	15,875	18,082	10
Kilninver and Kilmelford	51	6	-		6,909	5
Kilchrenan and Dalavich	24	6	-	16,421	11,299	8
Muckairn	99	14	-	24,510	15,042	-
Kilfinan	29	4	-		4,482	-
Kilmodan and Colintraive	52	5	-		13,972	-
Kyles	71	11	-		22,889	-
Kilmore and Oban	381	43	21	77,078	52,091	-
Kilmun, Strone and Ardentnny: The Shore Kirk	127	15	-		26,370	-
Lochgilphead	94	10	-	22,008	26,089	5
Lochgoilhead and Kilmorich	59	-	-	21,587	21,762	-
Strachur and Strachlachlan	93	10	10	18,714	16,293	-
North Mull	128	17	-	60,820	39,518	9
Rothesay: Trinity	274	32	17	57,776	33,345	1
Skipness	14	2	-	9,391	6,129	2
Tarbert, Loch Fyne and Kilberry	81	10	22	38,331	18,180	-
Tiree	45	5	-		8,538	2
West Lochfyneside: Cumlodden, Inveraray and Lochgair	102	14	14		29,397	-

10.2 Abernethy

Congregation	Com	Eld	G	In22	M&M	–18
Abernethy	121	11	-	52,363	34,409	16
Boat of Garten, Carrbridge and Kincardine	148	13	26	37,304	23,544	17
Alvie and Insh	49	6	-		19,518	5
Rothiemurchus and Aviemore	57	7	-	16,797	10,432	5
Cromdale and Advie	49	3	-	15,324	13,935	-
Dulnain Bridge	27	5	-	3,645	7,162	-
Grantown-on-Spey	150	12	-	52,562	28,343	15
Kingussie	57	13	-		16,212	10
Laggan and Newtonmore	87	15	-	42,699	33,052	-
Tomintoul, Glenlivet and Inveraven	110	7	-	12,896	16,782	-

10.3 Inverness

Congregation	Com	Eld	G	In22	M&M	–18
Alves and Burghead	92	14	23	30,573	21,441	8
Kinloss and Findhorn	61	18	-	30,697	21,214	-
Ardersier	35	-	-	23,184	12,971	-
Petty	30	-	-		8,876	-
Cawdor	138	-	-	20,052	19,309	-
Croy and Dalcross	34	6	12		12,389	-
Culloden: The Barn	140	17	-	83,803	50,973	-
Dallas	41	-	-	11,605	9,682	-
Forres: St Leonard's	112	34	24		30,876	10
Rafford	41	-	-		8,995	-
Daviot and Dunlichity	43	-	-	21,993	8,929	-
Moy, Dalarossie and Tomatin	30	6	15	6,405	6,192	7
Dores and Boleskine	50	5	-	8,311	12,260	-

Congregation	Com	Eld	G	In22	M&M	–18
Dyke and Edinkillie	143	10	11	32,004	27,335	28
Forres: St Laurence	292	15	13	61,722	42,996	-
Inverness: Crown	451	-	27	-	61,515	-
Inverness: Dalneigh and Bona	115	6	11	-	29,304	-
Inverness: East	164	16	-	101,788	67,175	10
Inverness: Hilton	204	12	-	88,800	43,059	28
Inverness: Inshes	222	13	-	249,834	102,275	75
Inverness: Kinmylies	61	7	-	47,260	24,258	50
Inverness: Ness Bank	445	37	21	179,674	87,959	135
Inverness: Old High St Stephen's	282	29	-	107,290	65,655	2
Inverness: St Columba	61	-	-	43,331	19,000	-
Inverness: Trinity	151	19	8	44,436	39,202	27
Kilmorack and Erchless	78	-	-	-	32,282	-
Kiltarlity and Kirkhill	97	12	-	46,607	28,693	40
Nairn: Old	294	35	16	94,676	69,329	15
Nairn: St Ninian's and Auldearn and Dalmore	151	11	28	57,644	39,728	4
Urquhart and Glenmoriston	83	-	-	39,282	34,598	-

10.4 Lochaber

Congregation	Com	Eld	G	In22	M&M	–18
Acharacle	27	4	-	-	10,058	5
Ardnamurchan	12	4	-	8,765	10,008	-
Ardgour and Kingairloch	38	7	9	-	7,394	5
Morvern	24	4	-	-	5,230	-
Strontian	24	3	-	-	3,459	-
Duror	35	6	15	16,751	7,560	-
Glencoe: St Munda's	26	2	-	6,475	9,003	-
Fort Augustus	55	7	-	-	10,986	2
Glengarry	24	5	10	-	6,627	2
Fort William Kilmallie	332	30	23	-	62,522	-
Kilmonivaig	44	12	10	-	17,577	6
Kinlochleven	39	5	9	20,104	12,933	-
Nether Lochaber	31	6	-	19,747	9,555	-
North West Lochaber	68	8	-	23,321	17,566	22

10.5 Ross

Congregation	Com	Eld	G	In22	M&M	–18
Alness	56	8	-	28,944	17,853	14
Avoch	16	-	-	11,691	8,173	-
Fortrose and Rosemarkie	68	4	-	33,565	20,713	5
Contin	33	8	-	26,219	10,271	2
Fodderty and Strathpeffer	90	-	-	30,140	17,641	-
Cromarty	15	5	-	11,417	7,970	-
Resolis and Urquhart	77	-	-	-	27,934	-
Dingwall: Castle Street	117	-	-	50,334	28,179	-
Dingwall: St Clement's	113	20	15	64,830	41,405	-
Fearn Abbey and Nigg	38	-	-	-	11,505	-
Tarbat	21	4	-	-	5,707	2
Ferintosh	134	-	18	43,087	29,696	-
Invergordon	85	-	-	64,594	34,795	-
Killearnan	71	-	-	30,504	29,454	-
Knockbain	22	-	-	6,820	9,326	-
Kilmuir and Logie Easter	58	9	14	25,478	22,562	4

Congregation	Com	Eld	G	In22	M&M	–18
Kiltearn	48	6	-	28,497	21,488	1
Lochbroom and Ullapool	28	5	-	27,080	20,262	9
Rosskeen	93	11	12	49,118	28,804	16
Tain	71	7	19	-	29,676	6
Urray and Kilchrist	69	14	-	58,365	32,905	12

10.6 Sutherland

Congregation	Com	Eld	G	In22	M&M	–18
Altnaharra and Farr	20	-	-	-	7,293	-
Melness and Tongue	16	2	-	-	11,780	-
Assynt and Stoer	10	2	-	22,798	6,656	13
Clyne	38	8	-	-	18,581	2
Kildonan and Loth Helmsdale	26	6	-	10,745	10,428	-
Creich	14	4	-	-	8,000	-
Kincardine Croick and Edderton	14	5	-	12,893	12,073	2
Rosehall	17	2	-	9,218	6,023	4
Dornoch Cathedral	252	20	41	-	73,512	50
Durness and Kinlochbervie	25	3	-	-	11,652	30
Eddrachillis	5	1	-	11,446	9,464	1
Golspie	25	5	-	17,181	16,119	-
Lairg	17	1	8	13,113	13,257	-
Rogart	11	4	-	-	8,100	-

10.7 Caithness

Congregation	Com	Eld	G	In22	M&M	–18
Halkirk Westerdale	71	6	8	14,586	6,462	-
Watten	11	1	-	4,268	3,651	-
Latheron	43	8	7	17,127	14,993	20
North Coast	29	8	17	15,235	11,731	8
Pentland	90	8	22	-	24,081	10
Thurso: St Peter's and St Andrew's	121	16	-	-	34,261	14
Thurso: West	129	21	17	54,294	30,541	4
Wick: Pulteneytown and Thrumster	169	8	16	-	33,281	102
Wick: St Fergus	117	17	-	35,614	25,783	-

10.8 Lochcarron-Skye

Congregation	Com	Eld	G	In22	M&M	–18
Applecross, Lochcarron and Torridon	59	4	5	-	20,609	-
Bracadale and Duirinish	30	4	6	-	19,938	3
Gairloch and Dundonnell	61	3	-	85,982	45,508	3
Glenelg Kintail and Lochalsh	57	8	8	37,457	25,187	-
Kilmuir and Stenscholl	28	4	-	26,567	19,511	3
Portree	77	14	-	59,516	40,713	4
Snizort	28	-	-	-	20,636	-
Strath and Sleat	96	6	-	95,102	64,482	-

10.9 Uist

Congregation	Com	Eld	G	In22	M&M	–18
Benbecula	59	-	15	31,583	24,111	-
Carinish	64	-	-	36,222	31,217	-
Berneray and Lochmaddy	25	-	7	13,026	10,131	-
Kilmuir and Paible	25	-	-	24,255	19,196	-
Manish-Scarista	20	-	-	19,972	19,251	-
Tarbert	69	-	-	69,601	37,679	-

Congregation	Com	Eld	G	In22	M&M	–18
11. Lewis						
Barvas	70	-	-	59,318	42,489	-
Carloway	44	-	-	29,591	16,741	-
Cross Ness	58	-	-	39,710	26,394	-
Kinloch	30	-	-	44,059	25,054	-
Knock	21	-	-	-	18,222	-
Lochs-Crossbost	8	-	-	12,241	9,189	-
Lochs-in-Bernera	28	-	-	-	9,399	-
Uig	13	-	-	20,408	11,167	-
Stornoway: High	82	-	-	79,361	38,413	-
Stornoway: Martin's Memorial	329	-	-	169,049	95,238	-
Stornoway: St Columba	124	-	34	-	60,527	-
12. England and Channel Islands						
Corby: St Andrew's	115	10	-	25,962	17,581	-
Corby: St Ninian's	129	10	-	60,932	20,602	20
Guernsey: St Andrew's in the Grange	163	19	-	63,523	41,893	16
Jersey: St Columba's	86	9	-	57,201	33,709	10
London: Crown Court	180	27	3	-	55,515	19
London: St Columba's	739	50	-	-	240,703	15
Newcastle: St Andrew's	103	14	-	-	8,903	15
13. International Charges						
Amsterdam: English Reformed Church	343	10	-	-	-	8
Bermuda: Christ Church Warwick	399	37	-	-	-	35
Brussels: St Andrew's	265	16	-	-	-	20
Budapest: St Columba's	27	-	-	-	-	-
Colombo, Sri Lanka: St Andrew's Scots Kirk	103	-	-	-	-	-
Geneva	214	12	-	-	-	8
Lausanne: The Scots Kirk	130	12	-	-	-	3
Lisbon: St Andrew's	66	6	-	-	-	8
Malta: St Andrew's Scots Church	44	6	-	-	-	1
Paris: The Scots Kirk	86	8	-	-	-	12
Rome: St Andrew's	81	-	-	-	-	-
Rotterdam: Scots International Church	173	9	-	-	-	28
Trinidad: Greyfriars St Ann's, Port of Spain with Arouca and Sangre Grande	227	-	-	-	-	-

INDEX OF MINISTERS

Ministers who are members of a Presbytery are designated:
  'A' if holding a parochial appointment in that Presbytery;
    'A-1, A-2' etc. indicate the numerical order of congregations in that Presbytery;
  'B' if in other appointments; or
  'C' if 'Retaining'.
Ministers who have resigned their seat but are registered by Presbytery are designated:
  'D' if in other appointments;
  'E' if 'Retaining'; or
  'F' if 'Inactive'.
Ministers serving overseas (List 6-E) are listed here under their Presbyteries.
Ordained Local Ministers and Auxiliary Ministers are listed here under their Presbyteries.
Ministers who have died since the compilation of the last *Year Book* are designated 'List 6-J'.
For reasons of spacing:
  Edinburgh and West Lothian is given as 'Edinburgh/W.L.';
  Forth Valley and Clydesdale is given as 'Forth V./C'dale';
  International Charges is given as 'Int. Charges'; and
  England and Channel Islands is given as 'England/C.I.'

For a list of the Diaconate, see List 6-B.

INDEX OF PARISHES AND PLACES

Numbers on the right of the column refer to the Presbytery in which the district lies. Names in brackets are given for ease of identification. They may refer to the name of the parish, which may be different from that of the district, or they distinguish places with the same name, or they indicate the first named place within a union.

INDEX OF SUBJECTS